CULT OF JOHN

The Secret Life of João de Deus
Spiritual Healer and Serial Rapist

Michael Bailot

ILUMINA
BOOKS

Copyright © 2025 by Michael R. Bailot

All rights reserved. No part of this book may be reproduced or used in any manner without the written permission of the copyright owner except for the use of quotations in a book review.

For more information contact:
mb@michaelbailot.com

First paperback edition April 2025

Cover photo: Creative Commons with permission of "Anonymous"
Cover design by Evgeniia Gurcheva

ISBN 979-8-9914116-0-8

Published by Ilumina Books–www.iluminabooks.com

Every effort has been made to trace or contact all copyright holders with the exception of brief quotes under Fair Use guidelines. The publishers will be pleased to make good any omissions or rectify any mistakes brought to their attention.

Trigger warning: physical assault, rape, pedophilia, spiritual abuse.

CONTENTS

Prologue

I.

A Long Time Ago in a Very Strange Land

Vagabond John: Taking a Spin

Quimbanda João

The Peregrinations of João

II.

GI João: Tailor for the Military

The Parrot's Perch & The Parrot's Beak:
Casa Azul—The Blue House of Terror

João and the Indian Genocide of the 1970s

III.

João the Garimpeiro: The Gold Digger

Serra Pelada: Naked Mountain Bonanza

IV.

Doctor John the Night Tripper: Babalaô João

João's Juju

Blood, Semen, and Tears

V.

Me and the Medium

City of Sycophants

Child of the Casa

VI.

Waiting for Godot

Santo de Pau Oco: The Hollow Log Saint

John the Con: The Wizard of Oz

VII.

The Enchanted Realm of Abadiânia

Silence is a Prayer

VIII.

The Shit Hits the Fan

In the Name of God

Cognitive Dissonance and the Casa Cargo Cult

IX.

What In Hell Happened Here?

Postscript

End Notes

EDITORIAL REVIEWS

"A masterful and unflinching revelation."

"Bravo, this is a really powerful personal and thoroughly researched exposé. It's both illuminating and disturbing in equal measure.

"Some books inform, some books expose—few manage to do both with the precision, depth, and courage found in this work. A personal and masterful account, it takes readers on an unflinching dive into a dark underworld of João de Deus that had been carefully and systematically concealed for so many years.

"As powerful as it is disturbing, the book weaves together an intricate narrative of Brazil, João, and the forces that shaped his practice. The author does not shy away from the complexities of the story, instead presenting a brave account that demands to be read with both an open mind and a critical eye.

"The fact that João was once endorsed by Oprah Winfrey serves as a stark reminder of the level of deception that can operate in plain sight. It underscores how easily charisma, power, and influence can be mistaken for virtue—often at a devastating cost.

"This book is not simply a story about one man from Brazil, but rather a story for our time, a cautionary tale about the dangers of blind faith in authority figures and the need for personal discernment. In an era where we are increasingly encouraged to outsource our own power, this book serves as a necessary wake-up call."

— Dr T. Edmunds, Clinical Psychologist, London

"An impassioned, revealing account of the dark side of a "miracle worker."

"Bailot explores João's background, from his birth in 1942 in a desolate part of Brazil to his possible involvement in clandestine operations with the military in the 1960s. The early pages of the book provide a wide swath of information: The text addresses subjects from the history of Brazil's capital of Brasilia to a crash course in Spiritism to the locations of João's postings while he was in the army.

"The story hits its real stride when the author gets to his personal account—his narrative of falling into João's orbit is vividly populated with people desperate for cures and others more than willing to exploit them. He pulls no punches in his criticism, noting that one woman who worked with João "could easily be cast as a Nazi prison guard." This is a brutal and honest telling, and altogether unsettling.

—Kirkus Reviews

"A brilliantly written historical account, this harrowing story of João de Deus not only exposes the shocking events but also immerses readers in the rich and complex society and culture of Brazil. At times difficult to read but even harder to put down, it is a gripping and deeply detailed exploration of power, deception, and the forces that shaped a nation."

—Debra Lynne Katz, PhD, author

"The tragedy of John of God - spirit healer, multi-millionaire, violent criminal, serial rapist - begs for explanation. How could a man blessed with such gifts and charisma, who clawed his way out of dire poverty, with such a capacity to do good for his fellow Brazilians, have so fully betrayed those who trusted him and, indeed, his lifelong legacy?

"Weaving together a thorough understanding of Brazil's complex colonial, military, and religious history, Michael Bailot paints a damning portrait of religious power corrupted and unchecked. Bailot writes from a unique, personal perspective, having had a relationship with John's healing Casa, but finding himself dangerously in the crosshairs of John's criminal enterprise. He brings comprehensive context to the enigma of John of God. It's an important book and well done.

"I found Cult of John to be powerfully compelling, at turns scary and enraging. It's well written and told with a good ear to engage the audience. I can see this being a true resource for anyone who wants to have the full picture of João. I've already been recommending it to friends."

—Dereck Daschke, PhD, Professor of Philosophy & Religion

PROLOGUE

João Teixeira de Faria aka João de Deus (John of God)

He appeared out of nowhere, angry and aggressive. As they say in Brazil, *he was standing on my toes*—sweating and red in the face. I noticed his bright blue eyes and the stubble on his jaw. He held me in his gaze so close that I could see the pores of his skin. He was raging and spewing saliva.

He snarled, "If you fuck with me, I'll kill you! They tell me I've killed nine, but I only remember one. Don't mess with *me*, man."

I awoke with a dry scream paralyzed in my throat, startling my wife with my nightmare. That raging face was João de Deus, the spirit healer of Abadiânia. His face would haunt me for twenty years.

Why did I wait so long to tell my story? We'll get into that later.

To be honest, I was afraid. This story is like a Hans Christian Andersen fairy tale. There is hell and terror to pay—a fight to the death between good and evil. Ultimately, there is a moral to digest and a truth that is hard to swallow.

The year was 2002. I walked to the Casa de Dom Inácio in Abadiânia, Brazil, a few blocks from my home. I was there to meditate with other children of the Casa in the Entities Room, as I had done for the past few years. I was one of a couple of dozen Casa *mediums* expected to attend every session at seven in the morning to warm up the current before the Great Healer arrived—the Miracle Man, João de Deus. Many believed John to be an impoverished saint who healed millions of people from all over the world—for free. Some even suggested he might be the second coming of Christ. I had my doubts.

Martin, a friend of mine for the past three years and someone close to João, accosted me on the street. He was angry, waving a copy of an email in my face and shouting, "What have you done? It's not true. He cured me. He cured my mother!"

I replied that people were being sexually assaulted and threatened. João was a fraud. I told him João molested one of my clients in the invisible surgery room. He removed her bra and fondled her breasts. We were advised to close our eyes, but an attendant was present if João wanted anything. My wife had been in attendance, and her eyes were open.

Martin protested, "No, he was healing her." I then reached under his polo shirt and squeezed his (surprisingly large) breasts, asking him if that was a healing technique. He was losing control as he shook the Xeroxed email in my face. I had sent it to thirty people who had contracted me to be their guide during their upcoming visit to the Casa de Dom Inácio. I was supposed to help them through the process, indoctrinating them in the myths of the Casa.

My email was brief:

"In good conscience, I cannot be your guide for your upcoming visit to Abadiânia. It has come to my attention that João de Deus engages in criminal activities and is a dangerous person. I can't encourage anyone to visit him and suggest you cancel your trip. The allegations that have come out include rape and murder. I am sorry to bring this to your attention and for any problems this might cause you."

One recipient was a friend of the Casa. This man sent my email to Martin. As João cannot read, Martin translated it for him.

Martin towered above me, spitting out his words. "I have a message for you from João." He said, *"You idiot, don't you understand that one can have a person killed here in Abadiânia for three hundred reais?"*

Yes, the story of João de Deus is tough to swallow. So, may we begin?

Brazil. Created with mapchart.net / Creative Commons.

I.
A LONG TIME AGO IN A VERY STRANGE LAND

It was a long time ago in a very strange land. João Teixeira de Faria was born in 1942, in the tiny village of Cachoeira de Fumaça in Goiás, Brazil. They were two hundred impoverished settlers on a forgotten dirt track in the middle of nowhere.[1]

All of them were fleeing the poverty of Minas Gerais and dreaming of staking out a plot of open land to claim as their own. Most were from the same family. Goiás was the end of the track, a no-man's-land where thousands of homeless peasants gathered.

The end of the track. Photo: Public Archive of Brazil.

João was the youngest of six children. He was born in a dirt-floored adobe hovel with a leaking roof and wooden shutters for windows. His mother cooked for the family on an outdoor rustic wood burning stove.

They did not have indoor plumbing or electricity.

João's father, Jose Nunes de Faria (Juca), was an itinerate tailor. His mother, Francisca Teixeira Damas (Dona Iucca), sold lunch to road workers and occasional travelers. The family was destitute, and they often missed meals.

Goiás was one of the most impoverished and undeveloped states in Brazil. The few roads were unpaved dirt tracks, a land of poor soil with no cities or industry. The government encouraged landless peasants to homestead in this wilderness. They offered small parcels of public land to those who dared to move there.[2]

It was a lawless frontier—a region populated by descendants of rogue miners and plantation owners and their ex-slaves. The Portuguese enslaved Indians and Africans to mine gold, silver, and gems.

These mines spawned small towns and villages, cut off from other settlements or linked only by riverways and paths. Goiás has a lot of dirty laundry in its history. This was a rough place.

Vast land holdings, thousands of square hectares, were ranches (fazendas) owned by single families. These families were the law, the court, the police, and the tax man. If you worked at all, it was for one of them. The top man, known as the Colonel, reigned like a king over his domain. If you share cropped for them—and for many, this was their only option—they owned you. The average yearly income for Brazilians in the early 1950s was $228, but in Goiás, it was much less.

The government programs were unsuccessful. Wealthy land barons cheated many of the homesteaders out of their holdings. A peasant revolt was in the making, and Goiás was the epicenter.

The Faria family moved to a nearby town, Itapaci, when João was three years old. They expelled João from school in the first grade. He remained illiterate his entire life. A fact that he found embarrassing and for which he overcompensated with arrogance. The story goes that the family was so poor that they couldn't afford the cost of schooling. However, they expelled him from the three schools he attended, not for lack of money, but for unacceptable behavior. João was a disobedient and unruly student. He completed only six months of school.[3]

Before we begin this tale, I need to clarify something. Much of João's history (as he narrates it) is more myth than substance. His past biographers' sole source for the account of his magical childhood and the next twenty-five years was João himself.

They quote the same sources: João, Liberato Póvoa (his longtime friend and attorney), or Sebastian Lima (his sidekick of forty years). The myth of João begins here. He is the sole author without a witness or a thread of proof.

Although a few of his stories are true, most are clichéd, exaggerated, and altered. Many are lies. He obscured or erased various unpleasant years and incidents. In the rare moments that João spoke about his past, unintended details slipped out. His biography is a process of gathering the broken pieces and gluing them back together.

The life story of João Teixeira de Faria reminds me of the film Forrest Gump. João shows up at many of Brazil's historical moments as a bystander. But he is not at all like the innocent and lovable Forrest. He is a grifter and a gangster, not a Gump.

What strikes me upon hearing João's official life story is that twenty-five years are missing. The myth says that authorities persecuted him for his healing work. He was often imprisoned and maltreated. He moved from state to state, one step ahead of the authorities in pursuit. Doctors and priests hounded him while he gave his healing passes to the povo, the common folk, at no cost. The truth is much darker than this.

When João was nine, the villagers called him the "little witch." His clairvoyant powers had frightened them. His mother, Dona Iucca, was also drawn to the psychic realm. She earned money from the occasional tarot card spread (cutting the deck). Dona Iucca also read palms and recited formal prayers of supplication. She was what rural folks called a benzedeira, one who recites formulaic prayers while blessing with water sprinkled with sacred leaves. This is like the Catholic priest and his holy water. One visits a benzedeira to resolve a problem or cure an illness. It is a form of folk magic.

One of Dona Iucca's prayers, which João often recited, was: "My son João, may God set you on a good path. Seven angels accompany you, and seven lights illuminate you… Pistols fired at you, my son, will not detonate; knives will be bent backward to the handle. Clubs will fall from any hand that threatens you. Your enemies will not see you, and if they have legs, they will not catch you. Their hands cannot grab you. Your enemies will become your friends."

João also read palms and told fortunes. These techniques are the commerce and specialty of gypsies. João's lifelong identification with the Gypsy Line of Umbanda and his family's ties with palm reading and cartomancy suggests Roma ancestry. Traditionally, mothers handed down fortune-telling skills to their daughters.

His mother's side of the family, Teixeira, has a branch linked to Portuguese Roma and Jews forced to convert to Catholicism. His father's line, Faria, also has offshoots of Roma and Jewish "converts." Exiles to the colony of Brazil were given a Brazilian name. For example, many converted Jews have surnames that are types of fruit trees.

In the late 1600s, unwelcome Roma were expelled from Portugal and forced to migrate to Brazil. In Goiás, several of their communities exist to this day.

At an early age, his mother took him to a New Age wonder of their times, the Prophet Master Yokaanam. He was passing through their town on a quest to create a utopian community in the region. Oceano de Sá (1911-1985) went by the mystical name Yokaanam. He and four hundred followers from Rio de Janeiro arrived in the area in 1946.

After Yokaanam made his presentation, they held a communal lunch. João and Yokaanam conversed. Impressed by João's potential, the Master asked Donna Iucca if she would give the nine-year-old boy to him to raise. He would train him to be a good doctor.

She replied, "My son is not like a dog to be given away." [4]

João began working as a child laborer. However, his rebellious nature prevented him from holding those jobs for very long.

One of his childhood friends mentioned wild times drinking cachaça (sugar cane alcohol) with João as a boy. He reminisced about their frequent visits to the local prostitutes. [5]

João threw a stone and struck the village priest in another act of defiance. Enraged at the lack of respect, the priest excommunicated him at age ten. João was already an outsider. Now, he had burned his bridges. Excommunication was a severe stigma for anyone in Goiás. Everyone was obedient to the Church during this era. They believed that the excommunicated go to Hell when they die.

Contrary to several of his devotees and biographers, João was never a practicing Catholic or a spiritually inclined person. He has been at war with religion ever since that fateful day in 1952.

Vagabond John: Taking a Spin

The family trained young João in the tailor's trade. He apprenticed with his father and older brother. Then, they loaned him out to his sister, also a seamstress. He lived with her for some time in three other cities.[6]

His family was in a crisis. João remembers times when he would pick up discarded watermelon rinds to satisfy his hunger. A steady decline in the mental health of his father further complicated the situation. When João was thirteen, Juca's condition had deteriorated to where he would eat only one thing—toothpaste. They committed him to a psychiatric hospital. This is where he disappears from João's narrative. Other sources say Juca had schizophrenia and died of electric shock therapy applications.

A year later, his mother abandoned João to his eldest brother, who put him to work as a bricklayer's laborer.

Dona Iucca followed the road crews on their relentless drive to open a highway from Goiás to Belém. João explains that they hired her as a cook for the laborers. Maybe so, but most women traveling with the road crews were prostitutes, an expected benefit of the crew. Dona Iucca also fades from his story at this point. But she reappears years later when João moves to Abadiânia.

By the age of fifteen, João was run out of town. He had created a political scandal as treasurer for a local politician's campaign funds. At this tender age, João decided to see the world. And here, he seems to have slipped off his biographer's maps. He claims to have never returned. But three of his children contradict this. They were born in that very town, his hometown of Itapaci.

His trajectory began at sixteen in Campo Grande, in the State of Mato Grosso do Sul. He would continue to repeat this story (some call it a myth) throughout his life.[7]

He traveled there to work as a tailor's assistant but was fired on his first day. Camping on the city's outskirts, penniless and hungry, he took a dip in a river beneath a bridge he had crossed. He recalls a beautiful woman who appeared out of nowhere, speaking his name and singing to him. It was like a waking dream.

He came back the next day, hoping to see her again. A column of light confronted him in a stern voice, giving him a spiritual warning. He claims the shaft of light guided him to the Spiritualist Christ the Redeemer Center. A place he had never visited before. Mysteriously, the center director greeted João by name at the door. He told him they had been waiting for him. They invited him to their Mesa Branca, a mediumistic healing ritual to contact and be possessed by spirits.

Mesa Branca rituals are exclusive to Umbanda, Brazil's popular Afro-Brazilian religion of trance possession. They are not a spiritist or spiritualist practice, *per se.* We are not dealing with a spiritist center.

João claimed that he had incorporated a spirit identifying himself as King Solomon of Biblical fame. In Brazil, they say a possessed person has incorporated a spirit. When João exited the trance three hours later, the congregation was astonished. They informed him that he had performed numerous surgeries and healed many people during the session.

He didn't remember any of this. João had no experience or interest in spirits or healing. He was a hungry, uneducated vagabond, never inclined to a spiritual path. It startled him when they invited him to have a meal with them and wanted to shake his hand. *I fainted. I don't remember doing any of this. They'll be mad and throw me out when they discover I'm a fraud. I'd better eat all I can now,* he thought.

They encouraged him to stay with room and board, and he participated in their services for three months. However, he soon felt the call of the road was much stronger than the call of the spirits.

João never surrendered to the spiritist faith's discipline, joined a spiritist group, or practiced its principles. This was his first experience with mediumistic incorporation.

This type of trance possession, known as the "blind medium," occurs when spirits take over a medium's body. The person does not remember any events while in a trance, leaving them unaware of their actions during possession.

The medium does and says many things, but the spirit entity has complete control over its host. This type of trance possession is fraught with danger. The medium is not accountable for what happens in their trance and has no self-control. Spirits can impersonate whomever they wish: Jesus, a dead doctor, or a famous saint. João, a lifelong blind medium, never remembers whom he incorporated or what transpired. He often works with spirits who refuse to give their names, which is even more dangerous.

A recent Google search lists over sixty spiritist centers in Campo Grande. Interestingly, Spiritualist Christ the Redeemer Center isn't among them. This occurred almost sixty-five years ago. No one can corroborate that this spiritist center ever existed. No one remembers João's time in Campo Grande. With this story, he created the beginning of his myth.

João claimed that the mysterious woman he saw by the river was Saint Rita of Cassia. Saint Rita entered into an arranged marriage at the age of twelve. Her husband was violently abusive for eighteen years. She is the patron saint of abuse victims, widows, those struggling with infertility, impossible causes, the sick, and the lonely. Campo Grande is home to twenty Umbanda Centers, including the Centro de Umbanda de Fé Santa Rita.

These two spirits, King Solomon and Saint Rita, are a theme throughout João's life story. Pay attention; they will return in strange alternative forms as the tale unfolds.

In 1956, Juscelino Kubitschek became the twenty-first President of Brazil. He was elected on promises to open Brazil's vast wilderness in the central and northern regions. He planned highways, railroad lines, hydroelectric plants, and cities. The centerpiece would be a new Capitol—built from scratch in the middle of nowhere.

He reckoned he wouldn't be re-elected. Therefore, he needed to complete the project in only four years, which was the length of his term. Kubitschek reasoned; "Because no President of Brazil has ever left office and had his successor continue his unfinished projects."

Kubitschek believed he was the reincarnated Egyptian Pharaoh Akhenaten (Amenhotep IV). He stated that he received the plan for Brazil's new capital in a spiritual vision and channeled a map of the city. Several pyramids are scattered across Brasilia, including Kubitschek's tomb. The layout of the Capitol, the geometry, and the location have many occult and Masonic references. A New Age fever was dragging Brazil into the future.[8]

By the time, in João's words, he took a spin and hit the road in 1958, Kubitschek's vision was rapidly unfolding on João's turf. The highways under construction were the key to Brazil's version of Manifest Destiny. Army helicopters airlifted hundreds of bulldozers into the region. Each one set a course cutting through the wilderness for months. Enormous chains linking two bulldozers dragged down millions of trees.

It was a time reminiscent of the Wild West. Men with pistols strapped to their legs, whorehouses, bars, murders and robberies. Following the conquest of this wilderness were tens of thousands of men longing for work. And here, they had finally found it. One of these roads, Highway BR-60, led from Campo Grande to João's hometown.

Nearby, they were carving another road through a dense jungle. This was the Belém-Brasília Highway, the first road through Brazil's central and middle north regions. The roadway connected the States of Para, Maranhão, Tocantins, and Goiás to the Capitol, which was under construction.

They were laying out the survey grids for Brasilia. The land was a tropical paradise of rivers, virgin forests, and the savanna ecosystem known as the Cerrado. It was replaced with an enormous artificial lake and a concrete metropolis. A futuristic Russian-style city was born.

João traveled the new highways from the Amazon to Goiás. Goiás was an enormous territory that included the current state of Tocantins and parts of Mato Grosso. According to João, he worked as a laborer, a barber, a tailor, a bricklayer, a street vendor, a bullfighter, a circus worker, an illegal gold miner, a tooth puller, and a wandering fortune teller.

He was always on the move. By his account, he was always one step ahead of the pursuing police. If you have seen the classic comedy film Bye-Bye Brazil, you can envision the rough and tumble life in this era.

João arrived in Brasilia at the height of the construction process, along with tens of thousands of Brazil's unemployed. In a television interview, he said, "I lived in Cidade Livre and in Cruzeiro Novo, being the first resident to move there. The military police were afraid to enter our encampment. I sold oranges on the streets of Cidade Livre." He also read palms. That would be from 1958 to 1960.

Brasilia under construction in 1958. Photo: Public Archive of Brazil.

By early 1957, they had transformed the majestic plains and forests of Planalto Central into a sea of bulldozed and treeless red earth. The rising spectacle of Brasilia attracted 80,000 impoverished laborers. They lived in scrapped-together wooden shanties without water or septic systems. Most of these migrant workers lived in Cidade Livre (meaning *Free City* in English).

Kubitschek and his architect, Oscar Niemeyer, encouraged the rapid completion of the project. They were often present on the construction sites. They had created a monster. When João arrived, they were coping with their problem.

Re-constructing the federal government and all its agencies was a challenge. They also needed schools, shopping centers, parks, and hundreds of high-rise apartments. Workers received wages three times more than their salaries back home. They were the problem child. The problem was, where to house all these men and police them? How do you persuade them to go back home (to unemployment and perhaps starvation) after they finish the job?

"Candangos," the builders of Brasilia. Photo: Public Archive of Brazil.

The laborers, already organized and aware of their rights, became an unruly and potentially dangerous presence. Many were promised a plot of land or their shack as a reward for their hard work. They often worked eighteen-hour days in harsh conditions. Temperatures frequently reached the nineties, and during the winter months, there was nearly daily rainfall for six months. The lack of shade made the heat unbearable, and finding potable water was difficult. Clouds of biting insects and the threat of infectious diseases only added to their discomfort. Several confrontations occurred between the squatters in the shantytowns and the government, resulting in a compromise that forever tainted their vision of a New Age World's Fair Fantasy Capital with a grand palace.

The planners envisioned a small city with a maximum population of 500,000 people. Everyone would be related to the function of the government and the city. Shanty towns were missing from the planning map.

Several essential details had not crossed the planners' minds. Where would they produce food in this wilderness? What about electricity, sanitation, and water lines? Capitalism and the military resolved this. Cidade Livre fixed the supply and demand problems. Their shantytown became a tax-free zone for impromptu commerce.

When João lived in Cidade Livre, it was a Wild West outpost with violence, prostitution, and the sale of almost anything. It became Brasilia's first favela. Wooden shacks, precariously stacked up to a second floor, housed shops, bordellos, and bars at the lower level. Families or cheap rooming houses occupied the second level. The military patrolled the streets at night, and folks carried pistols. A person selling oranges on street corners and peddling palm readings was socially at the bottom of this cesspool.

In time, the authorities evicted squatters from several of these multiplying favelas. This is probably why João moved to the forest near the construction site for the apartment complex they called Cruzeiro Novo. This encampment was primitive and forested. Wild animals, including ocelots and poisonous snakes, lurked in the night. People sat by fires and cooked their meals. It was a dangerous place. Those living there called it "The Cemetery."

There were dozens of construction sites and camps. Twice a month, trucks loaded with prostitutes would visit the construction sites. They allowed the men twenty minutes each. [10]

The situation was often worse for the construction workers hired by building contractors. Filthy dormitories infested with vermin and rancid food were the norm.[11]

As the building project progressed, various encampments were destroyed to make way for the next construction project. The

Cidade Livre in the late 1950s. Photo: Public Archive of District Federal.

government relocated 80,000 families to several pieces of undesirable raw land on the far outskirts of Brasilia. They gave each family a small lot to build on, abandoned to fend for themselves. These later became enormous favelas and cities as well.

The future satellite city of Brasilia in 1958. Photo: Public Archive of District Federal.

Quimbanda João

The new capital was officially inaugurated in 1960. It was also the year for João's mandatory registration with the military. All boys were required to register when they reached eighteen. Mysteriously, there are no records that confirm his registration.[12]

João moved on. For the next six years, he disappeared off the radar. In 1961, young João began attending Candomblé sessions in the northeast coastal state of Bahia, famous for its African trance cults.

João also attended healing works in the spiritist city of Palmelo, Goiás. He briefly interacted with Chico Xavier, Jeronimo Candinho, and Bortolo Damo, whom he called the popes of spiritism.

He spent time at Novo Jerusalem; the community led by Master Yokaanam founded near Brasilia. João visited the psychic healers Zé Arigó and Santa Dica. All these centers influenced his styling of the Casa de Dom Inácio.

Several of João's biographers felt a need to explain Spiritism and Occultism in Brazil. Umbanda also needed to be described. I assume that some of my readers won't know much about these things. We cannot understand João unless we understand this background. For the rest of you, please bear with me. I will keep this brief. Thousands of web pages and books are available to explain all this.[13]

Brazil was built on a deep foundation of slavery. Without slavery, Brazil wouldn't exist. In the sixteenth century, expeditions of *Bandeirantes* (armed, flag-waving, mercenary thugs) captured the native Indians. They laced together entire tribes with rawhide cords and marched them to the auction block for days or weeks. The women and children sold for twice the price of men. One expedition of Bandeirantes netted 60,000 Indians in a single campaign.[14]

With the growth of the sugar market and discoveries of gold and diamond deposits in the 1600s, Brazil began importing African slaves. The enslaved Indians' life expectancy was only nineteen years. The African slaves cost more than the indigenous ones, but they lived an average of twenty-three years. They were considered better workers (more submissive) and were in greater demand.

Brazil enslaved six million Africans from 1501 to 1866 (another source put the total at 12.5 million). For the first 250 years, the Portuguese colony's population was 70% slaves. Brazil was the last country in the Americas to abolish slavery, reluctantly doing so in 1888.

African slaves came from several regions of the continent, arriving with their languages, cultures, and religions. The slavers shattered these groups into splinters. Upon arrival in Brazil, families, clans, and villages were divided. Speaking their native languages was prohibited. The Africans prevailed by hiding their heritages and performing their rituals in secret.

The Afro-Brazilian religion of Candomblé blends the beliefs of three major tribal nations. These are called the fundamentals, the foundations of the cult. The largest nation is Nagô. Their language is Yoruba. The Nagô peoples came from several West Coast nations, including Nigeria, Benin, and Togo. Their ancient religion centered on a pantheon of archetypical deities called the Orixás. The Nagô conducted ritual dances with drums, chants, and trance possession. The Nagô influence is Candomblé's core.

The Ewe-speaking nation is a Gbe ethnic group from Ghana and Togo. The traditional Ewe religion is Vodun (Voodoo), which means spirit. They practiced ancestor worship. They were a cult of the dead.

Bantu-speaking Africans came from Angola, Congo, and several other tribal nations. Their language gave us the name of Candomblé (their sacred dances). They were famous practitioners of magic. The Bantu are the stereotyped and feared witch doctors. They practice ritual scarification and blood sacrifice.

Luanda, Angola, was the principal shipping port for the Brazilian slave trade. Here, an enormous market of slaves from all over Africa held daily auctions of fresh captives. They shipped most of them to Brazil. The major ports were Rio de Janeiro, Recife, and Salvador, the birthplace of Candomblé.

Candomblé has no central authority, doctrine, or sacred books. Each *terreiro* (backyard), their meeting place, is autonomous. Their beliefs vary from region to region. They believe in a supreme God, Olodumare, and the Orixás. The Orixás are archetypal spirits that mediate between the Creator and humanity. There are 401 Orixás.

Humans and Orixás are interdependent. One needs good relationships with them to remain balanced and secure. The Orixás are morally ambiguous, each with its virtues and flaws. Songs and offerings summon the Orixás. These might be alcohol, tobacco, honey, or specific African foods. The Bantu terreiros favor ritual bloodletting or animal sacrifices.

The cult of Candomblé spread throughout the slave communities of Brazil. Today, Brazil has over 170,000 practitioners.

The slave owners found all this disturbing and correctly understood this to be a seedbed for revolt and devilry. They did everything they could to stamp out this slave religion. The slaves held their rituals in the forest at night and in secret. This further provoked panic in their Portuguese *dons.*

Once they arrived in Brazil, the Africans were converted to Catholicism. They were indoctrinated into the story of Jesus and the saints of the church and attended segregated churches. Many of these Catholic icons seemed familiar to the Africans. They resembled various traits and powers of their Orixás. This led to *syncretism* (amalgamating several religions into one).

Syncretism has been an irresistible force in every Brazilian religion. It allowed the African religions to hide behind the skirts of the church yet not be in conflict with their fundamental tribal beliefs.

Each Orixá is associated with a color, healing herb, animal, mineral, and day of the week. A different Orixá rules each year and influences everything that happens. Candomblé added to this list by assigning a Catholic saint to correspond with each Orixá.

Thus, Oshun, who is the goddess of love, beauty, fresh water, and divination, becomes the pregnant Virgin Mary, Our Lady of Conception. Ogun, the God of war and iron, transforms into Saint George. Candomblé has elaborate folk art altars, and many statues of saints crowd the space.

In Candomblé, every individual is born with an Orixá. This is determined by divination. This Orixá is the *Don de Cabeça,* the owner of the head.

Candomblé also works with other types of spirits. One of these is the Exus. The Exus are slaves of the Orishas. They are also defined as devils or demons. Candomblé blurs the line between good and evil. Exus do both good and bad magic. Exus can open or close the roads of fate—to help or to harm.[15]

In Candomblé, one works with Axé, the vital life force. You either have enough, or you lack it. Another term for the life force is *o corrente* (the current or the chain), generated during their rituals. Axé can be wielded and transmitted. People can attract and share this current during the ceremonies. Blood contains Axé in its most concentrated form; thus, blood offerings have the most efficacy.[16]

Throughout the 1800s, Candomblé mutated and spread to many slave communities, even though it was forbidden by law and persecuted. By the 1930s, Candomblé had become widespread. Even upper-class white Brazilians participated. They often blended

Catholic influences into their practices. Sometimes, it was mandatory to be a Catholic to join one of the terreiros.

As a result, the work with the morally ambivalent Exus splintered off from Candomblé. Their followers founded separate, secret sects called Quimbanda and Macumba.

This divorce of the Exus is called the *whitening* of Candomblé. It made it more palatable to the average Brazilian. The whitening process continued as Spiritism and Umbanda entered the stage. A growing population of people interested in spirit communication and incorporation encouraged this.

Another influence in the styling of João was *Espiritismo*. Spiritism has always been with humanity. Christianity and Islam held it hostage and hidden for centuries. The earliest Christian churches practiced spiritism.[17]

In the 1800s, French professor Allan Kardec influenced the spiritual philosophy of Brazil. The Spiritualism movement, experimenting with seances, Ouija boards, and hypnotism, inspired Kardec. His ambition was to create a science taught by the spirits of the dead to human students: a systematic guide on how to speak with them, behave with them, and use their wisdom to benefit humanity. By using mediums to channel these spirits, Kardec wrote five books.

He tried to synthesize Eastern philosophy, such as reincarnation, with Western philosophies, like the concept of Heaven and Hell. Kardec was not a channeler or a medium. Because of his influence, his ideas sound a lot like modern New Age philosophy.

The religion of Spiritism believes in a *Supreme Intelligence and Primary Cause of Everything.* Spirits exist. They begin their evolution in ignorance. They have the potential for improvement in each incarnation. Spirits can communicate with living people and even affect their lives.

Spiritists have few rituals or rites other than their healing passes (a bit like Reiki) and the sharing of spiritually charged water. They meet regularly and study Kardec's books with a fine-tooth comb. The meetings are open to the public.

It's a bit like Sunday school or catechism. The confirmed mediums in the group occasionally hold private channeling sessions that are not open to non-members. Their philosophy is that charity is the highest virtue. Spiritual and healing services should never be monetized. High moral principles are the Spiritist goal.

Brazil's famous spiritists were channelers, authoring hundreds of channeled books. The first thing that a budding spiritist practices is automatic writing. Brazil enthusiastically embraced Kardec's philosophy. It has the largest number of Spiritist centers in the world.

Up to 40 million Brazilians are members or attend the study sessions. Spiritism arrived in Brazil at the time Candomblé was blossoming. They both presented a conflict of interest to the Catholic Church. Umbanda set out to resolve the issue, taking syncretism to another level.[18]

It began in Niterói, a neighborhood near Rio de Janeiro, in the early twentieth century. It was started by the medium Zélio Fernandino de Moraes (a Spiritist). He envisioned blending Roman Catholicism, Candomblé, Spiritism, occultism, and the shamanic traditions of Brazil's Indians. His creation, Umbanda, sought to unite all these spiritual paths into a balanced whole.

Umbanda has it all: African Orixás and their lesser deities, trance drumming, ecstatic possession dance, and received songs of invocation. There are Catholic Saints in abundance and mediums of every persuasion. A good dose of esoteric occult ideas, consultations with wise old African slaves from days gone by, and healing performed by spirits of the vanishing Brazilian tribes add to the mix. Angels, ETs, ascended masters, even gypsies, rogues, and the devil are brought under the wraps of Umbanda.

In the sixties, Umbanda was a relatively new religion. It spread like wildfire and mutated rapidly. They believe there are three types of spirits:

1. Pure Spirits: angels, those who have attained spiritual perfection.

2. Good Spirits: the ones the mediums incorporate (ideally). They can become one's spiritual guide. These might be Orishas, Saints, or members of the Great White Brotherhood. Or Caboclos (Indian Shamans), Preto Velhos (wise old African slaves), or Crianças (children's spirits, innocent and full of joy). Deceased cowboys, gypsies, sailors, mythical spirits of enchantment, and mermaids work with Umbanda. Many types of ancestor spirits might be one's guide as well.

3. Bad Spirits: also known as Kiumbas, are not welcome, but they frequently appear at Umbanda rituals. They are obsessive spirits or suffering spirits. Kiumbas sometimes possess or confuse a medium, which can cause pandemonium, violence, or terrible sobbing.

The mediums interrogate and indoctrinate these spirits, trying to guide them toward the light and a higher vibration. This is the service performed by all Umbanda terreiros, assisting lost souls.

A sub-group of spirits exists in some Umbanda groups, the Exus. In the Umbanda tradition, the Exus are benign. These spirits do the dirty work of dealing with obsessive spirits. Those who cause bad luck, violence, perversion, addiction, and depression. Some terreiros claim that the Exus never do black magic but protect people from all destructive energies.

The Exus, however, are low spirits—often personified as pimps and criminals. Female Exus, Pombagiras, are spirits of promiscuous women or prostitutes.

One other low spirit in Umbanda is Zé Pilintra. He is the patron saint of barrooms, gambling dens, and whorehouses. Zé Pilintra is a partying low-life drifter and personifies the trickster. Brazilians have taken to calling João de Deus, João Pilintra, and for good reason.

As we follow João Pilintra Faria on his adventures through Bahia in the sixties, we can only imagine what he was up to. He has revealed very few details of this history to his biographers. Whatever it was, the police were always in pursuit, and he kept moving on.

All his biographers mention Umbanda and Quimbanda as the rituals he participated in during this epoch. Umbanda is the practice of white magic, improving life through the supernatural—but not at others' expense. Quimbanda is black magic, a subject that I reluctantly need to address.

Over the years, various styles of Umbanda have separated from the mainstream. One of these splinter groups was more like a rupture. Candomblé and Umbanda rejoiced when Quimbanda split from their paths and forged a new one. They thought they had rid themselves of a problem, but it remained.

Free of the restrictions of the original cults, Quimbanda is black magic. Its services include harming others, enriching yourself at the expense of others, and breaking bonds of karma. Quimbanda delivers justice with vengeance. It is the *left-hand path.*

Quimbanda also has healing spirits that can remove physical and psychological illnesses. Exus can create both beneficial and harmful magic. They claim to open all roads, alter one's karma, and eliminate all obstacles. The spirits of Quimbanda can kill an enemy, seduce the object of your desire, or evaporate any problem. They can secure drug deals, crimes, and any dark human revenge you can think of. They can even help you find gold and gems and win at gambling.

In Quimbanda, the mediums work solely with Exus and Pombagiras. The Exus can cure cancer, heal a broken heart, and guarantee business deals. They save lost causes and fix the unfixable. Exus can manifest miracles.

Quimbanda is also syncretic. It gave the many Exus pseudonyms to disguise their true identity. The Exus have a supreme leader. Initiates understand him to be Lucifer, but one of his syncretic aliases is the biblical figure of King Solomon. The same spirit possessed João in Campo Grande and stands by him now: Rei Solomon / Exu Rei. King Exu is always accompanied by his Falange, by his countless troops of lesser spirits.[19]

As João refined his brand, the concept of a *phalange* (a military phalanx) was his constant theme. Falange (the Portuguese spelling) was also the name of the Spanish Fascist movement under General Franco.

In Quimbanda, the *lesser spirits* of the Exu (his phalange) are the deceased scum of the earth. Exus claim they work with humans to improve their karma. An example might be a Nazi Doctor who performed torturous science studies on helpless subjects. These spirits comprise the phalange of the seven primary Exus. Once the initiate has captured one of these low spirits, it becomes their slave and vice versa.

The primary Exus are fallen angels and demons. They adopt syncretic identities of prestige. Exus pose as doctors, professors, saints, and historical figures. In contemporary Brazil, many politicians and organized crime figures consult Quimbanda. There is a neighborhood north of Brasilia that is renowned for this. The town is famous for its *trabalhos* (works) of black magic. One will see dozens of status cars parked in front of the many terreiros.

The Peregrinations of João

As João began his saga of the sixties, one of his influences was Master Yokaanam (Oceano de Sá, 1911-1985). He had met him as a child in 1956 while the Master and his group were on a long pilgrimage that started in Rio de Janeiro. Yokaanam was searching for the ideal power spot in Goiás to create his visionary city. He struck a dramatic figure, wearing his hair and beard like Jesus, and walked with a staff in long white robes. [20]

This group of pilgrims numbered 300 families. Before they found their ideal location, they lived in Anápolis, the largest city in Goiás at the time. It is the hometown of João and various family members to this day.

In 1956, Yokaanam (John the Baptist in Greek) founded the community of Novo Jerusalem, which still exists near Brasilia. The Master promoted an alternative form of Umbanda. His cult combined Umbanda with the philosophy of the Essenes, Freemasonry, and Spiritism. He called his new religion Ã Ecletica Espiritualista Universal.

Before he became Yokaanam, Oceano de Sá was raised by spiritists and trained to be a Franciscan monk. He was a lieutenant in the Brazilian Air Force and a personal pilot of Gethulium Vargas, the president of Brazil.

On a training flight, his trainee crashed their plane into Guanabara Bay, near Rio de Janeiro. Yokaanam accredited a female entity with saving his life and helping him recover. He sustained many injuries, and his companion died. During his recovery, another entity appeared. He called himself Master Lanuh, and Yokaanam channeled his messages.

Lanuh said the central highlands of Brazil would be one of the few places on Earth where people would survive a coming cataclysm. Master Lanuh warned Yokaanam that a rogue planet would sideswipe Earth. A planet 300 times the size of ours.

It would arrive in 2003 and kill two-thirds of humanity in an instant. Master Lanuh instructed him to gather his people and create an Eclectic City. In the rugged outback of Goiás, he would restore the original Essene Christianity and unite all religions around it.

Master Yokaanam on pilgrimage. Photo: Public Domain of Brazil.

Yokaanam predicted the relocation of Brazil's capital (then Rio de Janeiro) to this area. He prophesied it would become a glorious center of culture and civilization after the Apocalypse. Soon afterward, Oceano de Sá changed his name to Yokaanam. Young João visited this community several times. He was not a member and never embraced their religion.

He borrowed ideas from them, especially their hybrid style of Umbanda and Freemasonry. Yokaanam's cult practiced yearly pilgrimages. This resonated with João's persona of the Romani wanderer. As a fortune teller, he traveled from town to town, never staying long. Our gypsy was not yet posing as a spiritual healer. He pulled teeth, peddled pharmaceutical remedies, and produced rustic herbal syrups. He never did his work for free.

Another influence on João's style was the Spiritist community of Palmelo, Goiás. He visited there when he was in his twenties—mediums founded this village in 1929. In 1936, a famous political figure, Jerônimo Cândido Gomide, transformed Palmelo into a small city. He built a hospital staffed by mediums. It became famous for its spiritual surgeries performed without anesthesia.

Another Palmelo founding father was Bortolo Damo. He opened a Spiritist Sanatorium. They treated the mentally disabled and persons having spiritual emergencies. The mediums in Palmelo specialized in delivering messages from the dead. Palmelo was a famous healing center in those days. It attracted celebrities and many lost souls.

João did not become a Spiritist nor join the community. On one of these visits, Jerônimo Cândido Gomide reprimanded João. He told him to grow up because he was joking around, grabbing crutches and eyeglasses from the patients, and aping a cure. This compulsion lasted throughout João's career and became one of his hallmarks. Most of these people needed their eyeglasses and canes the next day. They expelled him from the center.[21]

The sixties were a turbulent time worldwide, and Brazil was no exception. Waves of migrant homeless families seeking work and labor union demands worried the government. The economy took a nosedive, bankrupted by the extravagant cost of loans to build Brasilia.

The next president lasted less than a year before he resigned. He was succeeded by the left-wing vice-president João Goulart. He ruled until 1964 when a Pentagon/CIA-sponsored military coup overthrew him.[22]

This was the height of the Cold War, the Cuban missile crises, atomic bomb tests, Fidel Castro, Che Guevara, and Chairman Mao Tse Tung. Poor folks and college students were agitating for socialism or outright Marxism. Capitalism had Brazil by the throat as things unraveled. They found Goulart guilty of the sin of allowing land reform and nationalizing some essential services. The paranoid powers that be smelled a commie.

Opening the vast wilderness regions of Brazil created social havoc. People poured into the Amazon states with promises of free land, but the Green Hell quickly defeated them. These pioneer states, including Goiás and Bahia, became political and military flashpoints. João was in the maelstrom.

João and his biographers all mention that he did his work during this epoch, concealed in Quimbanda/Umbanda rituals often held in the forest. In reality, he was a *practitioner* of Quimbanda.[23]

If you are a member of such a cult, you do not do your own thing, using their centers to promote your healing work. Instead, you practice the art of Quimbanda. They arrested him for this, along with a lot of other people. Quimbanda was illegal, as was practicing medicine without a license, particularly as a way of earning a living.

"There was a time in the past when I had to stay in hiding in order to attend to the people wanting my help. People were saying, here comes the healer. I said I'm not a healer; I'm a tailor.

"Or some would say, here comes the Macumbeiro, and I'd reply, I'm not a Macumbeiro. I just come with the Word of God. I don't even have the knowledge to do Macumba. *But if someday somebody comes to me and says I must do my work through Macumba to be at God's side, then I will.*" From João de Deus's speech on November 22, 2000, recorded by Josie Ravenwing, in *The Book of Miracles*.

João was incidental to a more significant issue. Black magic was rampant in the regions João traveled. The authorities pledged to stamp it out in the name of *charlatanism* (witchery). They did not falsely accuse and persecute him; he was breaking the laws of Brazil.

Apparently, the money was pretty good, and João, who was also a pool shark during this time, leveraged his earnings gambling at the pool tables and, according to him, always winning. Although João was a participant in African trance cults, he didn't take his mediumship seriously and ignored the advice of other mediums who wished to train him properly.[24]

From 1963 to 1967, João's story gets sketchy. He mentions living in Barreiras, the largest city in western Bahia—near the border of Goiás. Nowadays, it is a major transit conduit for all drugs trafficked in Brazil. It ranks as Brazil's fourteenth most violent city—home to over forty drug gangs. It was an Amazon boom town of commerce and river trade in the early sixties.

It was, and is, the home of many Quimbanda and Candomblé terreiros. Bahia is the holy land of Candomblé—Salvador is its Mecca. In this era, Candomblé, Umbanda, and Quimbanda were morphing and changing into one another. We can say the same for João's studies in Bahia.

Another place João lived during these times was Cana Brava, a small neighborhood in Salvador. It was a favela that sprung up around an enormous landfill. The residents were trash pickers. It was a dangerous neighborhood, but it gave João easy access to Salvador's 5,000 terreiros. Today, a park covers the old landfill.[25]

João mentions incorporating Caboclo Gentil during this time, which is a clue about the true nature of the rituals he attended. But before descending that rabbit hole, we need to discuss other topics.

In the early sixties, João visited the two most famous spiritual healers Brazil has known. Both mediums were at the height of their careers. João witnessed true supernatural healing at their centers. These brief encounters left a lasting impression on young João. Years later, their influence manifested as the Casa de Dom Inácio in Abadiânia.

Benedita Cipriano Gomes was born in 1903 in a tiny village two hours from Anápolis, or Abadiânia. When she was seven years old, she became very ill and died. She had lost all her vital signs. While the family was preparing her body for burial with a ritual bath, they noticed she was sweating profusely. They held the wake but waited three days to bury her, *just in case.*[26]

Three days later, her vital signs returned. She had returned from the dead. She became famous. The simple country folk flocked to her home for her blessing or perhaps a miracle.

Lovingly nicknamed Dica, Benedita attracted hundreds of disciples within just a few years. While she was still a child, her followers built a village around her home, calling it Lagolândia.

Dica believed in communal land use and was an advocate of land reform. Her budding community abolished the use of money, and their lands had no fences. The crops were distributed equally among the villagers. She preached racial equality, abolition of taxes, and free land for all.

Dica gathered 15,000 followers. She built a small army of 1,500 men, trained and armed. She also counted 4,000 registered voters among her numbers. The powerful colonels of the region who acted as Mafia Dons were not pleased. They feared an armed uprising was being fomented.

Dica's popularity was because of her healing work. Pilgrims poured in from afar to take part in the masses she held. They came to receive her healing touch or surgery performed by the spirit of a German doctor named Dr. Fritz.

Her fame spread throughout Goiás. Newspapers condemned her and asked for her arrest. It incensed them that many diqueiros sought refuge with her. These ex-slaves had only recently escaped from the plantations where they were born. Legal slavery had ended almost forty years earlier.

Dica's devotees were armed and ready to protect her from arrest, and the local authorities of the region avoided confronting them.

In 1925, a military detachment was sent from the State Capital, Goiás Velho. They were instructed to attack the village and capture Dica. They fired machine guns at her home and the village when they arrived. Dica and her villagers jumped into the nearby river and fled into the forest, but she was captured.

They brought her to Goiás Velho and put her in a basement cell with guards at the padlocked gate. In the morning, she was gone. She continued her mission, married, and had several children. Her popularity grew.

Dica was arrested again and imprisoned in Rio de Janeiro. Rio's poor would line up at her prison cell window to receive a healing. An archive in Rio de Janeiro chronicles the many cures she enabled while imprisoned.

After her release, she returned to her home and her mission as a healer. Her simple dirt-floored farmstead became a spiritual hospital. Her patients spent days, weeks, or even months under her care. She provided for the helpless and hungry, doing her healing work for free.

Dica continued her work, incorporating Doctor Fritz, until she died in 1970. Known as Brazil's Joan of Arc, folks in Goiás call her Saint Dica or *Santa Dica*.

Santa Dica. Photo: Public Domain of Brazil.

One of Dica's close friends told me João visited her center in the sixties. Her "hospital" continued for many years after her passing, with the help of her loved ones.

Zé Arigó (José Pedro de Freitas, 1921-1971) was known as "The Surgeon of the Rusty Knife." He was the other well-known and beloved Brazilian healer of João's time. Like João, Zé was poor, with only three years of schooling. At fourteen, Zé started working in the mines of Conghonas do Campo in Minas Gerais.[27]

In 1950, he suffered from headaches and insomnia. Then, he entered trances and had visions. He heard a voice, and it wouldn't leave him alone. One day, as this voice chased him, a bald man wearing a white apron possessed Zé. He led a group of doctors in a giant operating theater. The bald doctor told Zé he was Dr. Adolf Fritz, lately of Poland but now serving humanity to pay off his karmic debts—the same Doctor Fritz that Dica incorporated.

Soon afterward, Arigó performed operations with kitchen knives and needles. He also scribbled complicated and archaic pharmaceutical prescriptions. They could only be formulated in his brother's pharmacy. One of Arigó's hallmark operations was poking a knife's blade into his patient's eye sockets without them feeling pain.

Arigó's fame spread throughout Brazil after he removed a lung tumor from a famous Brazilian Senator. Thousands of people came to Arigó for his healing powers.

In 1956, he was arrested for illegally practicing medicine and sentenced to prison, but President Kubitschek pardoned him. In 1962, the authorities arrested him again, and he spent seven months in prison. However, the wardens allowed him to continue healing people while jailed—he was *that* famous.

When João witnessed Zé Arigó's surgeries and popularity, one can picture the envy this aroused. Arigó became João's model for much of his later work. The spiritually minded Arigó denounced Quimbanda and African magic. I imagine this soured any student and master sentiments that may have crossed João's mind. Not that it mattered. João was there to learn more tricks. He had picked up three from Arigó: the eye scraping, the cuts, and the indecipherable prescriptions.

Arigó died soon after Santa Dica in an auto accident in 1971. Fritz had warned Zé never to accept donations for the Doctor's work, with the caveat that Fritz would kill him if he did so.

Later allegations suggest that he had accepted contributions before his untimely death at age forty-nine. This created a vacuum. Young João Curador had ambitions to fill it, and his spirits didn't mind if he made money. He needed to acquire his own spirit doctor.

He found him in Quimbanda. Salvador, Bahia, was Brazil's first capital, an epicenter of slavery, and a focal point of Candomblé and hundreds of its sub-cults. This incubator hatched João Curador and his Quimbanda spirit, Caboclo Gentil. Shall we peek down that rabbit hole?[28]

Umbanda and Quimbanda are like day and night, black and white. Umbanda embraces Christianity, while Quimbanda wants nothing to do with it. They consider themselves disciples of Lucifer and his Exus.

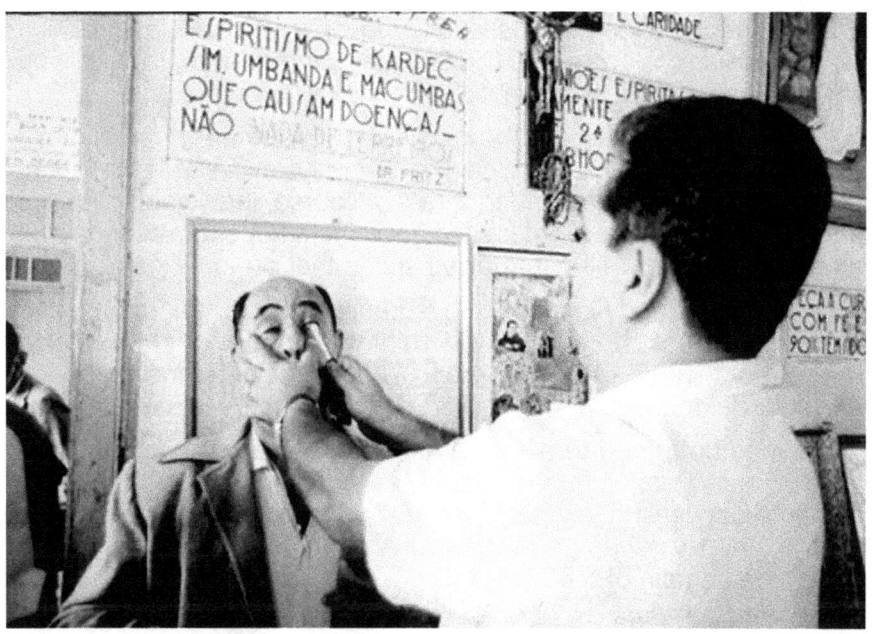

Zé Arigó, inserting a knife blade into a man's eye socket. Note the framed declaration: Spiritism of Kardec? Yes. Umbanda and Macumbas that cause illnesses? No. Nothing to do with Terreiros! Dr. Fritz. Photo: Archive of ESTADÃO CONTEÚDO/AE.

Umbanda works with spirits who exist on the astral plane, spiritual beings. Quimbanda works with fallen angels, demon spirits, and low-life dead people. They use the term *entity* for these spirits.

If it could only be that simple. It was anything but black and white. In João's time, one could attend hundreds of possession rites in Bahia. This part of his history is something neither he nor his disciples wanted to be known. We must sift through the infrequent hints João shared with his trusted confidants to find the truth.

The terreiros João frequented were Candomblé, not Umbanda. Bahia was steeped in African traditions, but Umbanda only arrived in the late 1950s. Most of Bahia's terreiros practiced various traditional forms of Nagô/Yoruba Candomblé. However, João gravitated toward the cults of the Ewe and Bantu nations, with their ritual magic and blood sacrifice. None of these tribes were Christian.

Afro-Brazilian religions had an identity crisis. Catholicism and Spiritism didn't mix well with Bahia's African traditions. Umbanda was a white person's approach to trance possession. White culture believed in right and wrong, angels versus demons.

Quimbanda doesn't believe good or evil exists in the spirit realm. The spirits are neutral. Feed them and treat them well, and they will help you. Disrespect them, and they will harm you.

Can anyone imagine the psychic state of the African slaves? Prisoners with no human rights, living in filth and semi-starvation, and always prey to rape and torture? Of course, they wanted justice and freedom. Their ancient beliefs gave them hope for revenge and an end to suffering. They preferred spirits that could kick ass.

Umbanda and Candomblé eventually became mainstream and legalized. However, the left-hand cults were feared and prohibited by law. For that reason, it isn't easy to define the difference between Quimbanda and Umbanda.

They both tried to avoid persecution and used syncretism to hide their secrets. Quimbanda often called itself Umbanda to avoid scrutiny. Concealing secrets, particularly for the left-hand path, has always been a fundamental part of their creed. This was João's world, the domain of the Trickster.[29]

In Quimbanda, the Major Exus are named by their qualities. They derive their secret names from the fallen biblical angels, one of whom is the Baphomet of the Knights Templar and the Freemasons.

The king of the Exus is Lucifer, The Prince of Light. He goes by syncretic names like King Solomon (aka Exu Mor). The Exus of Africa merged with the fallen angels of the Middle East and blended with European Occultism. This is left-hand Quimbanda.

Caboclo Gentil, whom João incorporated during this epoch, is a minor Exu. He is unknown in conventional Umbanda terreiros. A Caboclo signifies an indigenous spirit. They are an important element in Umbanda rites.

There are three categories of caboclo spirits: forest Indians, acculturated Indians, and *caboclos* (mixed-race or non-Indian).

Caboclo Gentil is usually from the mixed-race line that includes gypsies and European nobles. The Gentiles are a separate group of spirits. They have deep roots in Vodun and Angola-inspired cults. They don't exist outside this context.

From 1960 to 1980, João incorporated spirits in various cults straddling Quimbanda, Umbanda-flavored Voodoo, and the occult and magic traditions. He was from the line of the *Curadores Pajés* and the *Gentileiros*. In other words, he was a shamanic healer practicing the left-hand Quimbanda arts.

We now need to turn to events in Brazil in 1964. This was a dramatic and pivotal year for Brazil and João. He was twenty-two years old. Brazil's President was on the CIA's hit list. The United States stepped into Brazil's sovereign affairs.

Their mission was to replace the democratically elected civilian president with a military coup and junta. Brazil became a pawn in the intensifying Cold War. The U.S. feared another situation like Cuba was brewing, and the CIA decided drastic measures had to be taken.

The economy was in shambles. The land reform movement was large and dangerous. Students in the universities were converting to communism. They attempted to influence the poor and dispossessed of Brazil to embrace the idea of a popular revolt.

President João Goulart was overthrown in the military coup of 1964. He was a popular president, and the polls showed he would win re-election. The power brokers of Brazil and the United States saw his reform policies as too left-wing. They orchestrated an anti-Communist hysteria.

This swelled into a mass protest in Sao Paulo of 400,000 right-wing Christians hell-bent on deposing Goulart. Others came forward to anoint the coup, such as Volkswagen and American car manufacturers in Brazil. The Chicago School of Economics also supported the coup with its Shock Doctrine.

The CIA's *Operation Condor* provoked the turmoil. The U.S. Navy's *Operation Brother Sam* was set in motion. A U.S. aircraft carrier and backup warships off the coast of Rio de Janeiro waited on standby should Brazil's military need help.

The problems had only begun. The military dictatorship wouldn't end for twenty-one years. In 1964, the military government rewrote Brazil's Constitution. They stifled freedom of speech and all political opposition. The military regime was anti-communist and nationalistic. They were also paranoid and out of their minds.

They dragged the population into a collective trauma. Before it was over, the military had arrested and tortured around fifty thousand Brazilians. Another eight thousand were exiled. They were politicians, academics, writers, and entertainers. Four hundred thirty-four were killed or *disappeared* (likely much more). Eight hundred were tried and convicted in military courts. The clamp down on the press was universal.

Not one Brazilian politician of presidential stature agreed with the new agenda. The military chose Marshal Humberto de Alencar Castelo Branco as the new president. He had four successors, each appointed by the last president. They were always marshals or generals.

The economy boomed while the quality of life for the poor plummeted. The government implemented grand projects to open the Amazon region to commerce, transportation, and exploitation.

Bahia had already been smoldering with grievances. It now became a hotbed of protest and resistance to the military regime. Across the state border in Goiás, one of João's older brothers, Valdivino, had become a communist.[30]

He joined a popular peasant movement led by José Porfirio. Porfirio gained fame as the leader of two homeless land revolts, which led to land titles for the armed squatters. Porfirio became a wanted man, fleeing into the jungles of Pará and becoming one of the *disappeared.*

These famous rebellions of Formosa and Trombas inspired many homeless wanderers to organize and arm themselves. They came toe to toe with the military police. Everywhere João Teixeira de Faria lived were regions permeated with this tension. Also, they were centers of Afro-Brazilian religions harassed by the police.

João was arrested for charlatanism in Barreiras, Bahia in the mid 1960s. He was brought to trial and confronted the judge with private details from her life. João said she was so frightened by his powers that she didn't prosecute him but made him leave town.

He also told how he was jailed and severely beaten in Bahia. When his torturers interrogated him, the police began screaming in pain as they invisibly received the same beating they had dished out.[31]

João is fond of these portraits of a victim's revenge. It must be helpful to have entities who do this type of work. Where can one find entities like this?

We can find them in the *Candomblé of the Caboclos,* which originated in Bahia. The spirit entity Caboclo Gentil exists in a few obscure cults. Gentil was João's primary spirit for decades. A person possessed by Caboclo Gentil must attend rituals specifically for calling him. He is summoned with songs, dance, and offerings of sacred foods, honey, and mind-altering herbs. On other occasions, chickens and small birds are sacrificed for a blood offering. Blood calls Caboclo Gentil and the Exu he obeys.[32]

Candomblé of the Caboclos works with Voduns, Caboclos *(called Entities)*, Exus, and Gentileiros. Macumba, which is similar, works with the same spirits. In this cult, mediums incorporate many spirits—the more, the better. Candomblé of the Caboclos is rooted in Angolan Candomblé.

Another popular Quimbanda sect of this era that welcomed Caboclo Gentil was the cult of Jurema, prevalent in Bahia. Jurema is an Indian goddess and the forest's protectress. She is also a psychoactive plant.

Gira with Caboclo Gentil. Photo: Public domain of Brazil.

Gentil is famed for his knowledge of herbs and forest spirits. The terreiros working with Jurema make tea from this powerful psychotropic tree root containing high levels of the mind-altering molecule DMT, also found in ayahuasca. This would lead to spirit possessions and trance states. The Jurema line calls him Caboclo Gentil das Matas (Gentil of the Forests). He is a healer and an herbalist—*a curador.* Several people at the Casa told me João drank a sacred tea in those days, but not ayahuasca.

Another type of Bahian terreiro that would have welcomed João and his Caboclo Gentil would be the houses working with Vodun

(Voodoo). The Ewé and Fon people of West Africa brought Vodun to Bahia. Candomblé Jeje is one such sect. This style of Vodun works with disincarnate spirits (Vodun), Gentil spirits, and Caboclo spirits.

These various cults hosting Caboclo Gentil are all sects of Candomblé. The authorities of Bahia were closing many of their terreiros. The government had persecuted Candomblé since the 1920s.

Until the late 1970s, one needed a special license to open a terreiro, perform the rituals, or initiate new members. As a result, there were hundreds of unlicensed houses of Candomblé, such as those João attended. These houses were vulnerable to raids, where their ritual objects were confiscated, and the participants were jailed.

The military regime erased more and more of Brazilians' constitutional rights. The Constitution was outlawed and replaced with a dictatorial set of laws. Beatings and torture sessions fueled an angry population with resistance and fear. The military created secret programs. They trained Brazil's various police forces in CIA torture methods. Hands-on workshops were the norm, with detainees or street people as practice victims.

By the late sixties, anyone brought into a police station for questioning had no right to a lawyer, bail, or habeas corpus. As soon as they were photographed and fingerprinted, they were intimidated or tortured. If they broke, their interrogators would recruit them as informants, spies, or secret vigilantes. If they refused the job, they risked being killed. The military government created these projects. Civilians (or police officers in civilian clothing) did the dirty work.

It wasn't just vagabonds like João, or black magic cultists being rounded up. Thousands of ordinary citizens ended up in these secret torture centers. Many died there and became the disappeared. Bahia was exploding with union unrest and student uprisings. Homeless squatters, radical insurgents, and a rising black power movement resisted the oppression.

We will probably never know how João began working with the intelligence service or his role. Thousands of official documents that catalog these events are withheld as national security classified documents. Many were destroyed decades ago or are buried in dust in a repository where one might spend years piecing together more details.

The truth is, there were no records kept at the torture centers. Victims were tortured with a black hood covering their heads, so they couldn't identify their tormentors if they survived. The people operating these places had no face, name, uniform, rank, or identity.

They all had code names. Brazil has been in denial for over sixty years about the crimes against humanity perpetrated on its citizens.[33]

Of course, João might have chosen the easy way out and become an informant. This likely occurred in Bahia, at one of the clandestine torture centers run by The Department of Political and Social Order (DOPS). Before 1966, their primary function was to curb crimes related to *vagrancy* (João's lifestyle), the practice of capoeira (African martial arts), and Afro-Brazilian religious cults.

They used the local police to enforce this. That is how they came to know João, who was frequently under their scrutiny. Perhaps they used him to penetrate and report suspicious activities in the terreiros. But, by 1967, they had bigger plans for João.

The DOPS mission was now morphing into a cleansing of subversive elements within Brazil's infrastructure. They harassed rival politicians and anyone who disagreed with the regime. Their policy of torture as an interrogation tool had gotten messy. Civil police were the henchmen, and they were out of control. They were being funded by shadowing figures of power and wealth. This needed to be kept well hidden. The government reined them in by placing the military high command as their regulatory body. Two hundred and forty-two secret detention and torture centers were created.[34]

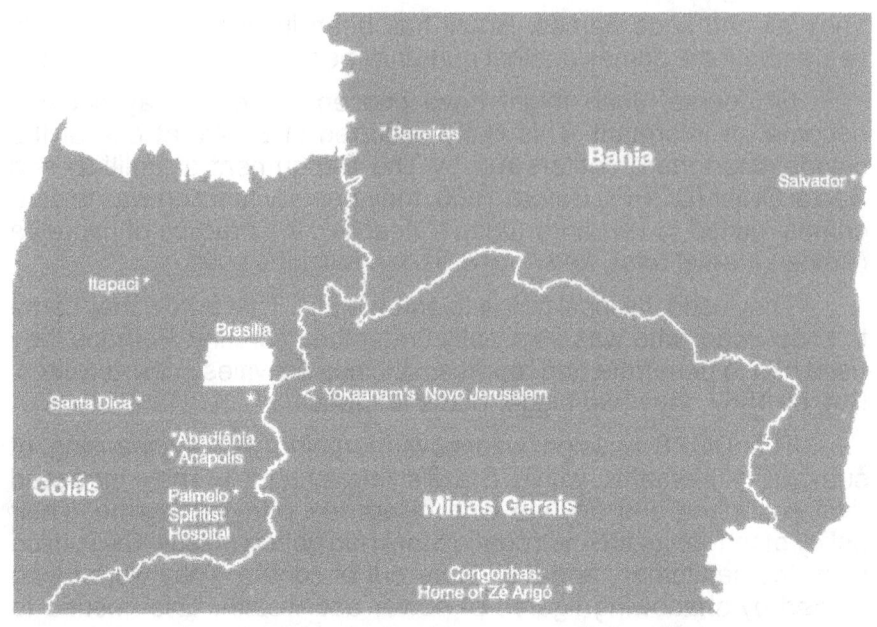

João's neighborhood. Created with mapchart.net / Creative Commons.

II.
G.I. JOÃO: TAILOR for the ARMY

The official story is that in 1967, at twenty-five years of age, João found refuge with the military as a tailor. Then, his eight years of suffering persecution ended.[35]

What puzzles me is how João, a drifter and grifter always flaunting the law, gets a job as an *alfaiate* (tailor) for the military. He had only three years of training, from ten to thirteen years old. João never succeeded at practicing the art and never owned a tailor shop. He is a man who cannot hold down a job and hasn't practiced the tailor's art for twelve years or more. João didn't even register for the draft—a crime. How does this guy get such a professional and cushy job and enjoy the military's protection?[36]

I remember a few stories I heard when I lived in Abadiânia. During the '60s, he was in such trouble with the police that they gave him an ultimatum: join the army or go to prison.

His biographers have a different version. For example, Robert Pellegrino wrote: "After eight long and difficult years, he could not endure the persecutions any longer and sought refuge in the military barracks at Brasilia as a civilian tailor. In return for protection, he healed the sick amongst the military personnel and their families, remaining under the army's protection for nine years."

Dictator Castelo Branco removed power from parliament, legal courts, and opposition parties. He dissolved Congress and revoked the Constitution. He disbanded the thirteen political parties and began selecting all governors by military panels.

The Press and television were censored. Brazil was in turmoil. Many elected officials were deposed, and important people were tortured and imprisoned. Small armed groups were spreading like wildfire. The Amazon was a flash point—the military rushed in.

In 1967, Joao began working as an informant or perhaps a tailor (or something worse) and moved to Brasilia. The military junta appointed Marshal Costa e Silva as Brazil's new dictator. He began a terrible regime known as the Years of Lead (*Anos de Chumbo*), which is also remembered as the Brazilian Economic Miracle. Many wealthy and middle-class people supported the coup.[37]

The other Brazilians did not. They had a low opinion of the situation. Afro-Brazilians, Catholics, and homeless people were now seen as subversives. The junta stripped universities, media empires, senators, governors, and the famous of their civil rights. All were subject to a towering wave of terror and paranoia. Mass protests broke out in most cities. These problematic people were now dealt with by military law in military courts. The armed forces superseded civilian law.

João had fallen into their net. From his perspective, this was Heaven. His narrative has him living in the military barracks in Brasilia, acting as a tailor while healing the officers and their families. He lived a charmed life doing as he wished with Caboclo Gentil and his Quimbanda ways. The military set him up with at least one tailor shop, which was likely a front for intelligence operatives. The military could visit his shop, and this wouldn't look suspicious. João kept the community under surveillance. He hacked the system, achieving financial security for the first time.[38]

Why was he sent to Brasilia? Why not use him in Bahia, where he lived? In 1967, the dictatorship created the Army Information Center, CIE, something like the KGB. This was an intelligence gathering agency and a secret murder and torture operation. The CIE now oversaw the entire pre-existing repression apparatus of Brazil. Its roots reached deep into all regions of Brazil and every level of civil order.

Their spies penetrated daily life, and the CIE now administered all police agencies. The CIE infiltrated student movements, unions, and any suspect group. They trained the agents to look like supporters and dress like them. They had fake IDs and assumed names, and very few people knew of their existence. Sometimes, these agents were arrested along with the group members they had penetrated. They only escaped torture with a password given to them by their superiors.

The CIE also sponsored a radical right-wing vigilante organization, the Secret Group. These terrorists planted bombs in public places, often at colleges and theaters. Afterward, the military blamed it on the communist rebel groups. The American CIA guided the CIE, strategizing their every act of repression.[39]

Brasilia, the new capital, was home to the Army High Command. This evil penetrated the largest cities and the tiniest villages of Brazil. If João was there to stitch uniforms, why didn't he stay? As we will see, João claims he served at eleven or more military bases in the nine years he spent in their service. That's a lot! Why? Was he really altering the length of officers' pant legs? I will pose a larger question. Is it a mere coincidence that every one of these bases concealed clandestine torture centers?

Torture, false imprisonment, and disappearing people were

illegal, even for the military government. The intelligence agencies did their dirty work in unofficial, civilian-funded, clandestine torture centers. The military administered and designed these programs. But culpability did not rest on their shoulders.

Because their activities were secret, it was difficult to identify the players in this torture culture. Indeed, writing about it would have been suicidal. Brazil's government has recently revealed a bit of its secret and horrifying history. The CIA also declassified some files on their involvement.

I have no documentation that João was arrested and brought to a torture center. But his descriptions of being severely beaten by the police in Bahia suggest so. In at least two interviews, João mentioned being stationed in Bahia. This would place him in or near Salvador and her several torture camps sometime between 1966 and 1967.

When he transferred to Brasilia in 1967 and was reborn as a tailor, he may have also visited their torture centers. They encouraged informants to try it themselves, sometimes forced to do so. Did he receive training in espionage, kidnapping, or sabotage?

Many police were trained to become assassins or torturers with the help of CIA intelligence schools. Informants and undercover agents for these agencies knew, *up close and intimate*, what the torture looked and smelled like. It was obvious what would happen if they disobeyed their new master.

President Marshal Arthur da Costa Silva signed the fifth emergency decree in 1968. This was the final blow to democracy in Brazil. The military began a hardline offensive against its detractors, and the president now held absolute extraordinary powers.

Armed groups robbed banks, killed cops, and kidnapped foreign ambassadors. They were like the Black Panthers and the Weathermen. The military panicked and amped up the covert war against subversion. Their new policy was to capture-torture-execute and conceal the corpse.

DOI-CODI was the new agency overseeing this Orwellian civil repression project. This became Brazil's Homeland Security. They divided Brazil into six military zones of internal defense. The country was now at war with itself.

All intelligence agencies answered to the SNI, the National Intelligence Service.

The DOI (Department of Information Operations) was an illegal and secret intelligence organization. It comprised police and select military leaders, but private donations funded it. The DOI acted like the Gestapo to eliminate political and intellectual resistance to the dictatorship.

Every state had a DOI unit, directed and overseen by a central agency called CODI (Center of Internal Defense Operations). The government denied the agencies existed.

CODI analyzed all the information gathered by the DOI, made combat decisions, and planned region-wide troop deployments. An Army Major commanded each DOI unit and oversaw the three armed forces, plus state, military, and civilian police.

DOI-CODI operated hidden torture centers. Some were at private ranches and homes. Others were at local police stations or jails, even a soccer stadium. They hid them in agencies like the Highway Department or military barracks.

I suspect it is not coincidental that João began his career as a military tailor while DOI-CODI was implemented throughout Brazil.

Forty years later, João funded a slick documentary film starring himself and directed by a close friend. It is the most intimate cinematic look at João's personal life to date. He's relaxed and talkative.

At one point in the film, he is sitting in a rustic lawn chair with cow pens behind him. His shirt is unbuttoned, and gold jewelry is displayed around his red neck.

Redneck John. Artistic reproduction.

He explained he was stationed at several military bases as a tailor for the army. My jaw dropped when I heard this.[40] He even listed them:

1. Brasilia. The nation's capital was home to all extra-judicial agencies. The CIE trained informants in espionage and personal interrogation (torture) methods. DOI-CODI operated several illegal torture sites in the city itself—including within the ministries of the army and navy.

The SNI, which oversaw the recruitment and training of secret agents, was also in Brasilia. Their spies reported on their workmates. Agents penetrated government and private institutions at every level, looking for people to neutralize (kill). The SNI had a liaison relationship with the American CIA, which used them as a channel for information about communists and such. The intelligence data traveled in both directions.

Brasilia had its own worries. In 1968, military and federal police invaded the University of Brasilia. They detained five hundred students and professors. One was shot in the head, and sixty were imprisoned. Two hundred twenty-three of the professors at the University resigned in protest. Many were arrested and tortured in the neighborhood of the ministries and parliament. This was the third attack on the University in the last few years.

Fifty-thousand protesters marched in the streets of Rio de Janeiro. Violent resistance spread everywhere. Dictator Costa e Silva created The Superior Council of Censorship. This killed freedom of speech in Brazil.

Three of Brazil's most loved and famous musicians were arrested and exiled. Many bombs exploded in various cities.

We stand at a crossroads here. Is João an alfaiate for the military, a mere tailor seeking refuge in the military barracks? Or is something hidden in his story—a secret? Let's explore some other locations he says they sent him to after training in Brasilia. Three are in the Northeast region:

2. Salvador, Bahia. Sixth Military Region DOI-CODI. Also, Alagoinhas military base with secret torture farms far from neighbors. These clandestine encampments were nicknamed *Grandma's House*—DOI's black humor.

3. The State of Pernambuco. Recife (the 4th Military Command) and Olinda were the military bases. Both were DOI-CODI torture centers. Recife's nightmare began on the day news of the military coup reached them. The military police expected this, meeting the

protesters head-on. Recife was one of the epicenters of rebellion.

4. The State of Piauí had four clandestine torture centers. All were in the capital of Teresina. There was widespread civil unrest in Piauí beginning in 1964. Anti-communist rhetoric and police violence were viral. Actual communists were in grave danger in Piauí.

Thousands of regular citizens spied on their friends and neighbors for the military. Everyone was afraid of being labeled a communist. Being a "communist" often meant being Catholic or a member of a rural cooperative. Students of a left-leaning professor reading the wrong books might be implicated.

João spent most of his military career in the Amazon, stationed at four bases there:

5. Pará is an essential Amazon State in this story. João was stationed in Belém (8th Military Command) and Marabá, both DOI-CODI torture centers. In Belém, problems arose overnight in 1964.

The military had a significant presence in Belém, the port city at the mouth of the Amazon. The mayor of Belem denounced the coup. Students began a formidable resistance movement. They arrested hundreds of militants from left-wing parties—unionists and high school students as well.

The Junta deposed the Governor of Pará and the Mayor of Belem. They replaced them with military appointees. Catholic youth groups were singled out for arrests, then large union groups.

6. In Marabá, Pará, João was associated with the notorious Army Information Center hidden in the highway department office. This was the largest and most horrifying of the hidden serial killing centers. A high-level DOI-CODI military observer from Brasilia commanded the death house. They called it Casa Azul (The Blue House). Few captives survived the tortures and executions. João spent four years in service to the military in Marabá at the same time the Casa Azul functioned. This explains everything.

7. Tocantinópolis, Tocantins. Nearby villages of Xambioa and Bacaba were other torture centers in the Marabá orbit. The extermination of the communist rebels of the War of Araguaia occurred in this region.

João mentioned staying at four other bases, all of which had

DOI-CODI torture centers:
- 8. Imperatriz, Maranhão.
- 9. Anápolis and Goiânia, Goiás.
- 10. Niterói, State of Rio de Janeiro.
- 11. Rio Grande de Sul.

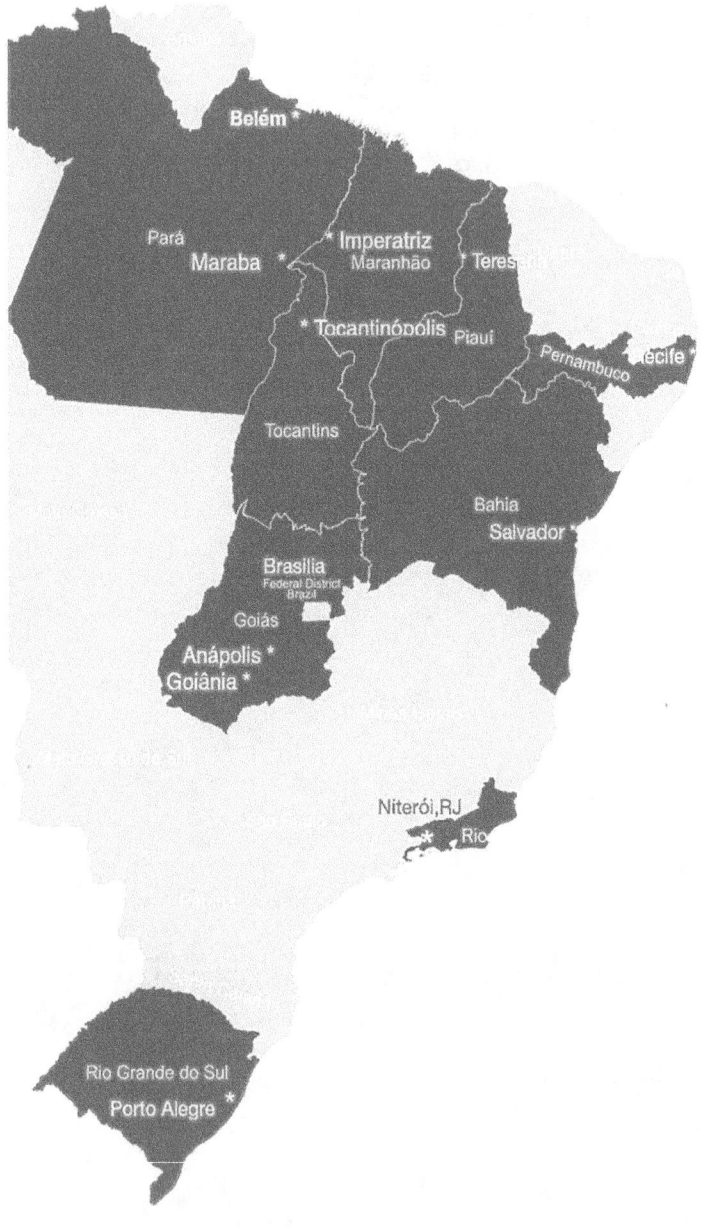

Places João claims to have been stationed with the military. All were clandestine torture centers.
Created with mapchart.net / Creative Commons.

In 1969, Dictator Costa e Silva had a stroke. A military panel replaced him with General Médici—another tough character. This year, several notorious kidnappings of foreign ambassadors by resistance groups occurred. Brazil was spiraling into hysteria while its economy was breaking all growth records.

The Regime decided to "develop" the Amazon. To do this, it needed roads. It also required a significant military presence. Why an army presence in the least populated region of Brazil?

A small segment of the resistance had taken their cause from Rio de Janeiro and São Paulo and hid in the Amazon. They trained Indians and locals in self-defense and self-sufficiency. These idealists imagined a peasant uprising like Castro's. They pictured the Amazon states seceding from the Military Regime.

It was a foolish and deadly mistake on their part. A vast military and espionage net was cast over the Amazon. Any local tempted to listen to the revolutionists would pay the price. Various popular grassroots movements also drew the military's ire.

The military sent João Faria to the Northeast and the Amazon trouble zones. Was he embedded as an intelligence operative in the disguise of a tailor? Every place he was based had a Grandma's Farm or torture room in the barracks. Coincidence?

So, did he stop working with Quimbanda? No, although each region had its peculiar version of the cult. All the military bases were in areas where Quimbanda cults were prevalent. Things were different in the Amazon. Candomblé hadn't taken root there. During João's nine-year career as a "tailor," he explored many types of cults found in this region.[41]

Caboclo Gentil would be welcome to incorporate in the local terreiros. Catimbó, Jurema, Xangô, and Vodun Jeje dominate the region. Blood sacrifice and shamanic magic were the norms.

This wasn't a stronghold of Umbanda. The roots were ancient Native and African rituals. The phrase "we do not trace this terreiro to Umbanda" is common among the local terreiros. Here, João first encountered popular cults of left-hand spirits and jokesters, such as the Exus, Mestre Zé Pilintra, and Mestre Inácio of Jurema.

In Piauí, our military tailor was stationed in Teresina. There are over 400 umbanda and quimbanda terreiros in Teresina. João was also stationed in Belém, the capital of Pará. The states of Pará, Piauí, and Maranhão are notorious for their left-hand cults.

João would spend the next ten years in this region, famous

for its *feiticeira* (black magic) and *pajelança* (magical healing). Here he entered the Oriental line and the Gypsy line of Umbanda—Quimbanda in disguise.

Many soldiers and police were members of Umbanda and Spiritist centers. In Pará and Maranhão, the police were fond of Quimbanda. Corruption within the military invited abuse in licensing terreiros. A cleansing of Umbanda and all the Afro-Brazilian sects ensued. Military agencies now regulated these cults.[42]

A color line was drawn. Afro-Brazilians were harassed and persecuted for decades. It didn't end with the racist regime in control. Complicated laws defined the terreiros permissible activities. Many were prohibited from initiating new members. The military attempted to strangle the weeds infesting Umbanda.

One needed recommendation from the authorities to practice your cult. This often involved background checks, old boy connections, and bribes to become legal. Many terreiros registered themselves as spiritist centers to get licenses. It was easier if you showed you supported the regime, staunch anti-communists willing to denounce anyone who wasn't.

Throughout the seventies, João moved from base to base. He was in Anápolis in 1973, which is considered a strategic area for the defense of Brasilia, a couple of hours away. The Dictator Emílio Médici decreed the city a national security site and deposed the elected mayor. The junta selected their mayor for the next twelve years.

They constructed an air force base in Anápolis the year before. The military presence and intelligence services were firmly planted in João's hometown. Goiânia, the new capital, had a DOI-CODI torture and interrogation center linked to Anápolis. It was a focal point for the statewide military strikes against the opposition.

Early in 1973, the medium João Curador held healing sessions in Anápolis. He claimed to be channeling the famous spirit doctor Adolph Fritz. Zé Arigó had died two years before, and young João aspired to follow in his illustrious footsteps.

He still wielded his gypsy knife when incorporated, working with his three dozen entities. Dr. Fritz was the first doctor entity he would try out. More would follow. This is the earliest sign that João Teixeira de Faria had begun practicing psychic surgeries. It is also the first year he is accused of rape and attempted murder.[43]

Maria was sixteen years old, a thin and shy girl who weighed ninety pounds. She was an innocent country girl visiting her aunt in the big city of Anápolis. Recently engaged, her aunt was to help her make her wedding dress. The aunt had health problems and was being treated by João Curador. One day, soon after Maria's arrival, she was at João's house, where his disciples were preparing food. João wanted to drive to a farm and get some chickens.

The girl and two women accompanied João. Along the way, he convinced the two older women to stay behind. Maria wasn't concerned because she was in good hands with the Curador. She didn't know where they were going. After they passed through the village of Alexânia, he turned onto a dirt road. She became nervous, thinking she should jump out of the car.

Parking beside a bridge, he told her to come down to the riverbank. He was going to do a cleansing for her with Dr. Fritz.

Beneath the bridge, he raped her. Maria begged him to stop; she was a virgin promised to another man. She says she was a tiny thing—only skin and bones.

After the act, she hemorrhaged, and João decided to kill her. He picked up a large rock and smashed her head. He shot her in the head three times when he saw she was still alive. One bullet knocked out all her teeth. Then he threw her into the river and drove away.

A fisherman found her, took her to the hospital, and saved her life. Her family fled Goiás in fear for their lives. She stayed silent and hidden for forty-six years before going public in 2019. One bullet is still lodged in her skull.

The Parrot's Perch & The Parrot's Beak
(Casa Azul—The Blue House of Terror)

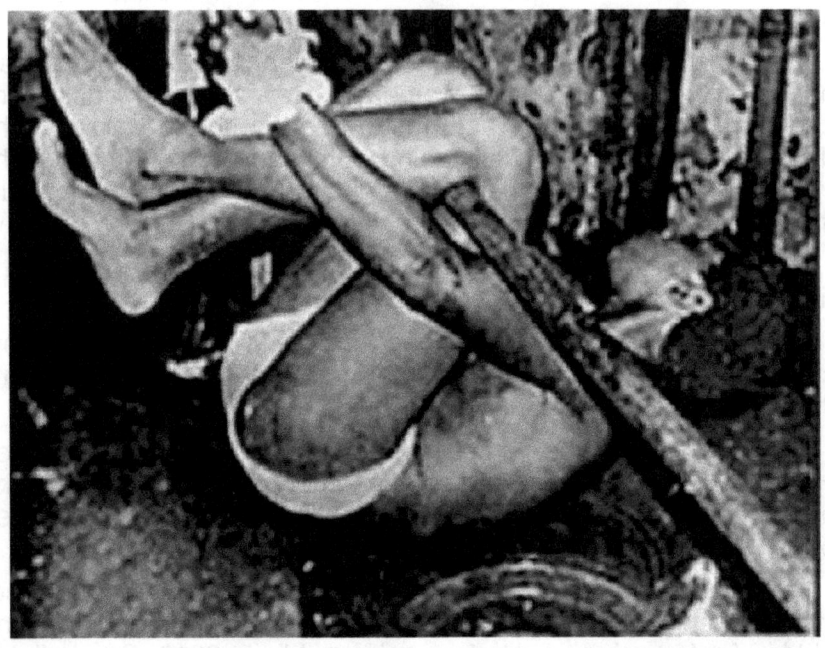

The Parrot's Perch. Photo: Archive of ESTADÃO CONTEÚDO/AE.

"For four years, João resided at a military base in Marabá, in southeastern Pará, which was beginning to gain political importance due to its mineral wealth and strategic location for the national security doctrine in force during the dictatorship years. At the time, he was able to enjoy stability and constant protection for the first time in his life." Machado, Maria Helena P. T. João de Deus: Um Médium no Coração do Brasil, 2016. [44]

The National Commission on Truth reported, "A report by Manuel Messias Guido Ribeiro, a former Army soldier who served in the Casa Azul between 1974 and 1980, asserted that *all soldiers who participated in military operations in the region witnessed and were aware of the torture practiced on the spot* and says that the same structure was used to torture military personnel who showed a more humanized conduct with the prisoners."[45]

The Parrot's Perch, *Pau de Arara,* is a Portuguese torture technique first used to punish slaves. Torture is a tradition in Brazil, beginning with its inception and continuing today. The perch works like this: They place a pole over the victim's biceps and behind the knees while the wrists and ankles are bound together with a cord. This person is then suspended upside down like a dead animal, the pole supporting their weight.

This would be torture enough, causing extreme joint and muscle pain, but the sadists in the torture centers also stripped the victim naked and applied electric shocks to the genitals and other sensitive places. Women were raped, and men were sodomized on the parrot's perch.

As one was restrained, the perch allowed other torture techniques such as waterboarding, tearing out fingernails, and branding. The perch was only one of their terrible torture methods. This technique was also used in Auschwitz during World War II, where it was known as Boger's Seesaw.

The Parrot's Beak, *Bico do Papagaio*, is an Amazonian region shaped like an isthmus of forest and rivers in the northern point of the state of Tocantins (the northernmost part of Goiás in João's time). It penetrates, in the shape of a parrot's beak, the adjoining states of Pará and Maranhão.

Here lies hidden the darkest history of the military regime and those who helped them. This is Brazil's dirty little secret. João was stationed at several places in the Bico do Papagaio that were known torture centers. Let's begin with Marabá, Pará.[46]

Marabá was connected to the Belém-Brasília highway in 1969. The same road project his mother had disappeared on several years before. Marabá was a sleepy jungle outpost about to experience an overnight boom. It grew to 20,000 residents when the highway reached their town. In the past, Marabá was only accessible by riverboat. João opened a small tailor shop in the early 1970s in downtown Marabá. A few people today remember his office in those times.

Marabá was not your typical military base. It had a secret torture camp with no accountability or records. The public didn't know it existed. It was at the edge of town in an agency that oversaw the highway department. They called it the Casa Azul. Unspeakable tortures and horrors occurred in those rooms for the four years João lived in Marabá. The photos of Casa Azul from this epoch are hauntingly similar to the early version of Casa de Dom Inácio, with the same white and blue paint job.

Casa Azul—Marabá, PA. Maíra Heinen/Rádios EBC. Public domain of Brazil.

The Amazon was about to become a militarized zone. In 1970, the government declared Marabá a National Security Area. This permitted direct intervention by the central government. They began Operation Mesopotamia in the Parrot's Beak. They aimed to eliminate (murder) all subversive elements and communist infiltrators. A civil war was their boogie man. *Kill the commies* was their war cry.

In the late sixties, a small group of students and opponents of the dictatorship created a movement. They were located along the Araguaia River in the Bico do Papagaio. Under the banner of the Communist Party of Brazil, the PCdoB, they arrived with simple rifles and medicine. They offered to help the poor Indians and caboclos (Brazilian phrase for mixed-race jungle dwellers) of this sparsely settled forest.[47]

A few had received military training in Mao Tse Tung's China. Women were in the group, too. They opened free primitive health clinics and schools in an outreach to the locals. Their dream was to spark a popular socialist revolt like Castro's in Cuba. Most of them had come from São Paulo, city kids with few skills to cope with the Amazon's harsh environment.

There were only sixty-nine of them. They made friends with the locals as they adopted their social customs of sharing and independence. These tragic idealists would foment the *Guerrilha do Araguaia,* the guerrilla war of Araguaia.

By April 1972, this tiny group of guerrillas had set up several jungle camps deep in the forest. They began attacking military posts in the Araguaia River region. The army responded with Operation Papagaio, deploying five thousand heavily armed soldiers. They even sprayed napalm from helicopters. The army suffered ten casualties, and they captured only a few guerrillas. This embarrassed the military.

They changed their tactics in 1973. The Guerrilla War of Araguaia was not a war but a hunting expedition that spread throughout the jungle regions of Goiás, Pará, and Maranhão.

The rebels were established a short distance from Marabá. Intelligence operatives arrived on flatbed trucks concealed within huge wooden crates. They were disguised as employees of various agencies. Others were embedded into communities as laborers, shop owners, salesmen, and rubber tappers. Agents were smuggled into remote areas with fake IDs.

Each man had a pseudonym everyone in the military called him—for instance, Zé, the mechanic, and Carlos, the cook. Perhaps João the tailor was one of those names. These undercover agents acted as informants. It was called *Operação Sucuri* (Operation Boa Constrictor).

From 1972 to 1975, the region was flooded with fake caboclos who dressed and spoke like locals. They ran riverside bars, became street vendors, and traded in local produce. Others opened barbershops, tailor shops, and lumber camps. Some even sold ammunition to the rebels. These spies kept records of what they heard and saw. They passed this on weekly to a pseudo-civilian agricultural engineer from the government agency INCRA (National Institute of Colonization and Agrarian Reform).

He went by the name of Dr. Luchini and was stationed in Xambioá. Actually, he was the supreme military commander Captain Sebastião Rodrigues de Moura, aka the notorious Curió. He dressed as a civilian. Unlike the battle against armed struggle in the cities, there were no police or military inquiries or court sentences. His order was to take no prisoners, killing them after prolonged torture sessions.

Innocuous agencies such as anti-malarial services, agricultural substations, and engineering offices disguised the military programs and implemented them.

The next phase was Operation Marajoara, which lasted through 1974. About 400 soldiers specialized in counterinsurgency infiltrated the region. They enlisted those who had previously collaborated with the guerrillas. The guerrillas' supply posts were located and destroyed.

The guerrillas faced starvation and jungle diseases as they were hunted down, tortured for information, and exterminated. The peasants and Indians were offered 1,000 cruzeiro bounties, leading to the capture of a rebel or a sympathizer. This was enough to buy a good piece of land. Many were denounced this way. Perhaps João became *financially secure for the first time in his life* through similar transactions.

Non-compliant locals who sold food or tools to the rebels or provided canoe transport, and even priests who helped them, were also tortured and disappeared. Homesteads were burned down. Over 400 locals were detained and tortured, several of them murdered.

The women suffered horrifying acts of sadism. One of their victims testified, "I was barbarously tortured into giving information. The torture was so violent that they closed the doors of the HQ because the soldiers were watching. They stuck a steel truncheon about this size [she measures with her hands, alluding to something about 8 inches] in my buttocks with electric shocks. I was already wounded. I was in no condition to be tortured. They hung me up on a fence; that blood that pus oozed out. I fainted. Then they lowered the rope and put me there. After they found out who I was, I started to walk around hooded. I was in my seventh month of pregnancy. I was visibly belly fat. I spent, day and night, day and night, in interrogation."[48]

By late 1974, the soldiers had murdered, either by execution or torture, all sixty-nine guerrillas. Sixty-one of the guerrillas are still listed as *disappeared* because, in 1975, the army implemented a secret clean-up operation.

They dug up the victim's graves and scattered the dismembered corpses from helicopters over the jungle. Others were tossed in rivers or cremated on the spot. The records were burned. Casa Azul was erased from memory.

THE PARROT'S BEAK

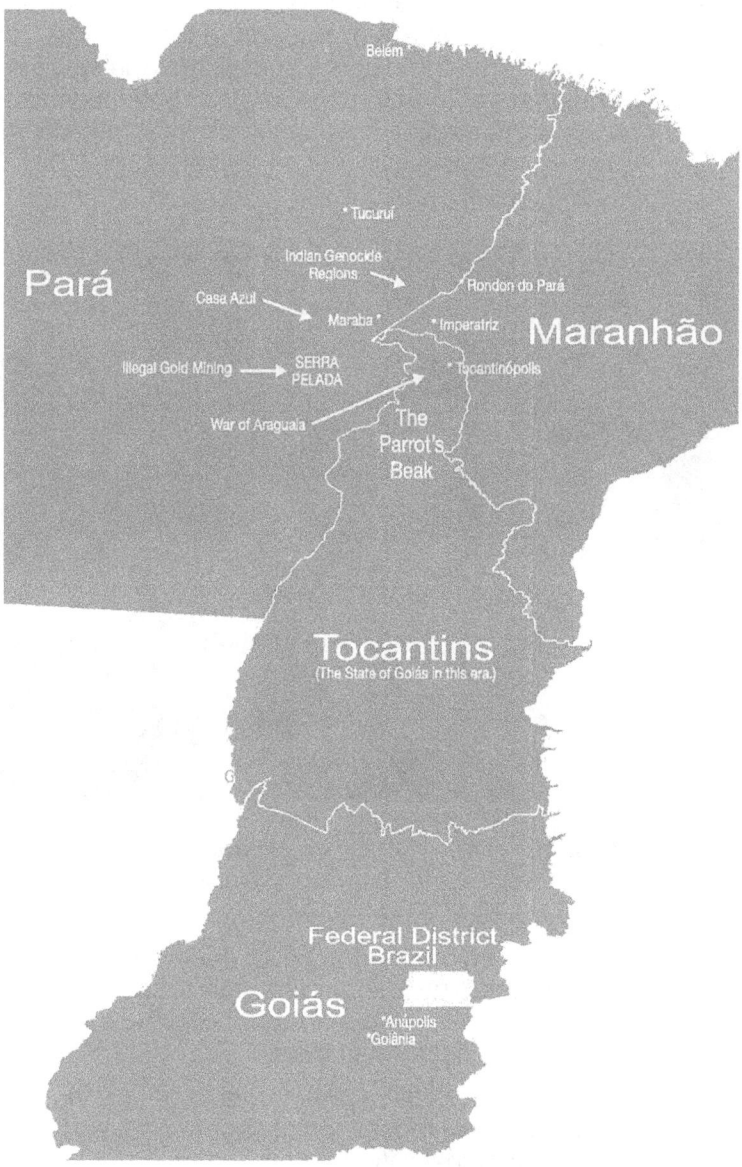

Created with mapchart.net / Creative Commons.

João and the Indian Genocide of the 1970s

Brazil's new President, General Emílio Geisel, took office in 1974. The rebels of Araguaia had been eliminated, but there was still more work to do. João became a participant in the Grande Carajás Program. This project aimed to explore and extract the world's most significant mineral deposit. The Grande Carajás contained incredible amounts of iron, gold, tin, bauxite (for aluminum), manganese, nickel, and copper. There were also diamond and gemstone deposits.[49]

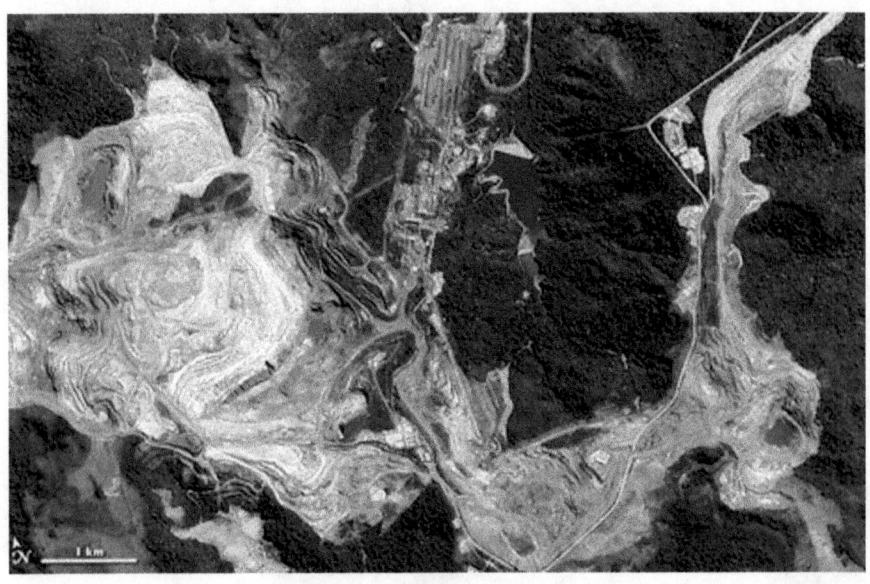

The Serra do Carajás iron mine in Pará, near Marabá, is run by Vale Mining Company. Photo courtesy of NASA.

This Amazonian region, where João spent ten years (1970 to 1980), was dominated by the military for reasons other than communist rebels. The military penetrated the jungle by building roads where none should have been made.

The roads were built to extract minerals in enormous open-pit mines, clear-cut hundreds of thousands of square hectares for exotic lumber, and produce charcoal with the rest.

They were built to create and access enormous dam projects (which powered the energy-hungry smelters that process the ores into aluminum and steel). They were made to transport the thousands of tons of beef and the millions of tons of soybeans and sugar cane that the regime imagined the region could produce if they only got rid of the trees and the Indians. Highways are the death of the Amazon, transporting the spoils to Amazon/Atlantic ports for export.

Throughout Brazil, the military regime stole Indian lands and committed genocide. Indigenous people were, by far, the largest group murdered and disappeared during the military's dirty war. The official figure is 8,000. The actual figures are much higher and uncounted.[50]

FUNAI is a Brazilian agency created by the military in 1967. It governs and determines the destiny of all Brazilian Indian tribes. FUNAI was declared to be the military government's resolution for oversights in earlier Indian agencies. It was not created to end corruption.

FUNAI leadership was high-level military henchmen appointed to dominate the Indians. They forced them off their mineral-rich lands and into assimilation: homelessness, alcoholism, slavery, and prostitution at jungle posts.

In the military's endless battle to stamp out dissent and resistance, the tribes were expected to assist in their efforts. Those who agreed became hunters of men and betrayers of their tribes. Indians who didn't were deemed enemies for their disobedience.

The military created secret concentration camps and torture sites specifically for Indians. They trained an elite troop of Indians to capture, torture, and imprison their fellow tribesmen. We know little about the Indian genocide during the dictatorship.

One of the few documents illustrating this tragic history is *The Figueiredo Report,* a study commissioned by the military in 1967. It investigated the National Indian Service, the predecessor of FUNAI. The report disappeared for forty-four years. The authorities claimed a fire destroyed it. It was found almost intact in 2013 and reported from one hundred and thirty indigenous reserves around the country. The published record is shocking.[51]

Entire tribes were killed. Large landowners, vigilante posse, and police were granted permission to capture and torture Indians in the way of progress. Over 5,000 pages chronicle massacres of tribes by machine guns and dynamite dropped from planes.

Secret inoculations of smallpox, meningitis, and measles, and handouts of sugar and children's toys laced with strychnine or ant poison (a nerve toxin) killed thousands. Many were captured for slavery and prostitution.

FUNAI amplified the problem. The military implemented an enormous project to claim and secure the Amazon for exploitation. They displaced more than a million people. Intrusive colonization by immigrants from other states left no region unoccupied. Dozens of Indian tribes were in the way of the advancing highways. The 100-kilometer clear-cut zone along the sides of the highway (where the government foolishly planned to settle 500,000 people in agricultural villages) was often within Indian reservations.

FUNAI's program was to divest the tribes of their ancestral lands, forcing them to become "Brazilian" or to eliminate them. The Indians became the next national security threat and were subjected to abject cruelty and almost exterminated.

Many tribes lost their lands to mega-scale dams that inundated dozens of small settlements; several of the tribes were uncontacted or remote and primitive. The Indians attempted to defend themselves with arrows and spears. They were no match for machine guns and aerial bombing.

The integrationist indigenous policy saw converting the Indian into a worker as a civilizing process under the terms of the regime. In 1972, Funai's superintendent, General Ismarth de Araújo, explained to the newspaper O Estado de S. Paulo that "An integrated Indian is one who becomes labor."[52]

One tribe, the Waimiri Atroari Indians, resisted in the northern Amazon region. They refused to be run off their lands for the construction of the gigantic Balbina hydroelectric plant, the BR-174 Highway, and bauxite mining explorations.

In 1974, a large festive gathering of this tribe and their neighboring tribes was interrupted by the sound of airplanes buzzing the group. The children ran out of the orca and looked up. Then, machine gun fire mowed down thirty-two members. It began raining a white powder. Soon, the Indians were writhing in burning pain, paralyzed and dying. They were victims of chemical warfare.[53]

Afterward, vigilante groups entered their villages armed with guns and machetes and finished the job. They murdered 2,650 Indians. Another tribe in the region, The Cinta-Larga, lost 3,500 to genocide through poisoning, germ warfare, and mass execution.

Another project, the Trans-Amazon Highway, which traversed the Amazon from the far west to the east and joined the Brasilia/Belem Highway, was destroying the lives of twenty-nine indigenous groups, including eleven tribes that had never been contacted.

João lived in Vila Rondon, Tucuruí, Tocantinópolis, and

Imperatriz from 1976 to 1980. These were all Indian forced-removal sites during that period. No records show that he ever worked for the military while he lived in these cities. [54]

Two biographers—Liberato Póvoa and Ismar Garcia—mention his presence in these locales. Póvoa is João's longtime attorney, champion, and close friend, and Garcia is now a lawyer for João's ex-wife, Ana Keyla Teixeira, in the cases implicating her involvement in his crimes.

The military planners decided Marabá needed access to the Brasilia/Belem highway and a route to Imperatriz. They gouged out a dirt track through the virgin forest, penetrating the traditional lands of several tribes. The Indians resisted the aggression.

These dear people, yet to enter the Stone Age, didn't know what they were up against. They barely had any contact at all with Brazilians. They didn't wear clothing. The military began a war of pacification to confront the elusive tribes in their own territory.

What began as a tiny riverside military outpost within an Indian mission and a highway department office (as was the Casa Azul of Marabá) grew from a few dozen people to 35,000 by 1982. The name of this new town would become Villa Rondon, bordering the states of Maranhão and Pará, near Marabá. This was João's new home. The year was 1975, and João was thirty-two.

Somehow, the "army" required João's services. Villa Rondon was one of at least four cities where he lived during a time of forced relocations and violent confrontations with indigenous people. Vigilante groups did much of this (overseen by the military), so it is hard to say whom João worked for or what he did. After all, he wasn't living in the middle of the jungle for pleasure. Indeed, this region is the poster child for the destruction of the Amazon ecosystem.

In Pará, the first and largest hydroelectric dam project in the Amazon was shaping up, and João was there as well. Over 34,000 reluctant occupants and many Indians (although the government did not count them in this statistic) needed to be forcefully evicted from their native lands. Many resisted, and nine tribes were displaced.[55]

The completed dam flooded 1,400,000 acres of former virgin forest and wreaked havoc on the ecosystem and the population. João was now stationed at the epicenter of this chaos in the village of Tucuruí. It was late 1975, and the work had just begun.

They were not concerned with the project's environmental or social impact. If you have seen the famous Hollywood film *The Emerald Forest,* the dam featured in the plot was the brand-new mega-turbines at Tucuruí.

First, the forest needed to be removed. The army used Agent Orange. They had more than they needed to destroy the forest. They tossed the unused full drums of the toxin into the grand excavation now unfolding. The residue contaminated the water. It caused the death of many animals. People downstream suffer from neurological disorders, congenital malformations, miscarriages, and cancer.

The flooded area is in the Tocantins-Araguaia-Maranhão ecoregion, the most degraded forest in the Amazon. You see this region frequently in the news. Illegal logging and infringement into native reserves by gold miners often turn violent. They like to kill protestors and Indians here. This part of Amazon now burns out of control each year. It will become the world's largest soybean producer and has many more cows than people. The forest is just about gone.

All this, for an electric plant meant to fuel steel foundries waiting to be built. The iron ore had not been mined yet. They needed a train line through the jungle to transport the ore; a separate highway gouged out of the unspoiled forest for access, and a clear-cut path for power lines. And, of course, one of the largest open pit iron mines on earth.

Indian reserves were in the way of these projects. Many of the Indians throughout Brazil who resisted—died. The survivors were placed in other parts of the forest, often a government-made shanty town on a speck of land, and sometimes with other tribes who were not their friends or in their linguistic group. Some of these tribes had only recently been contacted, and several had never been contacted.

The same thing happened to hundreds of quilombos, the remote villages founded by escaped African slaves in the past centuries. It was the end of the hunter's life, their rituals, and freedom. It happened overnight. The ancestral lands of six tribes were buried beneath the enormous artificial lake. The power lines and the railway displaced three other tribes. Part of those Indian lands is now the city of Tucuruí, where the dam and turbines of the Tucuruí Hydro Plant reside.

Tucuruí Hydro Plant. Photo by Repórter do Futuro Creative Commons Attribution 2.0 Generic license / Mongobay.

In 1976, João moved to Tocantinópolis. The Trans-Amazon Highway displaced the local Apinajé tribe, whose land it now crossed. The clear-cut zone on either side of the highway was promised to cattle ranchers and thousands of (white) homesteaders. As the homesteaders were desperately poor, they would contract the 250-acre parcel the government had given them to a lumber mill, and the unused forest debris would be made into charcoal. They would earn enough money to build a shack, buy a chainsaw, and begin their new life. Like termites, these folks eat the edges of the Amazon forest. Ranchers clear-cut a larger bite, thousands of square kilometers, needing more than an hour to traverse by highway.

Tocantinópolis was a military base with a landing strip used on bombing missions and an army concentration camp. João's move to Tocantinópolis heralded a new epoch in his story. In 1976, the military regime engaged in a second Guerrilha do Araguaia. This time, it was against peasant squatters.[56]

In Tocantinópolis, João had access to a variety of terreiros offering exotic left-hand paths.[57] This city had a torture center linked to the Casa Azul in Marabá. They often moved prisoners from one to another. Some were sent to Brasilia for their final act on INCA chartered airplanes. Tocantinópolis also had strong ties with the military base in Imperatriz, Maranhão, where João moved next.

Indians resisted the military with wooden spears.'Os Fuzis e as Setas', Rubens Valente. Photo: Public archive of Brasil.

III.
JOÃO the GARIMPEIRO (The Gold Digger)

Most of João's biographers say that 1976 was the year João left the military. This agrees with João's account that he spent nine years in their service. When you finish reading this book, perhaps you will agree with me. *He never left the intelligence service of this clandestine branch of the military police.*[58]

While researching this book, I referenced many sources. One author set me on a path of discovery about João's roots in Umbanda. Professor Cristina Rocha's book *John of God: The Globalization of Brazilian Faith Healing* helped place João in Imperatriz, Maranhão, and as a founder of Umbanda centers there from 1978 to 1980. In her chapter: *How Does He Get His Magic?* she recalls wandering into the room at the Casa, piled high with crutches, antique wheelchairs, and various braces. She noticed several framed honorary certificates and stumbled upon three documents about Umbanda.[59]

Rocha says, "One affirmed that in 1978 João Teixeira de Faria was head of the Umbanda temple Faith, Hope, and Charity in Imperatriz, and affiliated with the Umbanda Spiritist Association of Maranhão State."

In 2019, I visited the Casa de Dom Inácio and verified several documents related to Umbanda. This led me to renew my research into the *real* João Faria. What I found was puzzling.

He had three lives happening at the same time in different regions of Brazil. He began leaving a trail of rape accusations wherever he traveled. Various sources place João either in Anápolis, Abadiânia, Imperatriz, or Serra Pelada from 1976 to 1980. Those four years saw a lot of water rush beneath the bridge.

Freed of his four-year tenure in Marabá, he revived his traveling road show. Nineteen-seventy-six finds João in Tocantinópolis, where he sexually assaults a minor. A woman testifying against João Teixeira de Faria said the medium molested her when she was fourteen years old. Her mother was a hotel manager where João stayed. He did a private healing for the woman, then told her he needed to be alone with her child. He forced the girl to remove her clothes, telling her that the assault that followed was to improve her low energy.[60]

For the next forty years, his many victims reported the same comment. Had this been going on for years earlier while he served in the military?

But wait. In 1976, João also seemed to be living in Anápolis, where he opened an Umbanda center. He was not well received and soon found himself under the eye of the law. He began searching for a locale in Goiás/Tocantins where he could establish his terreiro and be left alone.

João began going by the name João Curador (Healer John).[61] He still incorporated Caboclo Gentil but found a new direction in the Parrot's Beak in the cults of the Ciganos and the Orient. These two paths are fringe groups. The line of the gypsies (ciganos) is at least three separate cults.[62]

Brazilian Roma adapted their traditional fireside rituals, dance, and fortune-telling to the Umbanda format of the Gira. It is a party of incorporation with lots of good food and alcohol and joking around. Their various entities wear gypsy clothing and speak of their past life as living Roma with a history to tell.

The male entities carry a knife when incorporated. This reminds me of the stainless-steel tray loaded with knives and scalpels, always by João's side when he works. And, of course, they can tell your fortune or prescribe herbs. This line works with the right-hand and the left-hand paths.

The second cult is not made up of gypsies living their culture. The mediums are from different races, occasionally a real Romani. Cigano entities mingle with other exotic spirits. This includes the Masters, the Enchanted Ones, the Nobility, Exus, Pomba Giras, Zé Pilintra, and Povo da Estrada (street people). This cult works with left and right-hand paths. I would argue that the scale tips to the left.

The third gypsy cult is within the line of the Exus and Pombagiras. Here, the entities go by gypsy names but with the prefix—Exu.

The line of Ciganos has its roots in the Candomblé of Angola. Practitioners of the cult of the dead ancestors (Vodun), which allows the gypsies' ancestors membership. Here, the gypsy entity is a Vodun.

This line is famous for magic, outwitting fate, and eliminating bad karma. Its members break the rules of the terreiros, drink hard alcohol during rituals, and perform shameful or insulting acts. They are the tricksters.

The Oriental Line, the line of the East, is a mutating type of Umbanda stripped of most of the Orixás and African influence. It is Umbanda's ultimate whitening agent. This line also conceals murky waters that go left or right, depending on the circumstances.[63]

The Oriental line in Umbanda channels entities from the East, such as Hindus, Arabs, Asians, Romans, and Egyptians. It is also called the Eastern line.

Their various cultures are broken down into *legions,* each led by a famous *entity.* Joseph of Arimathea heads the legion of doctors and scientists. The Roman Emperor Marcus leads the legion of Roman and European races. The Oriental line also has legions of Caboclo and Gypsy entities.

Some might interpret the Oriental Line as being New Age. Their fascination with crystals, palmistry, and occultism suggests this. I see it as a niche for every type of entity that was never incorporated in Umbanda terreiros before. It was a brand-new cult in this era (1960 to 1980). The Oriental Line experimented with many kinds of alternative practices.

John the Baptist leads the Oriental Line (syncretic with Xangô). It has seven phalanges. One of these is the phalange of medical doctors and healers. João claims that each of his entities leads a legion of spirits under his command. The dominant spirit of the Casa, Dr. Augusto, brags, "My phalange is not made up of ten, or a hundred, but of millions. I am the one who goes to the depths of the abyss to save a soul." [64]

These exact words are found in Quimbanda. The King of the Exus goes to the depths of the abyss to rescue a lost soul. He leads a phalange of countless hordes.

Quimbanda also has seven phalanges. The last two are the Line of Coboclos and the Mixed Line. The Line of Coboclos (Coboclo Gentil is among them) can perform the most terrible forms of magic. These spirits can cure the incurable and enrich their disciples. The leader of this line is Exu Curador.

The mixed line does not work with Exus but rather with Kiumbas—spirit slaves of the Exus. These spirits are responsible for obsessions, emotional suffering, and spiritual diseases. They even cause madness. These low spirits are also referred to as Eguns. The Casa phalanges are Eguns.

João was under the cultural influence of his military friends for nine years. He shared their fascination with Quimbanda and magic. His favored terreiros *appeared* to distance themselves from black magic. João created his peculiar type of Quimbanda. It was legal, secret, profitable, and invisible to the authorities. He would conceal his spirits in the cloak of Spiritism, Catholicism, and Umbanda.

The terreiros of Maranhão (and of Pará and Tocantins) are renowned for practicing black magic. Many received the coveted legal certificates, which deemed them houses of Umbanda or Spiritism. João got several of these licenses through his connections and opened centers in Maranhão, Goiás, and Bahia.[65]

The Federação de Umbanda Espírita e Culto Afro-Brasileiro do Maranhão (Umbanda Spiritist Association of Maranhão) confirmed that João was the head of the Umbanda temple Faith, Hope, and Charity in Imperatriz in 1978. This association was part of the apparatus that led to legalizing Umbanda under the military regime.[66]

Registration of Umbanda centers was transferred from police jurisdiction to civil. The Umbanda Associations were now responsible for policing the Umbandistas. In the 1960s, Umbanda was listed as an official religion in the national census. Several of its religious holidays became local and national holidays.

Many terreiros that were macumbeiros (witches/bruxas) became registered Umbanda and Spiritist churches. Their practices continued as before, now condoned by the authorities. It came at a price and sometimes compromised their beliefs and rituals. Unregistered centers continued to be prosecuted. They went underground and moved from the cities to isolated rural areas.

Politicians and their friends created The Federation of Umbanda in Maranhão. Some were initiates of Quimbanda centers. Using lawyers and media crusades, they brought Afro-Brazilian cults into mainstream Brazilian culture.

The military saw it as a strategy to counter the power of the Catholics. The Church was now in open conflict with the regime with many tortured priests. It also brought under its control an enormous body of black Brazilians. They had been using the terreiros to promote the empowering of the Afro-Brazilian religions and culture. Another imagined threat to the regime was being neutralized.

The government cultivated a nationalistic image for Umbanda. What else could a military government imagine? Umbanda was a National Religion, a National Treasure, and a cultural tribute to Brazil's diverse peoples.

Umbanda festivals were now legal and held for the public in large cities. They attracted tourists and their money, and they became the dictatorship's poster boy for the beauty, music, and culture of Brazil.

A foundation with thousands of members, now certified all terreiros in a vast region. Without their permission, one could not perform rituals. This group was attempting, by bureaucracy, to standardize Umbanda into one cult and to permit or prohibit certain rituals, spirits, and protocols. Money, politics, and the subterfuge of the dictatorship lurked beneath the surface.

Their concept didn't work out well in Maranhão. Things continued as before. Codó, in central Maranhão, is a city of 120,000 with 400 terreiros. Considered the *Capital of Macumba,* Codó is a short distance from Teresina, Piauí, where João lived in the early 1970s. Most of the population is Catholic and Evangelical. Yet, they are members or participate in the terreiros' rituals.

They are Catholic, but they incorporate vodun and caboclos. They are Evangelical, yet they pay a witch to avoid trouble or to win back their lover.

A secret network of lines is inscribed in the earth beneath Codó. Only the initiated know this. They delineate one terreiro and their spirits from another. An invisible web of spirits wrote the rules for Codó and their cults—laws an association couldn't override.

Afro-Brazilian magic is widespread in Maranhão. Politicians often pay hefty prices to the bruxas (witches) of Maranhão—those who can guarantee a lucrative campaign fund and a sure win in the election. People with power frequent these houses.

The traditions are as old as Africa, as ancient as the Indians along the Codó River. These are roots that refuse to die and keep sprouting new limbs. If you had money, a competent lawyer, and friends in high places, you could legalize your terreiro and carry on as usual.

Codó is Portuguese slang for a tree stump. Maranhão was first exploited for rubber tapping and Brazil nuts. In João's time, hundreds of lumber mills were clear-cutting the largest and rarest trees for lumber exports. Codó, and most of the state, is now a ghost forest of codós, cows, and soybeans.

From 1976 to 1977, João also lived in Anápolis. He opened a terreiro (registered with the Brazilian Academy of Umbanda) and gathered a following. His official story has grown murky and convoluted, with confusion over the years and incidents during this epoch.

In August 1977, João made his first appearance in Abadiânia. Back in Anápolis, his work had caused controversy, and he was chased out of town. There are different versions of this story about why and when. Regardless, he was looking for a haven in a storm.

The official Casa version is that he was being persecuted by the Regional Council of Medicine of Goiás. They denounced him for practicing surgery without a degree, and the police were in pursuit. However, the President of this Council has written that they never brought a case against João. They have no record of him. Yet, a criminal case was brought against João in Anápolis in 1977, and that charge was murder.

Chico Felitti wrote, "According to his followers and one biographer, João had been charged with the murder of Jardel Sousa, and two witnesses claimed João was the shooter. Months later, while João awaited trial, another man confessed to the crime."[67]

Abadiânia was a picturesque colonial farming village. A tiny gem tucked into a small valley. One had to travel a dirt track to reach the place. Ten miles away, the first paved road in the region was passing Abadiânia by. She was going to miss her first opportunity for commerce, doomed to obscurity.

This fancy two-lane highway stretched from Brasilia to São Paulo, opening Goiás to the world. The government offered the town free land along the side of this road if they wished to relocate. Most of her residents moved to the highway, and those left behind now lived in *Old Abadiânia*. The new Abadiânia was only fourteen years old when João arrived. It was a ragged work in progress.

He arrived at the town hall with the past mayor of Abadiânia, the district attorney of Anápolis, and soon-to-be Mayor of Anápolis, Decil de Sá Abreu (and past district attorney as well). The Junta appointed him Mayor. He was not elected by popular vote. They were followers of this charismatic young man and his dramatic spirit possessions. The old boy network of Anápolis was passing João to the old boy network in Abadiânia.

Here, we see that João's Anápolis connections are military and judicial. His cronies in the secret army underground delivered him. His connections with the shadow government continue to this day.

Having lived there, I can assure you that Abadiânia is one of the ugliest run-of-the-mill towns in a state full of them. It is not charming. The landscape is the aftermath of clear-cutting the Cerrado. Most of the locals are poor. There are few opportunities to escape. The minimum wage is the lifestyle.

When João arrived that day in August, it was worse. The town had no paved streets and few facilities. A vast panorama of stunted trees, termite mounds, and overgrazed cattle ranches was all around.

João's cronies brought him to Abadiânia's young mayor, Hamilton Pereira. On this first meeting, João bragged about the healing powers of over thirty entities he incorporated. More strings were pulled.

They consulted with those in power. All agreed that João's idea of a healing center in their new town sounded like a potential moneymaker. Today, Hamilton Pereira is the administrator of the still functioning Casa de Dom Inácio.

Well, now we know. As early as 1977, João had powerful friends in high places. Where did he get these guys? He was under investigation for murder and was run out of town. Three prominent officials arranged for his protection in an obscure village without a police station. Two of them were district attorneys.

Maybe we should follow the money back to the Years of Lead, i.e.: *associated with the military, and under their protection.*

Abadiânia, in 1977, was a few blocks of simple homes on the edge of the highway. The mayor and friends gave João the town's former and only ice cream parlor. Its owner had gone bankrupt, and the building was abandoned. This was the first center of João Curador in Abadiânia. By the next year, he was in business.

One of the first Brazilian friends I made when I moved to Abadiânia was a seventy-eight-year-old local, Seu Lazaro. He was a very good herbalist. He prepared a variety of exotic garrafadas for what ails you. Rattlesnake oil for sore muscles and lagging libido was his hallmark remedy.

When he learned I worked at the Casa, he refused to sell me his tonics and grew nervous. Over the course of a year, our friendship deepened, and he opened up about his history with João Curador.

Lazaro said, "João arrived in town with nothing but a wristwatch and a cardboard suitcase. He and his mother would sit by the side of the highway and flag down drivers passing by as they slowed down for the speed bumps. *Would they like a card or palm reading, maybe an herbal remedy, or laying on of hands?"*

João wasn't much of an herbalist. He envied Lazaro's position as the town *Raizeiro.* The *Curandero* you would turn to if the antibiotics or the Novena didn't work. Lazaro was a healer.

João bullied and harassed Seu Lazaro for all their lives and obsessively coveted his land. João prohibited Lazaro from selling his herbal remedies to folks visiting or working at the Casa.

On the other side of the highway, João hung a sign—his hallmark triangle within a triangle—directing visitors to his terreiro. It would be several years before his work morphed into The Casa de Dom Inácio and his new persona as João de Deus, Medium João. He began attracting clients. By the end of 1978, buses arrived from other states for sessions with the *Curador*.

João would say that the entity he incorporated for the first session of the center was Dom Inácio, the Casa's namesake.

Casa is another term in the Umbanda vocabulary for a terreiro or center, as is the term tenda (Umbanda tent). A terreiro is the backyard, where initiates dance the giras.

The Casa is where the consultations and offerings occur and is a place of healing. The house's mother and father often live there with their families, and the house is always open to visitors.

Somehow, in 1978, João also opened an Umbanda terreiro in Imperatriz, Maranhão. Its logo and slogan were the same as the one in Abadiânia. This was *João #2*, who was on the verge of morphing into *João #3*. *João #2* lived in Imperatriz, Maranhão. It is 1,350 kilometers north of Anápolis!

Here, he was a Babalaô registered with the Federação de Umbanda Espírita e Culto Afro-Brasileiro do Maranhão. The same federation was used by hundreds of macumba cults in Maranhão. Their strategy was to become invisible to persecution. Whatever João was doing became legal at this moment.

It's messy work deconstructing this part of the story. Imperatriz began as an Indian Mission. The dictatorship transformed it into a large commercial and military city. The 50th Infantry and Jungle Battalion were overseen by the Infantry Brigade in Marabá, Pará.

It was a small world for João. Although people say he left the military in 1976, we once again find him living in a Quimbanda hotspot and a place with an aggressive military presence and violent removal of squatters and Indians. Imperatriz was now connected by road to every other place where João had lived in the Parrot's Beak. All within a short distance of each other.

Imperatriz became one of Brazil's largest construction camps while building the Belém-Brasília highway. By 1977, Imperatriz had over 300 timber industries processing the massacred forests. Serious tensions arose between the military and the peasants. They had been chased off their lands. Their smallholdings were swallowed up by illegal mines, mega cattle ranches, and lumber camps—all armed with aggressive thugs.

When João lived in Imperatriz, there were many Umbanda/

Quimbanda centers, among which were well-known left-hand cults.

To open his *Tenda Fé, Esperança, e Caridade* João needed to meet specific requirements. He would need to be initiated in at least one of these regional cults to qualify for registration in the Federation.

What did this mean for João? He could practice his preferred spirit possession without legal repercussions. As he was no longer bound to the rules of other terreiros, his Casa was independent and different. This was João's House.

As 1978 slipped into 1979, João Faria moved between his two terreiros and his home in Anápolis. An unexpected twist in the plot revealed two sides of João that few people knew about.

On August 28, 1979, The Amnesty Law was enacted. It granted amnesty to all who committed political and electoral crimes from 1961 to 1979. João and his buddies heaved a collective sigh of relief. They could put all that ugliness behind them and never pay for their crimes. The torturers (and the tortured) were granted complete amnesty from prosecution. All those *disappeared people* would remain so. A dark cloak of invisibility concealed a thousand crimes, and João, alfaiate for the military, disappeared as well.

This is the year that João first began sexually molesting his nine-year-old daughter, Dalva. A pattern of rape and molestation is documented for the next forty years. In February 1979, João #1 was thrown out of Abadiânia. He didn't last a year. His allies hadn't asked permission from the person with more political clout than any of them—the village priest, Father Antonio Rocha.[68]

One could have predicted this. The original village of Abadiânia was a tiny, let us say, ingrown community and staunch Catholics. One of their founding colonial daughters was a famous visionary. Nothing changed when they moved to the highway, only fewer people. They all knew each other, and many had never left the county in their life. Most of them are related to one another. They left their church, a beautiful work of colonial folk art, behind in their exodus.

It was clear to everyone in Abadiânia that João was a charlatan, a witch, or worse. The Father prevailed, and Mayor Hamilton Pereira had to condescend.

But they reached a compromise. João Curador exited Abadiânia and never returned. He moved about half a mile away across the highway to a dismal wasteland where no one had wished to live. There were no services, no water, and no neighbors. They called this place Pau Torto. An expression suggesting rocky, infertile soil. A burned desert with small, twisted trees (pau torto)—an image of Hell.

Jacinto da Silva, mayor of Abadiânia from 1966 to 1970, was the land's owner and João's sponsor. His family also opened the first hotel, which exists to this day.

From that moment on, João divorced Abadiânia. He didn't visit there, and no one from there visited him. His battle with the Catholic Church and Abadiânia's several succeeding priests continues to this day.

Without fanfare, he created a third Abadiânia across the highway. It later became known as Gringolândia. He and his buddies constructed a primitive brick structure, his version of Casa Azul.

João would disappear for days or weeks, and no one knew where he was. He would visit his new *tenda* unannounced, do his healing work with Caboclo Gentil, and then disappear again. After a few months, they hung his sign out on the highway again. It pointed in a new direction, a blue triangle on a white background with the words João Curador.

The groups traveling by chartered bus returned. Folks slept in tents or on the buses. Rustic restaurants and lodgings would follow. This land on the other side of the highway would one day be called Barrio Lindo Horizonte—Neighborhood with a Beautiful View.

When João was in attendance in Abadiânia, he lived in Anápolis with his wife, Tereza Cordeiro Azevedo. On January 27, 1980, 34-year-old taxi driver Delvanir Cardoso Fonseca, aka Bigode, was murdered in Anápolis. He had been shot once in the back and thrown out of a car into a ditch, where he hemorrhaged to death.

The man had been having a sexual affair with João's wife, Tereza. He was a married man with four children. Sebastiana Geralda Costa, a friend of the victim, testified that João had threatened him for months because of his involvement with João's wife. He told Bigode he would end his life weeks before he was shot. Two days after the murder, João and Tereza separated.

The police named João as a murder-for-hire suspect, but two months after the crime, they arrested Nady Antunes Cintra. He wore a gold chain that belonged to Bigode. They implicated him in robbery for the murder motive, and João was dropped as a suspect.

The trial was held in Anápolis, and on December 23, 1982, a sentence of twenty years in prison was decreed. But Nady had disappeared, and although convicted, the police couldn't find him. In 2004, the Public Prosecutor's Office closed the case. He was never apprehended, and the statute of limitations had passed.

In the trial, Tereza and the wife of Bigode denied under oath that there had been an affair. They testified they all were friends. They both had many reasons to be afraid. João had no prior convictions, so the judge ruled that there was insufficient evidence to prosecute him. Intimidation and a clever lawyer remained João's get-out-of-jail card for decades.

As our sordid story of João unfolds, let me explain something. By 2019, over five hundred women had denounced João for sexual crimes. Perhaps a thousand or more rapes were unreported or never brought to trial. I know of several. It preoccupied the Brazilian press for four years and came to international attention. Three documentaries and numberless social media postings focused on this in the public eye.

Many of his victims kept their rapes a secret from their spouses and family, sometimes for decades. This type of shameful act is not something any woman wants to be splashed in the media. Not to mention the death threats. Yet, in these brave women's attempt to get justice, many of them went public, their names and hometowns revealed.

I do not want to take part in dragging their names through the dirt any further. In the pages that follow, I will refer to them as survivors rather than by name to show respect for their privacy. You'll find copious links to their cases in the footnotes, all in the public record.

However, there are a few of his victims that I will name. They received the lion's share of the media attention, appearing on camera of their own free will.

Of all these women, one has touched my heart the deepest. Her history crossed my own when I lived in Abadiânia (2000 to 2002). I remember her well.

In several interviews, Dalva (the name of a female Exu in Quimbanda) Teixeira narrates how, at nine years old, her mother told her that her father was going to visit soon. Dalva had never met him. Born in the village of Itapaci, Goiás, João's hometown, she only knew a poor country girl's hard but happy life. This was about to change dramatically. Her mother told Dalva and her brother that their father was a rich and powerful man who could care for them much better than she was. He said that he would buy them nice things and arrange for schooling.

She'd already decided without advising the children. Dalva didn't want to go with this strange man with whom she felt no connection, but her fate was sealed. In 1979, Dalva and her brother, Zezinho, began living with João in Anápolis.

In one of her video interviews, Dalva said, "This began the hell of my life. One night, he had an ugly fight with my stepmother Tereza. It was around nine or ten p.m. on the weekend. He told me he needed to do a spiritual work for me *with Dom Inácio* and called me into his room."[69]

"He handed me a white candle and asked me to scratch it with my fingernail. He told me he would need to do the ritual until the flame burned down to that scratched line.

"Then he took off all my clothes, and his as well, and began rubbing his penis all over my body and trying to penetrate me. I cried. Ow, it's hurting me. But he was on top of me all night.

"The next morning, I woke up early to go to school and was sitting at the table with my brothers. He sat down with a cup of coffee, giving me the hush sign. A month later, my stepmother died!" *[I was unable to confirm details of Tereza's death. Simone Soares and several people in Abadiânia mention a wife who died in a car crash—the brake lines cut. This was in 1980.]*

Then, he arranged a trip to Bahia. Dalva said, "My Dad and I sat in the back seat. He took off my panties and fingered me for the entire trip. When we arrived in Santa Maria da Vitória, we stayed at the home of a family friend.

"There were two single beds. He stayed with me in mine and messed up the other bed to pretend we had slept in separate beds." With Tereza out of the way, João had his way with his daughter for many years to come.

Soon after these incidents, João returned to Imperatriz and Marabá. While his devotees were creating the Casa across the highway from Abadiânia, João was embarking on a forty-year career in illegal gold and gemstone mining. João, struck it rich at Serra Pelada.[70]

Serra Pelada (Naked Mountain)

In December 1979, a cowboy was bathing in a remote creek at the Três Barras farm in the Serra dos Carajas region of Pará, near the city of Marabá, where João had lived for four years. The ranch hand showed off a shiny golden pebble he had found in the stream. The farm owner had the stone assayed. The report he received in reply stated that he was sitting on an enormous gold deposit.

Genésio Ferreira da Silva, the farmer, began prospecting the area without permits. The Vale mining company already held the rights to all minerals in this region.

He found a thirteen-kilogram (28-pound) nugget of gold. Word got out, and by February 1980, a thousand illegal fortune hunters had arrived at the farm. At first, it was possible to pick up pebbles of gold along the stream bed.

By March of the same year, there were 30,000 illegal miners (garimpeiros) at the site. They staked 4,000 claims. By June, the amount swelled to 55,000 and then to 80,000 before the year's end. Soon afterward, there were 120,000. They cut down the canopy forest that hid this treasure. A hole to hell took its place.

Like a fisherman's tale, João stated he was one of the first to arrive at the location. He claimed he found a 250-kilogram (550-pound) boulder of solid gold. Serra Pelada's largest legal recorded find weighed 60.8 kilograms (134 pounds). It is the largest specimen in the world. Named the Pepita Canaã, it is on display in Brasilia. In João's prison interview with Veja in 2019, he revised this story, claiming he found over four kilograms of gold.

Only three months after the initial discovery, 30,000 men were carrying 60 to 80-pound gunny sacks of rock and clay up impossibly long rustic ladders, known as *bye-bye mamas*. With only picks and shovels, the garimpeiros leveled a 500-foot-high hill. Then, they dug a 258,000 square-foot open pit mine, all by hand. It became the largest gold mine in the world, and over 45 tons of gold were mined. It is estimated that this figure amounted to only 10% of the gold extracted.

The other 90% left the site unreported.

Ants at work, Serra Pelada. Photo: Public archive of Brazil.

SERRA PELADA (NAKED MOUNTAIN)

Bye-bye mamas. Photo: Public Archive of Brazil.

In those beginning months, men fought with force and pistols to secure their area to dig. It turned to riots and chaos. The nearest city was Marabá. Thousands of new garimpeiros arrived every week. After flying thirty minutes to a tiny airstrip via Marabá or Imperatriz, Serra Pelada was accessible only by a jeep road. It cost a fortune just to get to the mine.

The miners paid exorbitant prices for taxis to take them from the airstrip to the end of a dirt road, from which they would walk nine miles to the site.

Once there, water, food, and tools were priced several times over their price in Marabá. Eighty people a month were murdered in claim conflicts and drunken barroom fights. The essential tool needed at the camp was a pistol.

One day, next to the pit, a Caixa Econômica Federal office appeared. This was the government's first step in controlling illegal mining. By law, it was the only place where miners could sell the mined ore. The bank took 60% of the gold's value. The Caixa had scales and paid the garimpeiros in cash. They didn't process and refine the gold.

That was done in and above the pit, using mercury in vast quantities to separate the nuggets and flakes of gold embedded in the clay. Of course, many people found larger nuggets and never reported this. They sold them elsewhere on the black market. This probably included João's bonanza.

A pecking order evolved from the chaos. They divided the land into *ribbons,* each about six by ten feet (two meters by three meters). This was a claim. At first, it was one man to a claim.

Later, the *capitalists* purchased these small claims. They employed many people and kept most of the profit. At its height, Serra Pelada had 300 *ravines* controlled by the capitalists. These lords of the ravines were the first people to arrive, seasoned garimpeiros or predators who bought out the claims of the weak.

Below the capitalist was the *half square,* the iron-fisted boss who ran the show and gave orders. He was the middle class of the system. He worked on commission; two to five percent of the gold was his.

The *ants* bore the brunt of the labor. Under the command of the half square, the mud hogs broke up the rocks and clay with pickaxes.

Others loaded it into gunny sacks. The ants balanced the sacks on their shoulders as they navigated the mud and trenches. Then they began the torturous ascent of the bye-bye mamas. The wage was about twenty cents per sack for their labor, averaging forty-five sacks in a twenty-four-hour work shift.

They could keep any gold found in every tenth sack. It was like the lottery—very few jackpot winners. Yes, sometimes they worked twenty-four-hour shifts. The mining went on day and night.

If you've seen the film *Powaqqatsi,*[71] Godfrey Reggio's 1988 documentary, you can never forget the opening segment. The pounding and rhythmic soundtrack by Philip Glass set the mood. Thousands of filthy and struggling *ants* climb 1,300 feet of *bye-bye mamas* in a perpetual state of exhaustion. They dug a crater over 400 feet deep and ascended in stages via the rickety ladders.

The gunny sacks were hefted to the washers and the sifters, who sorted for nuggets and flakes of gold. Most of the gold was in the form of dust. Separating the gold from the clay entailed washing it in mercury—barehanded and barefooted. The mercury would combine with the gold, forming an alloy of the two metals. This mixture was then heated in a metal pan until all the mercury evaporated, leaving behind refined gold. The process produced toxic fumes.

The living conditions were toxic, too, as were their entertainment options. In its heyday, thousands of underage girls, as young as twelve, arrived for work, with the hope of a better future, as prostitutes.[72]

Bars and gambling dens acted as stages for frequent dramas of drunken violence. There were many riots as well. In response, the government sent shock troops of the civil and federal police.

Serra Pelada: Relaxing with pistols at the hip. Photo: Public Archive of Brazil.

In June 1980, they sent the notorious Major Sebastião Rodrigues de Moura, the President's trusted man. He is known for his leadership role in fighting the Guerrilha do Araguaia and as a torturer and murderer. His nickname was Major Curió.

He was a secret agent for the SNI and the top commander in Marabá when João served there.

In Serra Pelada, he enforced the new government policy of intervention and control. He represented the National Security Council, SNI. João and Curió were again in the same town and in the same business.

Curió arrived with fanfare by helicopter. He immediately imposed his authority and demanded total obedience. Anyone stupid enough to disobey him faced public humiliation and was run out of town at gunpoint. The mine became a concentration camp patrolled by federal and military police. Curió outlawed women, guns, and alcohol at the mine. All that was moved some kilometers away and became a city of sin, Curionópolis (his namesake). It grew to 120,000 miners between 1982 to 1986. He also became the mayor for decades to follow.[73]

The violence and killings continued, but mainly on weekends. As most of the garimpeiros were already armed, Major Curió made them into an enormous, obedient militia. If someone got out of line, he was tortured in front of the others. If you stole, your head was shaved, and a mob expelled you forever.

Major Curió, the notorious Dr. Luchini. Photo: Wikimedia Commons.

Serra Pelada is in the Amazon, where temperatures hover at 90 to 100 degrees Fahrenheit. Months of rain are typical in the wet season. The pit was muddy, humid, and suffocating. The excavations opened several springs, making everything slippery. Workers were caked in wet clay and sweat; their minimal clothing was saturated with gray muck. It was a dangerous workplace with toxic clouds of iron monoxide dust day and night. Treacherous cliffs, broken ladders, and landslides caused frequent accidents and many deaths. It became a system of oppression. Most workers were essentially slaves. An unequaled environmental catastrophe unfolded.

One of several garimpeiros who knew João at Serra Pelada, George Grunupp, says that João would lead dozens of miners in morning rituals where they linked hands and created a corrente (chain) to invoke good luck. This leads one to the conclusion that he was a capitalist or a half square, as he was perceived as a leader. An ant was not his style.[74]

Grunupp said that when João made his big find, he left Serra Pelada and never returned. Others contradict this. People who knew João at Serra Pelada attest to his psychic ability to find gold. One of them became his right-hand man.

João Américo França Vieira is an airplane pilot, garimpeiro, and smuggler who flew miners into Serra Pelada and various other illegal mines. He was the pilot of João's private plane (an Embraer two-engine plane that seats eight) and his sidekick for decades. He was João's partner and *iron foreman* in other illegal mining operations. Their friendship and partnership lasted for over thirty years.[75]

Vieira says João has a supernatural knack for predicting where gold will be found. João used his powers to locate a new mine in Pará, marking a point on a map and telling Vieira to dig there. He did so and found gold.

João Américo França Vieira gained notoriety through his other partner in crime, Márcio Martins da Costa. Known as Rambo do Pará, he was killed by the Pará Military Police in 1992. His friends called him Rambo because he wore a red headband and carried several weapons like Sylvester Stallone. He was a gangster accused of murdering people to gain control of small gold mines in the jungles of Pará.[76]

Nine hundred kilometers southwest of Marabá is a community of garimpeiros hidden in the jungle. Indian lands are routinely invaded there and appropriated by white immigrants—thugs with cows, chainsaws, rifles, and gold dredges.

The Valley of Hope (Vale da Esperança) had a problem. The local Kayapo Indians were not happy with the encroaching chainsaws. They began attacking the sawyers.

The government "occupied" 75 million acres of public land (Kayapo lands). They deeded it in parcels to settlers from the south of Brazil. Léo Heck was one of these lucky migrants. In 1988, he found gold on his land and made a small settlement for miners. He named it after a popular song of the times, Castelo dos Sonhos (Castle of Dreams). He began exploiting the arriving garimpeiros, selling lots at inflated prices. His gold strike would spread to an area of 100,000 acres. Eight illegal mines were born, and six thousand garimpeiros worked there. The eight mine owners were a rough lot.

Márcio Martins, aka Rambo, a pilot and garimpeiro, arrived in 1989 when he was twenty-three. He started transporting miners but wanted more. He bribed a judge with five pounds of gold and stole one of the mines with false documents.

This led to a feud. Léo Heck expelled him from Castelo dos Sonhos, dragging him by the leg behind his truck. Rambo soon returned with a helicopter and two Ingram submachine guns. He fired on the miners at Garimpo Esperança IV, killing five.

He was now the king of a mine. The garimpeiros had to pay him a tribute in gold. He created his own mining company, an aviation company, equipment stores for gold miners, gas stations, and trading posts. He inflated the price of goods several times the regular price and insisted on payment in gold only.

Within three years, Rambo owned several dozen airstrips, seventeen airplanes, six gas stations, many trucks, and thousands of acres of land. He produced over a ton of gold per year and had an armed militia of men who policed his forty gold mines. Six thousand garimpeiros worked for him.

Rambo seemed invincible, with governors, mayors, police, and judges bribed and enemies silenced. Accused of killing at least 300 people, he tortured many of them for fun. Sometimes, he filmed his executions and mutilation of corpses. He even assassinated a senator, which implicated several other politicians.

His group began refining and smuggling cocaine on a large scale. The south of Pará became infested with bandits, fugitives, and armed gangs trafficking drugs and weapons. Planes carrying miners into the area departed loaded with drugs and gold and destined for power brokers in Belém and Brasília. His organization paid off politicians in Brasilia not to bomb their airstrips. The alleged bribes were 50 kilograms of gold (110 pounds) per month.

Adding to the ugliness, a court convicted Rambo of enslaving twenty workers. His guachebas (goons) controlled an empire of car thieves, drug dealers, and human traffickers. Human trafficking and slavery were big businesses in Pará, Tocantins (Goiás), and Mato Grosso. To this day, numerous isolated ranches and mines have captive unpaid workers (slaves).

The Sadi Rambo had support from influential people in Pará

and other states. His group included João Faria de Teixeira's right-hand man, João Américo França Vieira.

In 1992, the Military Police ambushed and killed Rambo. But Vieira remained a business partner with two of Rambo's closest associates. Vieira and others were accused of participating in another Rambo-style massacre at Garimpo Trairão in 1991. It took fifteen years to go to trial. They were acquitted of the murder of twelve miners.

João Faria opened several illegal gold and gem mines throughout the eighties in Pará, Tocantins, Goiás, Bahia, and Minas Gerais. He partnered with many criminals and remained invisible to the authorities. Viera became João's right-hand man and piloted João's airplane for decades to come. They co-owned several illegal mining operations.

João began cultivating a long list of people who might do him a favor or bend the rules with a bribe. He bought airplanes and ranches and hung out with smugglers, drug runners, and killers.

The phenomena at Serra Pelada continued until 1986. The open pit is now an enormous lake. Below the surface, buried beneath mercury-contaminated muck, lies most of the gold deposit, still to be mined. The remaining settlers live in poverty, with memories of bloodshed and greed and false hopes of striking it rich again.

João lived a double life. One half was the lifestyle of a garimpeiro, pistol and all. The other half had a home in Anápolis with a new wife and his sex slave daughter, Dalva. When he had time, he pursued his hobbies: the Casa and the Federaçao de Umbanda e Candomblé de Goiás (founded in 1979). He was a board member and friend of the founder during this era. One source claims he was their president.[77]

In 1979, the Casa had just been founded when he began abusing a girl whose family attended the Casa. In a recent interview with the newspaper *O Popular,* she reported being molested for several weeks in 1979 when she was fifteen.[78]

She said, "On the third day, he put me beside him, along with the mediums. Then it started. Everyone stopped by to pray, and he left me last *to do it with him alone.* And he wouldn't let anyone in my family inside. Then he would stand up, take my hand and put it inside his pants, hold my other hand, touch his face to mine, and say, "Daughter, pray now."

This went on for a month. Then he began groping her in her panties. He told her this was to call the guides for a blessing. When she reported the abuse to her aunt, she was reprimanded. Her aunt said the blessing would be nullified if she discussed what happened inside the Casa.

IV.
DOCTOR JOHN THE NIGHT TRIPPER—BABALAÔ JOÃO

It is now 1980. Marabá and Imperatriz were the lifelines of Serra Pelada. Everything needed at the mine came by air from these two cities. Here, one did their wheeling and dealing. They were the home base for João and his buddies.

One document Cristina Rocha mentioned declared, *The Spiritist Association of the Vale do Tocantins at Imperatriz, Maranhão State, recognized João Teixeira de Faria as the spiritual babalaô and teacher of occult sciences.* The certificate allowed him to practice Kardecism (Spiritism) in the country, asserting that Dom Inácio de Loyola was his don de cabeça (spiritual protector and guide).

I couldn't find any reference to this spiritist association. The phrasing of the certificate is strange. Why would a spiritist association recognize João as a Babalaô? And why would a *babalaô* have anything to do with occult sciences or want to practice Kardecism? And where would you find Inácio de Loyola ever being a *don de cabeça?*

These are contradictions. Spiritists never work with entities associated with Afro-Brazilian cults. If a spiritist strays, they become an Umbandista. A practitioner in a terreiro in Maranhão would not be interested in Kardecism. It would be unheard of to initiate someone into one of the African cults with Santo Inácio de Loyola (a Catholic Saint) as their principal guide.

However, if you were initiated as a Babalaô, with *Dom Inácio of the Enchanted Line* or the Catimbó line as your guide, that would be normal. Mediums of these two cults incorporate many doms.

The name of João's Casa in Abadiânia has always been The Casa of Dom Inácio. Casa de Dom Inácio de *Loyola* is their non-profit business name. In any case, Casa de São Inácio de Loyola would be the correct name of the Casa, Saint Ignatius' House. João channeled a different Inácio altogether.

The New Oxford American Dictionary: *"Dominion, abbreviated as Dom, is a title for male members of Portuguese and Brazilian royalty, aristocracy, and hierarchy, preceding the given name."*

Granted, St. Ignatius of Loyola was a nobleman worthy of the title of Dom. He was also a soldier and a mercenary killer with much blood on his hands. When he embraced his Catholicism and took a monk's vow, he founded the Knights of the Vatican, the Jesuits.

Jesuits have a long and dismal history with Brazil as custodians of her native people and with the Inquisition as well. The Brazilian military loves this story. They appointed the Knight from Loyola as their patron saint. The Catholic church claims him as the saint of all soldiers. In Imperatriz, the Infantry and Jungle Battalion built a military chapel dedicated to their saint.

We can see that either of these entities, the Dom or the Saint, is well suited to *sit on João's head* (don de *cabeça*). A perfect syncretic twist to the plot. This tacky and forgotten certificate from long ago explains how his Casa of Quimbanda became a Casa of Spiritism. Here, we can decipher João's intent. His style of healing was black magic in terms of Brazilian law. The Umbanda Federations provided a smokescreen to obscure his history.

Thus, his terreiro became a house of spiritism, but only on paper. His magic entities became wise old teachers of occult science while tipping their hats to Alan Kardec.

Several more years would pass before João whitewashed his roots as a Babalaô. So, what in the world is a Babalaô? Professor Rocha explains that a Babalaô is just another term for Pai de Santo (holy father), the phrase used for the head of Umbanda and Candomblé terreiros.[79]

If João was certified as the leader of terreiros, why didn't they use the usual word for it? The choice of Babalaô rather than Pai de Santo wasn't an accident. After all, the person requesting certification was João. He chose this rare and obscure title.

A Babalaô (*Babalawo*, in the Caribbean and West Africa) means *Father of the Mysteries.* It is a spiritual title that defines a high priest of the Ifá oracle. The Ifá cult is part of the Yoruba religions of the Jeje and Nagô cultures. The title is given to someone initiated into this African system of divination. His chief function is initiating other babalaôs and transmitting the secret knowledge of the Ifá cult to them.

This tradition was almost lost in Brazil. A revival occurred after slavery ended. Several Brazilians visited Africa and received the initiations, returning home to teach others. The cult succeeded more in the Caribbean colonies, especially in Cuba, Puerto Rico, Haiti, and Venezuela. It spread south from there into the north of Brazil.

This revival was occurring when João received his initiation in the late 1970s. João had practiced the oracle of the cards and palmistry for decades. Mastering this African oracle demonstrated a continuum of fortune-telling in his history.

The term Babalaô is used in several African cults. Most of these cults practice sacrifice rituals, frequently requiring a blood offering— usually through self-applied cuts or from sacrificed birds. Tobacco, incense, African foods, fruits, honey, and alcohol are other favorite sacrifices. One consults with the Babalaô and his wooden divination tray. He then advises which spirit you need to appease and their preferred offerings. The oblations will resolve the problem.

Here is a list of some sects using the term Babalaô, cults João likely attended for 20 years or more: Candomblé de Caboclos, Quimbanda, Culto dos Eguns, Tambor de Mina, Xangô de Pernambuco, Jeje, and Terecô.

Umbanda does not use this title. Other sects that employ the title Babalaô are Vodun and Santeria (The Way of the Saints). They require blood offerings and have the same roots as Candomblé. Both cults had advanced into the very places where João spent time. Santeria, the Caribbean version of the cult, uses the Ifá oracle, and a Babalawo is the diviner.

Meanwhile, João #2 was back at the Casa de Dom Inácio, although he was prone to disappear for weeks. A handful of his devotees moved into the Casa. They were doing their independent study of mediumship. He was back in business. The tour buses returned, and a camping area was set up with tarps to provide shade. The first hotel opened, Pousada Santa Rita, owned by the Jacinto da Silva family. Someone began preparing meals for the visitors.

João saw an opportunity for money. He began perfecting his stage show of pseudo-surgeries, but the garrafadas were still the real moneymakers. The problem was that he learned a bit about the herbs and baths of Candomblé. And he knew a little of the Jurema herbal tradition of pajelança. He knew how to make rudimentary garrafadas (medicinal alcohol tinctures) from the herbal roots of the Amazon and the Northeast.

But he was not much of an herbalist. João lied to his followers. His long absences were not wilderness treks with Caboclo Gentil, learning the medicinal herbs.

He never mentioned his teacher in Anápolis. According to Chico Felitti, João befriended an herbalist in Anápolis who identified all the endemic Cerrado healing plants for João and taught him how to prepare the tinctures.[80]

In Anápolis, João was a charismatic Umbandista with several followers. He was young, handsome, self-assured, rich, and powerful—a woman magnet. Friends and devotees drew in others, and his fame spread by word of mouth. João de Abadiânia and Medium João became his new monikers.

When I arrived in Abadiânia in 1999, he still sold a few garrafadas. These included remedies for weak livers, backaches, colds, and female problems. The tinctures had no set price. It could cost you a fortune if it looked like you had money. If you appeared poor, it might be twenty reais.

The herbalist's daughter (they both wish to remain anonymous) began attending the weekly works at the Casa and became a helper. She said João only had two tricks back then: the eye scraping and the nose job. These were his "visible surgeries." Then, he experimented with another technique. He would suck the pus and liquid from infected wounds and spit it into a bucket.

One day, a group of wealthy clients arrived from Brasilia, and João asked the herbalist's daughter to help him. He had her pretend she was paralyzed, stand up, and proclaim a cure to the audience. She did it as a lark, but she knew many others who feigned a cure at João's request.[81]

She saw other new tricks when she worked there. He would secretly chew a particular medicinal tablet and rub it on his hands. He'd ask the patients to pour the blessed water on his hands. The powder would turn blood red and appear to flow from his hands, suggesting that the holy water had manifested the patient's blood on João's hands after he touched them. This illusion coincided with selling the energized water, which became a big business for the Casa.

Eventually, João copied the other spirit doctors and began making his cuts. Patients at the Casa often spent days or weeks in the infirmary. The herbalist's daughter witnessed many people in the infirmary in pain. They received injections of painkillers and antibiotics.

In the early days, the Medium didn't have the magic of painless surgeries. Some people did not recover, returned home, and died. The herbalist's daughter became disillusioned and moved away from the Casa.[82]

The last straw, she says, was João Faria's mother. Dona Iuca had a cancerous tumor on her face, which turned her nose into a grotesque mass. Instead of taking her to Abadiânia for treatment at the Casa (or to a hospital), João left his mother in Anápolis. He hid her so that none of his clients would see her condition.

Nineteen-eighty had been a hectic year for Medium João. It

wasn't over yet. In September, criminal charges were brought against him by the family of a sixteen-year-old girl.[83]

Her parents had brought her to the Casa to see if they could help her with difficult menstruations and migraine headaches. Her first visit with the medium, alone in a private room with him for three hours, was the first rape. João advised her parents that she needed to be hospitalized. They did not know he had just raped her, so they left her alone with him for three weeks. He abused her the entire time.

When she told her parents what had happened, they tried to have João arrested. Brazil has archaic, often bizarre, laws about sexual abuse, even more so in the 1980s. The laws had a loophole. The crime would be erased if the rapist agreed to marry his victim. João proposed to her. She didn't accept. Like all the cases against him, the case was dropped after being dragged out for years. In 1986, this family stopped appearing for court hearings.

Two other accusations of alleged rapes occurred in 1980. One of these was a pregnant woman, twenty-six-years-old. The medium recommended a private session and told her to close her eyes.

He said, "An entity has arrived, and he insists on possessing you sexually. When he has done so, he will show you his face. You do not have the strength to argue with him." The face she saw was João's.[84]

In 1981, there would be two new rape accusations and an arrest for charlatanism. This was the year he began penetration rape of his daughter Dalva, who was now eleven years old and still under his care, along with three of his sons, in Anápolis.[85]

From 1981 to 1985, details about João's whereabouts are vague. He began prospecting and opening mines in the north of Goiás (now Tocantins). He ran with a rough crowd.

When he wasn't occupied with his illegal mining ventures, he continued living in Anápolis and attended the Casa three days a week, which is about a thirty-minute drive from there. João has lived in Anápolis since the seventies. Caboclo Gentil was working at his side. The young people attracted to João considered themselves apprentices.

But he wasn't a teacher or a trainer of mediums. João was a one-man show and didn't share his technique with anyone. This inner core of devotees numbered twelve, his twelve disciples.

Left on their own when João was absent, the Casa was their bedroom in the evening. The little group evolved independently of

João. They pursued their interests and mediumistic style. They had chores they did for João, such as bottling the blessed water they decanted from the waterfall and acting as guides and nurses for visitors.

The Casa had no rules back then, and it did not have the spiritist aura that would later be adopted. The Indian guru Osho inspired this Casa family of devotees. So did esoteric Umbanda and Quimbanda.[86]

There were romances, and João was sexually involved with some of his disciples. It was at this time that he created his notorious private office. The disciples frequented the Casa waterfall to meditate and incorporate. Some were possessed by Pombagiras and the same entities as Medium João. Disciples were speaking in tongues. People screamed and cried during the surgeries.

Meanwhile, João's life in Anápolis was going on parallel to Abadiânia. He had a new wife in 1982, Ligia Bueno, yet he continued abusing Dalva, who lived with them. A rape charge was also filed against him that year.

The big drama of the year was an attempt on his life. According to João, two cars ran his car off the road. Four men approached him with pistols drawn. He escaped. One cannot confirm if this happened, as in so many of João's tales. He claimed that a doctor and a politician had plotted his assassination.

But he never went to the police and accused them. For the rest of his life, he surrounded himself with pistoleiros, armed thugs. His excuse almost made this appear normal. The ambush myth was always given as an explanation for his bodyguards.

When João would disappear for weeks at a time, he was prospecting for gold and emeralds. As this was without documents or permission, it was illegal. João found ways around this. He became an anonymous partner in various garimpos (clandestine mines). He preferred gold and emeralds but also dabbled in crystals and other minerals. A new gold strike was happening in Crixás, Goiás. João and his partner João Américo França Vieira opened their mining enterprise there. This was another enormous find like that at Serra Pelada.

The tiny village of Lavra, near Crixás, Goiás, attracted 30,000 illegal miners in the 1970s to 1980s. They found gold veins in the bedrock and began opening crude shafts with dynamite and brute force.

João made his fortune here. He leveraged his profits by investing in more mines and large ranches (where he also explored for mineral wealth).

Lavra once housed thousands of miners and their bars and gambling halls. It is almost a ghost town now. The gold is still there, but an international enterprise owns the rights. They dug one of the world's deepest gold mines (8,000 feet deep) to reach the mother lode. It is one of the three most productive South American gold mines.

If you are having difficulty imagining what his world was like, I understand. It is disconcerting to me as well. João is becoming a famous faith healer. He is also having an incestuous affair with his young daughter. He's a man living the pistol-packing life of an outlaw. How can this be?

He and Viera opened another illegal mine in Santa Terezinha, Goiás, this one for emeralds. It was about twenty miles away from their gold mine in Crixás.[87]

The new mining ventures were near Anápolis. João shifted his operations from Pará and Maranhão to Goiás—his sideline as a garimpeiro now focused on emerald mining, all without permits. A quality emerald is one of the most expensive gems in the world and is worth much more per gram than gold. These clandestine mines are dangerous shafts hand-dug into the rock.

They go down many meters in a cramped, almost airless tunnel that one must crawl through. They use dynamite to break open more shafts, hoping to reveal a vein of emeralds. People are paid a daily wage for their hard work. João did not need to go down those shafts.

From 1980 to the 1990s, Santa Terezinha was called the Capital of Emeralds and was the world's largest emerald producer. Twenty-five thousand illegal miners arrived, giving birth to another city, Campos Verdes.

The mining continues to this day. João was hooked on emeralds and engaged in their illegal mining for almost forty years. He is always wearing an enormous cut emerald set in a gold ring.

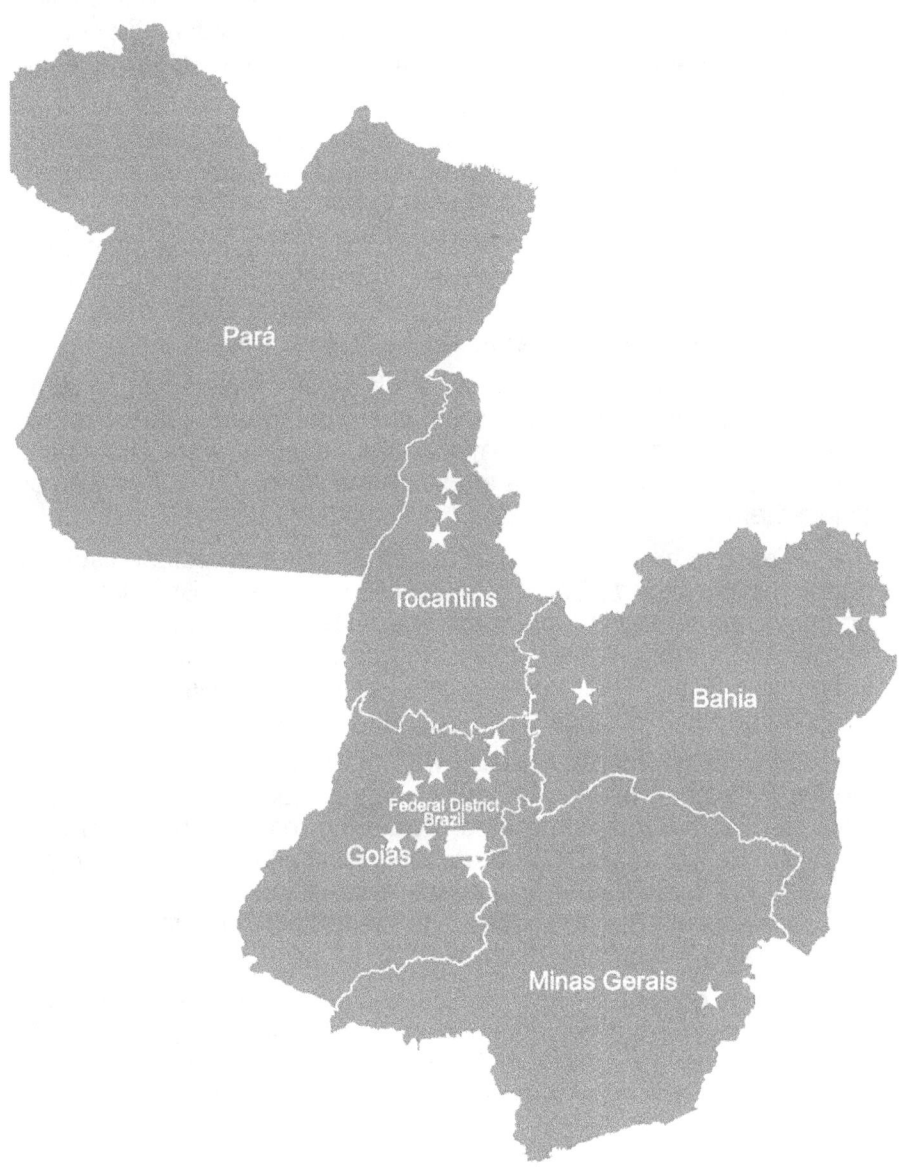

João's illegal mining ventures. Created with mapchart.net / Creative Commons.

Other places in Goiás where João was involved in illegal mining were Pilar de Goiás (gold), Cavalcante (gold and crystals), Pirenópolis (emeralds), Itaberaí (emeralds), Campos Belos (Cassiterite & uranium), and Cristalina (quartz crystals).[88]

João also had mining ventures near Guaraí, Tocantins (quartz crystals), Carnaíba, Bahia (emeralds), and Nova Era, Minas Gerais (emeralds). He continues in partnership with illegal miners.

Investigative journalists have uncovered these operations. His name is not on any document proving ownership of a mine. He never applied with the government for a mining contract, and there is no way to know how many other mines he was involved in.

The Casa was growing in popularity. He increased the garrafada production while polishing his style. He transformed his terreiro into a spiritual hospital. In 1982, several new mediums were channeling Doctor Fritz. It had become a media phenomenon, and João wanted to join them.

There is no evidence that Doctor Fritz, as an actual historical figure, ever existed. Several psychics and many Brazilian spirit doctors channeled his biography. They say he was born in Poland and served in World War One. One source claims his first appearance occurred in Bahia when he possessed a nun in the Sisters of Mercy. She charged for Fritz's services—things did not go well.

Edson Cavalcante Queiroz was the most famous of the new Doctor Fritz channelers. He was an actual doctor (a gynecologist) from Recife. When incorporated, he turned into a flamboyant mad scientist. He cut, sawed, and stabbed his patients with enormous needles in a manic state of glee while speaking nonstop in a thick German accent. Edson traveled to nine countries, including the United States, performing surgeries.[89]

Things got out of hand for Edson in 1991. He was convicted of manslaughter for the death of one of his patients who paid 500,000 reais for an unsuccessful psychic surgery. Before they could sentence him, his groundskeeper stabbed him to death. Edson was the next casualty of Doctor Fritz's curse against accepting money for his services. He was forty-one years old.

In Palmelo, the spiritist city João frequented in his twenties, another spirit doctor was at work. In José Nilton's spiritual hospital, O Centro de Amor e Caridade, Nilton operated on up to a hundred people a day.

He wasn't fooling around. He made deep cuts that required local anesthesia. A few years later, he was charged with the death of a patient. He fled to Paraguay, where he opened another spiritual hospital.

Another medium at Palmelo was the shocking Antonio de Palmelo. Under very unsanitary conditions, he performed operations best left to hospital surgeons. He was filmed opening the chest of a man with terminal heart disease with a carpenter's rusty circular saw. The man walked back to his posada after the surgery. He quickly recovered from the ragged ten-inch gash down his chest. According to his wife, the heart condition disappeared.[90]

After the deaths of Zé Arigó and Edson Cavalcante Queiroz, others appeared. Edivaldo de Oliveira Silva and Oscar Wilde, two brothers from Bahia, took on the mantle for a while. They both died in car crashes.

Rubens de Farias Junior began to work as Fritz in Rio de Janeiro soon after the death of Edson Queiroz. Dr. Fritz warned Rubens of violent death at a young age if he worked with him. Rubens disregarded the warning. In 1996, he was tried and found guilty after an unsuccessful surgery. In 1999, the Federal Police in Rio de Janeiro investigated Farias for international trafficking of cocaine. They also accused him of tax evasion and money laundering. The inquiry alleged he committed three homicides—clients who died on his operating table.[91]

Farias' career ended in scandal and controversy in 2000 with a tell-all book written by his ex-wife. Twenty-five years later, he is still trying to make a comeback.

Maurício Magalhães, from Mato Grosso, became the next Doctor Fritz. Fifty years after Arigó, Fritz continues to possess several mediums. He is still cutting and prescribing medicines.

In 1983, it was time for João to step up and join their ranks. He was having a hard time in Abadiânia, once again, and planned to move away. Here is a pivotal moment in João's myth. He wrote to the famous channeler, Chico Xavier, and asked his advice. His handwritten reply advised João to continue his mission in Abadiânia.[92]

He received the blessing of Dr. Bezerra de Menezes, the patron saint of Spiritists. The one whom Chico was channeling. João displayed this note as proof of his deep friendship (they barely knew each other) with Xavier. It implied his authorization of the Casa and the connection to Spiritism.

But he had another problem. His new wife, Ligia Bueno, confronted him about the affair with his daughter, threatening to make it public. Another problematic wife to deal with. She wasn't long for this world. The coroner decided that her cause of death was suicide, suicide by asphyxiation. He determined that a propane tank had leaked and caused her untimely death. This wouldn't be the last propane tank suicide death in Joao's world.[93]

Dalva explained that João cleaned up Ligia's crime scene and planted false evidence. He told her never to mention what she saw or what happened that day.

Sandro Teixeira, one of João's sons, an attorney in Anápolis, gave a different version in an interview with *O Popular* (12/16/2018). Sandro claims that he and Dalva discovered Ligia's body.

He said, "My father... had a truck and went to help a friend with a move. She (Ligia) woke up quietly in the morning. There was me, Dalva, Zezinho, and her in the house.

"She was there with us and went into the bedroom. When I went into the room, I found João Augusto [her child with João] lying on her lap and a glass of poison lying on the floor. I think she drank some poison first and shot herself in the head afterward. He (João Augusto) had just been born. He was five, six months old." [94]

Ligia's mother testified that her daughter had attempted suicide before. She claimed that she was the one who found her dead, contradicting Dalva and Sandro's statements. Ligia's brother worked for a long time for João de Deus, which may have influenced his mother's account.

In 1984, João was forty-two years old and accused of four more rapes. Meanwhile, Dalva discovered she was pregnant with João's baby. At fourteen years old, she escaped.[95]

She began a sexual relationship with one of João's employees. The young man later fathered her three children. He did not know that João was abusing her. When she told him, this subject became taboo. She avoided João. He knew.

When João found out she was pregnant, he attacked her with a leather bullwhip. A cat of nine tails with brass beads at the whip ends. He screamed that she couldn't get married to her boyfriend and began jumping on her stomach. He beat her so severely that they took her to the hospital. There, she miscarried. She still wears the scars from the whipping.

Dalva said, "I went to the hospital and then stayed for a while at an aunt's house, where I recovered. But I lost the baby. My relationship with my father has always been something out of the ordinary. It seems like a satanic thing. After a week, I got married. A month later, he was pressing me to get a divorce."

Rallies of hundreds of thousands of citizens were taking place in Brazil's major cities. People demanded free elections, and the military was losing its grip on Brazil.

João got involved with smuggling. He became part of an organized crime group. The SNI (National Information Service), perhaps his last employer, had been keeping a dossier on him throughout the eighties.[96]

In 1985, the Federal Police arrested João, his nephew Wagner Gonçalves, and three other accomplices. They were cited with illegal possession of one ton of radioactive material—an intrigue involving an Eastern European buyer.

The mineral autunite, which he mined in Campos Belos, is a rare and valuable radioactive mineral. The group was on their way to a secret airstrip in Alto Paraíso. From there, it would be flown to Suriname and then to Europe.

Everyone in the group was armed. João had a revolver in his belt when he exited the truck.

He told the police that he stored the ore at his ranch (not mentioning that he also stored it at the Casa) and that he had financed the operation. João would have been paid about one million dollars had they not been stopped. The three charges were dropped, although this was a serious crime.

There is a link here with corrupt officials, the SNI, and the Medium. Possession of this mineral was a national security risk. SNI archives have at least three reports regarding his involvement with this gang, including one where he confesses to the crime. He was accused of storing national security material for the second time. He stored the radioactive ore *in the Casa.*

This same year marked the end of the military regime and a new and freely elected president and government. João is accused of five more rapes, making these ten consecutive years of documented sexual abuse cases. This continued for thirty-four more years.

João's Juju

One might argue that the Casa de Dom Inácio really began in 1986—the year João laid down the law, ending the in-patient recovery program and banishing the volunteers from living there. This was when he recreated his Umbanda temple in the Casa's form. Since that time, the Casa has postured itself as a spiritist hospital.

Santa Dica, Zé Arigó, and the several spirit doctors of Palmelo were his models. They all opened spiritist hospitals in the region. João intended to copy Dr. Fritz's model of surgery and medicine. Several of his disciples were spiritists. He used his Spiritist Association license to align himself with spirit doctors. He didn't mention that the certificate granted him the title of Babalaô or that he was never a spiritist.

João bragged about the thirty-six spirits he incorporated and their phalanges. As we have seen, in Quimbanda, having as many guides as possible is important. This is a sign of authority and mastery. Some entities in his spirits list were only incorporated once or on rare occasions.

Three dominant spirits usually possess him. These spirits have no historical identity and are not incorporated by other mediums, leaving many spirits unnamed. There is a reason for this obscurity.

João's Casa avoided using Afro-Brazilian rituals. For thirty years, João attended terreiros of African heritage. These rituals revolved around communal trance. They all had roots in African magic. Most of them worked under the protection of one or more Orixás, all black-skinned entities. Over the years, João distanced himself from the African roots of his mediumship. His exploration of the Oriental and Gypsy lines began this separation process.

It should be no surprise that some people who know João describe him as a racist. He stripped the Casa of African entities, African rituals, and Afro-Brazilian administrators. He kept only the obligatory statue of Brazil's Patron Saint, Nossa Senhora da Conceição Aparecida. Our Lady of Conception is a black and pregnant Madonna.

João created the ultimate white-washed Quimbanda terreiro in the new Casa. He borrowed from the style of his contemporaries in the realm of spirit doctors, displaying their icons rather than those of Orixás and Exus. And yet, the Casa is a kissing cousin of any Umbanda house in Brazil. The only thing missing is the drums, dance, and African entities. Gone are the Enchanted and Caboclo spirits as well. He disguised such spirits as Catholic saints and within the Casa entities and rituals.

A typical terreiro is a humble house (casa) in a poor part of town or the countryside. Usually, there is a dirt-floored, rustic outbuilding or separate room. There, the mediums incorporate and give consultations and healing passes. They might have an outdoor area, preferably under a large tree, where the ritual dance of gira is performed. Often, there is a small shrine of the dead in the backyard.

If they had more money, they might use a larger hall-like structure or a circus tent for many of their rituals. If they were very fortunate, the terreiro would include a small waterfall, in which case, many rituals might be held there.

The mother and father of the house live there or nearby with their extended family. It is home to the entire congregation as well. For these are their spiritual parents, and the spirits of the house dwell here with their children.

Terreiros usually have a garden with at least seven sacred herbs planted on the grounds. Umbanda relies heavily on herbal knowledge, using over 140 plants. They make garrafadas as well. Most of the herbs are used to infuse magical and healing baths or as incense. The herbal infusions are poured over one's body—at a waterfall or stream, if possible.

Each terreiro is different. Their founders followed a specific line that had been morphing for centuries. They will add to that evolution. Their spirits dictate the rules and forms that they practice. Although rooted in the ancestors of their line, the spirits often have surprises. They shake up the rules from time to time. They are to be obeyed.

Incorporation occurs in several ways in the terreiro. It usually is a group effort. A variety of spirits simultaneously possesses members. The gira uses African drumming and chants to generate a powerful corrente (chain or current). This induces many to enter ecstatic trances. They dance and give healing blessings and passes (laying on of hands). Sometimes, they channel speeches or tell stories.

Incorporation in a calmer, more refined manner occurs in the Mesa Branca healing ritual. Music and chant alternate with meditation and healing work on individuals. The mediums incorporate, but their composure is more restrained. The head of the Casa often channels a message. This work is opened with Catholic invocations of the Lord's Prayer and The Hail Mary. Candles, crystals, incense, and holy water will be present. Many spirits will be called through song or invocation.

At one end of the room, an elaborate altar with many statues, framed paintings, and exotic objects is located. Two throne-like chairs in front of the altar are where the Mãe and Pai de Santo sit for consultations, as in João's Casa.

The most frequent type of incorporation in a Terreiro occurs in a separate room or building. It usually has a dirt floor. Here, various entities sit and give advice and treatment.

The patients wait in line for a consultation. They go to the medium of their choice, sit face to face, and explain their problem or need. The medium is provided with all the props needed to do the magical work. Usually, there is a food offering. Often, tobacco or alcohol is used. Advice will be given, and perhaps healing passes.

The consultation is brief; the advice is down-to-earth and simplistic. Herbs and baths are often prescribed. Witchery, or obsessive spirits, are frequently blamed for one's problems. The entity knows how to resolve this.

The Pai and Mãe de Santos, leaders of the Casa, and *the spirits they incorporate* are like an oligarchy. They have more power than others and dispense this power to their members. They resolve issues, maintain a balance in the Casa, and are the *go-to* for advice and solace. Their word is the law.

This same social model is practiced throughout Brazil on both the mundane and political levels. This is how Brazil works. João created his oligarchy in Abadiânia. The police are calling it organized crime.

João arrived in Abadiânia with many bad habits and secrets. He came with his spirits. The Medium was on a mission and liked to say that he made a deal with his spirit guides—take care of him financially, and he'd promise to do their work for the rest of his life. The type of spirits he works with demand a lifelong contract that is impossible to break. Where he went, so did they.

The first thing we notice amiss is that a Mãe de Santo does not accompany him. There will be no feminine side to balance his masculine.

As his early disciples attested, he was not an accomplished healer and was indeed a student. He could not submit to discipleship and initiation with the cults he attended despite other mediums' advice on its necessity.

As far as being a Pai, he was absent and aloof. He was charismatic and powerful, but few understood that he was a trickster.

His entities manifested João's future with their axé. João brought this to his Casa—his spirits and their axé, their magical current of power. He brought no Orixás with him to protect and guide the spirits of the house. Like most left-hand terreiros João had attended, the house was commanded by a king, in this case, King Solomon. [97]

This choice of a king underlies João's background in Quimbanda. King Solomon is syncretic with the king of the Exus, Exu Rei, who commands all Exus. He is the overlord of a phalange of spirits, any of which you might incorporate under his authority. Only three Exus can assume the role of King. The Exu associated with King Solomon is Exu Mor. Exu Mor *is* King Solomon.

In other words, Exu Mor is the king of the Casa de Dom Inácio. He's in charge of all the spirits incorporated there and in charge of João. He has been in charge since he first possessed João when he was sixteen.

He was in charge when João embraced the left-hand rituals of Catimbó and Jurema. Solomon is the supreme leader of these cults. In charge, when João incorporated the gypsy spirits, the gentil caboclo spirits, and the enchanted esoteric and royal spirits. Solomon is the King of one of their enchanted worlds on the astral plane.

The biblical King Solomon had 700 wives and 300 concubines (the most virile man in the world). He lived a life of luxury. He was renowned for his wealth (the richest man in the world) and unequaled wisdom (the wisest man in the world).

Known as a great warrior, but one who turned to false gods, having built altars to Ashtoreth and other foreign idols. Solomon built the *first* Temple in Jerusalem.

He was the last king of a united Israel. Jehovah rejected him as a disobedient sinner unworthy of a successor or an empire. Solomon was a magician and an exorcist. Many amulets made in the Hellenistic period invoke his name. The first-century Gnostic *Apocalypse of Adam* tells a tale in which Solomon sends an army of demons to capture a virgin who had escaped his clutches.

Later books described how he controlled demons and held them as slaves. Occultists wrote *The Greater and Lesser Keys of Solomon* during the Italian Renaissance. These are books of spells (grimoires) and arcane diagrams attributed to Solomon. They are used to cast magic spells.

Another spirit João brought to his Casa was, of course, Dom Inácio. As I pointed out earlier, this might be someone other than Ignatius of Loyola. I find it unimaginable that Saint Ignatius would want anything to do with possessing Medium João or anyone. It is not a very Catholic thing to do!

The official story claims that Dom Inácio was the first entity João incorporated when he opened the Casa. He became the Casa's namesake. Dom Inácio is one of the *Enchanted Doms.* João took part in various possession cults that work with the energies of the Enchanted Entities. Each entity is the leader of a city or empire that exists only in an enchanted realm. These spirits disappeared from the face of the earth. They will never return because they are enchanted.

This belief is found in most of the cults João participated in. These lines work with the left-hand entities, including Exus and Vodun. They all believe in the enchanted realms and their spirits. The cults he frequented in Maranhão and Pará have a variety of entities that go by the name of Dom.[98]

Doms incorporated by these terreiros include Dom Luis, Dom Ingrid, Dom João, Dom Rei Sebastião, Dom José, and many others. These enchanted entities frequent the Esoteric and Oriental lines as well.

And, yes, they incorporate a Dom Inácio. He was Dom Inácio de Azevedo, a famous mariner and a Jesuit martyr favored by the cult of Tambor de Mina. Or perhaps it is (Dom) Inácio Gonçalves de Barros, the mythic founder of the cult of Jurema.

As Dom Inácio is João's *don de cabeça,* he is his guiding spirit and the next in command of the Casa. These two leaders of the Casa are rarely and only briefly incorporated. It is below their status to do so. They appear to cause João great discomfort, a hallmark of Exu possession. I have observed him fail in attempts to be possessed by them. I have seen him fake their incorporation.

Caboclo Gentil, another enchanted entity, is the other guide with João most of his life. As João reformed his Casa into a spiritual hospital, poor Gentil disappeared. Or did he?

The first record of João working with Doctor Augusto (his primary spirit doctor) was in 1985. However, he may have appeared a year or two earlier when João began implementing his new surgical tricks. The myth goes that Caboclo Gentil was a great healer and herbalist at João's side for decades. Was he discarded so quickly for a new face? In Quimbanda, one's guides own you for life. You can't escape their presence and are bound to do their will.

Kleber Aran is another medium that incorporates Doctor Fritz. He currently works in several cities in northeastern Brazil. At seventeen, he began his mediumistic path by incorporating Caboclo

Arranca Toco. He opened an Umbanda center for his work. This went on for years. One day, Arranca Toco announced he would receive a new entity, *a spirit of light*. Kleber's experience of incorporation was powerful. He lost consciousness.

When he returned to his body, the congregation told him that the entity introduced himself as Doctor Fritz. Medium Aran realized that this spirit didn't belong in an Umbanda terreiro. He is associated with spiritists. Kleber built a separate center for spiritual surgeries and healing with energized water.

Could Caboclo Gentil have made a similar transformation and become Doctor Augusto? Aran's story sounds a lot like João's. Is Doctor Augusto the disguise used by one of his thirty-six entities? A mask that would permit him to erase his roots with black magic and replace them with a Casa free of African rituals? Free of a Mãe Santo and her female protective powers, and free of any other healers, teachers, or anyone equal to João?

Dr. Augusto de Almeida replaced Coboclo Gentil and Dr. Fritz. He remained João's primary entity of incorporation at the Casa de Dom Inácio until the end.

Dr. Augusto de Almeida *Monjardino* was a Portuguese surgeon. He was Dean of the University of Lisbon and a senator who lived in Lisbon, Portugal (1871-1941). Dr. Augusto specialized in hysterectomies. No other medium or spiritist center incorporates or works with this historical figure. He was not a spiritist.

João said that he knew him in past lives. He claimed Dr. Augusto was a Brazilian military officer, doctor, and rubber tapper. João states that the doctor performed surgery without anesthesia, as it had not yet been invented. However, it was in common use during Augusto de Almeida Monjardino's lifetime.

It's not the same fellow. No other *dead* Dr. Augusto (de Almeida) is referenced online (except with João), and no other medium has ever worked with this doctor.

But alongside portraits of Dr. Augusto, hang images of actual doctors in the Casa de Dom Inacio, just as they do in most spiritist and white mesa Umbanda temples. They are real doctors who lived and are now working in spirit, such as Dr. Bezerra de Menezes—the great Spiritist, Dr. Oswald Cruz—famous for his work on tropical diseases, and Doctor Gregorio Hernandez—a deified doctor of the poor in Venezuela. Like Jesus and John the Baptist, they are there to clue everyone that this place is safe and protected by good guys.

Dr. Augusto is the pseudonym of a shadow entity. He gave João the wealth and power he lusted for. We can't be sure when João got this spirit, but we can be fairly certain that it was in the State of Maranhão, and he didn't go by Doctor Augusto.

From 1985 forward, Caboclo Gentil is no longer the primary healing entity in the Casa. Doctor Augusto took over the role. He is under the command of Solomon and Inácio, the Exu, and the Enchanted Dom.

Doctor Augusto is the most active spirit in the Casa, with his phalange of countless others. This would be the same order of authority if this spirit were a caboclo or an exu. He is the one who possesses João—he and his legions.

The last style of Quimbanda that caught João's eye was the Esoteric Line, created by Woodrow Wilson da Matta e Silva, known as Pai Matta. He mastered Quimbanda in Pernambuco, working with the Enchanted Ones. When he moved to Rio de Janeiro in the 1950s, he received the teachings of his alternative path of Esoteric Umbanda. He worked with Exus and many other left-hand entities but not with blood offerings. Pai Matta was a Babalaô and famed for his divinations.[99]

He used the oracle of Ifá and divined with a glass of water he called the *glass of clairvoyance*. The medium could see a person's destiny in the glass.

Although he only had five years of education, he wrote nine books explaining Esoteric Umbanda. His system is reminiscent of the Freemasons or the Rosicrucians, with twenty-one grades of initiation. He trained successors who carried on his vision after his death. Some of João's earliest disciples knew this esoteric line, which also influenced João.

João was probably attracted to the Master's opinion of women. Although Matta had some female disciples, none were allowed to open a center. They weren't permitted to complete all stages of initiation or have a position of authority. Pai Matta believed women were ill-suited for training as mediums. They could not head a true terreiro or even walk a spiritual path. A woman's place was at home.

He was particularly antagonistic towards Candomblé, a religion usually led by a Mãe de Santo with a congregation predominantly of women. Pai Matta was a great whitewasher of Umbanda. He wanted to make it modern, clean, and intellectual—and more masculine as well.

The only female entity to enter the Casa was João's lifelong muse, Saint Rita. Santa Rita has a strange connection with Afro-Brazilian religions as well. She is revered in certain terreiros as a magical Catholic nun. In other terreiros, she is known as her syncretic version—Obá, an obscure Orixá of Candomblé. In Quimbanda, Santa Rita is powerful because they believe she persuaded Jesus to kill her two sons. This was to save them from going to Hell. They were her abusers. She feared they would kill a feuding neighbor to avenge their father's death (or kill her) and go directly to Hell. Santa Rita is part of the phalanx of enchanted entities.[100]

Obá is feared for her low spirituality. She is depicted as nearly naked, a fierce and feared warrior with a sword. Obá represents the aggressive, masculine aspect of a woman. Her devotees are brave fighters but misunderstood and dysfunctional in relationships and love. They tend to have difficult and unhappy lives.

With these four entities as the Casa's foundational pillars, João fashioned his twisted version of a spiritual hospital.

Blood, Semen, and Tears

All the left-hand paths João traversed are sometimes called Crossed Line Umbanda. This term signifies that the cult continues to make a blood sacrifice the centerpiece of their rituals.[101]

The offering of blood is usually from a sacrificed animal, or incisions made by the medium on their own body. They call it the cut. The entire history of Umbanda is this divide. The relentless pressure to rid Brazil of the blood cults. So, did Medium João remove this practice from his Casa as well? No, his spirits would never allow it. They would destroy him and withdraw their presence if they didn't get their offerings.

What became evident to me in the two years I worked at the Casa was that João's "visible" surgeries were blood offerings. The rituals in the Casa began with his possession and then the cut. Films of João's surgeries reveal something else. After completing his work, he stares at the blood on his hand or the knife with a wild look. Then he shakes it off onto the floor. He has made the cut. This is the act of the blood offering, casting the blood on the ground. Afterward, he washes the blood from his hands in a small water basin guarded by an assistant. This bloody water is another offering.

He also makes a sacrifice of tears. All bodily fluids contain Axé. When he scrapes his victims' eyes with a knife in his so-called surgery, they tear up profusely. Tears fall to the ground, as do the tissue and mucus he scrapes with his knife and then flicks off. When he molests a patient, and she instinctively cries, these teardrops are shed as an offering.

These sacrifices amplify the Axé. Their power is potent and creates a magical current, which everyone in his Casa now enters.

Of course, all this business is a secret known only to João and a few people in the Casa. The rest see a disturbing surgery, a supernatural miracle, or a magician's act.

The most shocking offering that Medium João introduced to the Casa is one that only a man can make. It was his deepest secret. It is a common and potent oblation made in black magic cults. This is the offering of semen.[102]

For forty years, the sorcerer João made his irresistible offering. He couldn't do his juju without it. Again and again, he told his victims that he must ejaculate to cure them or their loved ones. Inevitably, this was done soon before the stage show and the public healing session begins. It was done inside the Casa, in a room just a few yards from where he sat on his throne.

As our story progresses, it will be difficult not to assume that the semen offering was a daily event. Conducted within the Casa in secret but under the noses of everyone in attendance.

Blood, semen, and tears are precisely the type of offerings one needs to ensure possession by an Exu. These offerings preceded every work at the Casa. Doctor Augusto and his phalange are Exus.

Yes, I understand that many sincere people claim they received wonderful, loving vibes from the dear doctor. Any medium of Quimbanda would agree that many Exus and Pombagiras have loving vibes. People often fall in love with them. I'm not joking. Sometimes, they even get married and have sexual relationships.

As João seized control of the Casa from his disciples, new rules and a new ritual form unfolded. Now, the house mediums were authorized only by João, wore an identity badge, and no longer lived at the Casa. They were required to wear white clothing.

There would only be one healer in this house—no more spirit possession of the mediums, not even Pombagiras. The mediums could no longer preach or channel messages. They were to observe silence while sitting in the current.

Those who had served as volunteer workers received salaries and duties. Several people were expelled from the Casa. He posted formal rules of the house for the first time—wearing white clothes, not crossing your arms or legs, forming in lines for a consultation, bathing at the waterfall, and the restrictions for those receiving surgeries.

The rules of a Tenda of Umbanda mirror the Casa regime. But this is Umbanda neutered of its joy and ecstatic dance and with only one acting medium.

João's nephew, Urubatan Andrade da Mota, was the new Casa manager. He was treated like a son. Urubatan (Coboclo Urubatan is a gypsy entity from the enchanted realm of Quimbanda) produced the garrafadas and managed all financial matters. He assisted and accompanied João on his mining excursions and was a licensed pilot. Urubatan became João's partner while only in his twenties.

In 1987, João was featured on a popular national television show hosted by Luiz Gasparetto, a medium famous for channeling paintings in the styles of artists like Picasso, Monet, and Renoir. He was a close friend of the psychic Chico Xavier, who was renowned in this era.[103]

For the first time, Brazilians saw João of Abadiânia's bizarre surgeries. The presentation was dramatic and featured João in a sensational but sympathetic manner. Close-up shots of ugly incisions, probes, and crude stitches added to the shock value.

He performed several bloody surgeries and an exorcism. He

appeared to heal a paraplegic who got up and walked. The host was fawning over João, who received this blessing from the spiritist camp.

This same year, he was accused of six rapes. João would travel to independent spiritual hospitals under his sponsorship or alliance. He never ended his traveling road show. He'd sell his garrafadas and bottled water and stage surgeries. Sometimes, he would molest their daughters.

At one of these stops, he fainted during the session and was taken to a hospital. They did not hold him, as it was nothing critical. They made no exams to detect a stroke, but he claimed he had one when he returned to Abadiânia. So did most of his biographers.

He faked a crippled left side. When the sympathy level was at its peak, he pulled off a grand publicity stunt. He operated on himself! Making a slit in his left chest, he declared that the spirit doctor was doing heart surgery. They filmed this with hundreds of onlookers. Afterward, he claimed a complete cure for the stroke he never had.[104]

João wasn't aware that strokes occur in the brain, not the heart. Once again, it is on João's word with no medical documentation. With newfound confidence, his poor farmer myth, and the miracle man publicity, João began receiving more and more visitors to the Casa.

1988 had five accusations of rape. One of them, reported by Fantástico, says she was raped about ten times when she was just eleven years old, always at the Casa. She said, "He asked me to put my hand back, and I felt something strange. I started to cry and said, what is this?"[105]

"He said: 'It's what will cure you.' Then he came ahead of me and did what he did to me. Everything you can imagine. I said all the time, I want my mother. It hurts." He told me, 'Be quiet; otherwise, I'll kill your family.'

A Globo Play report claims João was arrested at this time for trafficking in cocaine via private airplanes. Globo obtained the original police reports, which show he was not prosecuted.[106]

In 1988, the State of Goiás was divided in half, and a new state, Tocantins, was created from the amputation. More posadas were added to João's side of the highway, and more followers arrived.

He was featured again on another television program, TV GLOBO, with live footage of his cutting and eye scrapping. Here, the national media began sensationalizing and promoting João. The crazy surgeries were the hook. Newspapers and magazines ran several articles on him.

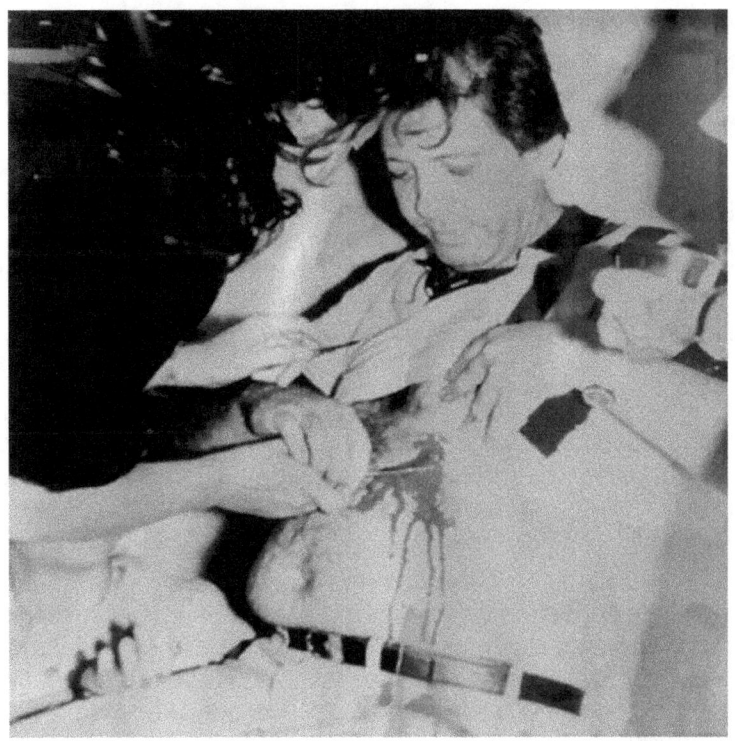

João makes the cut on himself—from a photo displayed at the Casa. Casa archives.

Urubatan and João were like twins. They lusted for young girls, power, and wealth. However, João was far cleverer than his nephew. Urubatan was caught having a sexual affair with two underage sisters at the same time. Unfortunately, their father was a family friend and a local police officer. João and Urubatan were challenged by this angry and threatening Sergeant Siqueira, who had been a regular at the Casa for years.[107]

Late on a Friday afternoon, the visiting sergeant left the Casa office just as the patients were exiting. Urubatan escorted him to his car. Two men were waiting there and, with a signal from Urubatan, shot him twice in the back of the head. A Casa full of clients witnessed the murder. The shooters fled but were captured later by the police. One was Urubatan's partner in a mining transport company they co-owned.

The prosecutors charged Urubatan with arranging the murder and his friends for being hired gunmen. It took a long time to go to court. In 1993, Urubatan was acquitted in the Abadiânia court by a jury voting seven to six. The other guys avoided trial for twenty-two years.

In 2010, they received twelve-year sentences. But the two shooters disappeared and were never imprisoned.

From 1989 to 1990, João was accused of twelve more rapes at the age of forty-eight. Dalva, now twenty, divorced her husband. She had three children and was impoverished. João began courting her again. He said that he would take care of her and his grandsons. He prepared an apartment for them next to his house in Anápolis. The first night she slept there, she saw João staring into her window. She felt his evil and was afraid.

Then it started all over again. He would arrive at night for sex. Her young boys knew what was going on with their grandfather. One of them hid under their bed the entire evening. João said he wanted to marry her, that they had also been married in past life. He called her his wife.[108]

She revisited the Casa, as she was suffering from migraines. Before the daily healing work began, he called her into the Medium's private room. He started massaging her until she became hypnotized, then he undressed her and forced her to have sex. One of the staff entered the room during the act, turned around, and said nothing. She got angry and told him it was over, never again.

"He said: 'So, there's no more car, no more sons, no more good life, now you're going to go hungry.' He took my car, my home, and my food. He didn't pay the rent anymore, and I had no more money. Then, I started using drugs. I got into this out of despair, grief, and suffering because the father I knew when I was almost ten years old was not a father. He was my destruction," said Dalva.

She moved to Goiânia and stayed with her mother and siblings. There were no more sexual encounters for the next six years. Dalva lost her sons, was broken and penniless, and sunk into a deep depression.

Patricia Melo began working at the Casa as an interpreter. She is one of the founding mediums of the Casa. Her responsibilities went far beyond the translations. Patricia is woven into João's web of deceit and secrets.

In 1991, the American actress Shirley MacLaine visited the Casa unannounced and incognito. She wore sunglasses and a red wig.[109]

Her flashy entourage of six arrived on a private plane. No one in Abadiânia recognized her. She had stomach cancer and had recently visited several Filipino psychic surgeons in the quest for a miracle cure she hadn't received.

When she attended the Casa, she was in a lot of pain. João treated her privately in a two-hour session, working only with his hands and no scalpel. He pronounced her healed, and she declared the pain was gone. The Congresswoman, Bella Abzug, was part of this group. She received one of his physical surgeries! The famous Brazilian actress of this time, Ruth Escobar, filmed the encounter.

A gossip magazine covered MacLaine's visit to an "unnamed healer" in central Brazil. It sparked international interest in the Casa. The rich and famous began finding their way to Abadiânia. Oddly, Shirley MacLaine never mentioned João de Deus in the memoirs of her spiritual adventures. Nor did she accredit him with curing her cancer.

Around the time of MacLaine's visit, a grieving family, devotees of the Casa, had just lost their patriarch. He died suddenly at forty-nine years old. João could not help them.

The daughter, a young woman in her twenties, was devastated. She started acting strange, fighting with her husband, seeing ghosts, and entering panic attacks.

Her grandparents, who worked at the Casa de Dom Inácio for two decades, thought her problem was spiritual. They accompanied her on her first visit to the Casa, along with her mother and aunt.

In an interview with Christina Fibe, narrated in her book *João de Deus—The Abuse of Faith*, the young woman remembers her first encounter with João. As soon as he caught sight of her in the line, his eyes were glued on her. When she reached the Medium, he told her to kneel as he held her hand and placed it near his groin.[110]

Then he forced her hand to grip his penis while unbuttoning her blouse and squeezing her nipple. She was horrified and embarrassed as her blouse was open, and everyone could see. Her grandparents and mother saw everything.

João told her family she needed to remain at the Casa for treatment or she would end up dead like her father. She refused, but João insisted that she stay. He paid for two months' lodgings at a posada. He convinced her that her father's death had caused her problems and that her husband's ex-wife had made black magic against her. She was young and naïve and believed him.

For two weeks, the victim was called to the Medium's rape office three times a day. She was abused every time. Between sessions, the Medium would hand her his slip of paper. There was always an assistant who would gather the people who had received the paper slip denoting a private session. She observed that they participated in this deception.

She discovered that this room had direct access to the Entities' Room. One could come and go with no one noticing. He would abuse her at seven a.m., before the first session.

She sat in the chair next to him in the Entities' Room. Around noon, when the work was finished, he'd lead her by the hand to the office. He abused her again until the start of the afternoon session.

João's assistants would encounter her alone with him in his office, tears running down her cheeks. They were all complicit. None of them attempted to save her from her fate as they served João his post-rape lunch. Around five p.m., João would take her back to his office and rape her again.

After a week, she couldn't sleep and was in a terrible state. One day, she stayed in her posada room, planning to avoid the Casa. João showed up with a group of people. The posada owner went to her room and escorted her to the waiting Medium. Her grandmother was proud that the Medium considered her important enough to summon to the session.

Like so many of João's vulnerable victims, she had been brainwashed and hypnotized into believing that this abuse was spiritual therapy. These abused girls are often criticized. Why did you go back for more? They were suffering from Stockholm Syndrome, a psychological coping mechanism where abuse victims bond with their abusers. It helps victims handle the trauma of a terrifying situation from which they cannot escape.

Their torturer and warden began each episode of molestation with a prayer. He faked incorporation, rolling his eyes upward and shuddering. He would magically start by speaking in English. She believed that an entity of wisdom and healing power dwelled in her tormentor.

She was forced to masturbate the Medium during each episode. He never achieved an erection. She noticed his deceit and realized it was all a lie. Confronting him, she said, "I'm going to expose what you did in here; you bum! You ruined my life. I don't even dare to look my husband in the eye with everything you made me do. You're the one who did it. There's nothing special about you. You're a big rascal, a scoundrel."

João threatened that he would destroy her life if she told anyone. She fled the Casa. She wanted to denounce him but feared he would kill her grandmother and family. After her case went public thirty years later, her cousin contacted her. João raped her when she was thirteen years old.

In 1991, João took his road show to another country for the first time, Peru, where he was enthusiastically received. A Peruvian patient paved the way with free airline tickets and much fanfare when his plane landed. The front page of the Lima newspapers heralded his arrival. The venue was a sports stadium near the capital of Lima. Soldiers guarded the stadium with machine guns.[111]

A frantic and uncontrollable mob of Peru's desperate poor crowded around the stadium. People waited several hours in a kilometer-long line to see the Curador for a few seconds. Of course, they received a prescription for his magical healing herbs and water.

The government wouldn't let him use his knives, so he touched each person instead, proclaiming them cured. He duplicated his usual theater, tossing canes and crutches aside. Global TV of Brazil accompanied him on this trip and filmed the action. Shills in the crowd loudly announced they had received a cure.

Global's coverage placed João in the national spotlight at a pivotal moment. Global is Brazil's largest media empire, more extensive than CNN. They are the dominant force in fashioning opinion and style for Brazilian audiences.

They introduced Medium João to the homes of most of the population. Global was very kind to João over the years, not questioning his official story. Global assisted in João's rise to fame. Thirty years later, it is quite an irony to watch them topple this myth and hammer the final nail in the coffin.

This busy year also saw a changing of the guard. The world-famous Doctor Fritz, as embodied in Edson Cavalcante Queiroz, had moved out and moved on. Edson was dead, stabbed to death by his groundskeeper. João was on his way to becoming the most famous healer in the world.[112]

In 1991, a family from Vitória da Conquista, Bahia, packed their belongings and moved to Anápolis. Their adoptive father, an officer in the military police, came to receive treatment from João at the Casa for his failing eyesight. He was a passionate student of spiritism and new-age ideas. They moved into João's neighborhood in Anápolis, and a friendship developed—a friendship from Hell.

This is the story of Simone Soares Silva. I mention her name because she also came forward publicly in 2018. She published a book about her experiences, *The Other Face of João*. I will leave her parents and her two sisters unnamed. She is another one of my heroes in this sad story.[113]

The three children were twelve, fourteen, and sixteen years old, with Simone being the youngest. The entire family was in awe of the self-assured Medium João.

Simone's cautionary tale is an essential key to understanding João. It unlocks his darkest secret. The family would hang out with João. They were regaled by his tales of gold mines, adventures, and spirits. He was like a guru to them. The girls volunteered at the Casa, and the family visited the weekly sessions.

Simone was very curious about what João had to say. Her two older sisters were getting all his attention. They were frequently called into the medium's private office for consultations, but Simone was not invited. She wanted to know what the entity could tell her about her destiny.

She remembers hiding outside the living room doorway to eavesdrop on the adults' conversations. Simone recalls João bragging about his powers. He said, "Do you know what I say before I do the surgeries? I can; I want, I do."

Then, he addressed her mother and asked her if she knew whom he had incorporated that afternoon. She replied, "No." He smiled and told her he had incorporated Exu do Lôdo.

Exu do Lôdo is a phalange of Exus with dark, dense energy. Most of his phalange were priests, witches, and sorcerers in past lives. He is the right-hand man of the King of Exus. His color is black, and he wears a black cape. His specialty is healing.[114]

He transmutes and manipulates stagnant energies, and he can turn lead into gold. He works with the merging of earth and water. Exu do Lôdo is often depicted covered in mud and slime (lôdo), like the bog monster. Exu do Lôdo is also the leader of the entire Quimbanda line.

When Simone turned thirteen, the medium called her to his private room—her day had come. She arrived with her aunt. A blind man was waiting as well. João told her aunt to wait outside. The blind man and Simone entered.

Simone was nervous and trembling. After all, this was the day she would know the mysteries of life and resolve the tragedy of her past. João instructed the blind man to sit a few yards away and meditate. Then he locked the door.

He told Simone he was going to develop her mediumship. The

Medium instructed her to stand with closed eyes and think of God. She was afraid that if she opened her eyes, she would die.

João began an incantation, and she fell into a hypnotic state of confusion and listlessness. She was unable to speak and felt him manipulating her mind.

Simone writes, "And in my concentration, in a fraction of a second, I felt a hand touching me from behind under my blouse. I froze, immobile, wanting to cry. I felt invaded. My soul was torn apart by shame and modesty because I was never even blouse-less in front of my sisters.

"João slowly took my blouse off. He said: 'Concentrate, elevate your thought on God,' He managed to unzip me, took my hand and put it on his member, and made me manipulate it. He was getting off on me until he came. He had a paper towel at hand and quickly cleaned up. I battled in my mind not to think badly of such an enlightened man. The anguish came, and the reproach in myself came as if I were a bad and obscure girl. A black sheep in front of the sisters and the family."

João told Simone that he would continue with this mediumship training and not to tell anyone. He invited her aunt in, who sat next to the blind man. He said to her that Simone was a natural medium and that he would develop her.

Her two sisters were enduring the same fate and worse. They were too embarrassed even to tell each other. He abused the three of them weekly for all of 1992. The psychological toll was devastating. Simone broke apart with depression and inner anguish. She had no one to console her or to tell her secret.

Meanwhile, João conspired to divide this family so he could own the girls. Simone describes how the sexual abuse was done as black magic rituals. She became overwhelmed and nearly destroyed by João's phalange of demons. At night, the spirits tormented her. She wanted to end her life.

Their live-in housekeeper saw many entities, including Zé Pilintra and a woman in a red dress with her hair standing on end.

João persuaded her adoptive father to move to Abadiânia and abandon his family in Anápolis. Her adoptive mother (her aunt) couldn't afford the rent, and they ran out of food. She told João, but he offered no help.

Simone said, "I was losing my life in that place. A man who claimed to be enlightened by God saw a family dying and destroying themselves, and he was the one who caused it all."

Simone's aunt decided to move back to Bahia without the father.

João hid their departure from the father. João arrived at their house in Anápolis the night before they left with his son, Zézinho (Dalva's brother), to do a ritual. It was one in the morning. There will be more of these late-night rituals in his unfolding history. He ordered the girls to gather all the magazines in the house addressed to the mother and built a bonfire. He wanted the father to discover the ashes and think the woman had made a macumba spell against him. Then João said, "I'm going to do a ritual, and you will come back in six months. You will be mine, or you will be nobody's." He conspired through magic to enslave Simone as a replacement for Dalva.

Then, he had the housekeeper write a note (João is illiterate) to the father, threatening that his wife had done a macumba spell against him and not to attempt to get her back. At 4 a.m., the Medium drove off. Simone said, "A piece of me had gone in that car. He stole it, locked my soul in the darkest darkness, and took the key." That day, her aunt and the three girls returned to Bahia, broken and penniless.

Exú do Lodo.

Ponto Cantado do Exú do Lodo *(Incantation to call Exú of Mud)*
Cold rain in the Kalunga* reminds me
My lord, who protects me and makes me see
That charity, humility, and wealth
Are worthless if they are done in vanity or for pleasure.
One day, son, he told me **I was a doctor,**
I did harm to the slave, to the maidservant, and to the master.
Today in Quimbanda, I have learned that charity
Transforms the darkness, the spell, and the evil.
Today, I praise you, oh my guardian.
Sentinel of souls, give me protection!
Exú do Lodo comes to help me!
He takes my pain into the mud.
Hail him, Hail Exú do Lodo!
Axé!
* *(Kalunga: The border between the worlds of life and death.)*

In 1993, Hamilton Pereira, ex-mayor of Abadiânia, became administrator of the Casa. He is still the administrator today. He promotes tourist visits, denies João's guilt, and ensures the Casa remains open.

This year there were three registered rape accusations. Six more occurred in 1994, the year João returned to Peru. A thousand visitors a day were propelling João to fame and riches. His entities channeled their influence and power into innocent and sick visitors. His traveling road show reaped further profits, as did several mining ventures. The poor, humble, illiterate farmer was doing pretty well for himself.

João returned to Peru with his latest wife, Myrian, his nephew Urubatan, and three lawyers. He always traveled with lawyers and bodyguards. This time he held his works in the Andean City of Puno, on the shores of Lake Titicaca. This was a different crowd and setting. Puno is at a very high altitude and bitterly cold. The unrestrained poor fighting for access to miracles frightened João.

He would return two more times to Peru but refused to attend to vast crowds of believers. João was treated like a head of state, and after the works in Puno, he was secretly flown to doctor Peru's new dictator, Alberto Fujimori. [115]

One of the lawyers traveling with João was Liberato Póvoa. In 1994, he published the first biography of the Medium, *João de Deus O Fenômeno de Abadiânia*. Póvoa was introduced to João through a dear mutual friend, João Américo, partner of the murderous Rambo of Pará. Póvoa was Faria's buddy for over twenty years. He is a well-known judge and professor of law.

A few months later, while on his road show, João was arrested at a farm in Pernambuco. The warrant cited illegal exercise of medicine and charlatanism. Most people think of a charlatan as a conman or a quack. In Brazil, it is the legal term for a practitioner of black magic, something that João was charged with multiple times. It was, and still is, illegal to practice black magic (charlatanism) in Brazil.[116]

João had his lawyers with him, of course, pleading *habeas corpus*. The judge recently received an operation from João. He also got arrested for charlatanism in Vitória, Espirito Santo, where he had sold 15,000 of his garrafadas. This year he is accused of two new rapes.

This was nothing compared to what happened at the end of 1995. His Exus demanded another blood sacrifice on the Casa grounds. It was seven years after the murder of Sergeant Siqueira.

The police accused Urubutan of ordering the murder of Mario Augusto dos Reis. He was one of the earliest members of the Casa.

He and his wife managed the Casa cafeteria—beloved community members. Urubutan and Mario argued over orange juice sales, leading to Augusto dos Reis' murder at the Casa. He was shot eleven times. That is a lot of blood. His family fled Brazil afterward.

Fifteen years later, they sentenced a lawyer to seven years for the murder of Mario. He had provided weapons and helped the shooters escape. They all answered to Urubutan. The convicted lawyer disappeared and never served his sentence.

Nineteen-ninety-six was an explosive year for João of Abadiânia, now fifty-four. In January, only twenty-one days after the death of Augusto dos Reis at the door of the Casa, Urubutan died when his airplane mysteriously malfunctioned, killing him, the pilot, and a passenger.

The official report on the accident cited several contributing factors: a problem with the fuel hoses, failure to make a test flight, lack of maintenance, and loss of control of the plane. He crashed into high-tension electrical lines, destroying the plane. The half-million-dollar craft belonged to João.

Simone Soares said, "I met a man named Gledson, and he told me about Urubatan and Mr. Mario and told me of their deaths. Urubatan died in an airplane crash in the Lourdes neighborhood. According to Gledson, João cried very hard when he saw his nephew's body all toasted on the ground. Yet, João was the one who had the plane sabotaged because he had found out that Urubatan was stealing from him." [117]

Leonor Vervloet Feu Rosa arrived in Abadiânia at age twenty-two. She and her boyfriend became central figures at the Casa, as did Robert and Catarina Pellegrino Estrich, who began bringing groups from Australia and Europe to the Casa.

Leonor's home was in Vitória, Espírito Santo, a state in southeastern Brazil on the Atlantic coast. João often brought his road show there, where a Spiritist center hosted him. The center accused João of several rapes. She accompanied him when he visited there, including one time when the police shut down the event.

She assisted João on the "surgery" stage and oversaw the infirmary, where "patients" recovered on rows of cots. It was a dismal, windowless room that smelled of alcohol and ammonia.

When I moved there, she had a small posada where foreigners liked to stay. She seemed a kind and sincere person. Leonor and

Martin's wife, Fernanda, were usually by the Medium's side. These beautiful women were always in his limelight, smiling and helpful.

When I arrived, Leonor's boyfriend, Charles (Charlie), was the Casa manager. He was emotionally distant and the enforcer of rules. He was one of the fixers. Charlie filmed the stage show every session. Some of these tapes inadvertently displayed João at his worst, even self-incriminating.

This year there are six rape allegations against him. One was a sixteen-year-old girl taken by her parents to Abadiânia from their home in Imperatriz, Maranhão—the city where João had his earlier Umbanda tenda.

She stayed there from April to June, seeking treatment for depression. She assisted Medium João by holding the surgical tray of knives, scalpels, and hemostats. Hundreds of victims were bearers of his surgical tray.

Soon, he summoned her to his private quarters at the end of the session. He handed her a glass of water suffused with rose petals and told her to drink it. She lost consciousness and claimed he drugged her.[118]

When she regained consciousness, she and João were naked. Terrified, she began to scream. João threatened her—if she told anyone and tried to flee, the bus carrying her would topple over and kill her. The girl remained there for two more months, abused repeatedly.

She descended deeper and deeper into depression. This led to several suicide attempts over the next three years. A spiritual group helped her recover from the traumas.

Three of his other victims in 1996 were from his satellite Casa in Três Coroas, Rio Grande do Sul. They were children of his devotees.

This year, Dalva's mother asked her to take her younger brother to the Casa to cure a problem. When they arrived, João's bodyguard, Antão, summoned her to talk with João. He was crying and asked her to wait in his office until the session ended.

João drove her back to Goiânia. He stopped at the mall and bought her expensive clothing. They passed the night at a motel. Then he took her to her mother's house and asked if Dalva could stay in Abadiânia for two weeks while he helped her sort her life out.[119]

Two weeks later, he bought her a condo in Goiânia. It was a surprise. He covered her eyes before he brought her into the apartment and then showed her around. The beautiful rooms for her three teenage children and *their* master bedroom. He announced they would be lovers again.

Sometime after this, he brought her to Anápolis. They were in a bar, and one of her estranged sons showed up. She cried. João asked her, do you want to have your sons back and live happily together? Thus began a new life with João, a life of terrible suffering. During these times, she knew of many sexual assaults by João on children. He had her sons beaten by thugs because they knew of his abuses and protested.[120]

As if all this wasn't enough for one year, he and his gang faced charges of trafficking cocaine. The other defendants arrested named him as their boss. He was also accused of brutally torturing Antonio Alves and another man. They were caught stealing from the Casa. The tortures occurred at the Abadiânia police headquarters, with their permission and participation.[121]

This incident points an ugly finger at the possibility that João was familiar with practicing torture. The December 10, 2018, edition of O Popular mentioned:

"In April 1996, according to the filed case, João was accused of having interrogated, psychologically and physically tortured, two suspects of having robbed the House of Dom Inácio de Loyola. The episode of violence allegedly took place inside the Civil Police Station of Abadiânia in the presence of police officers."[122]

Despite the serious accusation, the investigation was only concluded in January 2011. "Although the records contain over 242 pages, they took few steps to investigate, in an effective and correct manner, the crimes narrated. The victims themselves were not even heard."

In July, the case was dismissed by Judge Rosângela Rodrigues (she also dismissed other cases against João, including rape). She considered that there was no crime of torture *"As this criminal classification first appeared in 1997."* She wrote: *"The defendant could respond, at most, for bodily injury which, even in the serious modality, would have already reached the statute of limitations, which, in this case, is twelve years."*

The journal O Popular reported, "The current councilor of Abadiânia, Éder Martins [PTB], was a clerk at the police station when the torture was reported and condoned the interrogation. He said he did not remember the fact."

Simone Soares, now seventeen years old, was irresistibly drawn back to the Casa after a five-year absence. It was the Christmas season.[123]

João's curse had come true. What happened to Simone is called soul theft in many indigenous cultures, including most of those in Africa. In Haiti, the ultimate soul theft is when you turn a person into a zombie, a living but dead slave.

Capturing another's soul is like capturing their axé. They become helpless and under your control. João was a master sorcerer and a dangerous energy vampire who captured many souls.

For five years, Simone fell into a deep depression, possessed by João's entities, who dragged her into alcohol abuse, suicidal thoughts, and anger.

She couldn't love anyone. Everything in her life was crossed. She sensed the presence of death. João's power took over her soul, and she lost herself. A force was dragging her back to the Casa. She couldn't resist.

When Simone arrived at the Casa and stood in line to see the entity, she asked him if he remembered her. He said, "Yes, you should have come back a long time ago. I'll help you." He handed her the paper slip with his squiggles on it.

Medium João suggested she live in the Casa (something no one else did). He put her in his private room. Not his office where he committed the rapes, but a room beside it where he kept his clothing and personal things. He said he would undo her state but wove an even deeper spell.

She helped in the Casa, filming the surgeries, assisting patients, and cleaning up. She discovered her adoptive father was still working at the Casa, now completely blind. He told her he had received a vision. Two angels appeared, warning him not to let Simone attend the Casa. They were committed to protecting her life.

Simone said that in this room, João kept lots of anti-depressant medication. He awoke each night at two a.m. to make incantations. In his closet were black boots and black satin capes with burgundy embroidery. They were used for witchcraft. Every night, she endured frightening demons flying about the room.

One day, João angrily knocked on her door and told her he would take her as his own and bring her to his ranch outside of Anápolis. That evening, one of his bodyguards came to her door with a gun in his hand. He was shaking and said, "Get out of here because you are going to die."

Fortunately, she had the strength to run away. She was saved from this witchcraft through her devotion to Jesus.

Simone Soares Silva is now a pastor. She counsels victims of abuse and black magic. She is the author of ten books, has an internet presence, and is the mother of five children. Simone is one of the brave souls who exposed this terrifying history.

From 1997 to 1998, João was accused of seventeen more rapes. Once again, he was charged with charlatanism in Curitiba, Parana. He used the name João de Deus for the first time.

Robert Pellegrino-Estrich was featured in the new-age magazine *Nexus*. His unsubstantiated claims were the first chapters of a self-published book, *The Miracle Man*, which was published in 1998. His book about João reached an English-speaking audience for the first time.

Pellegrino-Estrich, a mustachioed flim-flam man, was single-handedly responsible for the spectacular fraud that João was about to perpetrate. *The Miracle Man* has been translated into sixteen languages, including Brazilian Portuguese. It calls people to the Casa to this day.[124]

Josie Ravenwing began bringing American tour groups. Josie became a crucial player in João's drama and a vocal denier of his guilt. She was the second English-speaking guide to write a book about him. Josie repeated the myths and pitched João and her services.

João published the first booklet of the Casa Rules. This is the era when Carlos and Rosane Carlotto arrived in Abadiânia with his parents and built the Posada Catarinense. They became millionaires and key figures in the unfolding scandal of the Casa.

Other newcomers were Martin and Fernanda Mosquera, who opened the popular Posada Brother Sun/Sister Moon. Martin (another millionaire in the making), who speaks four languages, became the English translator.

One of the original posadas, Posada Dom Ingrid, just across the street from the Casa, always had a strange vibe to me. Valdete Ferreira de Melo and her son Ricardo (one of João's bodyguards), the posada itself, had a dark aura.

She and her husband were part of the original group and practiced the Gypsy and Oriental Lines. Dom Ingrid is an enchanted royal from the left-hand path. Pellegrino-Estrich said, "Dom Ingrid, an extraordinarily powerful entity about whom nothing is known except that her energy is so strong that she will make Joao's nose start bleeding if she comes too close to him."

One of my anonymous contacts in Abadiânia told me a story that the locals know well. Valdete's husband died in a tragic hit-and-run accident. That week, he had argued about something with his wife and João. His car had been struck and run off the road by a large truck, which fled the scene. It is said that this was no accident, that it was arranged. No criminal charges were filed. My contact also told me that they know of more cases of mysterious hit-and-run deaths.[125]

The first time Clodoaldo Turcato visited the Casa was in 1996, seeking a cure for his ulcer. He spent the week, but the Entity asked him to stay another, then two months more. Turcato had a wife and child back home in Santa Catarina. He sent for them, and he and his wife began working for the Casa; she was a cashier, and he became the new Casa accountant.

He handled all the Casa's finances. Every Friday, he would close out the books, emptying the cash registers at the snack bar, the gift shop, and the herbal pharmacy. He also had monthly duties when he would collect the *Entity's salary.*

Turcato explains that everyone associated with the Casa and doing business paid a monthly tax directly to João. He said, "He charged a minimum (monthly) wage from each inn. And the taxi drivers paid half a monthly salary during that period."[126]

And woe to the person who could not pay their monthly Entity Tax. Turcato explains that delinquent accounts would receive a visit from João's enforcers. Soon after, the person would pay up.

He recalls an incident when a staff member embezzled funds from the Casa. João's thugs visited him and took everything of value in his house, including his car. They warned him of worse to come should he protest.

Turcato registered that the entire staff was each paid the minimum monthly wage. In reality, many received more than that. They were paid under the counter. He claims the Casa was grossing about two hundred thousand reais monthly in 1996. The exchange rate was one real for one dollar.

He says that half the Casa income came from selling water and passiflora. During this time, no money from those sales or the many donations was declared for taxes. Turcato says that 70% of the money went out the back door. The laundered money was deposited in João's business account, Casa de Dom Inácio, registered as a church. The government does not tax churches; they are like non-profit organizations. With this cooked money, João purchased ranches and other investments.

He usually had a co-signer/partner for these properties and enterprises. This illustrates the far-reaching arm of his mafia kingdom. And the strangling tentacles clutching his partners.

The remaining money was guarded in black trash bags stuffed in the ceiling above the soup kitchen. When the overhead space was full, the sacks would be transported to Anápolis. He kept João's crooked books for two years and looked the other way when the monster reared its head.

One day, Turcato's wife came home in tears. João had called her to his private room and made her masturbate him. He told her that Clodoaldo's ulcers would never heal unless she did as he wanted. It had happened two times. The family fled a week later.

It wasn't until 2019 that Turcato was interviewed about his history with the Casa. By then, he had moved far away, changed his name, and attempted to forget the unforgettable for twenty years.

V.
ME AND THE MEDIUM

In 1998, I was an ardent student of shamanism and indigenous folk healing. My companion, Theresa, had a similar focus. We lived in Santa Fe, New Mexico, and explored many of these paths in the rugged backdrop of the desert southwest.

One day in the city library, I pulled an out-of-print book from the shelf: Zé Arigó, *The Surgeon with the Rusty Knife* by John G. Fuller. A man in Brazil possessed by a dead German doctor, Doctor Oswaldo Fritz, was performing surgeries with a pocketknife, and miraculous cures occurred. I couldn't put that book down. I read it in two days. What a story! I would have visited Arigó if I had only known, but now he's gone; how sad.

Theresa had health problems, including Hashimoto's disease and 80% hearing loss. She began experiencing ovarian pain. We made a few trips to the hospital emergency room and her doctor. They couldn't make a diagnosis. As these attacks continued to drain her strength, we ran out of options.

A few months after I read the Zé Arigó book, I found a similar one about another Brazilian healer, *In Search of Brazil's Quantum Surgeon: The Dr. Fritz Phenomenon* by Masao Maki.

The healer's name was Rubens de Faria Júnior. He was alive and practicing his art on the poor streets of Rio de Janeiro. Rubens fell into a spontaneous trance while attending his first spiritist service. He channeled the same German doctor, Dr. Fritz.

Thousands of people lined up to enter his storefront healing center. He was famous for his hypodermic injections. He wielded an enormous veterinary syringe, dipping it repeatedly in a bucket at his feet. The bucket was a mixture of kerosene, alcohol, and ammonia. This was what he was injecting, at twenty reais each. He used the same needle thousands of times a day. Rio de Janeiro was having its first wave of the AIDS virus. People claimed miracle cures had occurred. He was about to eclipse the fame of the new star on the horizon, João de Deus.[127]

These books portrayed miraculous healing powers and unexplained phenomena. To me, they were hard to believe. But man, I wanted to believe. This is where my magical thinking began. I was well on my way to becoming a believer in miracles.

Theresa and I needed a miracle. We were both in poor health

and suffering from recent trauma as well. We had the good fortune to make connections in Brazil before we departed, which led to a fantastic journey.

We spoke with Rubens de Faria by phone, and he invited us to meet him in Rio de Janeiro and assured us he would cure Theresa.

We contacted a state senator in Minas Gerais. She invited us to receive treatment from another healer. He channeled Doctor Fritz in Belo Horizonte.

A friend, on a sabbatical in Salvador, Bahia, invited us to spend a week with her. She was studying Candomblé and Umbanda. Salvador is the epicenter of all this.

A month before we left for Brazil, another book came my way. *The Miracle Man, the Life Story of João de Deus* by Robert Pellegrino-Estrich. Yet another man, channeling a dead doctor and performing surgeries. His center in central Brazil was a couple hours south of Brazil's capital, Brasilia. We added him to our list.

A week before our flight to Brazil, we received an e-mail from Ruben's wife in Rio. He was arrested on a live TV program. He attempted open heart surgery with a kitchen knife and no anesthesia on a very trusting volunteer. Now, Rubens was in prison. One needs to be a licensed surgeon to perform surgeries. But she assured us we could still visit when he got out. We scratched him off the list.

Later, his wife would write a tell-all exposé about his teenage lover, lots of money laundered, and fraud. And the syringe? He never injected that vile concoction. The needle had a sealed, rounded end and didn't penetrate the skin. That's why no one felt any pain.

We flew to Salvador in August 1999, a beautiful colonial city with colorful buildings and homes overlooking the Atlantic Ocean. Our friend guided us on the night streets. We danced with The Sons of Gandhi Samba Band as they drummed and sang down the narrow cobblestone avenues.

We attended theater performances of traditional Nigerian Candomblé in full costume and regalia. We ventured into the barrios, participating in Umbanda rituals in dirt-floored terreiros. The locals consulted with spirits, asking for help with a multitude of life problems. In Salvador, we resonated with Africa's ancient roots—her traditions of drums, dance, and trance.

It was hard to say goodbye, but we were booked for a flight to Brasilia and a visit to Abadiânia's Casa de Dom Inácio. We arrived in the early evening but didn't know how to get to Abadiânia from the airport. We stopped at the information booth. Abadiânia was not even on a map, and they didn't speak English. We didn't get very far.

Off to the side, a woman was listening to our attempts to speak a little Portuguese and get to Abadiânia. She interrupted us and, in English, offered to drive us there and help sort things out with a room. Once again, serendipity was guiding our way.

It was the night before the first session of the week. We found a room at the Vila Verde Posada. It was the only hotel with rooms available. It was nearly empty. The only other guest I remember was Josie Ravenwing, a tour guide resting between back-to-back tours.

João's neighborhood in Abadiânia was much more rustic and disheveled than now. Every street was of dirt. The only paved road was the two-lane highway going to Brasilia or Goiânia. Most people lining up for treatments were Brazilian, and less than half were dressed in white. The only place to eat was at your posada. There was no internet, overseas phone lines, or gathering place.

A television mounted on the Casa wall ran poor-quality VHS films of some of João's bloodier cuts. A floor fan unsuccessfully tried to dispel the 90+ degree heat. As we didn't understand Portuguese, the Casa was exotic and surreal. It took a while to appreciate the theater. The VHS tapes were there to prepare you for what came next.

Let's begin with a question. Have you ever watched at proximity, someone sliced into with a scalpel? Or someone squeezing a stranger's eye until the pupil is half popped out of the socket while scooping under it with a paring knife? An average person isn't attracted to this. If you are like me, this is shocking. That drama is the theater of the Casa. It draws you into the con.

The Casa was simpler back then. It had the same blue and white paint, but the roof was corrugated asbestos. The cement floor was painted blood red. You waited while standing. This led many visitors to sit in white clothes on the exterior wall or the floor. There were no benches. The red color was made of wax and stained pants and dresses.

The theater became crowded, everyone pressing toward the tiny stage with the paintings of João and his healing entities. People stuffed scraps of paper and photos of sick loved ones into the giant wooden triangle. Then, they prayed or asked for help. Many poor Brazilians came by the busloads and stayed in a dozen run-down posadas, half the price of ours. Some would sleep on the buses, as they had no money for a room.

João emerged from a blue door in the white wall to the left of the stage, linked to his private office, and stood before us on the stage. Someone was filming him with an enormous antique VHS video camera. João's hair was long and disheveled. The Medium was a big guy with his shirt half open, exposing his chest and a heavy gold chain. He wore a gold watch, a gold bracelet, and a gold ring with an enormous emerald. He looked like a gypsy gangster or a disco king. We were in awe as he was about to perform some of those surgeries we saw on the TV. There was an excitement in the crowd as they pushed toward the stage, an anticipation of miracles.

No one translated what he said. He was with several people, all dressed in white. A woman carried a silver instrument tray with his knives, hemostats, and a glass of water.

When he entered his trance, it looked like he had received a painful electric shock. Then his eyes appeared wild, and he ripped off the paper wrapping of a scalpel. He walked up to a middle-aged woman leaning against the wall with her eyes closed. The Medium unbuttoned her blouse and drew the knife along her breast above the bra line. A bright crimson slit appeared. The woman was silent and unresponsive. His assistant then handed him a curved needle with a thick thread, and he sewed her wound with two stitches.

A tall guy had been standing beside her, rigid with his eyes closed, while this occurred. Two men arrived with a lawn chair and carried away the first patient who had fainted. João asked for the hemostat. It looks like slender long-nosed scissors but is a miniature vice grip. It's used in surgery to control bleeding by pinching severed veins.

He pushed the guy's head backward. He thrust the hemostat into the man's sinus cavity, twisting it rapidly several times. All the while, he was looking off into space with that crazy look. Suddenly, the surgeries were over, and he disappeared through another blue door.

Patricia Melo was our translator, and it was a rushed affair. She was a small, nervous person with very little patience. She handed us a ticket, directing us to a line that crept through a windowless room. A few hundred people waited for their turn to speak with the Entity. People were meditating on wooden benches. We then entered another room with more people meditating.

In these rooms, people are surrounded by music coming from a speaker system. A cassette tape mix of Goiás cowboy music, nostalgic Brazilian samba crooners, and awful synthesized new age music. An obnoxious folk singer priest and a sentimental song written for João by a local band completed the playlist. They only had two of these tapes, which played every day. They played so many times that they stretched and warped. The tapes slowed down and speeded up frequently. It was not conducive to meditation. Neither were the wooden benches and stifling heat in the windowless rooms.[128]

Patricia tugged on our arms when it was our turn to consult with the Medium. She told the entity about Theresa's problems and then mine. He handed us each a scrap of paper with some squiggles on it. Patricia escorted us to the window in the wall, where they sold the magical herbs.

In the first edition of Pellegrino's book, he claimed João used over 300 species of herbs. Each prescription was specific to your problem. Only the workers dispensing the sacks could decipher which bag to give you. They matched them to the squiggles on the piece of paper.

The entities directed everything here. The dosage was a teaspoon of the powder three times daily with meals. They cautioned us never to miss a dose. We were to observe several irrational food restrictions and thirty days of celibacy.

We adopted the regime, returning for a third day. We met an Argentinian named Martin, who spoke English. He owned a popular posada with his Brazilian wife, Fernanda. He was the only other English translator.

The next day, we were better oriented to the Casa. We attended two meditation sessions in what is known as the De-possession Room or the Medium's Room. There were some strange moments in this room. Someone shakes or weeps aloud or screeches. Many people fall asleep there. Your butt falls asleep on the wooden bench. Occasionally, someone faints. The sessions can be three hours or more, and if you need to exit for the bathroom, you must get in line again and wait to return.

One or two mediums pace around, and if the group appears restless (or is snoring), they give a pep talk or a prayer. They call this sitting in the current. This is the usual prescribed treatment along with the herbs. Some people sat in the current twenty years, still waiting for their cure. The fault was always theirs—bad karma.

Then, it was time to return to Brasilia and fly to Belo Horizonte, where we had a date with Dr. Fritz. Theresa was in pain and very weak when we arrived in Belo Horizonte, a large city and the capital of Minas Gerais in central Brazil.

Our contact had insisted we spend the weekend together so she could get to know us. She needed to determine if we were the type of person she would bring to the healer. We stayed in an inexpensive hotel, took a fantastic side trip to Ouro Preto, and passed the test with our new friend.

On Monday morning, she took us to a small house in a poor but tidy neighborhood. She ushered us into an office about the size of a small bedroom. It had a single window, and a massage table took up a quarter of the space.

The Senator brought a friend along, and they had spent the last hour preparing Theresa for the big event by telling her tales of the many cures this healer had performed and assuring her there would be no pain. The Senator reminded us of how he healed her of a chronic back problem and used a knife to cut people open. This was the real thing. He was the true Doctor Fritz.

We entered a room filled with cigarette smoke. Three people were puffing away, wearing stained white hospital scrubs. Squeezing his four guests into that space was difficult. Poor Theresa began shaking in fear of what was to come.

Doctor Fritz (after twenty years, I can't remember the gentleman's actual name) greeted us in English. We were the first Americans he had ever treated. He said, "I can't wait!"

But first came the introductions. The wrinkled old lady with bleached blond hair was a friend and patient. He introduced her as the ex-wife of the last dictator of Argentina. The healer stood about five-foot-four inches, a thin man in his seventies. He motioned for the young woman in the corner to greet us. "This is my wife. Yes, she is very young, twenty-four years old," he said.

He looked at me with a wink and asked if I thought he was a strong, macho man. He caught me by surprise. I was preoccupied with Theresa's suffering and fear and bewildered by the surrealistic room of crazies and thick smoke. I replied that I was sure he must be a strong man. He challenged me to test him. I deferred. He insisted. "Hit me hard in the stomach, punch me."

I gave him a light punch in the arm to humor him, feeling guilty for abusing this sweet old guy. He said, "No, I'm serious. Hit me with all you got right in my stomach. I can take it."

He persisted, and after a few pulled punches, which weren't enough for his taste, I slugged him hard in the gut. It was like punching a wall. He was grinning.

He turned to Theresa and asked her if she was afraid. She was pale and trembling. She whimpered, "Yes."

He said, "All illness results from problems with the spine."

Theresa reminded him that her problem was in the ovaries.

He replied, "Never mind, the problem is in the back. Don't worry; you won't feel anything. Get up on the exam table, but first, take off your blouse and bra."

"Say what? With all these people here," she asked.

The Senator and her friend stepped up and helped her undress. Theresa lay face down on the table. Things were happening fast now, too fast. This guy didn't go into a trance, say a prayer, or speak strangely. He appeared to be the same person but was more self-assured.

Theresa was sobbing. "You aren't going to cut me, are you?" But it was far too late for that. Dr. Fritz held a plastic-handled serrated steak knife gripped in his fist above Theresa's spine. We were both shaking at this point.

I thought, "Oh shit, what have I done? I brought her to this madman, and now he'll slice her open like a watermelon."

He turned to me, advising me to watch. Dr. Fritz secured the knife in both hands and plunged it into her spine at the upper vertebrae. He ran the razor-sharp blade down the length of her spine with a determined and skilled hand. I shuddered and waited for the blood to appear. He removed his hands, and a bright red welt ran down her back. The knife seemed to enter with significant force but never pierced her flesh. His thumbnail had scratched the red welt.

Then I perceived (but how) that he was pulling tiny white balls out of her spine. He tossed many of them on the floor. Dr. Fritz was a master of sleight of hand. Others might perceive this as a miraculous healing and closure of an open wound in an instant. I wasn't so convinced.

I was relieved he hadn't drawn blood.

The Doctor said, "Okay, you're healed. I'll give you some medicine to take back to America."

The Senator said, "Wait, now that he's fixed your ovaries, don't you want him to cure you of your deafness?"

Theresa panicked. "No, not my ears!"

The ladies helped her put on her clothes, and she sat in the only chair in the room.

Our Senator friend was doing all the talking now. In rapid-fire Portuguese, she explained that Theresa was 80% deaf and needed hearing aids and lip reading to communicate.

The good Doctor perked up again. He said, "Hearing aids? Let me see them."

Theresa protested, "Oh no, please. They are very expensive—be careful; each one costs five thousand dollars."

Dr. Fritz took out her hearing aids and asked if he could crush them and throw them away. "I'll heal you. You'll hear like normal again," he said.

Theresa was shaking and begging him to give back the hearing aids.

He set them on a metal tray with his surgery instruments, some cotton balls, the steak knife, and a hemostat.

He secured a cotton ball in the teeth of the hemostat. Without warning, he plunged it into Theresa's ear and began twisting the tool. He pulled it out a few times, examining the earwax and then plunging it again. I thought he punctured her eardrum.

When he got to her other ear, I heard a loud pop in my ears. I sensed every sound coming from the open window and the street. It was very loud, as if amplified. I could hear people talking in the house next door, birds singing, and children playing. None of this I noticed before.

Then, Theresa said, "Oh my God, I can hear! I can hear so well. I can't believe it—I can hear!" Theresa turned to Dr. Fritz and told him she wanted to put in the hearing aids to test. She didn't need them; they became a distraction. We cried.

Theresa put in the hearing aids and took them out in disbelief that they were no longer needed. She said, "I can't believe it, I can't believe it. I can hear."

Dr. Fritz's wife appeared with two paper shopping bags full of weird pharmaceutical products. The Senator explained that his wife was a pharmacist; they had a small drugstore in their home. Doctor Fritz whipped out a notepad and took the medicines from the sacks. He scribbled dosages and frequency for dozens of chemical medications.

He said, "Take two of these once a day for three weeks, and three of these after each meal until they're gone. Take a spoonful of this before sleeping, and this pill once a week on an empty stomach."

After he explained the first bag, he turned to me and told me the other bag was for me. I told him I wasn't sick; he hadn't treated me and that I only use herbal medicine. He insisted I take everything.

The Senator took us to our hotel.

Theresa repeatedly exclaimed, "I can't believe it! I can hear." She kept trying on the hearing aids and testing whether she could hear. She could. "I can't believe it. I can't believe it." We dumped our bags onto the bed and began an inventory. There were three types of antibiotics: sulfur, vitamin D, Epsom salts, liver tonic, powdered organs, and many pills with long chemical compositions. We would never use this junk! But he said we needed to take it all to get the cure.

After hours of hearing well and "I can't believe it," Theresa lost her hearing again at about ten o'clock at night. It never came back. We abandoned the medicines in the hotel room ($300 worth) and left for another week in Abadiânia. We were still on a quest for a miracle cure.

Upon arrival, I asked if I could film with my video camera during this visit. They liked the idea. I shot several surgeries up close. The next three sessions were a pleasure. I had powerful meditations with visions and spirits appearing. It was hypnotic to watch the surgeries; that raw shock grabbed you like a claw.

It announced you were in supernatural territory, and anything might be possible. We felt the pathos of hundreds of suffering folks passing through the lines. The simplicity of everything—no TV, cell phones, or internet. Nothing but the Casa and the never-ending stories. It was all hypnotic. I bought a crystal, a wooden triangle, and VHS tapes of his most radical and bloody projects. I was ready to spread the word back in the States.

What I hadn't noticed, how could I, were the four rapes he had been accused of this same year.

City of Sycophants

A Sycophant is someone who acts obsequiously toward someone important to gain an advantage. Denoting an informer.

After returning to our busy life in New Mexico, Theresa had not received her miracle cure. Sadly, we separated soon afterward. I couldn't get Brazil or the Casa off my mind. I had to return. This time, I traveled with two friends. One was the wife of a close buddy. She had health problems. The other was a friend studying Reiki who came out of curiosity. Word was spreading fast about João. I called Martin, reserved rooms, and went for an extended visit. We arrived in March 2000.

This was the year João had severe hypertension. Real surgeons installed three stents. He kept this a secret. After all, the most famous healer in the world should be able to heal himself. Everyone knows he did so before when the poor man suffered a stroke.

It was nearing the end of the rainy season and a completely different climate. Everything had turned from brown and burned to lush greens. Martin's Posada was full of English-speaking people. The tour guide and author Robert Pellegrino also had a large group in the Posada Dom Ingrid. There were more people than on my previous visit.

I did not know that Martin acted as my monitor. He assessed me and was ready to report any unapproved activities immediately to João. Unapproved activities would be anything João had heard about you and didn't like. The Entity would gruffly voice his disapproval. Maybe you had a friend he didn't trust, a gathering he suspected was a workshop, or you said something in public that he found offensive. I had to conceal my private life to avoid these confrontations. He kept a close eye on me for the next few years. Several times, I was summoned to speak with the Entity. It was always a reprimand.

The supreme lie of the Casa is that the Entity is omniscient. He knows your entire history of reincarnations. The Entity sees your actual state of health, including mental health. He knows what is good and bad for you and can read your thoughts. If you lie to him, he will know. He knows your deepest secrets, too—the ones no one wants to be made public. The Entity is a know-it-all. He can see right through you. Once, he reprimanded a young woman for wearing black panties beneath her white pants.

The Entity can also predict the future and is infallible in his advice. If he advises you to marry someone, do it. If he asks you to empty your bank account, do it. If he declares that you're now healed? You better believe it, even if your body is saying otherwise.

Not only that, but the Entity can also heal you of things the doctors and therapists cannot, and in an instant. He is all-powerful. He looks inside like an x-ray machine, scanning your aura and chakras. The Entity finds obsessive spirits lurking in your subconscious. He is so powerful that when he cuts you or tortures you with the hemostat, you don't feel a thing. No one ever gets an infection or complication from the surgeries. He has cured dozens of AIDS victims and thousands of terminal cancer cases. He has even brought people back from the dead.

Day after day, the children of the Casa (João's informants) indoctrinated the visitors into the myth. They shielded them from knowing anything about the dirty laundry. They posed as smiling, selfless servants of suffering humanity.

All the posada owners, tour guides, and taxi drivers served João this way. The Entity knew everything because his spies reported all interesting activities. João had modeled his Casa after the military regime's espionage network. Nothing at all escaped the overseers.

The visitors were captive in his system. We weren't allowed to cross the highway to the real Abadiânia—a town of poverty, alcoholism, cocaine, and prostitution. The four days a week, when João disappeared from the Casa was when independent-minded people left town for some sightseeing. You had to go through the line and ask the Entity if you could make such an excursion. The destinations allowed were minimal.

Robert Pellegrino took his groups to Brasilia on the free days. He didn't want his guests to see something awkward or hear any nasty rumors that continually circulated in the Casa.

They also spent a few days on arrival or departure, enjoying Rio de Janeiro in a nice hotel. Pellegrino's tours were pricey, especially for the year 2000, at $5,000 per person for a two-week tour. The posadas he used cost less than eight dollars per person per night, with meals included.

Because we didn't understand the intrigues behind our backs, we had a wonderful time at the Casa. Instant friendships abounded. Tales of healings and supernatural events passed from posada to posada. Those who had been there before were now an authority. Those people were happy to show you how everything worked.

An example is the triangle, the symbol of the Casa. This wooden triangle, with a cutout triangle space within, was the first thing explained. A constant stream of people waited to bring their prayers to the triangle. The open space in the middle, where one placed their forehead, had discolored the white paint from many years of contact with sweaty brows.

João's Spirit Catcher. Photo: Michael Bailot.

"The triangle symbolizes the Holy Family and three principles of the Casa—Faith, Charity, and Love—and it is a portal used to communicate with the entities." Rocha, Cristina. *John of God* (pp. 81-82). Oxford University Press.

It is the *portal* part that isn't explained well to the faithful. The triangle within a triangle is a well-known magical device that traps low spirits for their eventual enslavement and control.[129]

One drew it on the ground as described in one of the many grimoires. Magic incantations and objects placed around the triangle caused a demon to manifest. But he could only appear in the inner triangle. It was a trap. The magician sat outside the larger triangle and could safely tame the demon, who could never leave the triangle. This is the portal João asked everyone to use.

Quimbanda uses a similar triangle device to invoke and trap left-hand spirits. Two triangular mirrors are placed opposite and facing each other. A candle is lit in front of each one, capturing the spirit.

The Casa holds many esoteric secrets. Another example is the scrap of paper with the squiggles and dots. João sat for hours on his throne, licked his thumb, and extracted a single piece from a stack of paper. He scribbled on it and passed it to the next client. Only a few people could read the indecipherable scratches. Some markings directed one to buy the herb—they were the signature of an entity. Another symbol referred you to a private session with Medium João.[130]

João invested untold thousands of hours scribbling on his papers. Couldn't he have simplified the procedure, saving himself from potential carpal tunnel syndrome? Or hand out two different colored tickets as he used in the interview lines? He wouldn't even have to handle them. Well, no. The scribbles have a vital role in his work, almost indispensable. Quimbanda has a ritual called the *Pontos Riscado* (crossed-out dots). It reminds me of the childhood connect-the-dots coloring books. Drawing lines following the numeral sequence of dots reveals a cartoon.

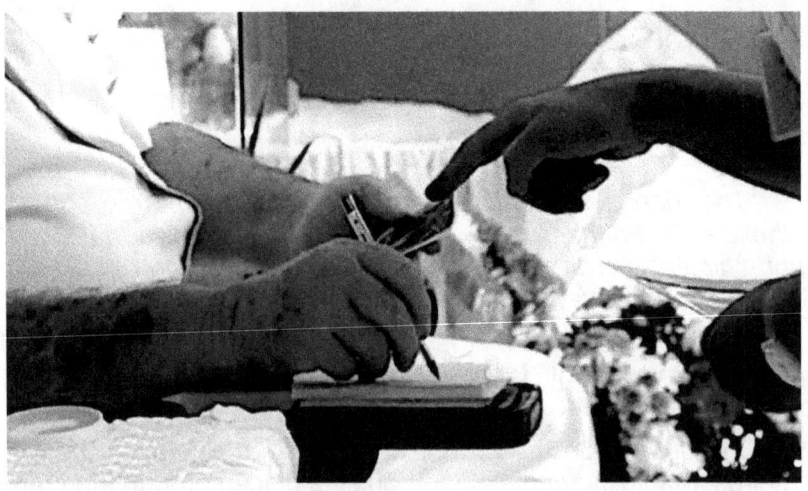

João's Pontos Riscado. Photo: Anonymous/Creative Commons.

A Pontos Riscado is a unique symbol belonging to the entity inscribing it. It is the entity's signature. The Pontos Riscado of Quimbanda summons the *don de cabeça,* the medium's head guide. Any other entities the medium incorporates on that day must also scratch their unique symbol. This authenticates for their don de cabeça that the entity has possessed the medium. The Pontos Riscado give the entity permission of the don de cabeça to work. Traditional terreiros scratch these marks into the earthen floor with chalk.

From the website *Cabana do Caboclo Gentil:* "Consulting the oracle of the búzios, the Mãe-de-Santo announced Caboclo Gentil's desire. He requested three roosters, two hens, and a couple of quails as an offering. Exu also responded to the oracle, showing his willingness to receive a rooster in sacrifice. In this terreiro, the caboclo is seated after knowing his Pontos Riscado. A kind of drawing he makes on the ground with white *pemba,* from which a tool is made in iron."[131]

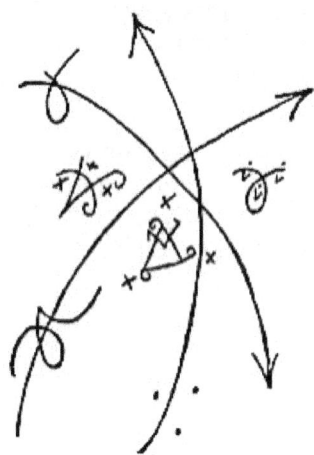

Pontos Riscado.

The few people who understand the Pontos Riscado can identify the spirit possessing João from the symbols on the paper scraps.

On my second visit, the Entity of the hour handed me one of these papers and told me it was his signature—José Xavier. *This illustrates that the entity he is channeling signs his name on the slip of paper.* The Pontos Riscado the Medium handed me for José Xavier was this symbol:

That evening, I dreamed about José Xavier. He appeared in a black hooded cape and said he would teach me hermetic wisdom. He explained that alchemy invokes the Divine Will to transform matter and human beings.

Xavier told me that it is important that I realize entities are real. He explained, "We have bodies. You can touch us." José Xavier showed me his Pontos Riscado again, this time enclosed in a triangle inside a circle. It was inscribed in bright light—scintillating like fire.

I discussed my dream and the symbol with Martin. He told me that the entity, José Xavier, was a warrior. The details of my dream surprised him. I told him I didn't know what hermeticism was. Martin understood. He recommended four books explaining the philosophy written by Franz Bardon.

Hermeticism is magic. It teaches an esoteric system of magic that evokes spirits and demons with symbols, glyphs, and the Hebrew alphabet. Bardon taught a multi-leveled discipline for developing magical powers and taming spirits. He warned his disciples that as the magician's power increases, so does his ability to harm, even unintentionally.

The Secret Seal of Solomon; note the Saturn symbol on the left and the several Pontos Riscado. The seal summons and traps spirits.

In researching this chapter, I referenced my journals from my time at the Casa. Another term that I noted from my dream was the Latin term Goetia. It refers to the summoning of evil spirits. It is linked to hermeticism and the Keys of Solomon.

Hermeticism influenced Freemasonry, the Rosicrucians, and The Hermetic Order of the Golden Dawn. It also influenced João and Martin. Over twenty years would pass before I re-read my journal of 2000 and discovered these references.

I researched the symbol. This is the symbol of Saturn, both the planet and the God—the Reaper. It is also known as the symbol for the Canaanite God Moloch, to whom they frequently sacrificed babies by throwing them into his statue's fiery mouth. For the alchemists, it symbolized the element of lead. Saturn is associated with black magic and hermeticism. It is the force of physical corruption.

When I returned to the Casa in March, rumors were abuzz. It was whispered that João had been arraigned in the federal court of Brasilia. Evil doctors and priests had pressured the court to close the Casa, but Medium João had won the case. It had been a tense moment.

He feared he might serve jail time. But now, *gracias a Deus,* everything was okay, and his spirits were more powerful than ever. This was not exactly true, but none of the tourists would know the back story.

João had gone to court in Brasilia accused of human trafficking (slavery) in his gold and emerald mines. Much of the human trafficking occurred at the illegal mines with enslaved prostitutes. He was also accused of selling babies on the black market.

Faria was also tried in Goiânia and convicted of practicing medicine without a license. The rumor was that the court decision mandated he couldn't sell his herbs and garrafadas anymore. They also prohibited his surgeries.

In June 2000, the public prosecutor Fernando Krebs signed a letter raising the need to investigate the suspected crimes of João Curador. Crimes that he said, "Had the connivance of the judicial police of that locality." [132]

The case in the higher court of Brasilia denounced João Teixeira de Faria for allegedly sexually enslaving women until they were pregnant and then marketing their babies. The girls traveled to a locale where the adoptive parents were waiting. [133]

Most of the babies went to foreign countries, where they were prepaid. After birth, the child went to the new parents. Bribed notary public offices and authorities created false papers.

They recorded the new parents as the actual blood parents or falsified adoption documents. That way, they would leave Brazil legally with the newborn. Some women were sent to other countries to give birth, and some never returned to Brazil.

The Prosecutor's Office claimed these allegations lacked evidence to continue an investigation. Therefore, these serious charges, which might have put him away for years, were dropped.

After the Court's decision, João stopped selling the herbs in sacks. He had a pharmaceutical laboratory in Anápolis produce thousands of bottled capsules with his label on the packaging. These were gelatin capsules filled with powdered passiflora (passionflower) leaves. Passiflora has tranquilizing, narcotic, and anti-depressant properties.

This remedy is listed in pharmaceutical and botanical references as harmless. It has no side effects or problems with long-term use. The herb is legal to import or export and a fail-safe choice for João. No 300 magic herbs were selected especially for a particular illness. Every sack contained powdered passiflora leaves with their bitter, dirty sock flavor.

The other restriction imposed on him was easy to circumvent. Of course, he needed to make the cut. Otherwise, his entities would not possess him. He circumvented this difficulty in his typical arrogant style.

Before the surgery theater began, he would ask if a doctor was in the house, maybe a surgeon or a nurse—even a dentist or a veterinarian would do.

He would select someone from the audience if no one came forward (they usually did). When his stage act began, he would hand the knife to one of these volunteers and announce that they would perform the surgery. Many of these doctors were put on the spot. They were in attendance as gawkers, not as believers. Now, he was directing them to cut.

If they hesitated (which was often), he took their hand in his and cut by moving their hand with his. He even had them doing the eye scraping.

The Casa was packed, and so were the posadas. We ate all our meals together. Friendships and circles formed. English was the shared language of most of his foreign visitors and we relied on Martin to translate our every need.

Martin escorted the newcomers through the lines to the Medium.

He translated everything and helped them afterward. Beforehand, he would ask exactly what they needed, either help or healing. He would write a brief note about the problem, nodding in sympathy. He read their request in their session with the Entity.

We all did this with Martin before we saw the Entity. He would line us up in order of his stack of papers to avoid confusing our illnesses. He read this note to João but was often out of earshot of the patient. That infernal music guaranteed it.

He then took the person to get their prescription and receive the medium's blessing. The Entity rarely had much to say unless you were a beautiful teenager or a rich guy. Patricia Melo did the same for the independent travelers who were not staying with Martin. Other posadas had their systems as well. Several guides served the same function as translators and intermediaries.

Martin would ask everyone to explain their issue. He played a role of sympathy and compassion and earnestly extolled the many virtues of Medium João. It was easy to relax with him and tell him about your cancer, skin disease, or leaky bowel syndrome.

Women felt safe describing their childhood abuse issues, infertility, or the terrible loss of a husband. This way, the "entity" on the throne knew your information before he said a word.

Medium João selected young women who were victims of sexual violence and pedophilia. I say the medium, and not the entity, noted this. When João was seated on his throne, he was rarely incorporated. That was João having the time of his life, a pervert playing God and Guru with strangers' lives.

None of us visiting Martin's Posada knew of this, but the translators sure did. They looked the other way.

He invited many women seeking healing for sexual abuse to his private office. There, he performed sexual abuse as a curing session. He offered the same services to women who couldn't get pregnant or suffered from depression.

My world during this visit was an incredible experience of divine grace that had been going on for a few years. I saw everything at the Casa through the lens of innocence. My inner vision reopened, and I found my spirit guides. I was open to spiritual inspiration and direction. The Casa might be the next step.

I hadn't meditated with a group for many years, although I was once accustomed to meditating for hours every day. The sessions sitting in the current were often uplifting. I was ready to spread my wings and pass a few more weeks at the Casa after my companions returned to the States.

A few days before my friends left, something strange happened. These were both women in their thirties. One of them was quite independent and chaffed at all the Casa rules. It bothered her that high walls surrounded our posada—walls topped with glass shards and electrified wire. Martin locked everyone in at ten p.m. and left the premises. We *had* to be back by then, or we were locked out or thrown out.

That night, she didn't return. I was concerned but knew she'd be back. She arrived in the morning for breakfast, her hair and clothing disheveled and dirty. Everyone at our dining table wanted to know where she had been. Nobody did this sort of thing in Abadiânia.

She told us she had made a friend. Some other visitors were going to take a short walk to an overlook above a valley. People had reported seeing flying saucers. This is about 100 yards from the Casa. They lay on the ground for hours, watching the stars, but they saw no flying saucers.

Around midnight, a group of people in white clothes and with drums appeared and began a ritual. They were at a crossroads, the ideal location for nighttime Quimbanda rituals.

My friend said they arrived as if by plan and invited her to enter their circle. She thought she might have entered a trance. Her next memory was waking up on the cold ground with everyone gone.

Martin asked to speak to me alone. He was agitated, having heard of the night's adventure. He informed me that if I brought others to the Casa, I was responsible for their behavior. I would need to scold my friend and never allow my guests to transgress the rules.

As I write this book, I often think about that Quimbanda ritual she accidentally attended. Many things that seemed inconsequential on this visit ended up being omens.

I spent more time with Martin. We had many conversations. I made new friends. I began eating dinner at different posadas to meet the other foreigners I'd see at the Casa. I befriended several people with terrible conditions. One was a young man in his early twenties, a paraplegic. Another had ALS and was rapidly declining into paralysis. Several were suffering from terminal cancer.

I met some guides and many curious, but not sick, tourists who came on tours. Several people with so-called psychosomatic diseases also came on tours. The Casa experience was their unanswered plea for help. There was camaraderie among these suffering souls. They all had one thing in common: an incurable and terrible condition and a desperate willingness to try anything for a cure.

It was comforting to know that they were in a community of others in the same predicament. The new-age tourists also had camaraderie. They shared tales of other healers and other adventures.

Many of these folks did Reiki, tarot readings, or various therapies. One was a color therapist, another an iridologist. There was a channeler of Carl Jung, a dowser, and a "hands of light" healer. Others had made the scene at one ashram or another or had visited Machu Pichu, Rishikesh, or Bali.

Quite a few of them had something to sell or something they wanted to impress you with. Abadiânia and your posada were worlds in themselves. Everyone fell into the rhythm and the spell if they stayed too long.

There was nothing to do but converse, eat, and sit in the current. Relentless indoctrination sucked us in. Everyone treated by the Entity lived by the no-alcohol and celibacy rule. In Abadiânia, there was indeed *nothing to do*.

Several of my first friendships there lasted for many years to come. Two of them fell into João's web, becoming well-known children of the Casa. I met Ultan O'Meara on my second visit. He had shelled out the $5,000 to Pellegrino but jumped ship and stayed. Ultan was a young Irish fellow in rough shape. He had been taking stiff doses of anti-depressants for eight years, addicted to them. Now, he was enduring their withdrawal effects. Ultan was a mess, collapsing on the Casa floor, groaning. I never saw him smile.

Ultan was emotionless and told me he had no sensation of touch. He was in a breakdown and had lost his bearings. He'd bang his head against the wall. His family couldn't help him, but they paid for his stay. He didn't leave for seventeen years.

The other friend was from the States, Rupert Drew. We lived in St. Louis as teenagers and are the same age. He claimed João had cured him of an eye disorder with his scraping technique.

We became a small circle that included Josie Ravenwing, Martin and Fernanda Mosquera, Robert and Catarina Pellegrino, Carlos Carlitto and family, and Leonor Rosa. They were participants in João's oligarchy.

Rupert and his girlfriend Lynn began bringing tourists and did so for many years. He hosts long-term paying guests in his elegant home just behind the Casa. Rupert still lives in Abadiânia.

Ultan founded Frutti's, Abadiânia's first hangout place—a landmark vegetarian juice bar. It was also the first time cappuccinos, long-distance phone booths, the internet, and live music and films were available on the weekend in Abadiânia.

Frutti's became the envy of a furious and calculating João. But I'm getting ahead of myself.

We didn't realize it, but Martin began grooming us as future Casa slaves. In my case, he started asking me to look after some of his guests, show them around, and help them if they were sick or had questions. This was only my second visit, and I was already sitting with the mediums in the Entities' Room and given responsibilities. The trap was set, and I took the bait. Curiosity killed the cat.

I remember one of his clients with cancer. She was very thin, weak, and dying. One morning, she confided in me that she had bloody diarrhea and was in pain. I explained this to Martin, assuming he would bring her to the Entity as soon as possible and help her. His knee-jerk reaction startled me when he told me to tell her she had to leave immediately. I didn't understand. Go where? He mumbled that the Posada Catarinense had already expelled her. If someone dies in his care, it is paperwork and problems with the authorities.

I gave this poor soul Martin's message. She cried. At his insistence, she was gone by the next day. I don't know where.

Other issues came to our attention. We would consult with Martin and ask for a resolution. One was a middle-aged woman, a nurse. That afternoon, João duped her into making the cut on the surgery stage. She was anxious afterward, somewhat paranoid. She worried that the VHS film documenting her act of surgery might reach her medical board in the States. It could cause her to lose her nursing license.

Martin directed us to Charles, the man filming everything and the general manager of the Casa. The woman wanted the original tape. The next day, a copy of each day's film went on sale. Theoretically, one could buy a video of any year or day you requested, going back a long time. Charles didn't like the idea and refused. She never got the tape, but he promised her that her film clip would be removed. It wasn't.

There was a couple from Canada. Their son was an autistic teenager who had violent fits, disturbing the current rooms as we meditated. The mother and father were stressed yet hopeful. After all, João had assured them he would cure the boy.

One day, they came to me in tears. They had taken the boy for a private session with João. He said he could cure him *only with a special crystal.* The parents asked him if he could get such a crystal for them. He said that he could, but it would be expensive—$20,000.

This dilemma overwhelmed the couple. Their friends and family donated a lot of money for airfare and the trip. They were frantic because they believed that this crystal would ensure a cure.

When they returned, they had no money and no jobs. João had suggested they borrow more money or mortgage their home. I was shocked. I told them not to buy the crystal, which wasn't necessary and ridiculously overpriced.

The week before, I heard about a South African devotee of João who purchased a unique crystal. João had chosen it for him. He paid $50,000.

I am an amateur connoisseur of gems and crystals. I collected them for years and understand a bit about quality and value. Brazil is the first place I encountered *fabricated crystals.* My interest is in natural crystals. Most of the 'crystals' sold in Brazil are cut from rock crystal or broken crystal chunks. They are faceted to have the appropriate number of sides and polish. This is all done with lapidary tools. They are not crystals.

I knew this when a guest asked me to look at a crystal he purchased from João. It wasn't a natural crystal. I had purchased one almost exactly like it. It was terminated at both ends, a rarity in genuine quartz crystals. I had paid about $8 for mine in Brasilia. His crystal cost $600. João assured him this was a powerful healing crystal. It was a fake.

João required every posada to sell his emeralds. Several posada owners pitched me. I took a close look. I know little about emeralds, but these had interior flaws and inclusions. Many lacked the deep transparent green of a quality cut emerald. João's emeralds were always promoted as the highest quality and a fantastic deal. We were told they were mined by the Medium, who found them on his impoverished farm.

The guy who bought the $600 crystal accompanied me to Cristalina, a town bordering Goiás and Bahia. João prohibited people from going there, but I found a taxi driver who broke the rule for the fare. And the 10% commission the gem dealers paid him for any sales he brought their way.

Cristalina was where João had a crystal mine. He bought many of the 'crystals' he sold in the Casa gift shop in Cristalina. Of course, we didn't know this. We visited a private dealer who had transformed his home into a crystal museum and showcase. He was a gemologist and an expert in faceted gems.

This same person who bought the overpriced crystal pulled out a jeweler's envelope. He asked the gemologist if he had received a good deal on the enormous, faceted aquamarine he had purchased from João. The gemologist returned it to the tourist and told him it was not aquamarine. It was an irradiated topaz, worth very little. Topaz is a colorless silicate mineral. It turns yellow or blue when subjected to radiation or heat. João ripped him off twice. He paid a fortune for his "aquamarine." The gemologist knew João and his subterfuge and told me he had unpleasant encounters with him. It went in one ear and out the other.

I purchased several small collector crystals and a kilo of unusual local crystals. I would ask the Entity to bless them and give them to friends as gifts.

Back at the Casa, another drama was unfolding. One guest was an older man with a hypertension problem and a heart condition. I remember the night he told all the diners at our table that he had received a complete cure for his hypertension. He stopped taking his medication. After all, the Entity cured him.

I often heard the Entity say, "Go, you are cured." I couldn't verify even one of these declarations as true. I wanted to, and needed to, see a miraculous cure.

Two weeks later, our group was gathered around the same table. One woman was a concert pianist who was losing her eyesight. She had submitted to the eye-scraping trick. Every session, João would do variations of the eye intrusions.

This one uses a sharpened kitchen knife, which he scrapes at an angle over the eye's membrane. I asked her if it hurt. She said it did. I asked how the recovery was going and couldn't help but notice that the whites of her eyes were blood red. She suffered from pain and blurriness for three days.

She introduced the older man accompanying her as her mentor, a doctor of psychiatry.

He said, "The problem with everyone here is that you are indoctrinated. I'm here to help my friend, but all I see here is brainwashing and fraud. I know enough about programming people to see this is a cult. That poor fool didn't even go for medical tests before he stopped his medicine. The entity didn't cure him; he killed him."

There was dead silence. No one agreed with him. I got defensive about his comment and scolded him for not having compassion for our friend, who was now in the hospital.

He had suffered a massive stroke, and the doctors said he might die. We never saw him again. João told tens of thousands of people he cured them, but how many were actually healed? How many made this man's mistake?

An amateur producer of a hokey community television channel program in Chicago invited a few of us to participate in an interview that would air later in 2000.

It was with Robert Pellegrino, author of the now-famous book *The Miracle Man.* I volunteered to ask him some questions that had been perplexing me. The first edition of his book made claims I couldn't substantiate with my experience. There have been several revisions over the years.

The original cover, now replaced, claimed João might be the returning Christ. In his opening chapter, a Brazilian crippled for life passed before João and was instantly healed. The paralyzed man got up and walked. Pellegrino claimed millions of people received cures, which were proven by scientific studies. In his book, he created the myth of a poor farmer compelled to help humanity and perform miracles for free.

A few others had their turn asking questions. None of them questioned his claims. When it was my turn, I quoted him his explanation of the herbs (as in the first and only edition available then). He claimed that João used over three hundred herbs in his remedies. He backed down on the claim and said that now seventeen herbs were used in the mix. In fact, it was only passiflora.

Then I questioned the source of the water we were buying. He claimed it came from João's sacred waterfall, one of only six obscure locales worldwide with this type of miracle-cure water.

I pointed out that the bottled water came from a nearby city and was sold at all the town markets. João had not caught on yet to buy this water with *his* label glued on the jug.

My last question regarded the instantaneous miracle cure described in his first chapter. He got defensive and explained that, actually, this man did not exist. He made a composite figure from several miracles he witnessed.

The episode made me see Pellegrino in a new light. He was a used car salesman, pitching a lemon. I was still a true believer all the same, but I began paying more attention.

João often took his show on the road on his four days off. They would load a commercial-size bus with bottled water and passiflora powder. He and his lawyers and thugs would travel to several spiritist centers that held him in high regard. Thousands of people would show up, considering him a saint.

The last week before I was to leave, in late April 2000, I waited in line to see the Entity with Martin at my side. When my turn came, I stood close to Martin and the medium. I understood some Portuguese words and phrases, but Martin wasn't aware of this.

He said, "Esse é o cara de quem eu estava falando. Ele daria um bom guia." (This is the guy I was telling you about. He'd make a good guide.) João took my hand and smiled. I now call this smile his *shit-eating grin.*

He rolled his eyes upward, speaking in the sweetest voice of Doctor Augusto. He said, "If you want to help my work, please go back to America and speak with people about my Casa. You took some videos and bought some of ours. You might show them at the public library or a school. Bring as many people as you can. You can charge whatever fee you wish."

Two days before leaving, I remembered I needed to have the Entity bless all those crystals. There were over forty. I put them in a plastic bag and waited in line, and when I presented the crystals to the Entity, he perked up.

This was the first time he paid me much attention.

"Where did you get these?" he asked.

"Cristalina," I replied.

He said, "The crystals from there are junk. They don't have spiritual energy. Put them on the table," (his little throne side table).

He rapidly sorted through them. He pushed the expensive crystals to one side. Rare ones like a rose quartz cluster and a crystal with a billion-year-old water drop trapped inside an air bubble.

"Don't use them; they're trash," he said.

He blessed the crystals I bought cheap, by the kilo, and shoved them back into the bag. My favored crystals remained on his table as Martin escorted me back to my bench, facing the medium.

I couldn't stop thinking about the crystals on the table. I took forbidden peeks at them throughout the session. I felt guilty about it, but I planned to run to the table as soon as the medium left the room and retrieve them. They might have been trash, but I wanted them back.

I waited until they shared the energized water and the cut flowers given to the ladies. Then, I moved toward the tiny table. The crystals had vanished! I spoke with Charles, the manager. No, he didn't see any crystals. The clean-up crew didn't find any crystals.

I imagined they threw them away, as worthless as he considered them. That evening, I discussed it with Martin. He said he would speak with João.

When I arrived for my last day at the Casa, I stopped by the gift shop, where one purchased the blessed water (I needed many liters). I glanced at the case displaying crystals for sale, thinking there might be a few I could buy to replace my loss.

I saw one that looked like the one I had purchased—three grey ghost pyramids inside the otherwise clear crystal. I realized my confiscated crystals were now on sale as I scanned the display. The prices were already marked. Rushing back to Martin's posada, I found him on his way to the Casa. I explained the situation.

After the lunch break, he told me João was aware of the details and wanted to speak to me in his office. This would be João and not the Entity. I had not met João yet.

The office was small. I remember there were some jars with enormous black insects in alcohol. One contained a human thumb floating inside. In a rage, João had called in the manager, his secretary, the bodyguards, and the shop personnel. João had them arranged in a circle. He didn't acknowledge my presence or speak to me.

João was out of control and began going around the circle, facing each person, and screaming. He asked, "What have you done? See how you've disgraced the Casa? Imagine if this American wasn't a close friend of the Casa. He might think badly of us. Shame on you inept fools!" He screamed insults at each person's face. They all took it in silence.

When his rage diminished, he handed me a plastic sack with most (but not all) of my missing crystals. I thanked him and reached out to shake his hand. He refused. He turned away without a word, storming out of the room.

I left the meeting perplexed by all the drama but certain that this was an accident. One of the staff probably picked them up and thought they were a donation. I was walking on clouds because the Entity had chosen me to be an emissary in America.

In my final afternoon session, I videotaped the surgeries on stage. I was filming very close to the Medium, trying to catch the details of the surgery. His eye caught mine, and I realized he wasn't in a trance. His arm shot out with his finger pointing in my face. "Get out of here. Go to the Entities' Room immediately," he said. I was stunned as though struck by a venomous snake. A lightning bolt of malice came out of his fingertip. I was instantly in a hypnotic trance. I couldn't move.

A lightning bolt of malice came out of his fingertip. Photo: Michael Bailot.

Two men escorted me to the Entities' Room. I sat down with much inner turmoil. I received a vision and was shown that Doctor Augusto had cured no one—that he didn't even exist and that the only people healed here had prayed directly to God. It took me hours to recover from the experience. I was still not paying attention.

I went before the Entity for my final consultation. He handed me my sixth paper slip. Each one had prescribed several sacks of the passiflora (I hoped they might contain the seventeen herbs Pellegrino mentioned). I couldn't escape the prescriptions if I hoped to speak to him in the line.

I had one more week before I left for the US. I planned to spend it in Brasilia. I met a very special woman there by a twist of spiritual fate. My life accelerated on a new trajectory, leading me to move to Brazil and marry Lucia.

I returned to the States with my suitcase bulging with powdered herbs. The moment I deplaned in Houston, a big drug dog came out of nowhere, pounced on my bag and guarded it. I reached out to pet him. I had no drugs, for sure.

Two burly guys in black uniforms escorted my baggage and me to a tiny windowless room. They unpacked everything, including my dirty socks, a pile of crystals, videos, and Brazilian knick-knacks. What's in the bags? What's with the bags? Explaining the twenty-four plastic bags of powder took a while—especially about João and his magical herbs. But I didn't miss my connecting flight.

I returned to the States to earn more money for another visit to Brazil. I was now a Casa guide. I lived in Santa Fe, New Mexico, the new-age capital of alternative healing. Soon, I'd assembled a small group committed to accompanying me to Brazil but was too shy to ask for deposits. We scheduled a September 2000 visit. I was anxious to see Lucia again.

About a month before departure, I received a phone call from a stranger. Her name was Heather Cumming, and she heard that I knew where João de Deus was and how to get there. She explained that she grew up on a cattle ranch in Brazil and spoke Portuguese.

Heather asked me if it was necessary to travel on a group tour. She was an experienced solo traveler and wondered how to visit independently. I thought the guides were abusing the charity aspect by charging thousands of dollars for a trip that only cost a few hundred dollars.

If João did all his work for free, why weren't the guides following his example? I told her to go alone, explained how to do it, and then didn't give it a second thought.

About two weeks before our group was to leave, I called the woman facilitating this group. They were all friends of hers. I reminded her that there was a $200 fee to pay before we departed for immediate expenses on arrival. She said, "We've decided to go with someone else. She knows all about the Casa."

I asked her who this person was, and she replied, Heather Cumming. My group disappeared into Heather's hands, and I returned to Brazil alone and unfunded. When she arrived with my stolen group, her first visit to the Casa, I avoided them. I didn't want anger or confrontation to spoil my visit.

I was more interested in seeing Lucia than visiting the Casa. But as things turned out, we spent a lot of time together at the Casa. She liked it too. This was another extended visit. I would stay for three months. The Casa proved to be an endless soap opera of João's dramas.

I began calling it the chaos factor. I still believed the Medium was infallible. I imagined that the powers of darkness were battling the forces of good. João was the good guy. Ultan and Rupert were still there, but many fresh faces had arrived.

When I returned in September 2000, the Entity informed me that I was now a Casa medium and should attend all the sessions seated in the Entities' Room. There was no initiation or ritual attached to this. A medium is a person able to go into a trance. I am certainly qualified for that. He recommended I attend the weekly Spiritist meeting some of the Casa mediums held. Martin helped me get an official Casa photo badge to declare my new status.

The first week of my return, a dozen people arrived with another new American guide, a doctor. He didn't know any Portuguese. This was his second visit to the Casa, and he didn't know what he was doing. The group from America joined the queue, waiting for their first consultation. They were all middle-aged or older. Most of them surpassed the sixty-year-old age limit the Casa imposed for visible surgeries.

Without warning, João entered the room, ripping off his shirt. He began performing visible surgeries on everyone in this group as they stood in line. This was not the standard procedure. They had arrived by a shuttle bus that hour. He caught them by surprise.

This was another one of those moments when I opened my eyes and broke the house rules. An attendant was asking the Entity, "Who are you? What is your name?" But the spirit didn't respond. I watched as he pulled up the blouse of a frail woman in her seventies and made his cut on her stomach. João likes that area. He can grab the stomach flab where there are no blood vessels. He inserted his ungloved finger in the wound and extracted a bit of fat. He quickly stitched her and moved on to the next in line, performing his "surgeries" on the entire tour group.

This story was a hot topic at the posada. I had returned to Martin's, of course. This group was staying at the posada Catarinense, owned by the Carlotto family. A few days later, a new entity arrived, yet another José. His wild nature would manifest again on this visit.

In the next session, João was preparing for his stage show. He waved a Xeroxed book with a plastic ring binder, weeping. I understood nothing he was saying. Later, I asked Martin what all the fuss was about. The book was a young Brazilian student's master's thesis. He was peddling it without the author's permission. It cost $100.

João declared that this book proved that he was a great healer. He was crying because he claimed the Casa was broke, and he needed to generate more money to keep it open. Please buy this outstanding book and save the Casa, was what he'd been saying through his crocodile tears. I noticed that emotional outbursts and public weeping were part of his style.

The thesis was far from proving anything and was quite dull. It studied, with maps, the layout of the Casa, the daily theater, and protocols. It did not establish a single cure.

A few days later, Martin approached many of the tourists. He asked for a one-hundred-dollar donation to help remodel the Casa and install tile floors. I asked him why they needed donations for this. Didn't the Casa take in lots of money daily? Martin explained that every penny from the Casa went into João's pocket without accounting. The transactions were always in cash. He refused to use any of this for remodeling. I was affronted and declined to donate.

A new guest arrived, a tall blond-haired German diva in her early thirties. She came with her right arm paralyzed and in a brace. Her doctors wanted to amputate it. She was at the Casa, hoping to revive the dead arm.

Until recently, she had been a surgeon. She was a professor at UCLA Medical Center in Los Angeles, a top-ranking teaching hospital. Her specialty was eye surgery. The car accident that destroyed her arm also destroyed her career. She would not accept this sitting down.

Being an actual surgeon and of elegant beauty, she captured João's attention. Soon, she was the one holding the instrument tray. One afternoon, as he performed his stage show, he asked her to scrutinize his eye surgery.

When he completed the violent scraping, he encouraged her to address the crowd. What was her opinion? The theater had a few hundred visitors, most of whom spoke only Portuguese.

She addressed them in English, speaking with authority. She said, "I have no idea how this would help repair the patient's impaired eyesight. He has traumatized the protective membrane, rupturing tiny blood vessels. This is not a medical procedure at all. I would be surprised if this didn't damage the eye."

Medium João thanked her in Portuguese for her testimony and

asked a staff member to translate it. The translator said, "The Doctor says this was the most amazing surgery she's ever seen. His skill level was above anything she or her colleagues could perform. He performed an impossible surgery, an amazing miracle."

The English-speaking guests didn't understand Portuguese, but the doctor had a basic grasp of the language and understood what he said. She shrugged her shoulders in disbelief.

Meanwhile, Viola Hamilton, the older woman who received unasked for surgery, became infected from the incision. She complained to the doctor leading her group, the posada owners, and the Entity himself. They told her not to worry. There were no infections in the Casa's history, and things would get better.

She passed in the line every session and asked the Entity to help her. The doctor leading the tour suspended his better judgment and deferred to the entity. All this came to my attention. Now that I was a house medium, I was available to help the visitors out when they had problems or requests. As her condition worsened daily—she had a raging staph infection, the Entity grew evasive, even defensive.

The Entity summoned the owners of her posada, the Carlotto family. He asked Violet where she had taken her meals and what she had eaten. He asked her if she had eaten any cucumber. She had. The Entity declared that the cucumber caused the infection. It was through the neglect of the posada Catarinense.

He demanded they remove cucumbers from the salad buffet and publicly humiliated them. He implied that Violet should be removed as soon as possible.

The day the group left, she was in terrible shape, debilitated. I asked for her email address and for her to confirm that she had arrived in Chicago and was okay. I also had her promise to go to the hospital immediately. That promise wasn't necessary. On the flight back, Viola had a cardiac arrest. A registered nurse on the same flight resuscitated her and attended her on the long flight home. An ambulance was waiting, and she underwent a six-hour-long emergency surgery.

She wrote me an email some months later. They removed a section of putrid flesh the size of a grapefruit. She would need to undergo plastic surgery later to repair the hole.

This was all from a one inch cut that turned septic as everyone ignored reality. I replied that she should sue the tour guide for medical negligence. She said she couldn't do that because he was an old family friend.

She asked, "But why didn't the Entity help me? Why didn't he see my infection as life-threatening? That's what I don't understand. Why didn't he cure me?"

My visit had one more surprise. I was still gliding along in the tourist current. Talk, talk, talk. That was Abadiânia for us. It seemed like we were in an enchanted world. Many signs were pointing toward danger and fraud, but we were oblivious to the threat. A significant part of the enchantment was that we felt a part of something bigger. We were helping humanity.

Two of my new Casa friends were Irish. They had arrived together without a guide. She was about twenty-two. He was her middle-aged uncle. She had a heroin habit she was kicking, caused by childhood sexual trauma. Her uncle brought her to Abadiânia for a miracle cure.

They needed to talk to me about a problem. The uncle and I spoke. He said, "My niece was in the line this afternoon. When she faced the Medium, he reached out, pulled her closer, and put her hand down into the open zipper of his pants. He held a little white towel over his groin so no one would notice. To her shock, she was handling his erect member, and her hand was sticky with semen. It all happened instantly, and then she returned to the meditation bench."

I was flummoxed. By now, I had seen many weird goings on at the Casa, but I had never encountered such a shocking event. Later, I spoke with his niece, who confirmed the story. I tried to console her and help. This new assault triggered an anxiety attack.

I hadn't made the connection between the translator's crib notes and the molestation. I didn't know what to do. Ultan and I began strategizing how to deal with this. We consulted with Martin. He feigned puzzlement and didn't think it had happened. He conjectured that this might be an arcane healing technique from the Middle Ages. Rare and obscure, but Medium João always knows what is best for the patient.

We visited Robert Pellegrino. He said, "João must be incorporating a European entity who uses an esoteric healing modality. The Entity knows how to cure with many techniques."

As we got nowhere with them, we asked the Entity for an explanation. We needed Martin's help to translate. The Entity denied doing anything of the sort and blamed João for the perversion. Later, we insisted that Martin ask João the same question. He blamed the Entity and denied anything had happened. Martin began damage control.

The victim and her uncle left Abadiânia with things unresolved.

Ultan, Rupert, and I became vigilant and questioned suspicious things. The issue hung in the air but was soon forgotten among the endless supply of new Casa dramas. We were not aware that several rapes occurred this year in the Casa.

During this visit, Lucia and I began our relationship. We traveled around the region when the Casa wasn't in session. I started meeting her Brazilian friends and their culture. This was a world apart from the Casa. Although I met her in Brasilia, her home was in the Amazon.

Child of the Casa

In October 2000, Lucia and I moved to Abadiânia and became official children of the Casa. We had asked the Entity, of course. One couldn't move there without his permission. We rented a house three blocks from the Casa, around the corner from where Frutti's now is. The current renter was eager to pass the place to us and vacated long before her rent was due.

Like most houses in Abadiânia, it had a tiny lot squeezed between other houses on tiny lots. A brick fence provided a hint of privacy. What happened in our neighbor's house was as obvious as what happened in ours.

The departing tenant showed us how to install the heavy double iron bars securing the doors. I asked about that. The neighbors were a poor family living in a crude brick hovel. Their twenty-year-old son was out of his mind on crack every night. He had broken down her door at three a.m., even as she screamed in protest. She was a medium at the Casa and was going back to where she came from.

Well, at least the doors had bars. The son lived up to his reputation the first weeks we were there. He shouted, and violent music throbbed at all hours. His parents were simple country folks and couldn't control the boy. I regretted our rental. Then, one day, the music changed to evangelical gospel music and preaching. The boy found religion, but the music remained atrocious.

When I returned to Santa Fe in late October, I had a lot on my plate. I decided to move to Brazil as soon as I could sell my business and belongings. One day, I was having coffee with a friend. I told her my tale of woe about the vanished tour group. She was sympathetic and offered to help me put together another group.

She was friends with the board of directors of a foundation that wanted to visit the Casa. They would come in a few months. We spoke and scheduled their trip.

Then, the unexpected occurred. My friend died in a car crash. The foundation called me. They wanted to cancel the tour and reschedule for later. She was a close friend, and they felt the visit would be sad and too close to her death. Once again, my attempts at being a tour guide met a brick wall.

I decided I wouldn't follow the others' example, charging a package price of $2,000 to $5,000 for a ten-to-fourteen-day visit. I posted an ad and a website advertising my services. For $200, I would pick them up at the airport and accompany them to the Casa.

I'd show them a variety of room options or had already reserved the best available. I would guide them through the Casa protocol and help them exchange money or buy toothpaste. I accompanied them in the interviews with the medium and was always available to help. We ate our meals together. They would only pay for their actual cost of transport and lodgings in Abadiânia.

A week before returning to Brazil in early December 2000, I was to participate in a ceremony in New Mexico. It required me to stand erect and unsupported for several hours. I was suffering from a pinched sciatic nerve, and standing was painful. A friend asked me if I would like to receive psychic healing from a famous Filipino spiritual surgeon. I thought, man, if I ever needed help, it's now. She had given me the last reservation.

She said to wear white and arrive at a home where he would be in attendance. The healer explained that he was the first psychic surgeon to receive international publicity. He had visited America several times but was now on a watchlist, preventing him from working there. He traveled incognito.

He stood behind a table with an enormous Bible in the center. An electric crock pot with steaming hot oil was to his right. He leafed through the Bible pages at random, landed on a verse, and read the scripture. Then he said that he would prove to us that he worked with the Holy Spirit's supernatural force.

He rolled up his shirt sleeve and plunged his forearm into the hot oil. He left it there for an extended number of seconds. It emerged pink but unburnt. He was smiling the whole time.

There were several of us, and we waited our turn for his treatment. He treated us in a private room with an exam table, each with him alone. He said to remove our clothes in a separate bathroom and enter wearing only our underwear. This isn't very American. It set a certain edge to the experience and put him, who was clothed, in a dominant position.

I told him my back was the problem. He had me lie face down and began passing his hands and massaging me. When he finished, he had a piece of chicken fat in his hand. He offered it for my examination, claiming he had removed it from my body and that now I would feel better.

I said I didn't need that to receive a cure, and he laughed and threw it in a waiting bucket. Shortly after this, I took part in my role in the ceremony with no sciatic pain.

The performance made me consider how all shamans and

folk healers have a 'miracle' and a magical outcome. The healer is a showman, an actor. He creates an environment that is shocking, even disturbing. He uses the shock to take his audience into a group hypnotic state. Then, suggestions and the placebo effect are at their strongest. If he is a true healer, he can manipulate things in a quantum manner—in other words, using the supernatural power of the Holy Spirit.

When I returned to Brazil for my fourth visit in early December 2000, Lucia and I traveled to her home in the Amazon around Christmas time and returned to Abadiânia in February. Then, the reality of our decision set in.

Martin was my handler, but Lucia's monitors were the Carlotto family. They explained the seriousness of what it means to become part of the Casa. They said, "For instance, you must ask the Entity for permission for whatever you plan to do. He doesn't always grant this. You need to be available to help the Casa when called. No one can open a business here without the Entity's permission. Don't go to other healers or bring clients there."

Lucia wanted to practice her vocation as a masseuse. She needed permission to do this, and João would set the price. She would also need permission to open an office.

Then Valeria Carlotto said, "First, you open your business. He gives you some time. One day, João will show up and want a commission on your sales." We were incredulous. "Oh no, everyone pays a commission," she said. "He comes here one night each month with his accountant, a ledger, and a bodyguard. He asks us to bring the accounting books and show his buddies the figures. We pay him twenty percent of our gross in cash. He counts it, stuffs it into a bag, and then on to the next posada."

I asked about the guides. "They too—when you make good money, he wants his share," she replied. I had little time to dwell on it. I was about to receive my first tour guests, most of whom were seeking a miracle cure.

The year is now 2001, the new millennium. João is fifty-nine years old. Two rape accusations against him from this year are now in court twenty years later.

I sat in the Entities' Room for each session at seven a.m. An hour or two later, crowds would throng the Casa, pouring into this room. I sat two benches back, directly facing João, and always kept this seat.

Casa Mediums 2001. Photo: Michael Bailot.

Most of the Casa mediums were Brazilian. We numbered a few dozen. João temporarily allowed many others to sit in the Entities' Room, but our small group consisted of the official house mediums who arrived dutifully every session to fulfill our obligation.

The same couple sat to my left every day. We meditated in silence. Soon, one of us would begin trembling, a hand or a leg twitching. Someone might raise their arm or make passes. A medium would make sounds or weep. The Entity selected everyone sitting in this room. Here is where the action was. We all entered a trance of sorts, incorporating God knows what. We were into it.

When the Medium João arrived and sat on his throne, anything might happen. He often threw canes, crutches, and eyeglasses to the floor. Many people fainted, wept, screamed, or were possessed against their will.

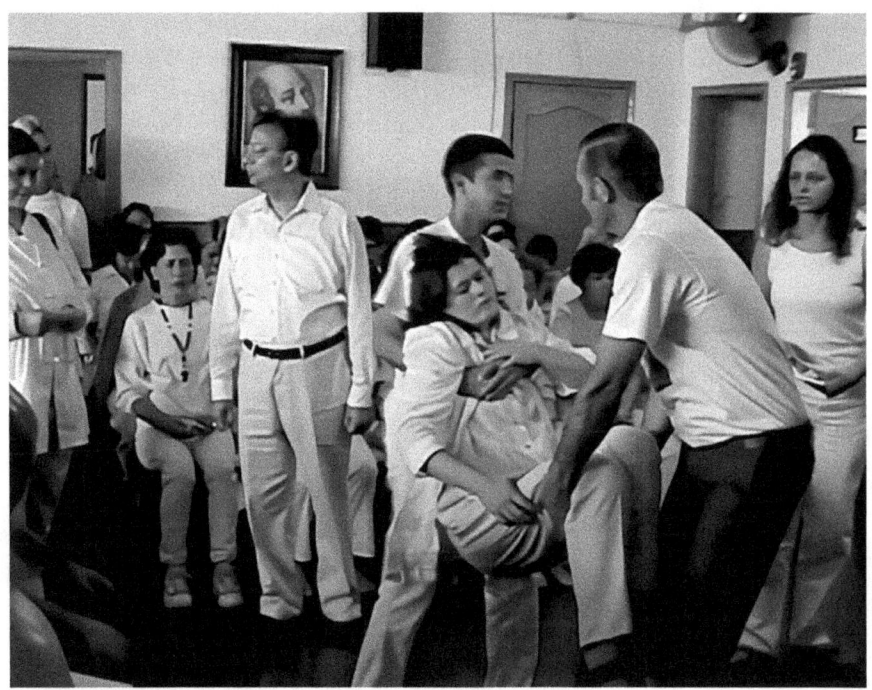

Possessed and incoherent. Photo: Michael Bailot.

Warped cassette tapes, stifling heat, rough benches, and boredom hobbled our meditation. Yet, for me, many wonderful journeys and visions unfolded. They were out-of-body spiritual experiences, visions of various spirits, and inspiring advice. Other times, I'd lose consciousness, my hand shaking and swooning for hours. The session would go on until eleven or twelve o'clock, and then we had a lunch break.

But first, we sampled the blessed soup. We lined up to sit at the long rustic tables. We made new friends, telling all the fantastic, enchanted stories of the Casa.

By the time I finished lunch, I was weak and drained of energy. Sitting in the current always resulted in this. The afternoon session was the same as the morning. A stage show with the same three techniques: the nose job, the minor incision, and the eye scraping. He usually worked on a few people each session, although there were days when he did the physical surgeries on up to a dozen volunteers.

I occasionally filmed or watched the surgeries with my new clients.

Once, the Entity summoned me from meditation to assist him with the tray of knives. That was an eyeful. My hands were shaking. Actual blood, real scraping, and gouging—enough to make one dizzy. Shoulder-to-shoulder with Doctor Augusto was shocking. I was nervous about the omniscient Doctor Augusto. There were some things I didn't want him to know. I worried that he'd find out.

He kept prescribing more herbs, too, and frankly, I was sick of them and wanted to avoid buying more. I had a three-year supply, and they came with dietary restrictions. It was obligatory for the Casa mediums to say hello to the Entity at least once a week, and he would give me another prescription every time. The passiflora drugs added to the dopiness and weariness of the sessions.

Every time I passed in line for an interview, I would ask Dr. Augusto if he would teach me how to be a healer, show me how to work with blessed water or teach me more about mediumship. His reply was always an abrupt and rude *não* (no).

It didn't take long before Doctor Augusto began calling me for a scolding. Rumors passed fast in Abadiânia. The Medium often knew an hour after the first news had broken. If one of my clients made a misstep, I was responsible. If a tourist or Casa staff observed that I had done or said something not the norm for the Casa, it would come to the "Entity's" attention.Ultan and I were best friends. When Rupert was in town, the three of us discussed the endless peculiarities of the Casa. We noticed the attention the medium always paid to pretty, young women. He stared at her in the line long before she reached her turn before him. He would hold her hand, tell her she was a powerful medium, and invite her to sit in the Entities' Room. Often, he summoned her to his private office after the session.

We noticed the incredible amount of passiflora prescriptions he handed out daily. Rupert bought a counting device. His handheld clicker displayed an ever-increasing number with each click. He stationed himself in front of the herbal dispensary after every session for a week. Rupert calculated that João was making at least half a million dollars a year selling passiflora.

This was in 2001, and the sales volume rose exponentially through the coming years. I discovered that a kilo (2.2 pounds) of passiflora powder cost $3.50. Each baggie he sold held about two ounces. His cost was around twenty cents, but we paid ten dollars. Soon, João stopped selling the powder in plastic baggies.

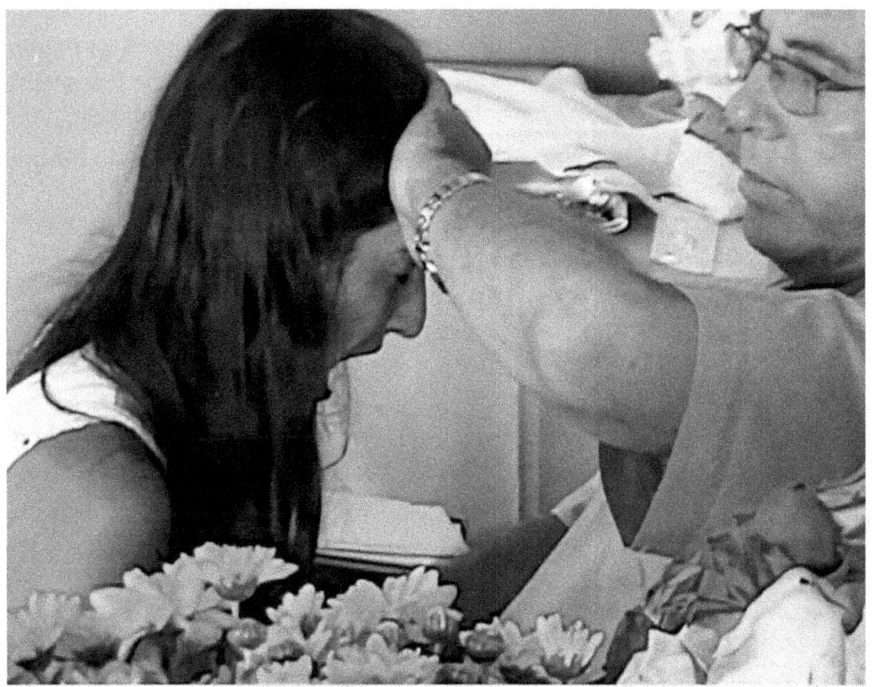

The Entity on his throne. Photo: Michael Bailot.

He upgraded to tiny bottles with thirty capsules, containing a minute fraction of a kilo. I found the laboratory where he purchased these pills. The wholesale cost per bottle with his custom label was about eighty centavos (less than forty cents). He was selling thousands of bottles weekly at a huge markup.

Rupert couldn't count the number of blessed water bottles sold, but the profits were enormous. They said the water was sold at cost. This was not true. Sales of crystals, books, films, knick-knacks, and donations added to the haul. João was reaping huge profits on a foundation of lies. He wasn't a poor farmer, and he did nothing for free.

One day, Rupert told me of another scam. João began courting the idea of traveling to other countries. Rupert, who lived part time in London, hoped to sponsor a trip there. He consulted with the Entity. The Entity needed a guarantee of $50,000 for the trip. He expected to fly first class with eight assistants. They would stay in the best hotel available and have all expenses paid. The sponsors would also rent a nice hall for his performance.

They would charge a price per head for the participants (not cheap), and he was to keep all the ticket sales after costs. And finally, he needed Rupert to secure a permit to ship a container full of the pills with import permits. All sales of passiflora were his as well.

Rupert and his friends couldn't imagine raising the funds for this and canceled the project. Many foreign friends of the Casa took the bait. They paid his price and hosted him in several countries in the years to come.

One of my first guests was a twenty-four-year-old woman with terminal cancer. She called me from America one night asking for my services.

I warned her that few people were healed, although his reputation was that he had cured millions. I tried to talk her out of it, but she arrived a week later with her best friend.

The first few days went well after finding rooms for them at the Posada Catarinense. On the fourth night, Valeria knocked on our door at ten. Our guest was screaming in pain. The other visitors couldn't sleep. We didn't understand. Her cancer had metastasized, and she was in agony. They wanted her to leave their posada immediately.

In the morning, I apologized, but she had not told me about her suffering. Their return flight didn't leave for some days. We gave her a room in our house, cared for her, and attempted to have the Entity help. No help at all, and this dear soul suffered terribly.

I asked Charles and Martin if there was a doctor at the Casa. I begged them to get a prescription for morphine so she could travel in a calmer state. It was obvious the airline might not allow her on the flight in her condition.

The day before their departure, the Casa "doctor" arrived—doctor of what, I couldn't say. I explained the situation and the urgent need for a painkiller for her long flight home. He resisted but prescribed two tabs of Tylenol with morphine. On our way to the airport in the morning, we stopped at many pharmacies. They would not accept his bogus prescription. We were in tears.

They boarded the plane with her in anguished pain. When I followed up after she returned to the States and a hospital, she said, "I don't understand why the Entity wouldn't help me."

Another couple with a posada were Elisabeth and Luiz. They had recently purchased the derelict and ramshackle Hotel Amazona at the insistence of the Entity. The Entity told them to return to their home city and sell their house and all they owned. With this, they had the deposit to buy the old hotel. João arranged the deal and the enormous loan they would owe. They had three reais left when they signed the deed. Try as they might, they couldn't make the mortgage payments.

I suspect their 20% kickback was unpaid as well. I remember how desperate they were because they began selling off the furniture in the lobby. We made several purchases, furnishing our empty rental house.

Beth (Betch) and Luiz struck me as good-hearted but unstable. I remember she had a brain tumor, and they first visited the Casa for a cure shortly before they purchased the hotel. There was an aura of chaos and desperation around them.

One day, Luiz showed us his new investment, an effort to raise funds to bail out the hotel. It was two bicycles, old-fashioned single-gear affairs painted pink. He would rent them to tourists by the hour.

Then he took me to see his other project. He had purchased an old pony that had spent its life dragging wooden carts of sand and bricks all over town. His prize would now carry tourists on her back, with Luiz leading the reins.

The Entity heard about their project. He had not given permission. This was the first time I saw João use his hemostat to punish, humiliate, and torture. The Entity summoned the couple. Those sitting in meditation with closed eyes were told we could watch.

The couple stood in front of us at the Entity's side. He questioned them about the purchases and aggressively accused them of recklessly jeopardizing the Casa. He shouted that a tourist might fall off the bike or the horse one day and sue the Casa. Although they had spent all they had on their project, he denied permission.

There is nothing worse for a Brazilian than being publicly shamed. Beth was holding back her tears as they fidgeted nervously. First, João tore into Luiz's nostrils, violently twisting and plunging the hemostat.

Luiz was wincing and struggling to endure. After traumatizing both nostrils, he turned to Beth and repeated the same horror. A bodyguard escorted them from the room. Watching this, silent and passive, was very unsettling for me.

Every week, we saw more strange events. I was beginning to doubt the Casa. I was still waiting to witness an instantaneous miracle cure, but it never occurred on my watch. João's frequent crying fits and angry tantrums were part of the show. The visitors brought their own dramas, amplified by the Casa spirits and atmosphere.

The Casa impressed a tourist from California, who had invented a contraption he called the crystal bed. He gifted one of his beds to the Casa. Immediately, João appropriated it as his creation. The Casa began selling twenty-minute sessions laying on the bed. It cost 40 reais per session.

Later, João started producing beds for sale to tourists. The purchasers then sold therapy sessions back where they lived. It wasn't a bed, more like a cheap portable massage table. Suspended from a bar above the cushion were several crystals. They were illuminated by different colored filters, one for each chakra. I booked a session. There was a long waiting list and only one bed.

When my turn came, I examined the bed. These were not crystals. They were cut lead glass like one might find dangling below a chandler or hanging in a window and casting rainbows. I fell asleep. Nothing had happened.

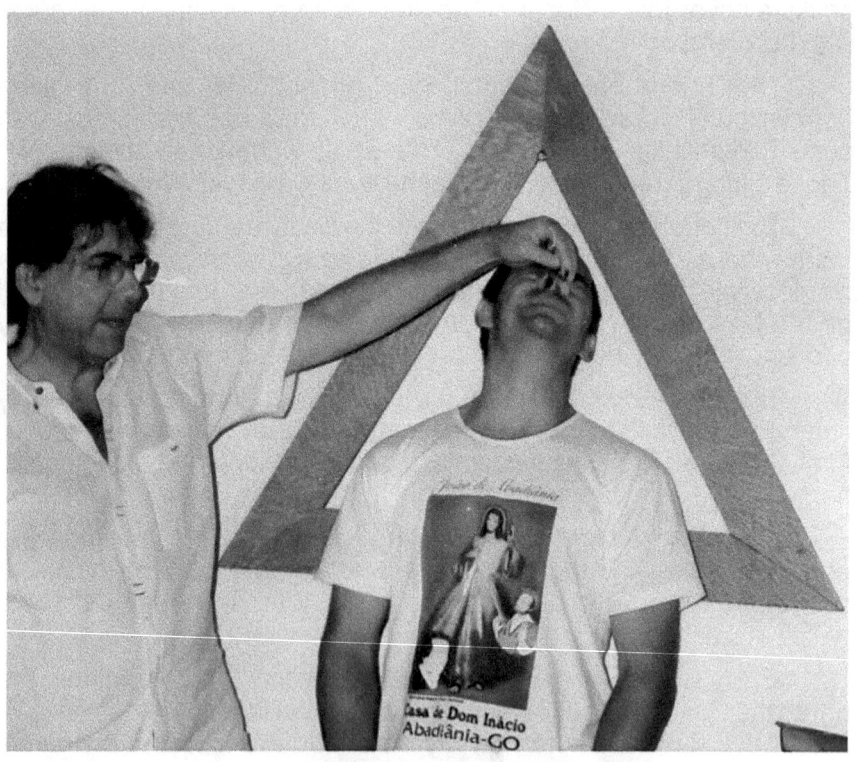

An example of disciplinary "surgery." Photo: Michael Bailot.

João copied this man's design and produced hundreds of beds, which he sold for $3,000 each. Only people authorized by the Entity could buy one, and that was anyone with the money.

João assured the purchasers that the Entities possess the bed—embedded, if you will. They would work with you through the colored lights!

Lucia had difficulties securing permission to give massages to the visitors. João had questioned her about who she was and where she came from. It made him nervous that she lived in the Amazon. He was suspicious of her, a powerful and good woman who tolerated no bullshit. She had appeared with no history at the Casa, and João was jealous of her immediate popularity.

There was already an entity-sanctioned masseur. One of the important Casa staff was a disciple of Osho. After he and João had a fight, he was prohibited from doing massages for the Casa.

Lucia could now perform massages for the Entity, but at a fee four times less than the masseur's. She could charge 25 reais for a one-hour massage (about $10). We rented a tiny one-room shed in front of the Catarinense, renovated it, and painted a mural on the wall. She was rewarded with many clients, and people called her a healer. This alerted João. He was always jealous if someone else gained attention.

The Entity asked Lucia to assist in the invisible surgery room every day. The room adjoined the Entities' Room, and when exiting the day's work, all filed through there. One went to this place for invisible surgery (bloodless)—another eyes-closed area. João would enter during the sessions. He performed these so-called surgeries and *sometimes other things.*

In her free time, Lucia gave massages. My guide service became popular because of its low cost. The Casa was now our sole source of income.

Meanwhile, the Casa saw a steady stream of new visitors, more and more from foreign countries. Some arrived with an agenda of their own. One was a famous defrocked priest from America. He offered his services to João. He wanted to heal people alongside the Medium! João denied him access to his show. He tolerated no competition and was very far from being a Catholic.

The man was resourceful. He hired those ubiquitous public announcement cars for advertising. The large speakers mounted on car tops blasted in Portuguese for two days. The announcer invited the town to receive free healing from the famous Catholic miracle priest. He rented a circus tent. Much of the Brazilian side of town attended. He moved with fanfare through the Casa like a Pope. João was seething with anger, but what could he do—attack a famous priest?

I had little free time, but when I did, I liked to explore the dirt tracks near the Casa. I decided to find the source of the magical waterfall that was so important in the Casa myth.

There was a small marshy area on the back lot of the Hotel Amazonas, right behind the kitchen. A gray water pipe coming from the Hotel emptied into this tiny seep along with their septic system.

This was the source of the magic waterfall. Water drained from this area in a ditch running by a poor woman's shack who took in laundry to support her several children.

Her laundry machine poured directly into the ditch. It continued to my friend Seu Lazaro's homestead. He captured its flow, and it ran out of a faucet (with no shut-off) installed in an outdoor sink. This is where he cleaned and skinned rattlesnakes, washed dishes, and prepared his garrafadas.

This water drained into another ditch that crossed his chicken yard. It continued into the cow pasture, full of manure, and finally to a small gray pond. I contemplated a swim, but the water was filthy. The pond drained into a channel that wandered through the pasture until it reached João's land where it formed a trickling "waterfall" six feet tall—the Entities' sacred healing waterfall (Cachoeira de Lazaro).

On the way back, I visited Lazaro. He told me João constantly pressured him to sell his land. The answer was always no. His resistance angered João even more. He was a terrible and menacing neighbor. Lazaro decided he had no choice but to sell. He contacted Faria to begin negotiations.

The next day, a woman visited Lazaro, explaining that she was João's aunt. She warned Lazaro never to sell to João and related her own experience. João had wanted her farm and pressured her the same way. Finally, she gave in. He arrived with a lawyer and a contract, paid her a 10% deposit on her price, and asked her to sign the documents. He promised she would receive the total price after his lawyer prepared the title. Being a simple person and his aunt, she signed the document without carefully reading it.

What she had signed was a confirmation that João had paid her in full and confirmed she had granted him the title to her farm. She lost the farm and all that money.

In late April 2001, I made one last trip to the States to sell my belongings and business and tie up loose ends. Lucia remained at home in Abadiânia.

I received a phone call from the foundation regarding their visit. They wouldn't need my services. I had heard nothing from them for nearly a year, which was a surprise. I assumed they decided not to come to Brazil at all. Then the director said, "Our group is coming with Heather Cumming." Here she was again.[134]

Days before leaving, another allegation of sexual molestation came up. Ultan and Rupert promised to continue our pursuit of the truth. Ultan kept me updated through e-mails while I was in the States.

There was only one place to send or receive e-mails in town, a posada owned by a staff member. She read everyone's e-mails and reported back to João anything suspicious. The Entity knows everything.

In rapid succession, three new molestations of patients occurred to women we knew. Ultan and Rupert persisted in sorting this out, but it didn't work out well. He sent me two e-mails outlining the incidents. There were witnesses, too.

While in the U.S., I received Ultan's third e-mail about this situation, dated April 26, 2001. Subject: Our Little Secret.

"Dear Michael, I'm sorry this has caused you much distress. Please forgive me that I can't give you all the details now. I want to get something to you as soon as possible because you are worried.

"I have been making a lot of noise around here, particularly yesterday, and I upset a few people—mainly those working at the Casa. Carlos has refused to allow emails to be sent out from the Catarinense. But we have no concrete facts.

"And the gossip needs to be contained. I have scarily seen this week how these things can very easily grow without necessarily there being meat behind them.

"With a lot of talk, it becomes hard to get to know what is real and what is people's hysteria. I'm pleased to say that the work in the Casa this week has been very powerful and seems to be good. Don't give up on this place. There is an accumulation of hearsay [sic] and circumstantial evidence, but nothing really concrete. I know Viola's case was a concern. But there are questions in the Casa about her adherence to how they were trying to help.

"They claim she didn't follow up on the course of antibiotics they prescribed [no one had prescribed antibiotics for her]. This is no justification, but I do believe it is the first case of its kind.

"I know that the money issue is of concern and still isn't clear, but this is Brazil, and standards are not the same. I know I sound like I'm backtracking, but I'm worried my last e-mail was too over the top, as it was written two nights ago in the heat of the way things were. I have done a lot of shouting in the Casa and have taken some risks in doing so. I have angered Martin and Charles by my insistent persistence.

"All the staff of the Casa think I'm mad, or at least very hot headed—and this woman who triggered the latest incident is questionable and refuses to talk to anyone. Rupert and Lynn have also made waves. Rupert feels happier about things, and so do I for the moment. I'm not sure Lynn is so easily placated.

"The Entity responded by doing a nice work at the Casa, which made us feel better." [He did a ritual for Ultan and Rupert. The Entity pierced them both with a needle in the web of skin between the base of the thumb and the first finger. He sewed their two webs to each other, joining the two men in spiritual brotherhood. Not surprisingly, this is a Quimbanda ritual. It ended their pursuit of the truth about those molestations].

"I know that's not a resolution, but I urge you not to keep riding the wave of hysteria. It sounds a lot worse in my e-mails than it is. Yes, this is serious. Yes, questions remain, but this is contained and blowing over.

"*I have to remark that when it comes to the sexual behavior, other than the seemingly petty molestations, about which I'm currently not getting upset, all the serious cases have questions hanging over them. All the women involved have had histories of sexual abuse.* Is it a possibility that to facilitate their healing, they are being forced to face their memories in some way that they can't get a grip on?[135]

"Anyway, nothing is out of hand here. Some people have been upset—a few hotheads. Good work still is happening at the Casa. Some questions remain. Let's not spread something that isn't yet sure and is based on an accumulation of people who all have their own issues.

"And I know it looks like quite a few people now, but a lot of disturbed people come to Abadiânia, so there is bound to be continual stuff. So far, the one that disturbs me most is Jane, but I have a lot of questions about Jane. Please keep well.

Regards, Ultan.

Addendum: "Michael, it turns out Teresa saw the Entity doing the same thing with the sheet the Australian woman saw, except that

Teresa saw nothing sexual occurring. The Australian woman did see something sexual." [The same Teresa with the web service who is monitoring Ultan's emails.]

I replied to Ultan: "Your earlier emails were explosive. I can't get this off my mind. I've been in touch with Josie Ravenwing lately. I said that there had been some more sexual incidents, nothing more. She wants details, as she has grown concerned as well. May I forward your emails to her or paraphrase them if you don't want her to know the source? I need to tell my wife about this. This impacts our lives."

I consulted the Chinese oracle, the book of *I-Ching*, asking about João and the Casa. This is what the *I-Ching* stated:

"The person in this position is lost in the memory of a compelling and harmonious experience. The time is past, and what is left is empty egotism. There is an impressive display of deterioration in nearly every aspect of the current affair. The lesser elements, and those who represent them, have gained complete control over the situation. It implies a situation in which there is little hope."

When I returned in late June, it was as if this hadn't happened. There had never been any molestations, only rumors spread by unstable women. What happened next was a whirlwind of experiences without chronological order. All this happened in the last six months of 2001.

Most of the rape and molestation charges against João came from Brazilians. Ultan, Rupert, and I were only informed of incidents involving English-speaking tourists. Only those brave enough to speak out. We were witnessing the tip of the iceberg. I brought this to Josie Ravenwing's attention (Casa guide and João's biographer).

She said, "Shit! I finally got my life back on track and earn sixty thousand dollars a year with the tours, and this had to happen. Well, it can't be. There must be a good explanation. You know, I counsel victims of abuse. I can't bring people here if this is true."

When I spoke with Robert Pellegrino, he said as much. He wasn't interested in all that. My next guests were free of crises, and Lucia blossomed with all the new foreign friends who adored her. We had a life outside the Casa and usually were away on weekends. Then, the craziness began anew.

One week, there were whispers that João's stepdaughter was visiting, and João was crying. He brought her up on the stage and then made a spectacle of her in the Entities' Room. I opened my eyes. João told the audience she didn't believe he had healing powers, but now she saw it was true.

From left to right: Tiãozinho—Casa Secretary, Medium João, and his daughter Dalva (in her early thirties). Circa 2000-2001. This is the Dalva I remember well from my time at the Casa. Photo: Casa archives.

She seemed stiff and artificial, dressed up in high heels, a thin and pretty blond, who looked like she was eighteen but was actually thirty-two. People said that he was in love with her. They were having a wild affair, and his wife knew and divorced him over it. We heard this stepdaughter was the wife's daughter from another marriage. Actually, it was Dalva, his blood daughter. We didn't know it, but she was the victim of twenty years of incest.

During one session, while I was in the Entities' Room, a man standing near the stage died of a heart attack. There was no effort to revive him or call an ambulance. They carried him off. Thirty minutes later, one of the taxi drivers took the body to Anápolis or Goiânia. There, matters were quietly taken care of. This was the protocol for the dreaded deaths at the Casa.

Get rid of the body as soon as possible, do immediate damage control, change the story, and make it a false rumor. Dead people only meant forms to fill out, penalties to pay, autopsies, and inquiries.

A visitor arrived from France. He was a small, middle-aged man, quiet and self-assured. He claimed he could remove negative energies with two copper dousing rods. Abadiânia was a boring place, especially when João was away. Any new-age diversion that came along caught people's attention. Soon, he booked the week ahead at 100 reais per person. The poor man didn't realize the penalty for encroaching on the Medium's domain.

He got away with this for a few days until João caught wind of it and summoned him to his office for a meeting. João raged. The Frenchman's appointment occurred as I was exiting the morning session. The door to the office was open. This was the public office, not his private rape office.

The Frenchman, the bodyguards, and Carlos from the Catarinense were present. Medium João was shouting. Someone was translating this into English on his behalf.

He said, "Who the hell do you think you are? You're no healer. You don't know shit. You can't heal a single person here. Let me show you something; see if you can heal him."

His arm shot out towards Carlos—in an instant, a violent spirit possessed him. Carlos began tearing the office apart, throwing chairs, and breaking glass.

The bodyguards couldn't subdue him. João taunted the Frenchman. If you're such a great healer, heal him. Get rid of this. The dowser guy froze in fear. He couldn't do anything or run out of there for his life. Then João made it all stop with one command. He said, "That's the power I have. What is yours?"

We all had much to discuss over lunch. Dozens of people witnessed this confrontation, and the story passed from table to table. João called everyone to the stage for a talk before the afternoon session. The Frenchman was by his side, but João was still raging.

He called a volunteer for eye surgery to join them. João handed the dowser a scalpel and shouted to everyone watching. "If you're such a great healer, heal this woman's blindness. Only I can do that. Prove your worth."

The Frenchman confessed he couldn't heal blindness and didn't want to use the knife. João insulted and intimidated the Frenchman until they escorted him off the stage.

Then João did what he often did after a spell of rage: he wept like a child, and he did not once apologize.

I took notice of all this. Especially the spirit possession of mild-mannered Carlos by an evil entity. Could this be true? Did João have command of evil spirits, or was Carlos staging a fake possession at João's command?

Josie Ravenwing had a different take on the event, although she had not witnessed it. Josie remembers, "He told the Frenchman that he liked him and respected his work. Joao simply felt that the Frenchman needed to be clear about what he actually was and wasn't capable of doing.

"Joao then told the group of people that he consistently—through exerting his own spiritual power and with God's help—was able to keep closed a particular spiritual portal that existed above the Casa and surrounding area. If left open, this portal would allow all kinds of negative entities to attack and create problems for those coming to the Casa seeking healing. Joao kept it closed for the protection of all those under his wing.

"But on this day, Joao said, if God permitted him to do so, for purposes of a demonstration for the French healer, he was going to open the portal and let into his cottage some negative spirits. He would then ask one of those spirits to choose someone from the group to temporarily attach itself to and then would give the Frenchman the opportunity to rid that person of the negative spirits.

"Joao then made a gesture with his hand, said a few words, and spiritually opened the portal. Once it was opened, he commanded that one of the spirits choose someone there to attach itself to. Immediately, Carlos, one of the Brazilians present who volunteers at the Casa and who generally has a mild, sweet disposition, turned into a raving lunatic."

My next guest was a singer/performer from Belgium. She was a beautiful young lady, all smiles. She didn't have a health problem. More and more people were coming to see the medium for spiritual help or out of curiosity. It was an in-place to have visited.

I was nervous for her as we waited in line for her first interview. João was checking her out. He asked her many questions. She told him she was living in Rio de Janeiro. He responded that he would give her a card, allowing her to enter a spiritist center there. She would be a medium registered with João's seal of approval.

He sent her to the invisible surgery room. She would wait there until the medium arrived to perform the invisible surgeries. Usually, it was a brief visit. He did very little in this room, which was quiet and dark. My wife was in attendance as his assistant.

João directed the woman to stand up. He slipped his hand up under her blouse and undid her bra. My wife saw him rubbing his hands on her exposed breasts and all over her body.

Lucia and I discussed this in private, but our guest didn't even realize this was a violation and did not mention it. My wife knew better and was very offended. This was our turning point. We would leave.

We kept vigilance on our guest and prevented her from being alone with the Medium.

The Hare Krishna Movement sent more and more British devotees to the Casa. A story was going around that the head of the London Hare Krishnas had arrived. João's scouts spotted a rich and influential person. João invited him and his associates to dinner at a popular restaurant in Anápolis. He expected them to pay for this, of course. It was a churrasqueiria, a high-end all-you-can-eat barbecue.

Of course, Hare Krishnas are strict vegetarians. Eating a cow is an affront and horror to them. João and his entourage gorged themselves on plates of meat while the Krishna crew had to settle for the salad bar.

The next day, one of the Krishna women turned blue (no pun intended). She passed out in the Entities' Room during our meditation and fell to the floor. I opened my eyes. She appeared dead but soon returned to her body. She screamed that an evil entity had attacked her and tried to steal her life force. She was hysterical and inconsolable.

Soon after this visit, the London group created a website warning their members away from the Casa. Over the years, more websites appeared and were posted by concerned victims and investigators. The sites all had brief lives because they only had a small audience of fellow victims. No website could take the Casa down.

My next guest arrived and was certain she wanted the physical surgery. She traveled only for that. I asked what her problem was, and she explained it was ovarian cysts. She couldn't bear having them removed in a hospital with regular procedures. She wanted the quick and easy method João offered. I tried to convince her that this wasn't necessary and might even be dangerous. She'd have nothing of it. She wanted the real thing, not any of that invisible surgery. We scheduled her surgery.

That morning, she was trembling with nervousness. João was to do the work in the Entities' Room, not on the stage.

Although many have insisted for years that João does not hypnotize people, he sure does. He hypnotizes the surgery volunteers in the Entities' Room before they come on stage, which is why they stand rigid and calm, leaning against the wall.

An assistant pulled my guest out of the line. João lifted her blouse and tore the wrapper off a scalpel. She was not hypnotized. Before he even touched her, she passed out and hit the ground. João announced she had received the surgery, and his crew carried her away. When she regained consciousness, she complained that he hadn't actually cut her open.

In the evening, my guest narrated a story about how she had been in the first bombing of the World Trade Towers in 1994. She had PTSD and still worked there.

A week later, on September 11, 2001, Carlos banged on our door early in the morning. He said, "Come, you must come." We went with him to the Catarinense, where a crowd gathered around their TV.

I arrived in time to see the second plane pierce the tower like a hot knife in butter. The Brazilians watched in horror as the towers collapsed, giving me their condolences. I didn't tell them what my first reaction was. It looked exactly like a controlled demolition.

My guest was at work that morning in one of the adjoining towers that did not collapse. She had not received a cure at the Casa. I wasn't in Kansas anymore.

The rumors of sexual molestation had disappeared. There were more indications of wrongdoing, but they were obscure and without details.

A young Portuguese man in a wheelchair and his elderly father had been there for a year or more. They attended every session, but no miracle occurred. Everyone liked them. One evening, the father spoke to us over dinner, explaining that they would leave the next day.

This was a shock. Why? The son defiantly kept his eyes open in the Entities' Room. This provoked João to create a scene and expel them both from Abadiânia. The man was in tears. His son saw some troubling things. After a year of treatment, the son remained paralyzed.

In one afternoon session, a new face was holding the instrument tray. She was very young, tiny, no more than eighteen, and exquisitely pretty. She wasn't smiling, and it didn't appear she was enjoying this. João selected his paring knife from the tray, a stubby kitchen knife. He took the tray from the girl, handed it to another assistant, and grabbed her. She began crying and protesting. No, no, not my eyes! She knew what that particular knife was for. He pried behind the eyeball with this. She resisted, but he held her firmly with the help of another man securing her head.

The Entity squeezed and thrust his fingers around her eyeball. He exerted so much pressure that it popped halfway out of the socket. I waited for it to fall out or reveal a nerve trailing from the backside. Then he pushed the knife blade into the space her eyeball had vacated. It was gruesome, and I was very close. The girl had a face of terror—João wore the expression of a madman.

The Entity granted my long-standing request to film a session in his room. Our eyes remain closed in that room, and they never document what goes on. Over the years, this policy changed, but in 2001, it was still in force. No cameras or video were allowed in that room.

I positioned myself in a front row with an unobstructed side view of the Medium. I caught the line of patients from another angle. I set up the tripod, turned the camera on, adjusted things, and left it running the entire session. Many people were staring at me. Who was this upstart with the gumption to film in this room?

I didn't notice exactly what I was filming until twenty years later when I offered the tape for Netflix's series about the Abadiânia scandal. I filmed a very bored, yawning João, who was not incorporated and trying not to fall asleep. He looked at me and the camera with a scowl. He didn't trust me.

In this film, I captured several key players in the Casa and the endless stream of patients. One moment Robert Pellegrino's wife and her twenty-year-old daughter spoke with the Medium. He had placed a white towel on his lap. In retrospect, he used that towel a lot. It was concealing something. Their daughter knelt on the floor before the entity. She was weeping, and her mother looked distraught. They often looked distraught. He pulled the young woman forward and positioned her head on his lap.

One could see the ongoing activity of the translators and fixers buzzing around the room, dealing with several things at once. Another regular appeared, a young man from Portugal. He arrived some months before in severe withdrawal from heroin.

He spoke English and became the Casa's third translator. He was always busy helping people and full of optimism and encouragement. This month, he would exit the scene at the Casa in a dramatic display of tears. He had seen something, he wouldn't say what, and he was gone. Unanswered questions hovered over his exit.

When the session finished and I left the Casa, a furious American fellow ran after me. He shouted something about my filming. He began threatening me. He said, "If you publish that footage, I'll sue the hell out of you. I have a very important group here who would be angry if their images went public. I forbid you to use your footage."

He continued harassing me as we moved through the crowd. I

told him I had received permission, and he stormed off, still threatening me. During lunch, Martin arrived at my home. The Entity had refused permission for me to return with the camera in the afternoon session.

Lucia and I had enough. With no other source of income and no backup plan, we were unclear on how to proceed. I began avoiding going through the line and missed some of the sessions. Around this time, the Entity addressed the crowd from the stage. He said, "I want to warn everyone; do not have massages from Lucia. Her salon is polluted with low energy." This was a surprise.

After that, I had many dark visions sitting in the Entities' Room. I saw scenes of the Medium and Patricia (the Casa translator) engaged in black magic rituals. I perceived that I was in danger. I had entered what Martin calls "the backstage" of the Casa. I sensed a vampire-like force draining me for months and became afraid of João and the Casa.

We needed to be aloof and secretive about our feelings, but it was time to go. We decided to take a few months off and revisit the Amazon. It was our delayed honeymoon.

In November 2001, soon before our journey to the Amazon, an incident would rock our world and the Casa. I received an email from Abadiânia's first French guide, a friendly, talkative fellow most of us knew well.

He was about to drop a bomb with an explosive ripple effect. His e-mail to the guides and translators explained that the former Casa manager, Charles, had been replaced some months ago by a new one, Mario Drago. I hadn't noticed this.

Mario had recently outed João about his rapes, mentioning this to several of the oldest Casa mediums, and was now a marked man. Mario had confided in Paul, this French guide, that he had lived at João's ranch for two years. He saw shocking events. He alleged João used the remote ranch to bring young women, whom he would then rape. The preferred method was anal rape. He accused João of several murders, tortures, and other illegal activities. Even rapes inside the Casa.

Mario Drago fled Abadiânia with two of the oldest Casa mediums: Valdeci, who had spent the past twenty years as a house medium, and Paxião, a fifteen-year veteran of the Casa. João threatened them with death. Paul's rental house had bold letters painted on the wall threatening, *leave now, or you are dead.*

They moved to a tiny village in Minas Gerais. The two mediums began incorporating some of João's entities and doing healing work.

Buses were arriving from Rio Grande do Sul, with ex-devotees of João from his center there.

I began asking discretely about the details in this e-mail. I warned Josie Ravenwing and others. All the major players at the Casa knew of this letter. Soon afterward, Lucia and I traveled to the Amazon, returning in February 2002. We arrived firmly convinced that we would leave as soon as we could find a place.

One afternoon, we were in Anápolis doing some shopping. I noticed a newspaper headline. *"João de Deus' son and his wife were arrested for sexually molesting her three-year-old daughter."*

Their photograph in front of the police headquarters showed them in handcuffs. We bought the paper, and Lucia translated it for me. As we thumbed through the journal, we saw another article. It said the daughter of João de Deus was suing him for rape and abuse. This was the same *"stepdaughter,"* Dalva, that João displayed on the Casa stage.

We realized we couldn't put off our move any longer. I considered our situation. Over thirty people had contracted a visit with me as their guide, and a few of them would arrive in a matter of weeks. In late March 2002, I wrote an email explaining that I would not be their guide and explaining the reasons why.

A few days later, I had my confrontation with Martin and received João's death threat message. We were gone within the week. But João's ugly presence wasn't gone. The Entity knew where we had moved. The first thing he did was announce from his stage that no one could ever visit the city we had moved to.

He called it a den of sin, drugs, and danger. He threatened the taxi drivers and told them never to go there. His prohibition continued for fifteen years. Once again, João had avoided exposure. I felt sure he would have us killed if we pursued this further.

Soon after our move, the bad dreams began—such as that vivid warning face-to-face with João in rage. Many nights, I dreamed of a shadowy figure following me. He ducked into alleys, sneaking behind trees. He filled me with anxiety.

Our personal affairs started on an excellent footing. Soon, we had unexpected obstacles and conflicts. A stronger force now crossed everything that had been moving forward. It was bad luck, and it made our life very difficult. I sensed João's presence, threatening us with ruin.

One night, the dream was very frightening. The shadow figure was right on my heels as I ran in terror. I stopped and confronted him.

He looked like a hoodlum. I asked him what he wanted. He said, "I'm looking for someone and can't find him. Medium João sent me. His name is Michael. Do you know where he is?"

I was invisible to the spirit hunting me.

After that, I understood that my protective spirits weren't about to let this witch invade my spiritual space. The dreams stopped, but the sense of being witched had not. It wasn't until 2004 that I completely rid myself of his magic. It was an education I needed, but I regret needing it.

Between 2001 and 2003, João was accused of thirteen more rapes. In 2003, only one of them went to trial. The others appeared in court sixteen years after the statute of limitations! They are witnesses to the cases of the more recent rapes. But will receive no judiciary resolution for their cases.

In Brazil, all rape cases remain sealed documents. The investigation details, the victim's name, and the trial transcripts are inaccessible. This is true of the many cases João faced. We only know about his victims because a couple dozen of them informed the public.

VI.
WAITING FOR GODOT

It wasn't until we escaped, and only in hindsight that I reflected on what had happened.

Who is João de Deus? João is a big man. He towers above most women. The first thing you notice is his bright blue eyes. The second thing you notice is that he avoids eye contact—he won't do it. He doesn't like to shake hands unless it is a politician. He offers a limp and unexpressive handshake.

He has dyed his hair dark for decades and had numerous plastic surgeries. He sports a full set of gleaming-white porcelain teeth. João is overweight, out of shape, and barely fits in his shirts. Sometimes, he leaves the last three buttons at the bottom open—to give his belly some space to sag. But mostly, he prefers shirts that allow him to open only the top three buttons so he can proudly display his chest hair and thick gold necklace. Like I said, he reminds me of a gypsy king or a disco star. He also reminds me of a Mafia don, a used car salesman, and a huckster at a carnival.

João is a cowboy with shit on his boots. He's a redneck, a hillbilly, and every image that brings up. João's greasy, sweaty, and aloof. He's a con and a thug. The man is crude, vulgar, and on a short fuse like a rattlesnake. João is as dumb as a rock and as clever as Rasputin. He's an avid carnivore—a drinker, partier, and playboy. He's never without sexual partners.

João takes the cake as the most arrogant person I ever met. He likes to display his wealth and power. He arrives before the morning session, slowly cruising the avenue in a cowboy truck and drawing stares all around. João's checking out his empire.

He always has a few armed bodyguards by his side. They arrive together and leave together. The bodyguards look even more like a thug than João does. His goons and most of the staff never consulted the Entity. They are on salary and not believers.

When I began receiving guests as a guide, I would arrive early at the Casa with my clients and wait for João's arrival, which usually came with some fanfare. In six months, I witnessed him arrive with six different SUVs, pickup trucks, and expensive sedans. He likes to show off his new purchases.

Medium João is a consummate actor, a pathological liar, and a full-blown narcissist—manic in his need for attention and control. At the Casa, he assumes his role as the saintly and infallible medium. He is unapproachable. One of my guests spotted João crossing the lawn after a session. He wasn't in a trance. She wanted me to introduce her. I reluctantly approached the unapproachable man to please the tourist. I said hello and attempted to introduce him to the woman. He immediately rolled his eyes upward, faking a trance, and walked right between us as if we were invisible.

Most people at the Casa only see João de Deus, the actor posing as a healer. Very few see the real man. Needless to say, he doesn't do Tai Chi, read the Bible, or have any spiritual path. He doesn't radiate divine love or anything spiritual. As he and many others say, *João is just a man—with a man's needs and a man's faults.* They got that right. He isn't a saintly man, nor a compassionate and loving one. It took me a while before I saw the man without the mask. That man is a frightening monster dressed in white. If there ever was an image of the Anti-Christ—he's the guy.

Despite the repeated psychic attacks, we created a new life without the evil energy of the Casa. I put it behind me, but not entirely. I felt that justice needed to be delivered and knew I would write a book about this one day. For the next sixteen years, I waited for the Medium to die, to be exposed, or to fall out of fashion.

It was like *Waiting for Godot.* I knew if I wrote this book, he would have me killed. To my shock, not only did he continue with his crimes, but he became increasingly famous every year and fabulously wealthy.

Even though tourists and residents were forbidden to visit our city, some disobeyed. Over those years, I received many visitors from Abadiânia. If they were receptive, I told them my story. If they were moon-eyed over João, I would keep my mouth shut. Otherwise, word would reach him within a day.

Every young woman, and not so young woman who had ears to hear, received my warning. *Never be alone with him in a room under any circumstance.* Yet, the bad news would reach me year after year.

I continued my friendship with Ultan, Rupert, and a few other people from Abadiânia. Ultan was someone I would see at least twice a month. I was his confidant. As he lived in Abadiânia, he couldn't tell anyone else what was on his mind. It wouldn't be secure.

With Rupert and Ultan, there were some unspoken rules of etiquette about our history with João. It was, *don't ask, don't tell.* Rupert never brought up the subject again. Ultan did. Over the next fifteen years, he related dozens of shocking events at the Casa. Only when they arrested João in December 2018 did details emerge, confirming his stories.

I had a few years free of thoughts of Medium João in my new life, far removed from his circus. I became a practitioner of Umbanda—a white altar spiritual Umbanda. My wonderful teachers, all of whom have been older women, trained me to incorporate and work with them. They helped me hone the medium's skill and learn the safe and ethical way to live that life. I came into balance again. When I speak about Umbanda, it comes with a degree of experience, yet I am only a student with much more to learn.

It took me years to recover from the loss of faith my collision with João had created. I've never been back to attend the Casa, set foot in a spiritist center, or visited a psychic healer again. It wasn't easy to believe in miracles after João. The New Age looks like a pathetic marketing scheme with nothing inside. But I recovered my faith in healing and healers. Now, it is with a different perspective that is more mature and informed.

Ultan visited many times over the next few years. He steered the conversation away from Abadiânia's shadow side. The focus was on his marriage and his new business, Frutti's. Our unspoken truce left me with many questions I didn't dare ask. Did he pay a kickback, too? Was he hiding things? What were his real feelings about the Casa and João? The molestations were a taboo subject. But in time, he revealed ongoing allegations and dramas.

Ultan was in a relationship with Fernanda's sister, Alessandra. The Entity sanctioned this. João had a long relationship with these two young women from Rio Grande do Sul. As Fernanda was Martin's wife, Ultan became their brother-in-law. I don't think Ultan ever realized Martin was his groomer and handler. Both Martin and Ultan became rich from their investments in the Casa world.

Over the years, Ultan had children with Alessandra. But their marriage was very rocky from beginning to end. I listened to his marital tales of woe and his attempts to escape it for years.

Ultan also told me many shocking things about Martin and Fernanda. The four of them were all intertwined in João's evil chess game. Much of the news Ultan brought me was like a soap opera.

Frutti's began in the little shack Lucia had rented for her massage business. They moved to its present location a year later. His success with Frutti's surprised me, as did his secretive therapy sessions and international travel photos. He peppered news of his latest blow-up with Alessandra with sordid tales of João's debauchery.

I kept my distance from all things of Abadiânia. But every time Ultan told me more about João's steady rise to fame and fortune, it hit me like a punch to my stomach. It would never be safe to write my book.

Ghost of Frutti's in 2024. Photo: Michael Bailot.

In 2002, Emma Bragdon published *Spiritual Alliances, Discovering the Roots of Health at the Casa de Dom Inácio.* Stanley Krippner wrote an introduction. Both of their PhDs were proudly displayed on the cover. Its oversized paperback format, with many photographs, was a flashy self-publishing effort. Here she sugar-glazed the fake science she was exploiting to sell tours. Now there were three books in English written by Casa guides shouting from their soapbox. "Come to magical Abadiânia. Could we interest you in one of our tours?"

How many times had the Entity said, "Go—you are healed?" Every day, he would make such announcements. But he never said, "Be sure to continue taking your medication. And don't cancel your appointment for surgery or chemotherapy." That would not be a very convincing declaration of a cure.

We will never know how many people took his advice and died or made matters worse by doing so. But we know about the American—Javier Villa Real Bustus. In 2003, this Catch-22 caught up with João. [137]

There have been rumors at the Casa about the AIDS virus from the beginning of the outbreak. At first, João refused to treat anyone with the virus. The house rules included this caveat. Later, some of his spokespeople claimed he cured three dozen people of AIDS. Pellegrino said that the Medium cured 390 cases. There are no such cures or documentation.

In 2020, the first AIDS survivor in the world was pronounced cured of HIV—virus-free for a long while. Healed by chemotherapy and dangerous bone marrow transplants, not by João.

Javier Bustus was a professional dancer from the U.S. He was being treated for HIV. His symptoms were in remission because of the new anti-viral drugs available. He was a devoted believer in the Casa and the powers of the Entity.

João pronounced him cured of HIV in 2003. He asked the Entity if he could stop using the pharmaceuticals. They made him feel bad. João said he could stop taking them. Javier wrote to his family about the good news in great detail.

After halting the anti-viral regime, his health deteriorated into full-blown AIDS. The only pills he'd been taking were the passiflora from the Casa. Eventually, he began to die. The Casa staff paid a stranger in Anápolis to take him to the hospital in a taxi. He had no identification with him. It took three different hospitals before they admitted him. The stranger couldn't speak English and was in a panic. Javier Bustus had been at the Casa for four months.

Admitted to a hospital in Goiânia and abandoned, he died.

The doctors attending him learned about his Casa experience. They filed second-degree murder charges. João testified he was not aware the patient had stopped taking his medication. He said he always tells his people to continue their medical treatment. They negated the case in 2015.

Leigh Hopkins, another American, also died while in the Casa's care in 2003. The Casa declared her healed after she expelled a large bloody tumor at one of the posadas. Because she received a cure, she didn't go for a hospital exam. Soon afterward, she died in the same lonely and heartless manner as Javier.[138]

This year João was in court again for rape. That case also disappeared under questionable circumstances.

In 2004, Ultan told me how a gang robbed the tourists at the Vila Verde Posada. A shuttle bus packed with foreign tourists arrived early one evening. As they checked in, a group of masked men entered the posada with pistols drawn. They robbed the entire tour group of everything, including their passports.

It sounded like a setup, an inside job. How did the thieves know they would arrive at that moment? Or that they all traveled with cash, per their guide's instructions? Why the Vila Verde?

As I researched this book, I often thought about the Vila Verde. There had never been such a robbery in Lindo Horizonte.

The Vila Verde was one of the earliest posadas in Abadiânia, circa 1979. When I first visited the Casa, I stayed there. It was clean and a grade above the standards of the other options. Yet, it was almost empty, while all the other inns were full. When I stayed there, the manager told us the owners no longer lived in Abadiânia. They had a falling out with João. They didn't know if they would have a job much longer.

When I moved to Abadiânia, the Vila Verde always had vacancies. There seemed to be a turnover of managers, and it felt like the place was cursed. It was. On more than one occasion, the Medium declared the posada sujo (dirty). He suggested folks stay elsewhere. The guides shunned it. Now I realize this was a case like my friend Lazaro. João bankrupted the hotel so he could buy it.

Within days of the robbery, João visited each posada, shop, and business in Lindo Horizonte. He explained that he hired a security force to patrol his side of the city twenty-four hours a day and charged everyone a monthly fee for the service.

Ultan paid 400 reais per month in the beginning. He was complaining shortly afterward because, despite the security service, his restaurant was robbed twice during daylight hours. They apprehended no suspects.

João sponsored a visit from the military police of Goiânia, who gave a photo presentation and lecture. They informed the community that their prisons were overflowing. Their prison held fifty excess inmates in a roofless cement pit in the exercise yard. They hauled up buckets of excrement and lowered buckets of rancid food to the prisoners. They had to take turns to lie down—as there wasn't enough room for all to lie down at once.

The message was explicit: don't expect any help from the police; be good citizens and pay for private service.

We would later learn that "off-duty" police were staffing the Casa security force. João had always been in bed with the police, but now he let them move into his house. Three rape charges rounded out 2004.

Heather Cumming had insinuated herself deeply into the affairs of the Casa. She became João's main assistant. A role usually filled by burly men. She was his primary translator and spokesperson. Heather assumed all the duties of her predecessors—especially instant and aggressive damage control. Heather was not well-liked by the children of the Casa; they feared her.

Heather Cumming was born on a farm in the State of São Paulo, Brazil in 1951. Her Scotch parents were hired as managers of a cattle ranch. She "grew up a cowgirl" but attended São Paulo's poshest English-speaking boarding school, St. Paul's. They moved back to Scotland, where she attended high school in another Catholic boarding school. This ended Heather's relationship with Brazil until 2001, when she first visited the Casa.

Heather wears her hair short and her clothing asexual. She is a no-nonsense, aggressive type-A personality and adopts an affected voice when speaking publicly. Her uncomely face is tired and worn. You don't often see her smile unless it's for a photo-op. She could easily be cast as a Nazi prison guard.

When she addresses the thousands of people visiting João, she does so in the syrupy, sing-song voice of an announcer. She uses new-age vocabulary and assures everyone that the Casa spirits and Medium João are agents of light and love, helping the suffering masses reach heavenly heights of abundance and goodwill.

She became a big boss at the Casa when they got serious about international venues. It was a prerequisite that she condoned João's predatory sexual behavior and mafia-like hierarchy. Heather speaks four languages, which earned her equal status as João's closest sidekicks. She groveled at João's feet and seemed glued to his side. She began opening every Casa session in three languages, attended João at all international events, and largely took control by 2005.

Having never met the woman, I am not the best judge of her aura's color. However, I am sure it is the same color as João's. They are soul mates. I asked around—I have yet to meet a person in Abadiânia who liked the woman or sang her praises.

Santo de Pau Oco: The Hollow Log Saint

Santo do Pau Oco.

The Santo do Pau Oco refers to the colonial epoch. The Portuguese crown demanded a stiff tax on everything extracted in Brazil. Those with a stash of gold or gems would hide them in a hollowed-out wooden sculpture of a Catholic saint—a piggy bank protected by its sacred appearance. This way, the tax collector would not suspect hoarding and tax evasion. Thus, the hollow log saint is a long tradition in Brazil.

It has become a colloquialism used in all regions of Brazil. The phrase denotes someone who appears to be something he is not—the name for hypocrites and conmen.

It is also used for garimpeiros, where it has its roots. They hide their finds and evade taxes and permits. His fellow illegal miners call

Joao the ultimate hollow log saint. The rise to fame of João de Deus is the ascension of a Santo do Pau Oco.

In 2005, the famous new age guru Ram Das (Richard Alpert) arrived from the States to visit João, one of a growing number of celebrities endorsing his work. Ram Das adored João and helped boost his rapid ascent to fame. But he did not receive a cure at the Casa.[139]

This was the last year João troubled me with witchery. I had been psychically assaulted many times over the past three years. My business ventures had all failed, and Lucia divorced me. My spiritual guide advised me how João was doing this and how to end it.

The last attack was shocking. I realized that he wanted to kill me with his psychic powers alone. It happened like this. I was in the south of Brazil, a subject in a scientific study. The scientists, a team from the U.S., acquired the world's most sensitive EEG (electroencephalography) device from Russia. It was more sophisticated than any in the States.

Their previous EEG studies were of monks and meditators. They wanted to measure my various brain waves as I entered a shamanic trance. Many small detectors (electrodes) were glued to locations on my scalp. Thin wires connect the electrodes to a device that records the brain waves in every region of the brain. A sneeze or a jerky movement would send the charts into ragged false readings. I was monitored like this for about two hours.

The glue smell was obnoxious, and after the session, when each electrode needed to be ripped away from my head, I hurried to the bathroom to shower and remove the residue and stench. I was still in a partial trance.

After I had undressed, I reached out to open the shower's sliding glass door. As I touched the handle, I saw a living figure of João de Deus projected on the frosted glass like a hologram.

At that moment, the glass door exploded into thousands of slivers. Hundreds of them covered my skin like needles. The crew rushed to the bathroom and panicked when they saw me. They tried to remove the shards of glass. This was the last time the sorcerer of Abadiânia troubled me. My spiritual guides created a failsafe system of protection.

One hallmark of the Casa de Dom Inácio is the daily communal serving of soup. This began as a show of charity for the poor, who rarely had the funds to buy lunch after purchasing the herbs. By the time I arrived at the Casa, this was symbolic.

One would be hard-pressed to make a soup cheaper than the Casa recipe. It is a watery soy oil broth with specks of potatoes, carrots, and pasta served in a shallow bowl. It costs a penny or two per serving. As far as charity goes, this was João's limit.

In a grandiose show of fake charity, João constructed an enormous box of a building in the center of the real Abadiânia. A place where he hadn't set foot for twenty-five years because he wasn't welcome. The building faces the police department. With much fanfare, his Soup Kitchen became a community center.

They distributed used clothing, Christmas toys, and, of course, free soup to the locals. All this was presented with Colonel João's garish taste in decor and style—an insulting edifice of self-worship. With this and donations to the police department, he tried to buy a good image from the town. He sure needed one.

The deserted Soup Kitchen. "Thank you, Abadiânia." Photo: Michael Bailot.

Seven more alleged rape incidents occurred this year. It was becoming difficult to keep this a secret. A tour guide, Amy Bryman, witnessed a sexual crime in the Casa and alerted many people earning their living from the Casa. No one responded. A copy follows (used with the author's permission): forwarded by Catalina Ely <catalinaely@yahoo.com 4 de out de 2005 às 11:33.

Hey guys, "I just got back to California from Abadiânia after a long flight. I was totally shocked on my visit there to learn that John of God is sexually molesting girls as young as twelve years old. I happened to know one of the families whose daughter it happened to. The Brazilian family totally worshiped John of God until the incident.[140]

"My friend in Australia is currently making a website which will give detailed accounts from all the young female victims who have been molested that he had contacted, but unfortunately, they are all too afraid to take John of God to court as he can be a very dangerous man when his authority is threatened.

"I know the healing is powerful, but I find it unfortunate that everyone is buying into the hype about John of God, believing everything Pellegrino falsely tells them that as a man, John of God is like Jesus. Please, people, try to be open-minded and don't start assuming that all the allegations against John of God are silly rumors made up because some strange people with nothing better to do are jealous of his healing powers. There's no doubt that healing is powerful there, but I mean, can you have a clear conscience when you know that the healer you are working with is molesting young girls? I know some people are desperate for healing, but other healers are out there. Martin, Arturo, and Pellegrino are all very aware of what is going on, but they turn a blind eye. They will vigorously deny that any wrongdoing goes on to protect their financial interests.

"When young girls go before the entity—the entity tells them to speak with medium João alone in his office, and then when alone, he proceeds with the molestation as often as he can, forcing young girls to perform all kinds of sexual acts.

"Sometimes he tries it on older women also, but he will back off and pretend he is just giving a special healing if he doesn't think he will get away with it. I know it's a lot to swallow, but trust me, the truth is about to come out as soon as someone has the courage to take him to justice. Also, please don't let the financial rewards that are to be made from Abadiânia get in the way of your conscience. Contrary to what it seems, he is a sick man, unfortunately, with a powerful gift, and he is totally abusing his power therefore, it's time now for everyone to stop supporting him, and it's time for him to go to jail, and it's time to look for a new healer. May you all be safe and peaceful, Amy Bryman."

One of these victims was an American in her early thirties. She had a brain injury from a car accident and turned to the Casa for a miracle cure. She visited three times, even contemplating becoming a volunteer translator. But on her last visit, João invited her to his rape office. There, he placed his hands on her hips, back, and head. She felt a strange sensation enter her, like a nervous tingle. He took her to his throne and placed her on her knees with her head between his thighs.[141]

She said, "He put his fingers between my teeth, opened my mouth, and placed it on his cock. I didn't understand what was going on—if this was a chakra alignment or sexual healing. But I thought that this was my opportunity, and I had to follow it; otherwise, I would miss a single chance of a cure. He said: 'Move your mouth deeper, deeper.' Now nine times, now eleven times. I moved my mouth like a fish. Then João ejaculated in my mouth. 'I didn't know what to do with that,' he said."

After the abuse, the woman was in shock. She hid in her room and didn't attend the sessions. She confided in one of the staff, Marisa, whom she had befriended. Marisa explained that she had gone through a deep spiritual cleansing. It was not a sexual assault. By this time, covering up João's crimes had become institutionalized.

Many residents of Abadiânia mentioned something obvious in recent interviews. Everyone knew.

The American said, "I spoke with guides from France, Canada, and England. They told me not to talk about what João had done to me. They told me that people had hope, and that hope brought healing."

She fled Abadiânia and flew to visit her family in Israel. She denounced João in a letter to the Brazilian Embassy but did not receive a response. She filed a formal complaint with the Brazilian Embassy in Austria two months later. Again, nothing happened.

In 2006, I was helping a friend immigrate to Brazil and needed to consult with an attorney who spoke English. I had a lawyer friend in Anápolis, and I chose him. My friend wanted to look into registering for a non-profit organization. The lawyer outlined the options and requirements.

He asked my buddy what kind of non-profit he was planning. My friend is a medical anthropologist with expertise in shamanism. He was thinking of opening a center to research alternative healing.

The lawyer grew alert, and I could feel the mood shift. He said, "A healing center? Like in Abadiânia?" There was tension in his voice, so I asked him about his response. To my surprise, he told me he had recently represented a foreigner in a wrongful death lawsuit against João. We assured him that something like the Casa was not the intent.

He was still on edge, so I asked him for more details. He explained that this was a scary business and that João played hardball. When the lawyer requested any past cases regarding João at the courthouse, they handed him a pile more than a meter tall. All the folders declare the *case closed for lack of evidence or not guilty.* The majority never had a hearing.

This year, there were ten rape accusations filed against João.

One woman arrived in Abadiânia with her father from Rio de Janeiro. He was dying of a stage four brain tumor. She was a petite young woman, five feet tall and twenty-three years old. She had just received her law degree. Although she did several interviews, I see no reason to mention her name. Her family practiced Spiritism and had much faith in the Casa. They planned an extended visit.[142]

On her first day at the Casa, she met an American with degenerative nerve disease who was in a wheelchair. He founded a group of people who would nurse visitors 24 hours a day for a salary. She was there to arrange one for her father. They became instant friends. That evening, he asked her to promise never to be alone with João in his office or anywhere. He was a silent recipient of Amy Bryman's e-mail.

She was innocent and never imagined he was referring to danger and sexual assault. She promised. The first time she passed in the line, the Entity requested her to visit the Medium's private office. The American accompanied her. Several times, he summoned her, but she always brought someone along. João would leave the office door open on these visits and compliment her on her care for her father.

One day, she sat in the current room earlier than usual. Someone tapped her on the shoulder. She opened her eyes, and it was João, motioning to follow him. He took her to his private office and then locked the door.

His eyes rolled up, and he began praying as he groped her. He forced her to masturbate him while he sat in a leather chair like the throne he used in the Entities' Room.

Then he made her give him oral sex. She was in shock. She froze and couldn't remember what had happened. He opened the door, and she returned to her place on the bench. She said, "I left my father's photo on the wooden bench. My sandals remained there. The people around knew I was in the Casa, and they must also have known where he had taken me. Immediately, he said the Caritas prayer and started with the surgeries. I was paralyzed. It was the longest morning of my life."[143]

After the session, she turned to one of the posada owners for help and told her what had happened. The woman slapped her in the face and said she was lying.

She spoke with the head nurse in charge of the recovery room. The woman pleaded with her to say nothing, or things would not go well for her father. She said that a gringa had spoken out and then disappeared.

Then, she asked her father to leave immediately. But she didn't dare to tell him about the rape, and he refused to go.

In defiance, she changed into her colored clothes and entered the Casa in a rebellious mood to confront João. She told him she was leaving. He told her she couldn't because she had caused her father's cancer. João said that this was karmic, that cancer is karma. She believed him. This naïve young woman would do anything to save her father's life.

She began going to his office every time he called her. When she protested, he threatened her with the death of her father by removing his healing power. The assaults became penetration. She no longer resisted.

It was 2006. Almost six months passed, and they took her father to the hospital in a coma. João called her to his office. He told her that her father was dying but not to worry. João would get her an apartment, and she would lead the prayers at the Casa.

She returned to Rio de Janeiro. João had her phone number and would call her at night. He'd say he has an apartment in Copacabana, and they would swim in the sea.

Ultan visited me in July. He had Casa news. A German tourist had been murdered just behind the Posada Catarinense. Police found a body at the gate of a Casa associate.[144]

Johanna Hannelore Bode, sixty-five years old, had been publicly denouncing João and the Casa. She threatened to post her accusations on the web. The official Casa story was that she died an accidental but natural death. Mighty efforts at damage control ensued. João was never implicated in the murder, nor was anyone else. The story was fishy.

The first person to "discover" the body was one of João's

enforcers. He then called a local military policeman. It was six in the morning, many hours after the murder occurred. The cop moved and examined the body and wrote it up as natural death and that it was a male corpse around fifty years old. He later amended this to a female corpse.

The next day, the civil police questioned the military policeman. He told them he found her body face down. He turned the body over and noticed a lot of blood beneath her chin. The wooden gate in front of the house had her blood on it. He testified that he believed she had tried to jump over the gate and suffered a deadly fall.

As he noticed no evidence of murder, he registered the death as natural. Her body was taken to the Legal Medicinal Institute in Goiânia to examine her cause of death. He claimed there was no money or identification found on her.

When they performed an autopsy, they confirmed she was a woman, not a man. They discovered her German passport.

The lab report noted, "The victim must have been subdued with the hands of the assailant, who bruised her skull, scalp, and forehead. She was killed while she was kneeling, looking down. She had wounds on her neck, and after the injuries, with the victim in a bent position, with her head down, the killer shot her."

In the conclusion, the forensics report said: "Barbaric homicide by subduing the old victim and firing a shot at close range in the face. The projectile entered through the chin and ended up in the thorax."[145]

The police officer affirmed that the local people who visited the scene said they didn't know the woman. The house's resident, José Robson Drumond, didn't know her either. In his statement, the police officer said that Drumond appeared suspicious and behaved strangely.

A report in the press said, "José Robson stated he was a volunteer [English translator] at Casa Dom Inácio. He was unaware of the German woman. He claims he was asleep when called by the policeman at the door of his house. Robson has not attended the Casa for some time. He does not remember any comments about João de Deus' alleged involvement in the murder after the case."

João denounced José Robson Drumond to the police a few years before this. The court convicted him of embezzling $10,000 from a foreigner, an older woman visiting the Casa. He had conned her into buying a crystal he owned that was *blessed by the entities.* He had pulled the same grift as João. The $10,000 vanished while constructing the house where they found the slain German. Drumond spent several months in prison.

The story that has passed around for many years in Abadiânia is different. Johanna Bode was very outspoken and specific in her charges. She threatened to *destroy* the Casa. Bode took a bus to Anápolis with her host, Izaíra Alves da Silva, to exchange money. Izaíra is a pioneer child of the Casa and owner of the posada where Johanna stayed—Abadiânia's first hotel. Her family gave João the land for the Casa back in the 1970s.

Drumond, who speaks English, was on the same bus. Johanna spoke to other tourists on the bus in English, in a loud voice, about the medium's indiscretions.

That same evening, she was shot. In 2016, they closed the case due to a lack of evidence. In 2018, someone came forward to the police with more information about this tragedy. The same state attorney for Abadiânia re-opened the investigation.[146]

An alternative account is whispered in Abadiânia that no one heard gunshots and that her body was dumped where it was found. A Casa bodyguard, Antão, found the body and enlisted the owner of a posada to help move it. They put her in the back of a pickup truck, wrapped her in a tarp, and drove to a *bribable* funeral home.

João first visited America and Australia in 2006. Heather Cumming promoted the U.S. event at a church in Atlanta, Georgia. His Casa-styled program cost $360 for the three-day event. About 1000 people were in attendance.[147]

Her advertising copy for the event said, "John of God is a simple, God-loving man from Brazil. He has extraordinary spiritual gifts and boundless compassion for humanity. His life's work is devoted to alleviating human suffering as directed by his spirit guides—beings who once lived in a physical body, just as you and me."

He was not allowed to perform the surgeries. Afterward, he was interviewed for the *ABC Primetime* program, appearing on American television for the first time. He was introduced as John of God. "Some people call him the most powerful spiritual healer since Jesus, and others call him a quack." They gave him a positive spin while pretending to be an impartial report.[148]

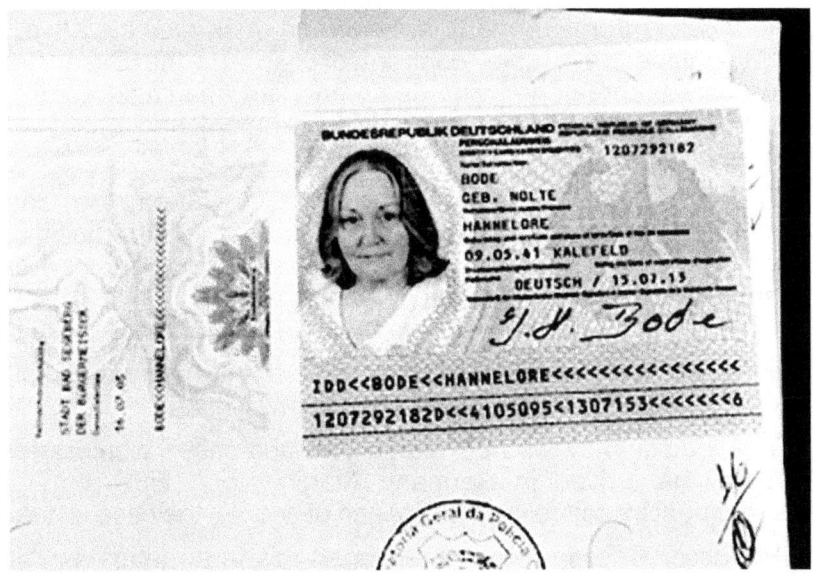

Johanna Hannelore Bode's passport.

In a prescient moment, ABC said, "There are also rumors that John of God has a much darker side. District attorney Juliana Almeida Franca says he sent her death threats. João is also accused of taking advantage of a woman who came for healing."

"There is a lot of jealousy. People talk. What dictates is the conscience toward God," he answered. He insisted his healings were legitimate.

The event in Australia involved his first alleged sexual molestation on foreign soil. Despite that, he created yet another Casa satellite in Sydney. He is accused of ten more rapes in Brazil, still a well-kept secret among the sycophants attending him.

Peter Waugh sponsored two John of God events in New Zealand in 2006 and 2007, which registered four thousand people a day. Waugh is one of the old-timers who have been bringing groups to the Casa from Australia and New Zealand since the 1990s. A sign posted in the Casa said, "If you have been authorized by an entity to bring groups to the House, please contact Peter Waugh."

He would explain the Casa rules for the new tour guides, which include a mandatory public contribution of $400 to $1,000 and a private 10% tax on their gross income.

In 2006, Ultan had more news from Abadiânia. He told me a large tour group from Germany arrived, and João molested five of them. The guides, a couple, confronted João and the Casa staff. The couple was threatened with death and fled Abadiânia abruptly, abandoning their group! They returned to Germany and spoke with the tour agency, which took legal action.[149]

Recently, I could confirm this. Martin Mosquera, the Casa translator, is fluent in German. He had made a lucrative business deal with Germany's best tourist agency. All their tour groups from Germany were being funneled into Martin's posada.

The agency's lawyers advised them to file the criminal complaints with the Brazilian Embassy in Germany, not in Abadiânia. João was scheduled to be in Germany in a few weeks.

The tour agency warned Martin that authorities would arrest João when he arrived in Germany. Martin saved him from this embarrassment by canceling the trip, and of course, the case is dead.

Professor Cristina Rocha mentioned this in an interview with the Sydney Morning Herald in 2018. She recalls how organizers in Germany in 2006 scrambled to cancel bookings after a German follower accused him of sexual assault.

In 2007, The Discovery Channel covered João. Broadcast internationally, their documentary highlighted him in a positive, if sensational, manner.[150]

The Casa became increasingly commercialized and glamorized. Faria was touted as the most famous healer in the world. Many Brazilian and international celebrities and politicians, often incognito, began visiting him. The list is impressive.

Heather had already refashioned his image for an English-speaking crowd when she brought him to America. Americans are so linguistically handicapped that most cannot pronounce João de Deus and display no desire to learn how to do so. Once again, João morphed into a new person, John of God. João is now sixty-five years old. Thirteen rape accusations occurred this year.

João and Heather had bigger fish to fry at the Omega Institute in Rhinebeck, NY. João was about to make his grandest appearance yet. Omega Institute is one of the largest and best-known new-age workshop centers. It hosts spiritual teachers, such as Deepak Chopra, Ram Dass, Thich Nhat Hanh, and Eckhart Tolle. It is a high-end venue.

One of the Institute's scouts had seen João in Atlanta, returning with a beaming report. Heather had opened the door for João to join their ranks.

Skip Backus, CEO of Omega Institute, visited the Casa and returned starry-eyed. Consequently, the Omega Institute hosted João for nine visits between 2007 and 2017.[151]

This was a gold seal of approval of his legitimacy, putting him among the stars of the New Age. His events always sold out immediately after being announced.

João and the entourage made their second trip to New Zealand. They opened another Casa clone center. There, one could receive the crystal bed treatment and buy triangles and herbs. They held meditations connecting them to the entities. Of course, they purchased an enormous crystal to stay in touch with the Mother Crystal by João's throne.

In 2007, Heather Cumming and Karen Leffler published *John of God; The Brazilian Healer Who's Touched the Lives of Millions.* This was the first book written about João that wasn't a self-published affair. A self-help imprint of Simon & Shuster published it. João entered the mainstream. The book was yet another self-aggrandizing tour pitch: the same tired biography, only this time, laced with new-age clichés. More books in this style were to follow.

Another character I knew from my time at the Casa was Arturo Rios. A short, limping troll who spied on everyone and sucked up to João. He had elbowed into the Casa Mafia and was rewarded with a small hotel. He was the Casa's connection with Greece, the next country the Medium took his flashy road show.

Heather Cumming, who was at his side for most of his foreign tours, was rewarded for her loyalty. She and João purchased the Vila Verde Hotel in partnership. They named their acquisition Hotel Rei Davi (King David, the father of King Solomon). It became known as the Hotel dos Gringos.[152]

Around the same time, João was accused of hiring someone to kill Ilion Fleury Junior—a high-profile doctor from an influential family in Goiás. The Doctor was a notorious womanizer who liked to seduce other men's wives.[153]

He was having an affair with João's wife. The civil police bungled this case as well, with no one charged. The prosecutor pointed out that there were other women as well. Their husbands might have also wanted revenge.

There were an astounding number of rape accusations this year, twenty-one. One was a sixteen-year-old girl suffering from anxiety attacks. Her father brought her to the Casa. The Medium selected her for a private meeting and also invited her father.[154]

Attorney Camilia Correia Ribeiro told Globo that João told her father to move a few meters away, turn his back, and pray. Under no circumstance was he to open his eyes. Then João fondled her and forced her to masturbate him. She broke down in uncontrollable tears, frozen in a panic attack. Her father did not know what was happening.

She told her mother and father what had happened when they returned home. The family filed a criminal case against the medium. It took five years before they had a court date. The female judge acquitted João. She said the victim's father could have saved her and that she could have screamed for help.

The televised interviews with Camilia illustrate the damage and sorrow João inflicted on the girl. She never received a cure for her anxiety attacks. She didn't find a resolution through the court system and has not healed from her trauma. We watch her bravely fight back her tears. Her face contorts into grimaces of bitterness and frustration. Her pain and helplessness are palpable.

"The wicked will always appear to be harmless and charismatic." (Mala de Queiroz)

Criminologist Aisla Carvalho writes about João, "The danger of perversity resides in the subtle form applied by the agent, who savors the agony it arouses in the victim. The enjoyment is in the reaction of embarrassment and fear it provokes, being in the power of control and domination.[155]

"Observing the medium's behavior in the face of overwhelming complaints, it is possible to identify similarities of psychopathic characteristics: eloquence, egocentrism, manipulation, absence of guilt, and empathy.

"Without seeking premature judgment, it can be said that the profile identified here resembles that of a serial rapist, in particular, because of the modus operandi reported in the reported cases.

"If so, we will be facing a real wolf in sheep's clothing, who uses multiple faces, typical acts of a pervert, as a way of posing as a good man. But his other face revealed to women that he was really looking to molest their true selves. For this profile of an abuser, the woman is seen as an object, and for this reason, his psychological/unconscious system does not know how to say no to his desires.

"He wants to do so all the time, seeking the satisfaction of his libido that seduces and deceives, behind a mask of a good man, *claiming he actually cures the pain* in others, while actually leaving scars on body and soul."

João, now sixty-nine years old, returned to the US and Omega Institute in 2009, drawing even larger crowds. The trip was also a holiday. He spent time in Manhattan and then visited Sedona, Arizona. He finalized the deal to open a Casa de Dom Inácio of America there. This year he is accused of nine rapes. One was an eight-year-old child (now twenty and testifying with others).

Another victim appeared on a televised program in 2018 that first broke the case. She reported that João de Deus abused her about twenty times from 2009 to 2010 when she was twenty years old. These occurred during services at the Casa. She recorded this in her daily diary. She displayed this for the camera, which is now evidence in the case.[156]

Diagnosed with leukemia, the medium told her she was very ill and would need to stay in Abadiânia for a long time. Soon after she arrived, João visited her in her hotel room. He forced her to give him oral sex. Afterward, she spit on him.

He said: "You be quiet, girl! From today on, you will say nothing about this. You will not leave. If you tell anyone, something terrible will happen to your son."

For two years, she was held captive by his spell. She became very depressed and contemplated suicide. She thought that this would never end. Her diary was the only means she had to talk to someone. She wrote in one of her entries, "This time, he went further. He entered my vagina and then penetrated my anus."

She became one of his attendants and often his tray carrier. João promised to develop her mediumship. The Medium ordered her never to lose weight. He promised to pay for her university tuition. She complained, "Man, you're making me sick. I'm getting worse and worse." He told her she was strong, and she could take it.

A fellow pilgrim at the Casa rescued this young woman—her future husband. Together, they fled to the United States, where they now live. The leukemia diagnosis was incorrect. She says that only now does she feel comfortable speaking about the abuse that scarred her life. "João gave me hope, and he took it away. He acted in the most cowardly way because he took away from me the faith I had in people."

John the Con: The Wizard of Oz

"You can fool people for one or two years, but you cannot fool people for fifty years."

João de Deus.

By 2010, I thought things couldn't get any weirder in Abadiânia. I had lost all hope while waiting for Godot. But, my God, things got weirder. Thousands of people from almost every country in the world flock to the Casa every week. The Casa underwent extensive renovations. The volunteers indulged in a major decorating binge. A new Casa embraced and consumed the form of the old one.

The old-timers invested in restaurants, gas stations, and real estate, channeling their profits into greater wealth. Some of them built mansions in Brazilian terms. They all had new cars.

Dozens of new posadas had sprouted up—dozens of new tour guides with their kitschy websites and unsubstantiated claims. Frutti's was overwhelmed by tourists. More and more trinket shops, crystal boutiques, and clothing stores (well stocked with white clothes) opened. They occupied the empty dirt lots or hovels that preceded them. There were even restaurants other than within the posadas.

Lindo Horizonte was crawling with pilgrims in white with rosaries hung around their necks and cell phone cameras at the ready. They were talking, talking, talking. I avoided this spooky place. Everyone was strung out on passiflora and cappuccinos.

This was the year I knew in my heart that nothing short of death could stop João. It was the year Oprah Winfrey produced the first episode in a two-part series about John of God. She didn't visit Abadiânia until they filmed the second episode. Millions of people watched her show, and she conveyed an enthusiastic message about how cool he was. Both episodes have been removed from the internet.

She interviewed three people who had been to Abadiânia. One was the editor-in-chief of *The Oprah Magazine,* who also authored an article about the Casa. The publicity brought to the Casa caused yet another tourist boom. A flood of celebrities followed. João was unstoppable. As his fame rocketed, his rapes continued, with fourteen accusations in 2010.

João was now touring wearing a white haute couture suit coat tailored to his weighty bulk. In this outfit, you sometimes saw him sporting a fedora, striking the figure of Zé Pilintra.

Zé Pilintra: patron saint of debauchery. Artistic reproduction.

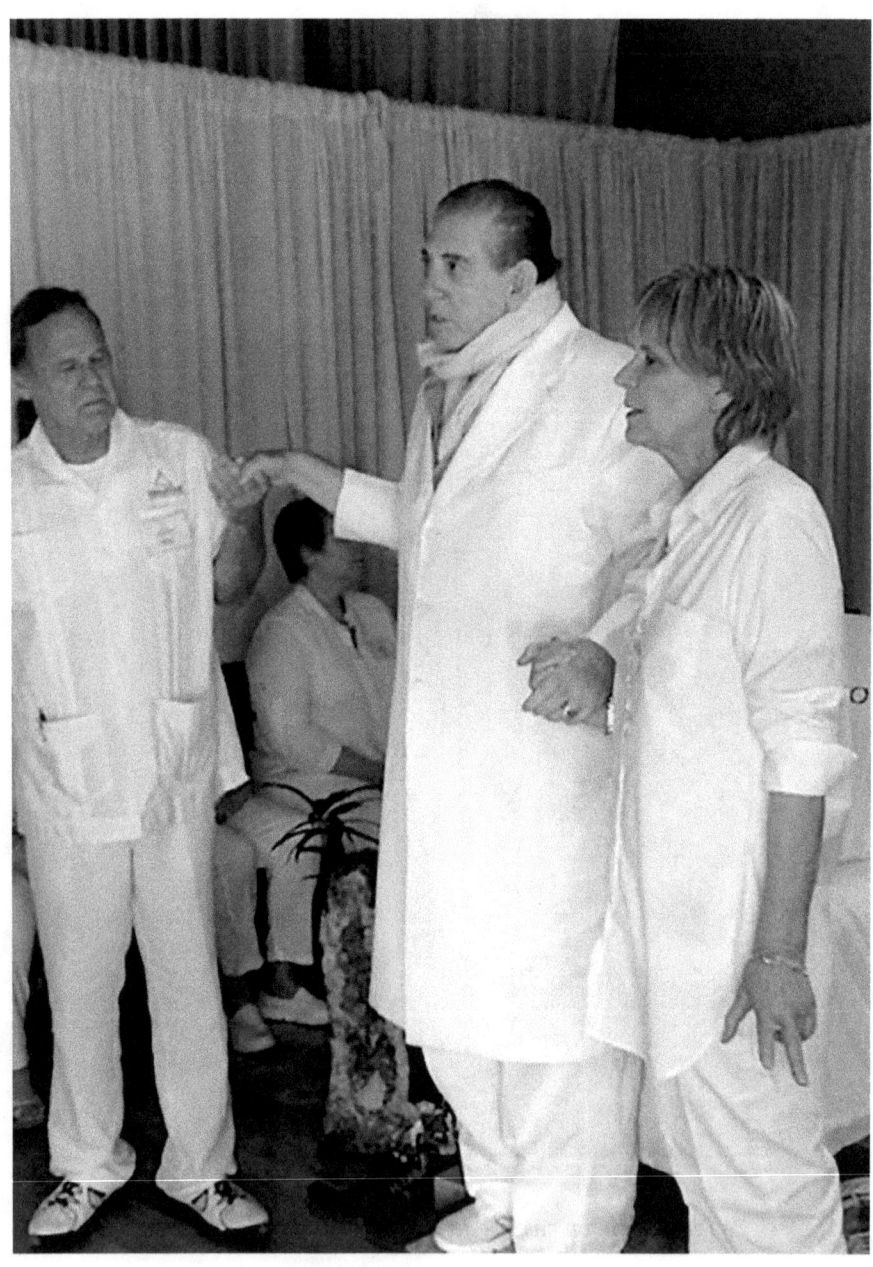

João Pilintra. Photo: Casa archives.

Gail Thackray, now that's a character. She arrived in Abadiânia in 2010. Gail was checking out the healer she heard about through the new-age grapevine of Hollywood. Within a year, she had filmed a slick but silly vanity "documentary." She also published a book (yes, another sales pitch with the fairy tale history of João). João gave her permission to bring tours. Overnight, she became another one of João's blessed groupies.[157]

When João's world crumbled in 2018, Gail was among the first to come to his defense. She uploaded two videos to YouTube, where I first learned of her existence. While all of Brazil was condemning and publicly humiliating the Medium, there was Gail with her finger in the dike, valiantly trying to hold back the waters behind the bursting dam.

I grew curious. Who is this woman? I Googled her, and a shocking history was here for all the world to see. Gail Thackray has a stage name as well: Gail Harris. Gail Harris is a washed-up porno queen with dozens of B-grade X-rated films to her credit. But wait, there's more. She owns the largest pornographic photograph archive in the world, which has earned her millions in royalties.

Many porno magazines in the 1980s featured Gail. She was on the front cover of Larry Flynt's Hustler with a centerfold and fourteen-page spread.

Harris/Thackray founded Falcon Foto—a porno photo licensing library of over two million images. In 2004, it had a net worth of twenty-five million dollars and licensed forty percent of all nude photos in distribution.

Gail Thackray created the first magazine for pedophiles, *Hustler's Barely Legal*. It was one of their best-selling titles and inspired many videos as well. Their models all appeared to be under eighteen years old. Had this been available in Brazil, you can bet João would have subscribed.

Gail returned to Abadiânia in early 2011 with big plans. We will return to her later. These were her first impressions:

"I now find myself about to be face to face with the great spirit that is incorporated in John of God. It is an awe-inspiring moment, such as one would expect if they were about to have physical contact with a saint. A moment in time that will be carved blissfully into my memory. I'm slightly nervous but in complete awe. I've been rushed through the Great Hall and into the sacred inner chapel, where John of God is seated.

Hustler's Barely Legal.

"This powerful being is holding court from an oversized, throne-like chair, adding to the grandeur of my experience. A huge rose quartz crystal adorned with rosaries and other catholic icons separates John of God's throne from the rest.

"I scan the room. Probably a hundred people are seated in church-like pews... Closer to John of God, the meditators are seated in more comfortable chairs. These are the Casa mediums, the established energy channelers. I had heard of these mediums back in Los Angeles, and part of me was thinking that my purpose here was to be chosen by John of God as a medium. I had fantasies that I would be recognized by him and called forward for my talent to heal people. After all, I could communicate with spirits, and I was a Reiki Master and healer."[158]

I remember Sedona, Arizona, in the 1970s: one motel, one gas station, and nothing else. I had the Oak Creek Canyon ruins to myself, not a tourist in sight. Now Sedona is the Disneyland of new-age style. There are several high-end golf resorts and many timeshares and condos. And hundreds of new-age therapies and gift shops. The theme is Native American, although no one there is Native American. It's *cowboy and Indian* style, a fake Santa Fe. They buy it because it's cool and you can't get it in Moline.

Sedona is a desert of dramatic views, wind-carved cliffs, and ancient ruins. These sit among hotels, tourist malls, spas, and restaurants. One can hike, ride horses, float in hot air balloons, and visit vortexes—the ultimate New Age come-on for Sedona. It is not a cheap visit—this pilgrimage to the various vortexes. Abadiânia, by comparison, is the made-in-Brazil hillbilly version.

João and his handlers decided Sedona was the ideal place to set up his Casa de Dom Inácio, USA—a perfect location for the Casa cult to take root. They could set up their very own vortex—a home away from home, where he could visit often and lucratively. Not only that, but they had found the perfect person to grift and foot the entire bill.

That person was Elisabetta Dami, Italy's most beloved author of children's stories. Dami was an adventurous soul who received her pilot's and parachutist's licenses at only twenty years old. At twenty-three, Dami traveled around the world on her own. She also crossed Africa, north to south, in a jeep. She raced the 100-km Sahara ultra-marathon and ran three New York marathons.

Elisabetta Dami is the creator of the internationally best-selling children's series *Geronimo Stilton* adventure stories, which have been translated into forty-nine languages and have sold over 161 million copies worldwide.[159]

João visited her in Sedona in 2009 and authorized the opening of this center (at her expense). She was one of his devotees, a generous woman who volunteered at children's hospitals.

He returned in 2010 to consecrate his most audacious con to date. The year before, she had purchased a one hundred pound, one-million-dollar crystal from him, which was a prerequisite for opening the center. Dami owned a million-dollar house in Sedona, where she spent a few months a year. She lived in Milan for the rest of the year.

She expanded her Sedona home into a small center housing the future Casa, where the crystal would be the centerpiece. Remember, Sedona is the world center of new-age crystal fanatics. It's unlikely Dami knew about João's criminal perversions. Yet, she became involved in a cover-up that ended any possibility of a Casa in Sedona.

She stored the crystal in an enormous empty garage. Upon arriving in October 2010, João wanted to see it. A couple, caretakers for Dami's property, who would be participants and staff for the Casa, greeted João. The previous year, he put the crystal in the care of their twelve-year-old daughter. He called her the purest person in the house. João invited the family to show him the crystal and perform a ritual.

He turned off all the lights and lit a candle. He asked the husband and daughter to stand together by the crystal. Then João and the wife stood apart and faced them. He ordered everyone to close their eyes and not open them. João stood behind the woman, his habitual molestation position. He held her hand and began caressing her fingers. He unzipped his pants and placed her hand around his penis. She recoiled and pulled away. He had her walk in circles and pray, abruptly ending the ritual. Had he hoped to anoint the crystal? Was this how he christened his new centers and seated his entities?

He told the family they would have a special ritual at the Dami home late in the evening. Late-night rituals are for his Exu. When they returned at ten p.m., their daughter had fallen asleep in the car. João had the husband stand outside and guard the door.

The Medium and the woman entered alone. When inside, he told her he would do a ceremony. He placed a white cloth over her head and attempted to pull down her skirt. Again, she backed away and told him he couldn't do this. There would be no ritual. The next day, he wanted to go to the nearby Grand Canyon, and the couple accompanied him. She drove. It would be a week before she told her husband.

In December 2010, this young woman appeared at the Sedona police department to report a sexual assault. She accused João Teixeira de Faria of forcing her to hold his penis in front of her husband and daughter.[160]

The police report says she feared John of God, a very powerful person. She was also afraid to tell Elisabetta Dami, her boss, and the owner of the home they were caretaking. She worried she would lose both her job and their home. She needed more time to process this.

She returned to the police in January 2011 and pressed charges against João. The police asked her if she would confront the healer when he returned for the grand opening in February. And wear a concealed recording device.

She agreed, but João never arrived, and the opening never happened. The victim had first recorded Elisabetta Dami and William Homann, Dami's partner.

She brought the police over three hours of recording. Dami and Homann said on the tape, "John of God may give up coming to America because of these rumors. You have to cancel your criminal complaint. I am asking you to cancel the deposition. You help us, and we help you." She offered them $150,000. She promised a first installment of $50,000 if the couple would sign a nondisclosure contract.

The document read: "We acknowledge that John of God, from Abadiânia, Goiás, Brazil, has not attempted to maintain any type of sexual contact, past or present, with any person in our family, including our daughter."

Tauber, Westland, and Bennett P.C. Attorneys drew up the document. Their contract stated that she would not seek compensation for the ceremony in Dami's home. Also, any claims she filed would be withdrawn. No future claims would be filed against Dami, Homann, and John of God.

Dami said, "We have a problem, which at the moment is not big but could become one. We need to work together to solve it. You know Sedona is a small place, so people talk and talk and talk. If you move to Peru [her husband's home country] before February 17, we'll give you an extra seven thousand dollars. We'll pay for plane tickets and the cost of the girl's private school."

She then explained that João de Deus had confirmed his presence at the opening scheduled for February 20.

The couple provided receipts for the received funds. The police accessed Dami's account and confirmed the payment. They also discovered a $3,500 check to the security company. Their cameras had captured João's incriminating behavior. They made their payment a few days after the incident. The video disappeared. Film the police wanted but never got.

Police filed charges against João Teixeira de Faria and separate ones for Dami and Homann. He canceled his upcoming visit. Dami and Homann fled to Italy, avoiding the police. In January 2012, the prosecutor's office dropped the case.

The separate charge against Dami and Homann for influencing witnesses to a crime was also dropped due to a lack of evidence. Elisabetta Dami never opened the Casa USA and refused to comment to the press. The couple kept their silence and left Sedona. João retained an American attorney, John Sears, who said that John of God had nothing to say.

It was an unbelievable year for John of God in 2011. He narrowly escaped arrest in Sedona for sexual assault. Then, he toured Austria in March, the United States in September, and Germany in November. Brazilian superstar Xuxa visited him. The American author of self-help books, Wayne Dyer, endorsed him.

João was accused of twenty sexual assaults, including two girls from his center in Rio Grande do Sul. The two Brazilian guides who chaperoned the girls to the Casa also raped the girls. The assaults by João and the guides were the girls' prescribed treatment by the entities.[161]

Gail Thackray filmed a vanity travelogue about her adventures in the "jungles" of Brazil with John of God. She imitated a newscaster, showing her bird's-eye view of a reality she knew nothing about. She repackaged snippets of João's cliff notes version of his life without understanding a word of Portuguese.[162]

Brazil's megastar Xuxa—the hostess of Brazil's favorite TV program for children, landed in Abadiânia by helicopter. She was filming a two-part segment on the Casa. The first episode of surgeries was filmed before her arrival. Abadiânia went crazy; I mean the real Abadiânia across the highway. The kids skipped school. The town flocked around the celebrity who took various photo ops with children. But her production never aired. Even so, her strong endorsement of João as 'an enlightened man' pushed the ante even higher.[163]

João always had a side business with the famous, the wealthy, the powerful, and the corrupt. They could count on receiving a private session and special services. They also arrived by helicopter and black Mercedes. João flew in his private plane to attend to those needing the utmost privacy.

In September, the John of God event at Omega Institute was another sold-out event. Blessed crystals and healing water were the hot items. One could book tours, buy a crystal bed, and books and videos about João. Dr. Wayne Dyer gave a testimony. He claimed that a long-distance intervention by the Medium had cured him of leukemia.

João told the author, "You are well."[164]

Dyer died four years later. His emotional speech elevated the Medium another notch in the self-help crowd.

After João's successful tour in Austria in March, he returned to Europe in November 2011. He held an event in Alsfeld, Germany, attending about 3,000 people daily for four days. Professor Cristina Rocha observed, "To many of them, he would say, 'Eu quero te ver no Brasil' [I want to see you in Brazil]. In the following months, most of them would spend two or more weeks at the Casa in Abadiânia. More often than not, they would be taken by tour guides (and the event organizers were also tour guides) in package tours." [165]

A European attendee said this about the event: "We saw that the only thing going on was to make money. After an operation, you had to buy six bottles of blessed water for €2 /liter. One ticket was €120 for one day. Some crazy guys were talking on the stage and telling us to be healed, things you can read in the telephone book. They sang Happy Birthday (Austrian version) for those with birthdays—praying into a wooden triangle and people for a long time.[166]

"A lot of sick, diseased people were around, and after hours of waiting, you come up to him, sitting in his white chair. The only thing he does is wave you into the next room, where a strange lady is doing a healing with you.

"After two seconds in front of João and five minutes of meditation, you are cleaned up. Nothing else happens. What happened there is a farce."

As John of God became a phenomenon, his gypsy roving took him to many places. Each one was a gold mine of unreported income. Besides the United States, he visited Canada, Germany, Austria, Portugal, Italy, Greece, Peru, Bolivia, Argentina, Australia, and New Zealand. He toured the United States at least ten times and Peru five times. These events generated millions of dollars for the Medium.

Ultan visited me with news from Germany. He said that João had been there recently with Heather Cumming and the gang for another session of his road show. I guess they weren't worried about his last incident with the Germans in Abadiânia.

Ultan said, "One of the German tour guides had asked for private counseling with the Medium in his hotel room. Her husband had left her, and she wanted him back. Could João help?"

Heather sat in an armchair next to João and translated. The victim remembered nothing after the Medium called her to kneel before him until she came out of her trance.

Ultan said, "She was giving João a blow job. Bewildered and not remembering how she had entered this shocking moment, she looked up to see Heather—who was grinning at her."

I asked Ultan to tell me her name, but he refused.[167]

João had hypertension for much of his life. After a day's work, he would measure himself, and at times, it reached 160/120, which is in the danger zone. Late in the year, João had a heart attack while returning from abroad. When he arrived in Brasilia, he underwent surgery. They inserted two stents. A year later, his doctor in São Paulo examined him and found more blockages of arteries. He installed four more stents.

Professor of History Maria Machado, author of *João de Deus: Um Médium no Coração do Brasil,* made her first visit to the Casa in January 2012. She returned many times, winning the trust of João. He granted her interviews and detailed things about his history not revealed before. Four years later, she would publish her book.

In February, Marta Rausche died in the Casa, an Austrian *living inside* the Casa. There was a police investigation, as the paperwork was questionable. Nothing came of the case. The coroner determined she died of a heart attack.

TV Anhanguera reported that The Civil Police of Abadiânia opened an investigation into the death of an 80-year-old Austrian woman at the request of the Public Ministry. Casa spokesman Chico Lobo talked about the case in the TV Anhanguera report. Contrary to what is stated in the investigation, he denied he was in the place at the time of the Austrian woman's death.[168]

According to Lobo, the medium was not present either. The police said, "How the Austrian woman's body was removed from the Casa calls attention. A witness, an employee of a funeral home in Anápolis, identified only as Junior, transported the body in an unmarked truck."

In March 2011, Oprah Winfrey arrived with a film crew at the Casa de Dom Inácio to cover her second episode about the Casa. This was her first and only visit. Oprah was impressed. Because she was impressed, her objectivity vanished. Heather Cumming translated as Oprah interviewed João on a rustic bench beneath a mango tree. She arrived incognito, dressed in white and in a limo. The locals didn't recognize her (of course not; she is not a Brazilian television personality).

She was escorted into the Entities' Room by a side door, invited to hold the surgery tray, and given a seat next to the Medium. Heather and the staff directed everything she experienced. She spent the day. Of course, she knew nothing about what was happening at the Casa, perhaps even under her nose.

As an advocate of the *Me-Too Movement*, we can imagine her embarrassment when the scandal broke in 2018. She removed all copies of her interview from her site and YouTube, but the damage had already been done in 2012.[169]

João and his Casa entered international celebrity status with her stamp of approval. It seemed there would be no turning back. Her interview with João added millions of dollars to his wealth.

It inspired a slew of other celebrities to add their rave reviews of the Casa. The free publicity drew more rape victims into his lair.

The young woman sexually assaulted while her father sat with his eyes closed three meters away in 2006 finally had her day in court six years later. João's defense lawyers called dozens of witnesses. Chico Lobo and Hamilton Pereira testified that the Medium was never alone in his office. João said, "I have to withdraw sometimes because people see me as God. They hug me; they grab me. In my room, no one goes in."[170]

When João arrived to testify, the court staff exited, fearing retribution. The press did not cover the case, and the hearing was conducted in secrecy. News reached the public, and a group gathered in front of the Catholic Church. They prayed for a conviction. João was found not guilty due to a lack of evidence and was acquitted on appeal.[171]

In 2012, a seventeen-year-old from Três Coroas, RS, plus three others, accused João of sexual assault. This is where João had a Casa extension, which he frequented a few times a year.

One said, "I went to the house for more than three years because I wanted a treatment to get pregnant. He led me into a room and ran his hand over me. He tried to get me to give him oral sex, but I resisted. Then he said, 'You are an expensive woman, right? If I pay you an allowance of ten thousand reais, will you live with me in Brasília?' He said he would reverse his vasectomy to give me twins and threatened that the treatment wouldn't work if I told anyone. After that, I stopped going to that place."

On his next visit to Rio Grande do Sul, the fathers, husbands, and leaders of the Casa in Três Coroas warned him never to return or that he would be killed.[172]

Martin Mosquera's wife, Fernanda, and another daughter of the Casa, Tãnia Appel, were sent to Três Coroas to attempt damage control (they came from there). It was not helpful, and the center was more or less abandoned.[173]

Another case, this one from Rio de Janeiro, happened in July. The victim was called to his office for a private consultation. She told him she was suffering from abdominal pain. João told her it was because she couldn't get pregnant and told her she needed to "get this thing out of you."[174]

She said, "I could feel his breath pulling and releasing the air on the back of my neck. He ran his hand over my belly and thighs. I thought it was a pass at the region where the disease was. He squeezed my buttocks. He squeezed with both hands, one on each side. His hands were big; they looked bigger than a normal man's." João said, 'Yeah, you're going to need a cleaning. A good cleaning.'

"I thought about screaming, but I couldn't. I didn't have the strength. You'll think I'm an idiot, but at the time, it made sense. It seemed that things inside were not the same as things outside. I believed I was going to find the cure there.

"I close my eyes and smell that day. Of Dove soap. The smell of the person you hate. It's not hatred, no. I guess I wish it was hatred. It is fear. I am afraid of him—even today. I'm afraid I'll come home one day, and he'll be here. Someone plays with your trust, with your faith.

"You stand there willing to believe in something that is mysterious and not normal. Everybody is open and talkative all day, seeing cure after cure. It creates trust. It is as if everybody there shares a secret that the world doesn't know yet—a miracle. And he abused that trust."

The woman hid in her posada room at Norberto Kist's guesthouse, terrified to tell anyone. She returned home. After suffering for two years, she was diagnosed with PTSD and anxiety disorder caused by her trauma at the Casa.

In late November 2012, João and the crew returned to Salzburg, Austria, and a week later to Alsfeld, Germany. He was on a roll.

João had declined the Omega Institute's invitation for this year over a dispute about how much they would pay him. He returned when they met his price of $100,000 per event.

Winterthur, Switzerland. João will serve 3,500 people at the Eulachhallen events space. The packages for the three days, 370 euros, are already sold out. Photo: event poster.

He also held his first event in Switzerland, where it is alleged that he sexually assaulted a Swiss woman. When he returned to Switzerland in July 2013, the police were waiting for him.

Maria do Carmo said, "In Switzerland, João was prohibited from entering the country, as there was a report of a sexual crime against him. He was only released because someone from the Brazilian Embassy negotiated that he could stay three days to attend. But under guard by the police of that country. I don't know the exact date, but I certainly have it recorded and saved to guarantee you the testimony of an informant/victim." [175]

VII.
The Enchanted Realm of Abadiânia

The 2012 interview with Oprah Winfrey was broadcast in 2013 to millions of viewers. She opened a floodgate that wouldn't be closed until the end of 2018. This year, João visited Toronto, Canada, Basel, Switzerland, and Germany once again. His John of God show was as finely tuned as a rock and roll tour.

Toronto, Ontario $188 (one day) to $514 (three days) — on sale now! Photo: Casa promotional material.

Gail Thackray brought João to Toronto. Her event literature said: "John of God is world renowned for his healing powers. People swear by him. Oprah has visited him. Acclaimed author Wayne Dyer credits him with healing his leukemia. Stories abound of people discarding their wheelchairs and crutches. But few can make the trek to this small Brazilian town in which he lives. Now, for the first time, John of God is coming to Toronto, Canada. In the words of this humble man, 'God is the one who heals; I am merely an instrument in God's divine hands.'"[176]

In a pre-event interview, Gail Thackray said, "She is a powerful healer and medium herself, has experienced this life-altering healing firsthand, as well as having her own psychic abilities increased many times, just from being in his presence. In her book, *Gail Thackray's Spiritual Journeys: Visiting John of God,* Gail shares stories of not only the physical healings, but emotional, relationship, and financial help as well. Readers report actually feeling the energy coming through the book, and some even say they have received a healing just from having the book by their bedside."[177]

There were rumors that João planned to open another Casa branch—this one in Italy. A web blog called *Dangerous Diane* published posts from women assaulted at the Casa. This query from a woman in Italy highlights Dami's role in this:

"I'm writing from Italy, sorry for my bad English. I'm looking for news about the case in Sedona because I have reason to believe that Elisabetta Dami wants to open a Casa of John of God or something like this near my town in Northern Italy. She is often here, and she bought a lot of old houses and miles of land nearby.

"The mayor of the town asked the citizens if they wanted to sell land or houses, and the people didn't know why, but when they saw money! The mayor says the business is great but won't say what is real. It is like a secret, something very strange. Someone knows, but nobody says a word. Who can I contact to have more information? See you soon. Thank you, C."[178]

In 2013, an anonymous guide, a volunteer at the Casa for twenty years, filed a police complaint accusing the Medium of sexual assault. She says that João's abuse of women was an open secret at the Casa. Many women had complained to her about such incidents.[179]

She said, "I remember them. I'm a witness to some of the abuse. I fought with João in 2013." She filed two police reports, but neither resulted in a conviction. The Global investigation found one case dismissed on appeal for lack of evidence.

Eight rape accusations occurred this year, including a victim, twenty-four at the time. An interview by Alberto Rocha in Folha Press explained she accompanied her grandmother, who sought a cure for a bruise on her arm. She thought of the visit as an opportunity to see something unusual. Surprisingly, the village revolved around João, with his photos plastered everywhere. She saw it as a peaceful and inspiring place surrounded by nature and good-intentioned people all looking for a cure. She fell into the group experience.

In line for their interview with the Medium, her grandmother was ahead of her. João ignored her, only passing a slip for the passiflora pills. Then the Entity asked the granddaughter what she was there for. She replied that she was a medium, which caused her problems, as she had no control over it. He told her to visit João in his private office after the session. At the office, she got in line with three other young women. The Medium shouted angrily from behind the door, saying he didn't want to see any more people today. An assistant sent them away.

She said: "At night, I had a horrible dream. João de Deus appeared in black beside my bed and sucked all my energy with his hands under my face. I could feel the fluids coming out of my body, but I couldn't move. I woke up with a scream. And I fell into uncontrollable crying. My grandmother was scared. I was twenty-four years old and asked to sleep in her bed—something I had never done before." [180]

The following morning, she spoke with the Medium before the session, mentioning her dream. He told her that this was normal. He was giving her energy, not robbing her of it.

João told her she was special and asked her to sit on his throne until he arrived for the session. He told her to close her eyes and "Command space energy." His assistant led her to the throne. People in the room stared at her in amazement. When João arrived, he had her sit in the chair next to him.

After the session, she returned to his office with her grandmother. Only women were waiting in line again. João sweet-talked her grandmother and suggested she eat lunch while he visited with her granddaughter for a while.

The young woman was nervous because he had screamed the day before. When they were alone in his office, he locked the door. He said she was a natural healer. He told her to stand up so he could re-energize her chakras. After touching her seven chakra areas, he opened the bathroom door and pushed her inside.

He had her turn around, place her hands on her hips, and move. She needed to release the energy. Her entire body turned cold. She resisted while he rolled her around and attempted to secure her hand around his flaccid penis. It repulsed her. He tried again, and she refused, telling him this was wrong.

They returned to the office, where she sat on the sofa in terror. João sent for her grandmother and began praising the girl, but she panicked and ran from the office.

She told her grandmother what had happened. She replied, "You're confused. João is a wonderful man who cured many people." The girl left the next day for São Paulo and spent three days crying in the fetal position in her mother's bed.

She said: "It makes you think it's our fault. Should I have screamed? Made a scandal? Therapy saved me from further trauma. I freed myself.

"Today, I know fully that he is a sick person who receives his victims in the hope of a cure and a search for spirituality. Today, I'm not ashamed of what happened to me. Who has to be ashamed is him!"

Ultan's cousin, a police lieutenant from Sydney, Australia, contacted me. He was visiting Ultan in Abadiânia. This made Ultan nervous because his cousin was on a mission. Ultan referred him to me. He visited my home, and we spoke for some hours.

He told me he was a detective for the Sydney police department. They were investigating João for an alleged rape that occurred on his last visit to Australia. They knew he would appear at another event in a matter of months. Australia didn't want a repeat of its years-long struggle with Scientology.

They planned a sting operation with a young police officer out of uniform. They planned to wire her with a hidden microphone and set up a trap in his hotel room. He wanted to know my opinion. Would this work? I told him that João had a criminal mind and already expected this. He preferred to do his molestations in Brazil, where he had protection from prosecution. I said João wouldn't risk another incident while traveling overseas. I was wrong. I wasn't aware that he sexually assaulted other foreigners in their own countries until the news broke in 2019.

The officer explained that authorities in Australia wanted to prevent João from holding events in their country. He told me they were working with INTERPOL, the international police force. INTERPOL had kept a dossier on João for three years (since 2010). They investigated João for international money laundering, tax evasion, fraud, and rape.

Thousands of daily guests at the Casa arrived with millions of dollars in revenue. More and more celebrities, journalists, and TV crews visited. The Casa needed an upgrade. The backwater, Goiás redneck image of Doctor João needed a facelift.

João was always a fan of reconstructive surgery; over the past few decades he had many plastic surgery procedures. He could understand the need to keep his image looking renewed.

His handlers thought it was time to update the Casa brand and bring it into the social media age. They decided hiring a publicist would be in João's best interest. Her name is Edna Gomez. She was a newcomer to the Casa and not a devotee or a child of the house. She lived in Goiânia, was an ex-model, a press agent, and a social columnist for the Diário da Manhã. Edna was a gossip columnist for politicians, the wealthy, and the influential scum of Goiânia.

Edna arrived at the Casa dressed for success. She wore a designer's white suit and a polished personality. She would visit the Casa only when needed, which turned out to be weekly. Her new job was to coax João out of his self-imposed hiding. João was nervous about the media and interviews. He had a lot to conceal. Her role was to attract publicity, not to avoid it.

This was a strange marriage. Pompous wealth and ego wed barbarian João. They spawned some weird children. She aimed to market the Casa brand and make João look bigger than life. Edna promoted a cult and a cult figure with a logo, jewelry, and wardrobes.

She was introduced to the staff as the new daughter of the Casa—anything involving the Casa's public image needed to go through her. The good news was that she was well-connected to famous people. She held the pulse of soap opera stars, governors, and billionaires. She knew her stuff. Edna showed up at the Casa when she needed to attend to journalists, influencers, or the famous. Edna created an Instagram profile for the Casa and was the respondent. The Casa and João became her *talk of the town.*

It wasn't only Edna creating a myth and a product. This had been going on for a long time. The tour guides, their books, and pseudo-documentaries all echoed tales of an enchanted realm in magical Brazil where the Casa becomes multi-dimensional.

Beneath the Casa lies a vast bed of crystals, or perhaps one gigantic crystal. It radiates healing powers. After blessing the sacred waterfall, it surges upward to the Astral plane—a spiritual hospital floats above the Casa, equipped with supernatural tools and a staff of dead doctors.

Millions have been cured of terminal diseases, and dozens of scientific studies prove it. He cures AIDS. The Pope and the Dalai Lama adore him. The lame walk, the blind see, the demons flee the madman, and yes, he can cure anything.

It's free, absolutely free. Medium João wouldn't have it any other way. Abadiânia is one of the world's rarest power spots, a virtual portal to the spirit realms. UFOs are abundant here; folks photograph floating specks of light, spirit chimeras. Magical surgical cuts appear unasked for. People come back to life after being declared dead. He saved my friends, aunt, daughter, and three Presidents of the Republic.

People grew so fond of this enchanted land that they brought it home to Hamburg, Sydney, and New York. They made their own rituals with their crystal bed, triangles, and blessed crystals. They even brought along the Casa music and prayers.

Like Jehovah's Witnesses, small groups popped up in living rooms and public spaces around the world. John and his spirits had become a full-blown cult fueled by a pyramid scheme of endless wealth. Everyone wanted to represent the Casa, buy a crystal bed, duplicate the vibe, and sit in the current. Above all, they wanted to stay connected to The Mother Crystal and the home of the phalange of entities. Tour guides and clients began claiming they could also channel the Casa entities.

The media and internet now amplified this myth, this meme — the greatest healer in the world. Everyone, from Newsweek to the BBC, parroted the standard monotonous biography of João.

João's Casa was, indeed, an enchanted realm. The supreme leader of this realm is the enchanted King Solomon. He is such a powerful sorcerer that he can never incarnate on Earth again. You can only know him and become his subject if you visit his enchanted land. There, all of his powers are manifest. People are cured, the poor are made rich, the abused receive justice, and the unloved find solace.

In Rei Solomon's enchanted Kingdom of Abadiânia, one can enter his world of wonder. Like Chico Xavier's novel *Nosso Lar*, where the recently departed live in a heavenly suburb of kindness, harmony, and love. A community of omniscient and selfless spirit friends welcomes you. You don't need to work here.

Cry, lay in bed all day, and eat ten bowls of ice cream; no one will judge you. All your sins are forgiven, and your weaknesses are erased. Your failures are given a second chance.

One is safe and made comfortable and peaceful in his magical kingdom. You could find your soul mate here, change your destiny, or receive a cure for cancer. Here, you might meet a strawman, a tinman, a cowardly lion, or even the wizard himself. Things turn inside out in the enchanted world. Everyone wears a mask or a disguise.

The Kingdom of Abadiânia is like Shangri-La. If you enter the hidden realm, you may never find your way back to the corrupted *real world*.

Gutta Monteiro writes about Catimbó. "It is a cult of trance and possession, where the masters take possession of the catimbozeiro's body. There are three distinct lines of work: trips to the Worlds of Enchantments, the manifestation of Masters, caboclos, trunqueiros, kings, and [incorporation of] the enchanted of Jurema, and other entities such as pretos-velhos, exus, and pomba-giras."

"Masters are neutral and can operate both good and bad deeds. The decision to manipulate the energies for the desired purpose is up to the catimbozeiro's ethics."[181]

Until you watch the interviews with João's victims and feel their emotions, you cannot understand. The trauma and ruin are written on their faces. There are thousands of faces.

Yes, thousands—most of his victims did not, and will not, come forward. There is no incentive. João threatened their lives. They were "witched" by black magic. They found no support from the Casa staff or the local police and courts.

Until Zahira made her bold denunciation on Globo TV in December 2018, there had not been a single rape case against João that resulted in a conviction. But before that could happen, Zahira Mous would suffer for four years in silence. Her story is mirrored in hundreds of other cases brought against João Teixeira de Faria.

When I watched the video interviews with Zahira Mous, I wept. I cried every time I watched them. This is the heroine of our story, the brave woman who brought down the mighty João de Deus and his house of cards. I had been waiting for Godot for sixteen years, and now *she* had arrived![182]

Zahira Lieneke Mous is a professional dancer and choreographer from Holland. She visited the Casa in 2014 when she was 30 years old. She sought healing for the sexual trauma she had suffered as a teenager. Unfortunately, João was always on the alert for this—a beautiful, traumatized young woman. She didn't see it coming. None of his victims did.

He always caught them by surprise with hypnotism, shock, and fear. His technique of entrapment was obsessive and predictable had we only known.

First, he made her feel special (and safe) by asking her to hold the coveted surgery tray. He offered to help her develop as a medium. She shook and trembled when he handed her the paper with the Pontos Riscado scribbled on it. She was the last in line when he called her to his room. He locked the door and told her she needed a private session.

How many women endured this same procedure? From the many denunciations pilling up, he had several young women scheduled for a private session most days the Casa was open. The staff was aware of this and assisted in the process!

In her televised interviews, Zahira said, "I walk into the office, and the people who were still there are gone. I'm left alone with him. He asked me why I came to the Casa. 'I am here to heal my trauma from being sexually abused.' João told me to stand in the middle of the room.

"In my head, I kept asking myself, 'What's going on?' He opened the door to the bathroom and told me to go in there. Then he positioned me in front of the mirror, standing up. He asked me, 'What do you see?' I didn't know what to say. I answered, 'A woman?' He then took my hand and placed it on his penis, which he had exposed.

"Then he made me kneel down as he sat on the sofa. He takes my hand and makes me move his cock. And he keeps talking while it's happening. He talked about my family as it was happening. He said, 'You should smile.'

"After ejaculating, he got up and went to a cabinet where there were crystals and cut stones. He offered me one. 'You can pick the one you want.'"

Some days after this assault, he called her to his room again. "This time, things got worse. He penetrated me. He penetrated me from behind." Zahira stayed silent for years out of fear. "I was afraid that they would send dark spirits after me. I was afraid that my life would be horrible. Like, that I wouldn't be able to sleep, that these spirits would start appearing in my dreams."

She narrated her experience with tears streaming down her cheeks. Her courage turned the tide against João. She encouraged hundreds of other victims to come forward and denounce the monster. Zahira's testimony is one of ten sexual assault charges registered against João from 2014.

The famous American singer-songwriter Paul Simon visited the Casa in the summer. His wife, musical artist Amie Brickell, encouraged the trip. She had visited the Casa the year before, received spiritual surgery, and was impressed.

Cathleen Falsani published an interview in *Sojourners* on June 6, 2016, *Paul Simon's Spiritual Fascination.* Simon arrived alone, guitar-less, and incognito. He had suffered from violent nightmares most of his life. When he visited the Casa, they were happening once or twice a week.

Dressed in white, he waited in line. The Medium sent him to the invisible surgery room and instructed him to close his eyes. He peeked. The medium entered the room, said a prayer, and then left. When everyone got up and began leaving the room, Simon asked his guide when he would receive his operation. She told him he had already received it. After his invisible surgery, Simon returned to the Posada and slept for eighteen hours. He stayed for ten days.

When Simon passed through the line for his first interview with the medium, he felt he didn't belong there. He imagined his parents would think this was ridiculous. Simon was the last person in line. He told the Medium that he wasn't sick and that many others really needed help. His only problem was that he had suffered from nightmares since he was four.

The Entity told him that this suffering wasn't less important than others. He took Paul's hand, called him a child of the Casa, and predicted he would return three times. Then, he asked him to sing one of his songs.

The request surprised him, but Simon agreed. Someone handed him a guitar, and he sang the only one that came to mind: his iconic 1969 song, *The Sound of Silence.* About 200 people were gathered in the Casa's three rooms as Simon began walking from room to room as he sang.

"As I walked toward people, some people would begin to weep, and some would fall down and ... I say to myself, *whoa, some big energy thing is happening that I don't understand. It's happening through me, but I don't know what it is, and nobody told me about it.* I don't know whether I'm doing anybody any good. It's pretty strong, so I'm afraid to get too close to people because the closer I get, the more they shake.

"Then I move over to the infirmary patients and let them weep for a while. There's something about this that makes me feel like this is okay. Whatever it is, I'm just playing The Sound of Silence. I walk into other rooms, and the same thing happens. People fall. They weep. I finish the song, hand the guitar to somebody, and leave. That's what happened ... I don't know how to describe it. It wasn't bad. It wasn't good. It was I-don't-know-what-happened. I hadn't experienced that before."[183]

Meanwhile, João had become a darling at the Omega Institute, according to an interview by Matthew Remski: Omega Institute, Rhinebeck, NY, September 30–October 2. "According to the institute's CEO, Skip Backus, the 2014 Omega event hosted approximately 1200 participants, paying $145 per day. The event revenue, not counting accommodation, would gross over $500,000.00."

Backus said such numbers were in line with other headliner presenters, like the Buddhist monk and peace activist Thich Nhat Hahn. He noted that many pilgrims returned year after year.

Nine such events between 2007 and 2017 may have grossed as much as $4.5 million.

"We never heavily marketed the thing at all," said Backus, who emphasized that hosting João de Deus was never about the money. "We didn't need to. It would go up on the site and sell out in ten minutes."

"Skip Backus said that João's handlers demanded a clear protocol restricting the medium from seeing pilgrims privately. Backus believed at the time that this was about protecting him from the draining effects of his endless empathy and service. He described overwhelmingly positive feedback from Omega participants. He also noted that when in the event room at Omega Institute, João was always flanked by an Omega security guard while meeting with pilgrims. Backus emphasized they received no negative reports from event participants."[184]

In October 2014, the TV show 60 Minutes Australia visited Abadiânia. They weren't there to promote the Medium but to expose him. He and his handlers hadn't seen it coming or thought they deflected it. Heather and the gang gave the moderator, Michael Usher, a list of questions he could use in his interview. She had a list like this for all interviews. They didn't know that he had already spent some days in Abadiânia. He investigated João's personal life and business.[185]

He was there with a small film crew and hired his own interpreter. Heather Cumming always hovered at his side. João arrived, looking both nervous and impatient. Usher began with one of the stock questions and got the standard spiel. His next question received a knee-jerk reaction from Cumming.

He asked, "There seems to be a big business around your spiritual clinic. Is it more about money than miracles?"

Cumming snapped, "That question wasn't on the list, was it?"

Usher protested. "Wasn't it a pertinent question to ask?"

As the interview disintegrates, even before it begins, you see

João's other handlers rushing in to intercede. The camera is rolling, and Usher still has his remote lapel mic turned on.

Heather summons everyone to leave, abandoning the film crew. Usher, running after him, shouts as he goes, "But João, what about these reports of sexual abuse? Do you have any comments about this? Have you sexually abused anyone, João?"

Usher's translator, a tiny Brazilian woman, tries to stay by João's side as he flees. She translates Usher's last question. "Have you ever sexually assaulted anyone?"

João turns to her and shouts, "Yes! Your Mother!"

They keep filming. Heather and João returned to Usher. João was pissed off. He reached out toward the camera and said, "I want to see what you have already filmed. Show it to me!"

The translator told him the bad news—no. João grabbed her arm, the way he does when he molests someone, with a restraining hold, and he barked, "No! I will see it!"

Usher removed João's hand from his translator's arm at that point and said, 'No, don't do that.'

The entire interview is over in a few minutes, but the impression it leaves is lasting.

The program aired around the time of João's scheduled event in Sydney in November. At the closing of his program, Usher said, "Don't go see him. To do so would be a waste of money. Please think twice before you go. I don't want Australians to be fooled by John Faria, John of God, or this circus that has formed around him."

But when João visited Sydney in November 2014, people paid up to $795 for a three-day ticket at the Sydney Showgrounds. Six thousand people were in attendance—a sold-out event.

Diego Coppola, who appeared at several other events, was the translator for this trip. He is one of the Casa insiders. We will discuss him later.

After the big show, the Casa group consecrated the Casa de Dom Inácio opening in Australia. It sported the obligatory giant crystal purchased from João. A couple from Sydney sponsored the Casa.

In 2019, the Brazilian prosecutor's office received reports from three Australian women. They were allegedly sexually abused by John of God. There were also allegations of the suicide of one of his Australian victims. And a denunciation by a woman involved with adopting Brazilian babies. However, very few people knew about this in 2014.

Back home in Abadiânia, this was the year that João tested the waters on the other side of the highway. A son of the Casa was getting married in the Catholic church and asked João to be his best man. The Medium arrived. In front of dozens of guests, the priest said he wouldn't hold the wedding if João attended. João didn't argue and left immediately. [186]

Ultan visited again and told me João's wife, Ana Keyla, wanted a divorce. This was a problem. He transferred the passiflora business to her name to avoid taxes and investigations. He was about to lose an enormously profitable business. João put her through law school, and she is now an attorney. He was much more concerned about the loss of revenue than threats of divorce. He refused to grant a divorce.

For some years, Ultan told me stories of his confrontations with João. According to Ultan, he no longer attended the Casa (YouTube videos refute this). His marriage to Alessandra was proving to be a problematic relationship. They would break up and then get back together. João was often in the middle of the drama, a provocateur.

He encouraged her to get a law degree. Ultan suspected her of having sexual encounters with the Medium. There were threats and extortions. Several times, João demanded certain things from Ultan. He threatened him directly or through his son or lawyers. João got violent in Frutti's with Ultan on one occasion and struck him.

Meanwhile, Ultan was getting richer and richer. He had many employees and a reputation as one of Abadiânia's most important players.

It was difficult for Ultan to avoid João, who opened an enormous crystal shop directly across the street from Frutti's—part of his strip mall where he also ran a travel agency and money-changing (money laundering) office. He even attempted to open a restaurant like Frutti's but was unsuccessful.

João was lusting for Frutti's and for Ultan's wife. According to Ultan, João provoked her to take many harmful actions. Over several years, he had created permanent tension within this family. The public knew nothing of this. For years, Ultan attempted to sell Frutti's and escape the harassment.

Ultan told me that João was a father again, this time with his most recent wife, Ana Keyla Teixeira Lourenço, thirty years younger than him. This is his eleventh child or so, but who knows? Ana Keyla had known João since she was ten years old. There were no more threats of divorce.

Ultan also had a story about Seu Lazaro's son. My friend Lazaro José Beira passed away. His son, Israel, inherited the homestead. He was a tough character, a hoodlum with a permanent scowl and a bad eye. Lazaro was afraid of him. His son pushed him around. After Lazaro died, his son revived the garrafada business. He learned how to make the remedies from his dad. He sold his remedies to João's tourists.

It seems there were confrontations. Remember the history Lazaro had with João? His son had the opposite disposition of Lazaro. Ultan told me they found Israel's body at the homestead—executed with his penis cut off and stuffed in his mouth.

Of course, Ultan didn't make any connection with João and this business. It was well known around town that Israel was into drugs and considered crazy. He was aggressive and threatening. Anyone he knew might have killed him. To my knowledge, this case also died due to a lack of evidence.

Much later, I would learn that Erika Beira, who inherited the homestead after the death of Israel, also had confrontations with João. She began investigating Israel's death, and then she received death threats. She died under mysterious circumstances in Brasilia. Her sister is married to one of João's thugs.[187]

Late in 2014, João complained of stomach pain. His exam showed he had stomach cancer. He kept this a secret. He received five months of chemotherapy at the Sírio-Libanês Hospital, one of Brazil's top hospitals. He would travel to São Paulo on the weekends, receive the therapy, and return for the following sessions at the Casa.

The chemotherapy wasn't enough to cure João's cancer. He returned to the same hospital in the summer for a dangerous and radical surgery. He spoke to the Casa and said, "Brothers and sisters, sons and daughters of the House. For the first time in many years, I am going to spend some time away. I'm going to have surgery that I can't do. It's a thing in my stomach. What do they call it? A hernia." [188]

The operation lasted ten hours, cutting out half of his stomach. The surgery and recovery process forced him to take his first vacation in thirty years. He disappeared from the Casa for five weeks. One was in New York, returning to the Omega Institute while hiding his condition. But even after he was cured, the leader kept this secret. The staff also lied about his health.

Heather Cumming said, "After routine examinations, a hernia was observed in his stomach, and the doctor chose to remove it [sic] at that time. But he is doing very well."

Amy Nolen. Photo from her Facebook page.

In February 2015, one of the Casa attendees was found dead in her apartment in Abadiânia. There were rumors of a suspicious death, a gas leak, or an accident.

Her name was Amy Sterling Nolen, age forty-six, and her passing was shrouded in mystery. Some people said she found out about the molestations and was making a fuss. The Abadiânia civil police investigated her death as a suicide, file #85-2015-03.03.2015.

The only record of Amy on the internet is her obituary and a Go Fund Me post. It raised over $5,000 to help defray the cost of returning her remains to America. She was an army veteran living in Fort Meyers, Florida. Her husband wrote that the authorities had not yet determined her cause of death.[189]

Seventeen rape allegations occurred in 2015—incredible under the circumstances. Around this time, one of my neighbors hosted a young woman and assisted her in taking a twenty-one-day liquid fast. I visited, and we had a cup of tea.

The girl mentioned finishing the fast the next day and visiting the Casa de Dom Inácio. This would be her first visit. She fasted to prepare herself for her healing with Medium João. I cringed as she was so earnest, frail, young, and pretty.

I warned her not to be alone with the Medium. She was too far off in the clouds to pay attention. A couple of weeks later, my neighbor told me that on the day she arrived in Abadiânia, João molested her. When the flood of denunciations against João began in 2019, she was not among them.

In February 2016, João was featured in a special edition of Newsweek, *Spiritual Living: The Secret to Peace and Happiness. Introduction with John of God, the Miracle Healer* was printed on the front cover. The article is in the voice of Gail Thackray, the only person interviewed. You can imagine the insipid content.[190]

Ultan finally escaped Frutti's and Abadiânia in 2016. He suffered many years of psychological abuse from João. He sold the restaurant for a fortune. Indeed, he saw the handwriting on the wall.

The Space in Between, a film by the world-famous performance artist Marina Abramović, debuted in May 2016. She traveled to Brazil from 2012 to 2015 and filmed her performance pieces, often cleverly embedded within other people's *performance pieces.*[191]

She enjoyed several of Brazil's exotic fringe hot spots, including the Casa, her first stop in 2012. Directed by the Brazilian Marco Del Fiol, the film follows Marina Abramović on her road trip. She experiences spiritual surgeries, ayahuasca rituals, shamanic ceremonies, Candomblé terreiros, and the surreal Valley of the Dawn cult outside of Brasilia. There are photo ops in caves, waterfalls, crystal mines, and the vast expanses of the Cerrado.

She liked the Casa. It is undoubtedly performance art. She has an affinity with all that cutting and blood. The shock value is seductive. Abramović's work is often about pain and shock. She was invited to hold the tray and watch (and film).

The artist said, "I came to Brazil looking for places of power and people with a certain type of energy."

Abramović captured a gruesome bit of film footage at close range. João squeezed a man's eyeball until it bulged out of the socket. He took the same paring knife he always uses and scraped the eye. A large dark bruise appeared, and the white turned blood red. The man didn't protest. The camera filmed this at close range in perfect focus. In her discussion, she tells us she wasn't shocked or shaken by the eyeball scraping and cuts. She is quite insensitive to physical pain.

The film did a great job capturing the wild, insane look João adopts when incorporated. They gave Abramović celebrity status and told her to sit in the chair next to João during the sessions. Although what she filmed in Abadiânia is brief, it is probably the only artsy film about the medium. The other Casa films were homemade travelogues crafted to sell tours.

She points out the crowds of poor Brazilians desperately hoping for a miracle and the last chance situation of many of his patients. With no wild claims, she portrayed the Casa as it was, or perhaps how it appeared to be. *The Space in Between* is a spooky presentation couched in new-age terms.

In late July, Carolina Pereira Lins Mesquita visited the Casa for the sixth time. She was a doctorate candidate writing her thesis with the Casa as her subject. This was her field project. She was a professor at the University Federal do Rio de Janeiro, with a doctorate in Judicial Science and a master's degree in Anthropology. She also worked as an adviser to a judge of the TRT in Rio de Janeiro.

This was her first field research. Her thesis (published in 2018) analyzes the judicial proceedings brought against the medium, "which has not been examined in detail and analytically in any research so far." She gathered investigations based on two hundred fifty-two pages of field notes and one hundred thirty-four pages of interview transcripts.[192]

On a previous visit, she made the mistake of asking the Medium about allegations made against him *before the end of the dictatorship.* This is a charged and taboo topic. João hadn't forgotten. He certainly didn't want her prying into his past associations with the military regime.

After a long drive to the Casa from Rio de Janeiro, she awoke early, dressed in white, and waited in line to speak to the Medium. She had been following all the Casa protocols, taking the passiflora, and observing the dietary restrictions.

This was her third visit to his private office. This time, he locked the door. He explained that this was the day of the Casa's celebration of the anniversary of Dom Inácio. He didn't want to be disturbed. João was well aware of the subject of her fieldwork to underline the audacity of what happened next. It was about criminal charges brought against him for sexual assault.

João told her he dreamed of her in a river and that he was waiting for her. This river theme is tangled in his rape history, Quimbanda roots, and devotion to Saint Rita.

He told her she must get married and that he would help. She replied that she wasn't interested in marrying. Then he scolded her for holding down three jobs as she was going through her doctoral process. He suggested she should drop her thesis project.

João directed her to stand with him behind her, her eyes closed and breathing deeply. He put his hands on her hips and told her to take deep breaths and "move it." He said, "Not just any man can handle you. You need a pulse and a lot of fire."

Carolina turned around and saw that João had taken out his erect and lubricated penis. She said nothing but made eye contact and shot him a look that could kill. It broke the spell.

He put it back in his pants and asked for her favorite color. He told her to reply with the first color to come to mind. He opened a cabinet and gave her a faceted smokey quartz crystal shaped like a heart. It was not the color she had chosen.

João frequently offered a crystal or cut gem after the assault. It's a hallmark of his perversion, like paying the prostitutes he frequented all his life. If the crystal isn't enough to silence her and fear doesn't have its desired effect, he threatens her and her loved ones with violence or death.

Then João brought up the subject of her thesis and the lawsuits she was researching. He called someone on his cell phone. In a few minutes, several people came to his office. They sat in a semicircle with João at the head. The staff who were usually called to intercede in such situations had convened.

Seated by Professor Mesquita were Hamilton Pereira, Chico Lobo, Heather Cumming, another well-known female staff member, and some people she had never met.

One of these strangers addressed her, saying he was a policeman, a lieutenant colonel. He said he was responsible for "the pacification of Rio de Janeiro's neighborhoods without deaths." Rio de Janeiro's pacification projects always result in shootouts and deaths. Or people are hunted down by secret police vigilante groups. The cop lifted his shirt and showed her a scar.

The professor felt intense fear. The policeman spoke about death and healing. He mentioned some ministers of the Supreme Court, whom he randomly quoted. She can't remember the entire conversation. It felt like hours of psychological torture. She pretended to be unaware of what had happened and played dumb.

Her impression was that everyone present in this meeting knew exactly what had happened. She was not the first victim. They were there for damage control. They arrived instantly, prepared to deal with a common problem at the Casa. The women present displayed no sympathy. Heather Cumming complained about the delay on this party day with a packed Casa.

The afternoon session had been delayed more than two hours. Professor Mesquita was told she must assist João and hold the instrument tray for his surgeries. A volunteer arrived and tried to escort her to the current room. The professor explained she needed to eat, not having eaten anything since seven a.m. Her escort insisted she must immediately assist with the tray.

She allowed her to use the bathroom first.

She said, "That's when I washed my face, did some yoga breaths, and organized myself internally. This was no time for resistance. Subterfuge, docility, passivity, and complacency protected me in this place, which became inhospitable. I was being watched, and my steps were being watched.

"I had finally accessed the profane space of the House of Dom Ignatius of Loyola, and I felt uncomfortable in it."

I read her account several times. I realized that part of João's macumba was having his victims hold the surgery tray after their molestation. Standing at the medium's side, they assist in his magic ritual of blood and sexual trauma. He initiates them in a trial of terror.

The entity uses the energy generated by the perversion to perform the surgeries. This current penetrates everyone sitting in meditation. The staff's insistence on her holding the tray suggests they knew the secret. Fortunately for Professor Mesquita, there were no surgeries in this session.

She was in a troublesome situation. Carolina called friends and told them what had happened. They cautioned her and advised her to leave immediately. She asked for advice and direction from her thesis mentors.

The reluctant tray holder. Photo: Michael Bailot.

Deciding to stay, she resumed her research with the legal documents at the Abadiânia courthouse. She was fearful and always looked over her shoulder. When at the Casa, Carolina pretended that there was no problem. Chico Lobo looked at her like, "What the hell is she still doing here?"

The film crew for *O Silêncio é Uma Prece,* directed by Candé Salles, was filming the surgeries on these days. The entity João was incorporating for these surgeries was José Penteado (Exu Penteado). The title, *Silence is a Prayer,* is a shocking reminder of the wall of silence that protected João Teixeira de Faria for fifty years. All of João's victims were forced to make the prayer of silence.

Carolina understood the shaky legal ground she stood on from the perspective of a woman who studies judicial law. If she denounced the Medium to the police, it was her word against him with no witnesses. She could be sued for slander or perhaps murdered. Professor Mesquita knew how casual and disinterested the police and judicial system were about sexual abuse.

Carolina divided her remaining days at the Casa between the sessions and nervous visits to the Abadiânia courthouse. She dressed like and posed as a busy attorney going about her business. But the files she requested were those of João Teixeira de Faria.

She continued her research. She said, "I had intuitively discovered in my first field research that kitchens, beauty salons, and OAB rooms are privileged places to uncover *behind the scenes* and get good informants."

Professor Mesquita's thesis was well received and applauded. *Me Too e as Decisões* is the real thing, a sound anthropological study of what the Casa *really* is in context with what Brazil *really* is. It is a study of bravery as well.

Another academic study of João and his Casa debuted in 2016. *João de Deus: Um Médium no Coração do Brasil,* by Professor Maria Machado, who had done field research at the Casa for four years.[193]

The publisher erroneously promoted her as "The only person to date to receive João de Deus' consent to write a book." As a historian, Professor Machado has published other academic books and papers.

Once again, we have a scholar drinking the Kool-Aid, only this time, she has chugged gallons of the stuff. I don't fault her. João has his secrets; you might overlook the obvious if you are not poking around for secrets.

As this is a biography of João and a discourse on the Casa philosophy, she tries to cover a lot of ground. It seems like a superficial attempt at objective historical analysis. Although her book is from a fan's perspective, it fills in a few of the missing pieces in João's mythic biography. Very few—most of her biographical information came through Faria himself and his cookie-cutter biographers. As we have seen, he is a suspect source of the truth. Her book became the publisher's best-seller. Her publisher, Companhia das Letras, is a Brazilian imprint of Random House.

After two episodes as João's young victim, Simone Soares

converted to the Evangelical faith. In 2016, she had a series of dreams where she was at the Casa and speaking directly to João about Jesus.[194]

Tormented by the dreams, Simone felt God was directing her to go there. She couldn't resist. She told a friend of her intention, who replied that she was crazy and that they would *finish her off there.*

When she arrived at the Casa, she was met by Tião (Sebastião de Lima). He was part of the Casa mafia, considered the second in command, and João's secretary for four decades. She knew him well from childhood when he was João's right-hand man. It was from him that she heard stories about how João had been married ten times, how some of his wives died suspiciously, including one who had the brake lines of her car cut. Tião welcomed her, and she continued her mission to find João.

She found the manager and told him she was there to see the Médium. He laughed at her sarcastically and told her things didn't work that way there. She would need the Entity's permission to speak to João.

Simone waited long until someone from the soup kitchen instructed her to sit outside João's office. He came to the doorway, and she was face to face with the man that had almost killed her twenty years prior. João abused her as a twelve-year-old child and again when she returned at eighteen. He also considered having her killed.

She asked him if he remembered her. He did but had forgotten her name. She entered and sat on the sofa, the same sofa and the same room where he abused her as a child.

João asked her, "What do you want? Do you want money?" She told him she had come to talk about Jesus and that he needed to repent for his sins. This startled João. She persisted in challenging him. Simone said she was a happy person because God had "delivered her from all evil work."

At first, he appeared intimidated. A few of his staff arrived at the door, and the Medium grew angry and said, "Preach to those who are almost believers. Don't come here and preach to me."

Then, three mediums escorted her out of the office. João took her hand as they exited and threatened her. "You are very audacious to come here and preach to me." João and Simone continued to lock horns, and he grew more upset.

One of the mediums asked her where she lived. She understood they wanted to know where to send entities to harm her. But Simone said, "I still didn't get out of there. I distributed many Bibles inside and talked about the love of God. Then I got in the car and left, confident of my mission accomplished."

João is now seventy-four years old. He is accused of abusing nine women this year. One of the cases entangled João, his son Sandro, a city councilor, a lawyer, and Edna, the Casa publicist, in a criminal case. It later went to trial in 2020. They were all acquitted; the evidence was deemed insupportable.[195]

What was alleged to have occurred was a sexual assault. The victim's friend who witnessed this was visited, unannounced, at her home by João and his son Sandro. The woman was threatened if she were to testify. When she refused, she claims Sandro lifted his shirt and displayed a pistol.

In late September 2016, João and his entourage returned to the Omega Institute for their eighth visit, an event organized by Heather Cumming. There were 1,760 attendees.

Silence is a Prayer

Dalva and João in a posed moment of remorse.
Photo: from video posted to Casa Facebook page.

João's daughter Dalva hit rock bottom since they last parted ways. She was addicted to crack cocaine, pimped, thin as a ghost, and without teeth. She landed back in Itapaci, João's childhood home—as well as hers. Her shocked family called on João for help. In 2016, he committed her to a rehabilitation center. He paid to get her fixed up and with new teeth. They held her there until João signed for her release.

Dalva's two sons, Paulo and João Paulo, now adults, sued their grandfather, João Teixeira de Faria, in 2017. They accused him of repeated acts of incest and rape within his family and lethal intimidation. For the first time, he was publicly accused of abusing their mother.[196]

Their valiant effort to help Dalva almost cost them their lives. Hired thugs beat them in a surprise attack as they sat in a restaurant. They endured repeated menacing threats to close the lawsuit.

Then, João showed up with his lawyer at the hospital where she was being held. Dalva said that her father told her that the lives of his grandsons were in grave danger. If she would renounce the abuse claims, she could save her boys.

In one of the most sickening episodes of this man's life, his lawyer positioned Dalva and her father sitting together on a sofa. He asked her to pet her father's hair to show her love and respect.

He videotaped them with his iPhone. As Dalva nervously strokes her father's head, she speaks into the camera, addressing her children.

In a forced sarcastic manner, she said, "Hi, Paulo Henrique, João Paulo, and Luana. I am very happy with you. The things you are doing, extorting money from my father, saying that I got into drugs through my father. And I am sure that you don't know what you are doing to my father. There is someone behind it.

"Because you wouldn't lie in my name. That my father was with me [sexually]. That I got pregnant by my father. That he was already [sexually] with Luana [Dalva's daughter]. If this had happened, the one who was extorting him would have been me, who was the most damaged one. I am ashamed that you say that *my father raped my mother and my grandmother.*

"Why don't you let him live in peace? Is this all about money? You could be nice—Grandpa, I need so much, and I need this just like he did for you all your life. The best clothes, the best schools, the best cars. He gave you everything you have. Didn't he?"

Later, the Casa posted this video on their Facebook page, denouncing Dalva as an insane drug addict.[197]

This year, twelve more women accused João of rape. The victim who suffered six months of João's rapes while her father died of cancer returned to the Casa.[198]

"I was there to heal," she said, "there to forgive the man that had nearly destroyed my life."

She passed through the line and finally found herself before the Medium. She said, "I came here to forgive someone who did me a lot of harm. To get it out of me." Eleven years had passed.

João smiled. He stared at her breasts and said, "Stop by the Medium's Room." She left without forgiving him or resolving her trauma.

In 2017, Oxford University Press published *John of God: The Globalization of Brazilian Faith Healing.* The author, Professor Cristina Rocha, studied João for ten years. She is a Professor of Anthropology at Western Sydney University. Rocha has written on Buddhism, New Age spirituality, and Pentecostal faiths.

Professor Rocha first visited the Casa in 2004. She visited

almost every year afterward and lived there for six months in 2007. Professor Rocha attended five John of God events in Germany, Australia, and New Zealand.

She participated in the cult's Australian circles and visited tour guides and followers. From 2004 to 2015, she was a member of a Kardecist Spiritist association. She also took a mediumship course. Later, she began making healing passes at the spiritist meetings. Although not considered a child of the Casa, she had permission to observe the workings of the house—*ten* years of fieldwork ensued.

From the perspective of many anthropologists, one might say that she had gone native and drank at least a few sips of the Kool-Aid. This is an anthropological study published by a prestigious university press. I suppose she hadn't crossed the professional line as had Emma Bragdon, who used her credentials to promote her tours. Did Professor Rocha promote the Casa and João? Of course.

Rocha said, "Following the approaches of experiential anthropology, anthropology of humanism and if people tell me that they have been healed by religious practices—be they prayer, rituals, or spiritual surgeries—I accept it."[199]

She gave credence to the popular myth from her perspective as a believer. The book is good, and the anthropology is well-studied and presented.

Her discussion of the internationalization of healers, gurus, and new-age philosophy is *right* on. Her book was helpful in my research as well. No one had written a better book about the Casa philosophy. Cambridge University Press! João might have been very proud of himself had he been able to read it. She added to his growing list of endorsements by respected people who should have known better.

Cristina Rocha relates the story of her first interview with João Teixeira de Faria. It occurred while she attended one of his events in New Zealand in 2006. No one had briefed him about her study, her credentials, or her questions for the interview.

She introduced herself, and immediately, João was on the defensive. He shouted angrily that he wasn't a charlatan. He mockingly confronted her, asking what a Brazilian was doing in Australia. Did she think she was a big deal because of her degree?

When she finally felt the courage to address why she was there—to write a book about him, he told her to talk to his lawyer. He pulled out a folder containing testimonies by right-wing politicians, journalists, and celebrities. All praised his integrity.

Professor Rocha points out, "The sharp disconnect between

the image of the healer as an enlightened, generous, loving being, painted by his followers in books and chats, and the reality of his absolute power caught me by surprise."

In October 2017, Heather Cumming hosted the ninth John of God event at the Omega Institute. A re-run of all the others, with 1,500 in attendance. Omega had installed a large portrait of John of God beside other revered guests. He joined the ranks of Gloria Steinem, Eckhart Tolle, Toni Morrison, Pema Chödrön, Maya Angelou, Woody Guthrie, and Al Gore. It would be his last visit. I wonder if his portrait still hangs there.

A few days after the Omega event, João and crew attended the premiere screening of *O Silêncio é Uma Prece (Silence is a Prayer)*. It was a gala event at the Rio de Janeiro Film Festival. A crowd of João's groupies and the notable in-crowd of Rio de Janeiro were in attendance. João made an emotional speech.[200]

This was the pinnacle of João Teixeira de Faria's life. Produced by Paris Films, the documentary film cost millions and was five years in the making. Some say that João helped bankroll the movie. The Casa's public relations chief, Edna Gomez, wrote the screenplay. The director, Candé Salles, was a close friend of the Medium.

O Silêncio é Uma Prece debuted in theaters in 2018. Most critics panned it for its complete lack of objectivity. It was a love fest praising João in exaggerated and sentimental tropes. Reviewers gave it a one or two-star rating. They considered it an institutional video of self-promotion. It starred John of God, actress Cissa Guitarães, and a cameo appearance of Marina Abramović, the filmmaker and performance artist.[201]

In one memorable scene (I think it was filmed at the Swiss event), João picks up a glass next to his throne and begins eating it! He bites off chunks, chews them, and washes them down with water. Someone shouts, "It's King Solomon." He was not allowed to make his cuts in foreign countries, and the Medium felt the show needed more drama.[202]

This shocking event was later explained in an interview with one of his staff who assisted at the event—his disillusioned nephew. The glass was a magician's prop made of crystallized sugar.

The Casa Newsletter of 2018 issued a press release. "John of God, known in Brazil as João de Deus, received the Order of Malta (Maltese Cross) in a special ceremony held on May 4, 2018, in Brazil. He was accompanied by his wife Ana and daughter Mariana Francisca. It's an ancient honor that originated in approximately 1099 at the time of the Knights Templar."[203]

The Casa newsletter did not mention that the Sovereign Order of Malta is similar to the Vatican. It issues its own passports and postage stamps, has foreign ambassadors, and positions itself as a charitable organization, something like the Red Cross.[204]

The group is actually a secretive international Military Order with a long and bloody history and unique status under international law. Based in Rome, it answers directly to the Pope. However, it is a controversial society often criticized and censured by the papacy. The Order has bilateral diplomatic relations with over 110 countries and is a Permanent Observer at the United Nations.

The Order of Malta is a secret society, membership by invitation only. It is rooted in the Knights Templar, Freemasonry, and Hermeticism and has a history of intrigues spanning over 900 years. Many politicians and important world figures have been nominated for the order. Its inductees have included thousands of members of European royalty over many centuries. King Charles and Queen Camilla are members.

Among the international political figures inducted were President George Bush, Sr., Tony Blair, William J. Donovan (ex-head of the OSS), William J. Casey (ex-head of the CIA), Alexandre Haig (former Secretary of State), Joseph P. Kennedy Jr (JFK's father), James Jesus Angleton (notorious former chief of counterintelligence for the CIA), and Benito Mussolini (Italian Fascist dictator during WW2).

Foreign Policy Explainer noted, "In 2011, Veteran New Yorker journalist Seymour Hersh alleged that the US military's Joint Special Operations Command [JSOC] had been infiltrated by Christian fanatics [The Order of Malta] who see themselves as modern-day Crusaders and aim to change mosques into cathedrals."

The order has been a popular target for conspiracy theorists. It is identified as an extreme right-wing group that aided the fascists and Nazis in WW2. They facilitated the ratlines and Operation Paper Clip, which helped thousands of Nazis war criminals escape after the fall of Berlin. Most of them ended up in the US, South America, and Russia.

Various theories have tied the Knights to the Kennedy assassination and to the spreading of AIDS through its clinics in Africa. In 2006, a newspaper article in the United Arab Emirates claimed that the Knights were directly influencing U.S. policy in Iraq and Afghanistan, reprising the Crusades.[205]

Fourteen rape accusations against Medium João occurred this year. Four of them were to become one of the first cases filed against João, in which he was found guilty and sentenced.

*The Sovereign Military Order of Saint John of Malta.
Photo: Creative Commons.*

João's induction in the Order of Malta, pictured with his wife and daughter. Photo: Casa press release.

It seems João's Exus felt neglected with all his absences during the road shows. They needed more blood. Dalva's sons were proceeding with their lawsuit. In July, their lawyer, Sergio Beze Prates, was shot point blank while sitting in his car conversing with a client, killing the attorney and wounding his passenger. The unidentified shooters fled in a black luxury car. Testimonies allege that Sergio had provoked João Teixeira de Faria, leaving him no way out of the situation. His grandsons had absolute proof against him. João stood to lose a lot of money and face an inglorious public shaming. The case is unresolved, a murder with no suspects. His grandsons wouldn't be hiring a new lawyer. [206]

One of João's staunchest allies is Marcos Eduardo Elias, a

high-profile Brazilian billionaire. In late August 2018, he was arrested in Switzerland and extradited to the US. The FBI detained him, and he faced charges of embezzling $750,000 from a New York bank. He was later convicted and sentenced to three and a half years.[207]

João and his crew, including Martin and Fernanda Mosquera, were briefly detained along with their billionaire buddy in Miami in late September. João was nervous that they would serve him with papers as well. He imagined there were charges against him still active in Sedona. We will have more to discuss regarding Mr. Elias later.

While compiling this chapter, I discovered one more letter posted by a Casa tour guide, who didn't return. She wrote, "My last trip to Brazil to see John of God with my group of people was in September 2018. Something deep within me knew it was my last trip. I was not ready to see what I saw on that day in September 2018. It was after the morning session in the current room.

"My group had returned to the posada where we were staying, and I stayed behind to gather my thoughts and feel the sunshine. I was sitting on the wall outside in the area where the King Solomon triangle is located and directly across from one of John of God's offices.

"I saw two very young girls dressed in daisy-duke-type shorts with high heels on. They were walking on the lawn outside of the wall where I was sitting. I said to myself that's odd, as they were not dressed in the white clothing, and their clothing appeared very sparse. I saw them knock on the door of John of God's office. They walked into the office, and one of them said in English, 'I brought you somebody new.' I thought that was odd, as I always believed John of God did not speak any English at all. After about fifteen or twenty minutes, I heard a loud screaming coming from John of God as I am very familiar with his voice and the sound of it. It was the sound of someone having an orgasm, and he was screaming at the top of his lungs.

"Directly thereafter, within five minutes, I saw the women leave his office. After the women left, I saw someone bring a tray of food to his office." I am certain I could not have been the only one that heard that loud scream from John of God. Feeling devastated and confused, I did not know what to do or what to think. I always heard people joking about his taste for young, pretty women, but I could not believe what I had seen.

"I knew it was wrong, as well as I knew he would be sitting in the afternoon sessions for the people. It was common knowledge that John of God was married to Ana and had a baby daughter, so I felt much sadness in my heart. The volume of his screams had to be heard, yet no one did anything except bring him his lunch. I have held this within my own being and shared it only with one dear friend. I can only imagine what the women feel like holding the secret of being sexually abused/or coerced. When I read Gail Thackray's blog, which stated there is no such thing as a private room and private bathroom, or private sessions—that is not true. John of God has a private office on those grounds, and there are always women lined up to go in there after sessions. I have seen this many, many times." [208]

Another sacrifice would be made to The Casa Exus. As Professor Mesquita wrote, "João de Deus had a harem, composed of those who consented and those who did not." Several victims succumbed to his magical control and were sexually enslaved for weeks or months. They were part of this harem. Other women consented, either to save their life (or a loved one's life), receive a promised cure, a favored position in the Casa, financial help, or by fatal attraction.

Gigi. Photo: Gigi's Facebook page.

We probably will never know which type of situation trapped Gigi in João's spider web. But Gigi, Giana Peres Pires, was in love with João Teixeira de Faria. She had frequented the Casa for two years and was living there. She was thirty-eight and came from Camaquã, Rio Grande do Sul. Her mysterious death on August 30, 2018, is listed as an unsolved murder.[209]

There are rumors, and there are documents. First, the rumors: she was in love with João, but it was unrequited. The Casa staff accused her of treason. She traveled to her home state for weight loss surgery. When she returned to Abadiânia, the Casa staff grilled her about where she had been and for what purpose. In a matter of days, she turned up dead. The Casa declared it was suicide. The police were considering murder for hire, mainly because the body disappeared overnight and was transported to the south of Brazil in Rio Grande do Sul and immediately buried.

The documents: The Abadiania civil police listed this as a suspected murder (Occurrence 8173323). They named no suspect. Was this a murder disguised as a suicide? Very few people can answer that question. Her last Facebook post was late in 2017. Her obituary said, "Giana Peres Pires dies at 38 years old. The body is being viewed at the Camaquense Funeral Home. The burial will be at Bom Pastor Cemetery," and nothing more.

VIII.
THE SHIT HITS THE FAN

December 7, 2018

A friend sent me an email. A television special about João, on Brazil's most popular channel, had aired the night before, exposing João as a rapist to almost everyone's surprise. There would be no turning back and no damage control. The situation immediately flew out of control. Brazil was to witness their version of Jeffrey Epstein. This was the birth of the Brazilian *Me-Too Movement.* The repercussions continue like strong aftershocks to this day.[210]

The program aired on Conversa com Bial, a popular talk show on TV Globo. Pedro Bial and reporter Camila Appel created a production that was not at all like his typical program. It came as a shock to all of Brazil. It aired while the Casa received up to 30,000 monthly visitors, and João was praised by three Brazilian presidents, governors, senators, and Supreme Court Justices.

First, there were Zahira Mous's raw and uncensored accusations, with tears streaming down her cheeks, knitting her hands, and gasping for composure. She was filmed live (in a talk show format) with an American tour guide, Amy Biank. They both spoke in English, as did Bial, with Portuguese subtitles.

Thirteen victims gave testimony to Bial. Mous, Biank, and three unidentified Brazilian women aired on the show. The unidentified women were Brazilian, their faces and voices obscured. They radiated the fear and the necessary anonymity permeating the program.

Amy Biank's interview was especially shocking. She recounts a day she brought one of her clients to the Medium's private office, where Amy was told to wait outside.

She said, "I heard a cry for help and went inside. He asked me to close my eyes and sit down. I saw that he had his pants open. She was on her knees, and he had a towel over his shoulder. She didn't want to give him oral sex; that's why she screamed. I sat on the couch and closed my eyes *because I was indoctrinated into thinking that everything was divine and special.* She screamed again. I opened my eyes, and he stopped. Then he told the girl that she had passed the test and rewarded her with a matched pair of crystals."

That evening, João visited Biank at her posada. He wanted to set the record straight, telling her that when he was not incorporated, he was an ordinary man with a man's needs.

Later, a Casa staff member said, "What goes on behind closed doors is nobody's business. You're a white woman, and white women disappear all the time in Brazil. You should get on a plane and leave now."

But before she left, she spoke with some of the Casa volunteer women who helped during the services. She told them what was going on and asked them to police João. Some of them wept.

One volunteer said she was told to clean the mouth of a little girl, about six or seven, of ectoplasm. It was semen. The Casa worker was shaking as she realized what had been going on. She explained that this happened often. The children were given a special lunch afterward. Biank brought groups to the Casa forty-eight times from 2002 to 2012.

Amy Biank has a lot of explaining to do. In her published remarks, it becomes apparent that she knew of these sexual assaults for some years yet continued to bring tour groups. It wasn't until she got caught in the middle of a crime and was threatened that she talked about her experiences. It was apparent early on that she would not be a reliable spokeswoman for the victims.[211]

She projected a strange image of a believer caught in an inconvenient moment. In a YouTube interview, she repeatedly laughs nervously when she talks about the molestations.

She says inappropriate things at the wrong time. One example is an embarrassing moment after Zahira tells Bial the details of her rape. She explained how she attended him on stage afterward with the instrument tray. Amy said, *"You know Zahira, that's considered an enormous honor to hold the surgery tray."* Zahira looked at Amy incredulously. What kind of honor is it to be raped and then conscripted to assist in his bloody fake surgeries?

Brazil and the media jumped into the fray. The program, *Conversations with Bial* exposed thirteen rape charges. The next morning, the newspaper O Globo revealed three new accusations. The following day, the Journal Nacional reported on two other victims. This began an avalanche of reports.

Three days after the televised program, the Public Prosecutor's offices of São Paulo and Goiás created a task force to deal with all the accusations. They publicized a toll-free number and an e-mail address where you could make your denouncement online.

Pedro, Zahira, and Amy. GLOBO—Conversa com Bial. Artistic reproduction.

Nearly eight hundred complaints were filed with the prosecutor's office. They continued to receive more complaints as of late 2022.

In December, the TV stations, news journals, and magazines all sent crews to tiny Abadiânia. They overwhelmed the streets of Lindo Horizonte and packed the Casa. All were hungry for interviews. They were met with a wall of silence and couldn't find anyone to denounce the Medium. The only people agreeing to an interview were defending João and the Casa.

The internet was flooded with postings about João. YouTube and Facebook were clogged with field reports. Conspiracy theorists, ex-guides, devotees, and victims venting their frustration added their opinions. The news hit the wire services. Overnight, it reached headline status around the world. The media pressure in Abadiânia didn't let up. They mingled with Casa staff and various tour groups who were just learning about the scandal themselves. There were heated discussions in Frutti's. Everyone associated with the Casa agreed that this was a conspiracy against their João. Those women were hysterical attention-grabbing sluts looking for money.

On December 11, the owners of Editora Companhia das Letras suspended the distribution of the book *João de Deus—A Medium in the Heart of Brazil.* Well-known historian Maria Helena Pereira Toledo Machado, a professor at UNICAMP University in São Paulo, is the author. The newspaper O Globo interviewed the historian right after the scandal broke. She said, "I talked to hundreds of people. I interviewed many, and none of this came to light. In none of the statements did any interviewee mention having suffered any embarrassment or harassment. I am dismayed."[212]

The same day, Paris Films announced it suspended marketing of the documentary *João de Deus–Silence is a Prayer* and withdrew it from all digital platforms. Both the book and the film were shameless accolades and veneration. It was not the time to sing the praises of the Casa de Dom Inácio. Many celebrities, politicians, and lawmakers made public statements washing their hands of Medium João.[213]

Then João disappeared. On December 12, five days after Pedro Bial's show aired, the Public Ministry of Goiás issued an order. They asked the court for João Teixeira de Faria's preventative detention (arrest). The same day, the press reported that one of his victims allegedly committed suicide. Behind the scenes, João and friends prepared his eight-seater airplane for flight. The police grounded the plane.

The Brazilian police requested that INTERPOL intervene should he flee the country. INTERPOL sent out a bulletin to intercept the fugitive.

The authorities also froze his primary bank account. A day or two before, he requested a transfer of thirty-five million reais into the account, which had a value of about ten million dollars at the time. The police suspected he planned to withdraw this and flee in an airplane to another country.[214]

On December 12, João returned to the Casa for the first time since the allegations were made on Conversa com Bial on the seventh. He and his lawyers and handlers had to fight through the enormous crowd of devotees and media crews. People were pushed and punched by his bodyguards. João didn't look good. He was sweating and haggard. He wasn't prepared for the role he was about to play.

His group finally gained access to the stage, and he addressed the crowd and a wall of cell phones, cameras, and microphones. The medium claimed he was innocent. He said, "My dear brothers and my dear sisters, I thank God that I am here. I am still a brother of God, but I want to comply with Brazilian law because I am in the hand of Brazilian law. João de Deus is still alive. The peace of God be with you."[215]

Then he fled, pursued by a crowd. He had spent less than ten minutes on what would be his last visit to the Casa. João asked to have the plaster statue of Saint Rita placed on his throne. He refused requests to hand over the Casa to another medium.

Publicist Edna Gomes said that the medium had a hypertension crisis and left abruptly for this reason. He was still a man avoiding arrest.

On December 13, João's attorney, Alberto Zacharias Toron, responded to the papers served for João's detention with his own request of the Court. Toron requested the court allow the medium to continue the Casa de Dom Inácio services.

In a matter of a few days, our poor, illiterate farmer had acquired one of Brazil's most sought-after criminal lawyers (and most expensive). It wasn't only a lawyer but a large law firm of aggressive specialists who were instantly on the defensive. Who had these connections? Who arranged this?[216]

Remember João's buddy, who was arrested for defrauding a New York City bank, Marcos Elias? Marcos Elias, Brazil's brash hedge fund billionaire, along with publicist Nizan Guanaes, arranged this. These two are very close friends and buddies of João. João often hung out with them when he was visiting São Paulo. Alberto Toron is a good friend of theirs as well.[217]

Nizan Guanaes is the most famous publicist in Brazil. His empire is international. Guanaes is an advertising giant and a consultant for many major corporations. He has impressive connections.

Marcos Elias's Laep Investments is known as the largest stock market fraud in Brazilian history. The government and 18,000 investors lost five billion reais (one billion dollars).[218]

His investment firm was run out of a post office box in Bermuda, with assets of 19 reais. He created 100 shell companies to move around his enormous assets, which he fraudulently gained by selling stock in a worthless enterprise. The prosecutor of this case said that probably ten crimes had been committed.

About 150 Casa staff, devotees, and local merchants held a protest march. They waved signs declaring *United for the Casa, Medium João We Are with You.* They prayed aloud as they marched down the main street by the Casa.

More and more critics and victims were going public. No one knew where João was hiding. The police began searching his dozens of properties, homes, and businesses. He had vanished. On December 14, the court ordered his apprehension for hundreds of sexual abuse and harassment allegations.

The prosecutors said, "Women heard by the Public Ministry stated that some employees of the medium João de Deus were colluding with the sexual abuse committed during the spiritual sessions in Abadiânia." According to the prosecutors, the victims named four employees. The Military Police of Goiás was investigating the case. Two of those employees are now dead.[219]

The Attorney General of Goiás, Benedito Torres Neto, opened the case. His team includes five prosecutors, two psychologists, and six delegates from various law enforcement agencies, including the agency that investigates organized crime. On December 15, they declared João Teixeira de Faria a fugitive from the law. They alerted INTERPOL and other authorities. They had searched for him at twenty of his properties to no avail.

He fled Goiás, according to his lawyer. Negotiations continued for his surrender. On December 16, his attorneys met the police on a secluded rural road near the Casa, where João surrendered. There was only one reporter at the scene. She tried to interview the Medium, who was in obvious shock. He was uncommunicative, even as she joined him in the police cruiser, hoping for a scoop. The look on his face told more than any interview could.[220]

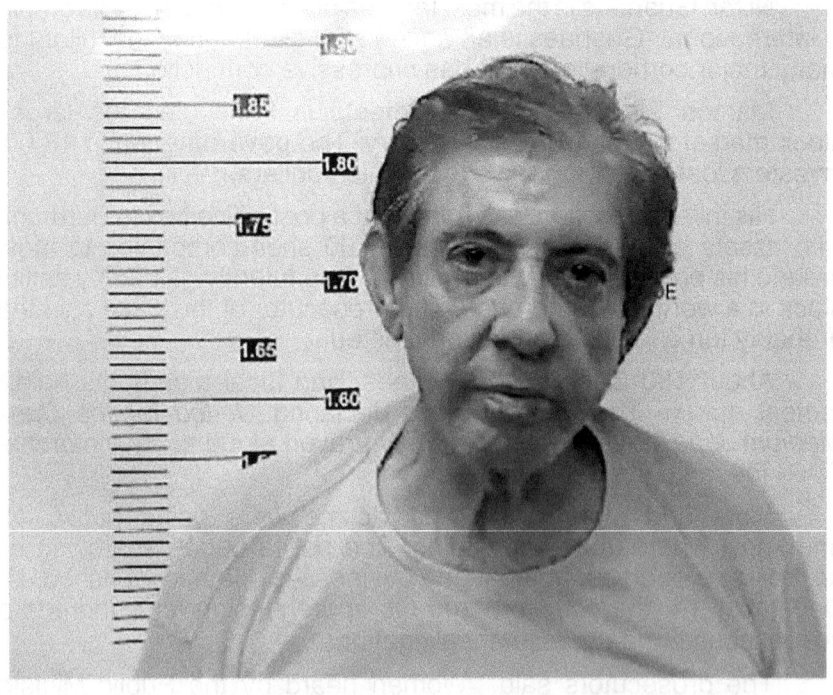

Photo: Divulgação, Federal Police of Goiás.

The police transported him to Goiânia for a preliminary booking and a two-hour interrogation. João's Exus were very pissed off. After all, he was their prisoner.

First, the clerk scheduled to record the hearing was run over on his way to the police station and broke his arm. When they began João's deposition, the computer they used to create the transcript suddenly became corrupted. Any key you pressed started typing OOOO.

The room was hot, and the interrogating officer connected the air conditioner. The extension cord exploded, burning out the refrigerator. The cops were spooked.[221]

The interrogation went nowhere. He said he did nothing he was accused of. He doesn't remember those women; he is never alone in his private office with a woman and never closes the door. He maintained his innocence.

His attorneys filed papers attempting to free the Medium from prison custody. It was tried in the high court, where his release under the right of Habeas Corpus was denied.

The same day, armed police dressed in black swarmed the Casa. They entered several of João's homes and ranches with search warrants. They found various currencies worth hundreds of thousands of dollars. Several illegal firearms were discovered. They were all unregistered, one with the serial number filed off. They also found a functioning bazooka and piles of emeralds.[222]

These searches took weeks. They found a suitcase with 1.2 million reais stuffed in it. He devised clever hiding places for the stored loot in every property he owned. In his main house, the police found hidden compartments in every drawer. A secret basement was hidden below the elevator shaft in his mansion.

They discovered his guns in a secret compartment beneath his wife's underwear drawer. They also found hidden safes. Most of the hiding places were already emptied of money, gems, and who knows what else. They found the suitcase stuffed with cash in a bunker with a cot, supplies, and more gemstones.

Around the middle of December, an exclusive interview was published in VEJA, Brazil's equivalent of Newsweek or Time. It was Dalva on their front cover, out of rehabilitation and with her terrible tale. The pretty blond Dalva that I remember from 2002 was unrecognizable. I doubted my memory when I saw her photos.[223]

By December 19, the police had received over 500 accusations of sexual assault. They came from seventeen states all over Brazil. Denunciations arrived from abroad. It included the United States (4),

Australia (3), Switzerland, Germany, Belgium, Bolivia, and Italy.[224]

Attendance dropped at the Casa by 90% in the first month. Brazilians stopped visiting, and tour groups canceled their reservations. Business came to a near standstill before the month was out. Hundreds of workers were laid off, and the posadas began closing, one after another. Most of the stragglers remaining in Abadiânia were foreigners and journalists. By New Year, it was a ghost town.[225]

Dalva Teixeira: "My Father is a Monster." VEJA cover of December 2018.

The press couldn't leave this story alone. Brazilians' overwhelming opinion was indignation. Few people came to his defense. Many tried to distance themselves from the scandal, including celebrities and politicians. Dozens of postings on YouTube denounced him and revealed more crimes.

The Prosecutors called this the most extensive sexual abuse

case in Brazilian history and perhaps in the world. They used the terms invisible web of protection, the law of silence, and conspiracy to conceal crimes. They spoke of João's personal mafia. The ongoing reportage echoed around the world. More women came forward and gave televised interviews.[226]

The State Attorney revealed the first bad news. There was a recent change in Brazilian law on sex crimes. Only accusations filed with the police within six months of the alleged crime would be permitted in court.[227]

Another law prohibited cases over ten years old from being reopened for sexual abuse if the accused is over seventy. Most of the claims against the Medium filed in the past were void. The statute of limitations was cut in half because of his age. Many cases they brought against him had occurred in the past six months!

With all these restrictions, one hundred eighty women qualified to register their accusations. Another one hundred eighty could testify to support the other victims. But they would find no legal relief for their assaults.

On December 23, the State of Goiás Health Surveillance Agency raided the Casa de Dom Inácio herbal pharmacy and closed it for thirty days. Although the Casa has a licensed pharmacist on staff, it produced the pills at industrial levels without a permit. It would reopen a month later.

The Casa upgraded its license to reflect the industrial quantity tax bracket. Chico Lobo told the police that about 10,000 people attend the Casa weekly.[228]

One bottle of passiflora pills sells for fifty reais, and a bottle of blessed water ten reais. Everyone gets a prescription. This would account for potential sales of the pills of 1 1/2 million reais per week—about 350,000 dollars. The water would gross 750,000 reais monthly.

This does not include the pills and water sold at his traveling events, revenues from the gate fees at the events, crystal bed sales and rental, gift shop sales, voluntary donations, and outright grifts.

Calculate the mandatory ten percent Entities Tax paid by tour guides, posada owners, and others, and his weekly income was astronomical. Taxi drivers, restaurants, and gift shops would also contribute a percentage. Most of these monies were paid in cash, untraceable sales.

We are looking at millions of dollars a year channeled into João's hands. As yet, the tax authorities have not addressed this issue. This may result in charges of tax evasion and money laundering, not to mention his organized crime syndicate.

Brasilia: "Judge Liciomar Fernandes da Silva, who ordered the arrest of João de Deus for illegal possession of firearms [a serious charge in Brazil] on Friday, stated that investigations show that the medium heads a criminal organization that operates mainly in the city of Abadiânia."[229]

On December 28, they filed the first formal charge. It accused João of four of his most recent rapes from the last six months. The Prosecutor explained that the charges needed to be filed within fifteen days of his arrest.

Future cases were being prepared. By 2021, they had brought fourteen separate sexual assault accusations against him. Each was made in the name of many women. More followed. The Court froze 50 million reais (more than 12 million dollars at the time) in his various bank accounts. This will compensate the victims.

The lawyer Antônio Carlos de Almeida Castro joined the defense team of the medium João de Deus. He is famous for defending those accused of Operation Lava Jato.[230]

In early January, João and his wife, Ana Keyla, were charged with illegal possession of firearms, the second case to be brought against him. Ana Keyla denied knowing of the guns.[231]

Later in the month, João was charged with a third set of crimes, along with his son Sandro Teixeira and two employees of the Casa. They accused Sandro and his father of traveling to a village in northern Goiás to intimidate a witness of one of his victims who had filed charges against him in 2016. They were accused of offering her emeralds valued at 15,000 reais if she would renege on her testimony. The woman claims that Sandro displayed a pistol when she refused the bribe.

The State claimed that João, Sandro, Edna Gomez, an attorney, and a city council member falsified and registered a document attributed to the victim. The document declared that no such abuse had happened. They were charged with witness corruption, ideological falsehood, obstruction of justice, and providing false information to forge the medium's innocence.

The city councilor is the same person mentioned in allegations brought against João of torture at the local police station, where he was a clerk decades before. There has not been another word about the rape victim or any related charges. His publicist and the councilor were charged with a lesser crime. They were only accused of falsifying a document about this case, and all were acquitted in

2021.

A new charge was filed against João, this one for the rape of five vulnerable people. The rapes occurred between 2010 to 2011. Six other women João had allegedly assaulted testified to support the victims. However, their cases would not go to trial because of the statute of limitations.

João's son, Sandro Teixeira, is the same son I read about on the front page of the newspapers in 2002. He was arrested, along with his girlfriend, for allegedly sexually molesting and torturing her three-year-old child. She lost custody of the child.[232]

Later in the month, João was interrogated for the second time by the police. He denied having committed any crimes.

In January 2019, Chico Felitti published his investigative book about João, *A Casa: A História da Seita de João de Deus (The Casa: A History of the Sect of John of God)*. This was the first book ever published that was critical of João.[233]

Felitti made several visits to collect interviews and impressions in Abadiânia. He described many of João's crimes, his checkered past, and shocking details about the town and his devotees. He portrayed the cloud of fear and silence that shrouds the Casa.

He is another brave person who opened the floodgates of suppressed information about Medium João. Mr. Felitti's work inspired me in my own peek down the rabbit hole. It was very helpful and confirmed my own experiences.

How courageous; he stayed in posadas in that miserable colony after João's imprisonment. He attempted to interview people who were too nervous or too implicated to talk. Through his persistence, he spoke with a hundred people. Abadiânia has always felt scary since I left, and more so now that it is a ghost town. Abadiânia has hugged fear to her breast and cannot escape its embrace.

The newspapers and investigative journalists began digging into João's history. They revealed more and more creepy details of his life. *More than a third of his victims were under the age of seventeen.* Fifty-seven *children* were victims and still counting. Rape by penetration was his favored method with young girls. Fifteen of them were three years old or younger at the time of the assaults.[234]

Every week, more women came forward, describing his history of forty-five years of sexual assaults. What was being revealed was a modus operandi. The women reported almost identical experiences and forms of rape.

Parallel to this, three women went public about their private investigations into João. They had gathered hundreds of reports from João's victims before the scandal was revealed.

One investigator is Maria do Carmo dos Santos, a founder of Vítimas Unidas (Victims United). She created her support group after the repercussions of a sexual abuse case committed in a fertilization clinic. Dos Santos followed João's case and maintained direct contact with dozens of women he had abused. She claimed she spoke to victims in eleven countries, and the actual number of cases is much higher than reported because of a lack of confidence in the judicial system.[235]

Lu Sudréin reported in the journal Brasil de Facto, "The group Vítimas Unidas accused supporters of João de Deus of threatening women who denounced the medium, as well as the activists who work in the support network. Maria do Carmo, for example, requested protection from the Organization of American States."

"The fear of retaliation is not an accident. Respondents repeat several times that, in Abadiânia, there are many rumors that the medium has already murdered or ordered the murder of women whom he raped so as not to be denounced."[236]

One of dos Santos' associates was Sabrina Bittencourt, a Brazilian social activist. Sabrina co-founded, with Maria do Carmo, another group working with victims of sexual assault, COAME (Combating Abuse in the Middle). Bittencourt was already involved in denouncing human trafficking in European countries. She turned her attention to Brazil and men known for their sexual abuse of patients and disciples. Bittencourt herself was raped as a teenager and was a victim of child sex trafficking as a young girl.

Sabrina registered complaints with the Public Ministry of São Paulo and Goiás about crimes committed by João Faria. They included international trafficking of children and women and illegal mining activities. She gave them documents substantiating her claims. "We have received reports from the adoptive mothers of these children who were sold for $20,000 to $50,000 in Europe, the US, and Australia," Bittencourt posted on Facebook.[237]

Her frequent postings on YouTube and Facebook brought her under scrutiny from the Casa camp. She received death threats. She also stirred up much attention in the international press. Sabrina's posts became increasingly paranoid. She claimed to be on the run, moving from country to country every couple of weeks. In a YouTube posting (she said was filmed in Morocco), we can see the hysteria that had overwhelmed her.

Meanwhile, the legal agencies investigating João were silent about her allegations. They said only that they were being investigated. In reality, the investigation was under tight wraps of secrecy. The public got their information from interviews with the victims and social media platforms—not from the prosecution or the police.

The press began putting the spotlight on Sabrina's unusual past. They interviewed ex-husbands and dug up old videos from before the Casa controversy. They portrayed her as a psychologically unstable person. For many watching her intense videos, she was clearly out of control. How much of this was fake news and an attempt to discredit her is unknown. The death threats, however, were the real thing. I had serious doubts after watching several YouTube videos by or about Sabrina.

Sabrina was fighting another YouTube figure over video accusations. He was well known in Brazil as a radical right-wing proponent and was on an obsessive and venomous campaign to discredit her whenever she posted.

Bittencourt posted this appeal shortly before her alleged suicide. "I am being persecuted by a man by the name of Paolo Pavesi. He is a guide at the Casa de Dom Inácio. And he has asked several of João's professional killers to find me."

Sabrina Bittencourt from her YouTube post in Morocco.

Bittencourt also posted this WhatsApp text shortly before her disappearance. "I confirm that Sandro Teixeira has been threatening our witnesses, coercing them, and entering people's homes. He forbade them from talking to me, Maria do Carmo Santos, and Vana Lopes from the United Victims Group. We are protecting several of these victims and witnesses. Besides offering precious stones, they have offered houses from the Minha Casa Minha Vida program in Itapaci-GO. These were "gifted" by politicians and facilitated for relatives, "oranges," employees and killers of João de Deus' gang."

"We activists have already forwarded all reports, evidence, and proof of this scandal either to the MP-GO, MP-SP, MPF, and civil deputies of Goiás responsible for the case. We requested an immediate investigation. The question remains: why are all the honest detectives being removed from the João de Deus case? How does Governor Caiado explain this, since he has said that João Teixeira de Faria is like one of his family? Please publish in full. Thank you."

Then, the drama took a turn. On February 3, 2019, Sabrina committed suicide, according to her teenage son. This looked suspicious from the very beginning. No corpse. No funeral. No police inquiry, and most importantly—no public record of her suicide or an autopsy. I could not find a single document in either Barcelona or Lebanon—the two places her family claimed were the suicide locales.[238]

One of Sabrina's friends was Felipe Neto Rodrigues Vieira, a well-known YouTuber in Brazil with over 42 *million* subscribers. He posted this on Instagram shortly after the notice of her death:

"Brazil's biggest activist, Sabrina Bittencourt, called me in tears yesterday because she couldn't stand the pain and pressure of the murderous threats that pursued her around the world. Sabrina yesterday took her own life. What she left was not just a legacy of a struggle against abusive religious leaders and ringleaders for murder, child trafficking, and kidnapping. She also left all the clues, witnesses, and letters in the hands of justice.

"I can't go into detail. I can't have these individuals after me. I'm not strong like Sabrina. I ask you from the bottom of my heart to find out who Sabrina Bittencourt was, whom she put behind bars, and whom she denounced before she died. They are powerful people who are now in control and who silenced our heroine."[239]

João, now seventy-seven years old, had been in prison for three months and was already a broken man. He lost thirty-seven pounds because he couldn't bring himself to eat the repulsive prison food.

He was self-medicating with many pills, and some were

unnecessary and made him sick. Not one friend or family member visited him, not even his wife. VEJA, the same magazine that had covered his daughter's story, was granted a prison interview.[240]

João tells them he is thinking about suicide. They describe a man who is dirty and unkempt. He urinates in his pants and cries a lot. His photos are reminiscent of Howard Hughes's last days. He is terrified at night when they turn off all the lights.

Demons torment him, and one of his cellmates has to hold his hand and comfort him during these panic attacks. João sleeps on the floor. He has had psychiatric exams, and they report he is in severe depression.

I was shocked when they said he had no other psychological disorders. If he isn't a psychopath, then what is he?

In late March, another television program, Fantástico, presented an exposé with new accusations. They revealed the case of Maria, from 1973, who alleged rape and attempted murder. They also reported the cocaine and radioactive material trafficking and murder cases and new rape allegations. All had been thrown out of court. Fantástico quoted the Public Ministry as saying, "The complaints against João indicate he had a protection network made up of authorities from Abadiânia, including the police."[241]

Also, in March, MST (an organization of homeless women) lost its appeal to INCRA (the authority administrating land reform issues). They were requesting the expropriation of one of João's ranches. The group of hundreds of homeless squatters had occupied his farm since soon after his arrest in December. They had hoped the government would grant them title to the land as a form of legal judgement against João. They moved on. [242]

In April, the Prosecutors brought another charge against the Medium involving multiple victims. His attorneys petitioned the court for his release from prison. They requested hospitalization for serious health problems not treated by the prison doctors. The judge agreed, and they took João to a private hospital. While in the hospital, he requested double servings at every meal.

The photos of his move to the hospital revealed a man in poor condition, barely able to walk. One report posted a photograph of him in an ambulance, looking longingly at a very young medical attendee sitting beside him. His hand is planted firmly on her inner thigh. Shortly afterward, the authorities prohibited female staff from being alone with him. [243]

Attendance at the Casa had dropped from a monthly high of

30,000 to about a hundred a week—residents of Abadiânia and small foreign tour groups. The posadas and gift shops closed.

In May, a ninth criminal charge was brought against him. One of his victims was blind. All six of the alleged assaults were rape of the vulnerable. The prosecution released more details to the media. Forty-eight victims had now filed criminal charges for sexual assault.

Recurring events clearly pointed to serial rape. Most of the victims were told by the Medium that they were his wives in past lives. All the victims experienced a freezing effect as he assaulted them and could not react or flee—a physical reaction of paralysis in abuse victims. Hypnotism can cause the same effect.

Also, in May, COAF (Council for Control of Financial Activities) gained access to the emails of people the prosecutors call "the healer's gang." They accessed correspondences between group members, property deeds, and witness statements.

The Justice Department of Goiás ordered the breach of the bank's security for twelve people close to João. The documents are from 2009 to 2019.[244]

On June 4, João returned to jail. Two new pleas for habeas corpus and a request for a continued hospital stay were denied. They brought a tenth criminal complaint against him, again for various rape allegations.

João de Deus' iron-fisted pistoleiro and former vice-mayor of Abadiânia, Chico Lobo, died of pneumonia in June. Chico Lobo had been hospitalized for about a month. Lobo acted as the Casa spokesman, defended the Medium, and denied all the accusations to the press.[245]

He had also been João's enforcer. The honcho who dealt with the women who confronted João with charges of sexual assault. He was a large, scary-looking brute. This was a blow to the Prosecutor's investigation, as Chico was their number one suspect after João in their efforts to reveal the Casa crime organization. They had plans to interrogate him and file charges.[246]

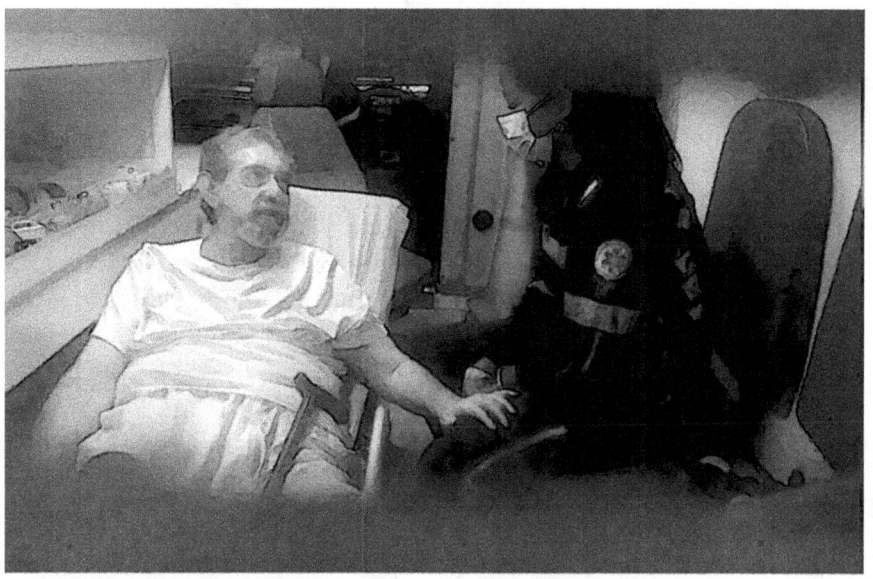

No woman is safe alone with João—artistic reproduction.

In the Name of God

At the end of June, Globoplay, Brazil's streaming equivalent of Netflix (and part of the Globo media empire), released a six-part series called In the Name of God about João de Deus and the unfolding scandal. Pedro Bial and Camila Appel emceed this documentary. They used a dramatic setting as their opening scene and reoccurring theme.[247]

Seven victims from Globo's first show (minus Amy Bianc) sat in a circle with moderator Camilla Appel. This time, everyone's face was revealed. They had never met one another, and all agreed to appear undisguised to pay homage to Zahira Mous's courage. They had been kept apart, even lodged in different hotels.

Each woman appeared and was introduced, creating a powerful emotional atmosphere. Then, they told their stories. Some of them were being heard for the first time. A fusion of solidarity and shared trauma overwhelmed the set.

The women sometimes wept and hugged their sisters in sympathy. They narrated their own stories, with gasps of shock from the other women or surprise at the similarity of their experiences. Raw emotion was on display for any sympathetic viewer.

The other sequences told the horrifying tale of sexual abuse and coverups. And the complicity of Casa staff, authorities, and the justice system. It laid open the entire dirty story for all of Brazil. This is a powerful and unforgettable portrayal by Globo. The series led to even more denunciations and cries of outrage from the public and the press.

On July 25, 2019, João's entire crew of nine lawyers quit without explanation. One of his lawyers said they resigned on ethical grounds but declined to elaborate. His top attorney, Alberto Toron, later claimed that João couldn't pay his bill. Much of João's liquid assets were frozen by the courts. He said they were charitable for a while, but they do not provide their services for free. João's pals, Nizan Guanaes and Marcos Elias, didn't bail him out.[248]

João hired a new attorney (just one this time), criminal lawyer Anderson Van Gualberto, who eagerly took up his cause. In August, another appeal for João's release was made. The Federal Supreme Court denied it. They cited "the need for preventive detention to ensure public order, in view of the amount of military material in the possession of João de Deus."[249]

This is the first time we've been informed that the authorities have collected such military evidence. In early August, the police entered the Faria home in Anápolis with a new search warrant. They discovered two mysterious documents. One was an identity card with his photograph, listing him as an agent of the Military Police Intelligence Unit of Goiás. The other was a badge naming him as a prison guard of the Penitentiary Administration of Goiás. Both agencies claimed the documents were false.[250]

These documents are one of the few public pieces of evidence that João may have been involved with intelligence agencies during the military regime. However, the prison guard badge is dated to 2000, well after the dictatorship.

Photo: Reprodução/ TV Anhanguera. Source: Prosecutors Office Goiânia.

Around this time, I visited Abadiânia and interviewed a friend living there who wishes to remain anonymous. My friend told me many rumors about the town.[251]

One was that the late Chico Lobo had been João's treasurer. While the police were searching for João, Chico cleared his many hidden stashes of millions of dollars—money that was not discovered by the police.

They had so much money that they decided the best place to hide it was in a cavern on one of João's ranches. There, they transported and concealed a fortune. Chico knew where the cave was, and he alone put the money there, in a place prepared some years before by João.

Photo: Reprodução/ TV Anhanguera. Source: Prosecutors Office Goiânia.

There was a problem no one foresaw. The cave was infested with bats and mountains of their droppings. Chico told friends that the smell of their shit was foul and overwhelming, yet he labored on. Sometime later, Chico fell ill. He was diagnosed with pneumonia and rushed to the hospital.

It wasn't pneumonia. Chico died of a hantavirus that infects bats and is spread by their feces and urine. It causes the lungs to fill with fluids, collapse, and drown the person in a few days. Near death, he finally mentioned the bats and the cave to the doctors. They had been treating pneumonia, not Hantavirus. It was way too late.

Another rumor my friend in Abadiânia recounted was that João raped an older woman in a wheelchair. She was in her sixties. She was a guest at a popular posada. The owner and another enforcer threatened this poor woman not to denounce Joao. She left immediately.

In a separate incident, the same posada owner threatened a young rape victim, insisting she leave and not say a word. She claimed he attempted to run her over with his vehicle at high speed when she refused to leave. She jumped just in time. Later, she filed a complaint with the local police. Nothing was done.

Several taxi drivers who serve the Casa tell stories of single women abruptly leaving the Casa and going straight to the airport.

They were agitated and crying, and when asked what was wrong, they said they couldn't talk about it.

And finally, one more rumor: a frequent visitor and fan of the Casa from South Africa told this story. João, with whom he was on friendly terms, asked him if he would come to his house and help him with something. The something was an enormous pile of money that needed to be put up in bundles of 100s. Eventually, they received visitors—the Federal Police. The money was for them. A well-known rumor in Abadiania is that João repeatedly paid off the local civil police, the military police, and even the federal police. This was the cost of doing business for João.

On this same visit, I dressed in white clothes and entered the Casa grounds with a camera, posing as a tourist. I entered an unlocked room. A couple of hundred framed documents, photos, and testimonies are proudly displayed. These are many items João used to carry with him in a briefcase when he traveled. They proved he was irreproachable and a man with friends in high places. There, I confirmed documents about Umbanda.

I was very nervous because the room, with its double glass doors, was visible to anyone passing by. I took some photographs and found certificates of membership in Umbanda centers. There were many testimonies by public and military officials and photos of celebrities posing with the Medium.

In late September, Faria complained of chest pains. He was admitted to the public hospital in Goiânia for observation. Around this time, he was charged with an eleventh criminal count of sexual assault.[252]

In October, an investigative journalist from São Paulo contacted me on behalf of Grifa Filmes, one of Brazil's top documentary film companies. She explained that Grifa was under contract with Netflix and producing a series about João de Deus and the unfolding scandal. Someone had given her my name. We arranged a meeting. I was so nervous when we met at a cafe that I spilled my drink. I agreed to help them with all my information but would not consider being filmed for an interview.

We communicated by e-mail. Soon, she put me in contact with the executive producer, Bianca Corona. I began a friendship with her and the staff.

João's trophy room: three walls, from floor to ceiling, with certificates. Photo: Michael Bailot.

Later, they conducted a lengthy interview at my home in November. We decided to disguise my face and voice. My name wouldn't appear. No one that they interviewed wanted to take part without their identities concealed. We were all afraid of the long reach of Faria's hand of retribution.

I frequently contacted Grifa, giving them information as things unfolded. None of the contacts or friends that I recommended would agree to speak about João. The Netflix project was having difficulty unveiling his secrets.

November 2019 was an eventful month in the unfolding saga of João de Deus. A twelfth case was brought against him. Fifteen women testified about rapes occurring from 2015 to 2016. Finally, they tried the first charge. They convicted João and sentenced him to four years in prison for illegally possessing firearms. The Court acquitted his wife, who was also charged.

The press covered an event that had occurred in prison. One of João's fellow prisoners entered an altered state and ran amuck.

The guards restrained him by tying him up with bedsheets. His wild trashing and screaming continued. One of the staff visited João's cell and asked him if he would help de-possess the crazed inmate. They took him to the high-security ward where this was happening. João began an incantation in an unknown tongue. The spirit exited the prisoner when he shouted, "Open your eyes!"[253]

An informant reported that João was giving secret treatments to important people in the government. He attempted to influence them and public opinion that he was a respectable citizen. He even sent his blessed water to the former president of the Supreme Court, Carlos Ayres Britto.

The news is a continuing soap opera of revelations. João's children accused one of his lawyers of robbing them of a suitcase filled with three million reais.[254]

This is a tale of hidden stashes of money. The transparent efforts of his family to snatch up whatever they can before the State steps in and confiscates everything João owns—and everything he owes. This includes his unpaid taxes, court fines, lawyers' fees, and compensation for his victims. Ana Keyla (João's wife at the time) and three of João's daughters spoke to the press without thinking about how self-incriminating this sounds.

Several suitcases full of money were delivered to certain trusted people. They were holding it in reserve for João. They mention one of these people, lawyer Ronivan Peixoto Júnior. The same lawyer who filmed Dalva's forced confession. He was the attorney who first represented João as the drama unfolded. Ronivan accompanied João when he turned himself in for arrest.

They say that João's wife, Ana Keyla, asked a Casa collaborator to store a suitcase and deliver it the next day to Peixoto Júnior. She was under surveillance as an accomplice. She wanted to pass it on to someone else. Agents of the Public Ministry were following her. The money disappeared.

One of João's daughters spoke of another allegation. "We know that our father had the caretaker of his farm in Anápolis deliver a large amount of money. It never showed up again."

Another daughter claimed Ronivan Peixoto was on a world tour with his family. He was spending beyond his means and posting all the extravagance on his Facebook page. She said, "Doctor Ronivan was without money before the imprisonment of our father. This is well known in Anápolis and Abadiânia. He and his family traveled to Europe in July. This can be checked on his social networks. Pictures of him and his family in Rome, Pisa, Florence, and Boston are available to everyone."

Ronivan Peixoto Júnior denied receiving any money from João de Deus for safekeeping. He said he would prove his innocence.

UOL, another Brazilian media company, released João de Deus, a short film inspired by the book A Casa by Chico Felitti. It featured Felitti and Vera Iaconelli, a psychoanalyst. She analyzed João's motivations. They interviewed Ana Paula São, a victim, and Clodoaldo Turcato, his former accountant.[255]

One more event in November sent shock waves through Abadiânia. A Casa visitor living there for the past two years, Hitomi Akamatsu, was found murdered at the Casa's sacred waterfall. An eighteen-year-old man was arrested. He confessed to killing the woman there. The forty-three-year-old Japanese woman was seeking a cure for cancer she acquired as a victim of the Fukushima nuclear accident. Had João's Exu been stalking the Cachoeira for a new person to possess? Was this another blood offering?[256]

In late December, I visited Grifa Films in São Paulo. They showed me their giant corkboard, which laid out the many aspects of their research. I also spent time in their editing studio, where we discussed aspects of the case.

They hosted a meeting with their staff of lawyers to determine what I could reveal in a future interview. I could name no one because of Brazil's archaic libel laws unless they were convicted of the accusations in a court of law. I realized how restrained their investigation was.

The executive producer and her staff were especially friendly and welcoming. They provided me with more research material for my project.

During this visit, news came to their office via the Prosecuting Attorney. They convicted João of his second charge—serial rape. He received a nineteen-year prison term. At that moment, I permitted them to use my interview without facial or voice alteration. We scheduled a second interview for the following year.

Yet, this was not to be. The Coronavirus was making the news that week, and their plans for more travel, interviews, and episodes died in the ensuing chaos.

By the end of the year, only two of the one hundred posadas in Abadiania were open. Most of the shops closed, and very few tourists walked the streets. João was denounced for the thirteenth time by seven more victims. There were eleven supportive testimonies from victims—rapes that occurred between 1999 and 2018.

On January 20, 2021, the court found Faria guilty of sexual abuse involving five victims. He was sentenced to another forty years in prison, his third conviction. Many of us celebrated in relief, learning that João now had an accumulated sentence of sixty-two years. The monster was caged. News reports continued to portray his deteriorating physical and mental health in prison.

Then, the unthinkable happened. Because of his age and the efforts of his new lawyer, Anderson Van Gualberto, João was released from prison, as were many other elderly prisoners in Brazil. This resulted from the Coronavirus' rapid spread through the prison system. They cited his poor health and seventy-nine years of age.

He had an ankle monitor installed and was placed under house arrest in his Anápolis mansion. It really is a mansion. Four stories high, six bedrooms, a private cinema, a three-story fountain encrusted with crystals in a huge interior courtyard, an elevator, and so much kitsch—you wouldn't believe it. There, he had the luxury of staff and all the comforts of a multi-million-dollar home.

Investigators secretly posted at the entrance recorded visitors entering with their cars and leaving unseen through a back exit. High walls and many security cameras surround the house.

His terms of house arrest prohibited him from contacting the Casa or his victims—nothing more. João could once again take control of his secret mafia and direct his affairs with broad freedom of activity. He allegedly began holding Zoom meetings with the Casa staff, but his terms of house arrest forbade this. His lawyer and others visited often.

He gave interviews, including one for the upcoming Netflix series. He sold them rights to personal documents, photos, and film archives for 80,000 reais. Once again, a chilling effect descended upon his victims, me included. What was stopping him from arranging murders for hire or obstruction of justice?[257]

Meanwhile, fresh revelations appeared. They exposed his vast real estate holdings and wealth. The press discovered that he owned twenty-seven properties in Abadiânia alone. This included a ranch of over 1,000 acres valued at nine million reais (about two million dollars at the time). His wealth included a private eight-seat airplane and many new cars.[258]

He also owned high-end apartment condominiums and properties in Anápolis and other cities. He owned several clandestine mines, with thirty million reais in one bank account alone (valued at six million dollars). He co-owned a dental clinic and several posadas. His discoverable real estate holdings amounted to over 100 million reais, which is twenty million dollars at today's valuation. This included seven enormous ranches.

Added to all this are uncounted millions in assets off the record and hidden in other people's names, as well as the unconfirmed stash in his secret cavern. The Casa was allowed to remain open and to make sales, including the notorious passiflora pills.

In May 2021, João was sentenced to an additional two years and six months in prison. This was for one count of a sexual violation through fraud, bringing the total to 64 years. So far, the prosecution has asked for 456 years as a minimum sentence for João de Deus, plus compensation for his victims.

In August, a new book about João appeared (in Portuguese). Titled João de Deus–O Abuso da Fé and published by Globo Livros. The author, Cristina Fibe, is a journalist who covered the case from the beginning. She obtained new information and exclusive interviews with more victims.[259]

Netflix debuted its four-part series titled *John of God: Crimes of a Spiritual Healer* in late August 2021. My interview is in the second part. The Netflix program unveiled more of the backstory. They used strong archival footage, demonstrating his rise to fame. The series received high ratings and was still trending high in 2023.[260]

They revealed, for the first time, the story of João de Deus to many countries and in many languages. It was a strange and disturbing tale, unknown to many who had never heard of João. The productions by Globo and UOL were only in Portuguese, so they didn't reach an international audience.

The crew at Grifa Films sifted through hundreds of hours of Casa archival footage. They found shocking moments that unmasked the real João de Deus.

The depiction is disturbing. We see a crude and volatile bully, threatening and reeking of arrogance. A poser pretending to perform surgery but actually performing carnival tricks.

One must wonder, what in the world prompted people to become devotees of this repulsive man? In one of the most disturbing scenes, he is shown speaking to the public on his stage. Flanked by three assistants, João denies and jokes about a recent revelation by a rape victim. He sarcastically says that if he had indeed raped her, he would have to marry the poor girl. The man by his side chuckles in commiseration. João suggests they bring her to the stage so he can propose.

This is a disturbing and ugly introduction for anyone who has never heard of João de Deus. As Dalva has said, "My father is a monster." Hearing the accounts of the women manipulated and abused in the name of God is shocking. The series juxtaposes interviews with his devotees, insisting João had cured them.

The production is a sensitive and sympathetic treatment of several of his victims. It amplifies the earlier work by Globo. The closing episode leaves one with a nagging sense of justice unserved. We are confronted with the image of a madman, a pathological liar, and many unanswered questions.

In a twist of irony, Faria returned to prison a week after the series first aired. Charged the fifteenth time for the vulnerable rape of another eight victims. Everyone was surprised when he was released again to house arrest a month after this new imprisonment. In October, he returned to the hospital for heart palpitations.

João's partner in crime for forty years, Secretary of the Casa and second in command, Sebastião de Lima, was now in the headlines. Tiãozinho, as he was known around the Casa, was an unforgettable character. A short and round, obviously gay ex-monk—who, for decades, was João's secretary, assistant, and liaison with the public, Tião reminded me of the Golem, a Peruvian version of the Golem.

He had direct access to the Medium and enjoyed his position of power. He directed the attendees, made announcements, and introduced João on stage. Heather Cumming assumed his role when he mysteriously vanished from the Casa in 2015. This followed an explosive fight with João amidst allegations of sexual harassment in the public men's room at the Casa. And embezzlement—the one sin João could never forgive.

Tião was as much a figure of the Casa as was João. No one saw this coming. But, in 2021, the crows came home to roost. The Journal Metrópoles, after a five-month-long investigation, reported about four male victims who suffered sexual abuse by de Lima. Clodoaldo Turcato, the Casa accountant from these times, recalls hearing about de Lima's sexual harassment in the 1990s.[261]

Tiãozinho was the only staff member other than João with a private office. He also held a concession within the Casa, which granted him the exclusive franchise of the rosaries and key chains marketed in the gift shop. He had been by João's side since the very beginning of the Casa.

Three of the four men interviewed in the journal Metropolis attended the Casa, hoping for a miracle cure for their HIV. The other man worked at the Casa for ten years. These testimonies relay events that happened over a wide span of years, from 1996 to 2015.

One might assume this was an ongoing and tolerated activity of Tiãozinho. Three former staff members attested to this. He wasn't the only one following in the footsteps of João's perverted style of healing.

João was aloof and unhelpful when a young Brazilian passed through his line asking for a cure for HIV. He was happy that the false rumor about the cures had worked so well. But the most this guy would get from João was lots of passiflora pills. He was looking for comfort, encouragement, and hope. Instead, he got João's left-hand man—the man with the cure for AIDS.

Tião had access to the medium. He led the patients to believe that they would get the healing they longed for if they followed his suggestions. It began in the public restrooms after he found out they had AIDS. He asked to see and touch their penis. He wanted to show his as well. They were all surprised, imagine, in the very public restroom of the Casa.

He got more aggressive in his office, where constant foot traffic passed by the glass doors. One of his victims claimed that he took him to the infirmary through the back door. He instructed him to lie on a gurney, and de Lima covered him with a sheet. There were several other people in the tiny infirmary. Tião told him he would need to handle his penis because that is where the virus started, and it would be cured there. As he attempted to masturbate the young man, he prayed aloud and asked his victim to do the same.

He told his victims that he wasn't gay, that this was a healing technique, and that he was married with children. After this episode, de Lima told the man he was cured of AIDS. When he returned to his hometown, he got an HIV test. He was, of course, positive.

The investigative reporter interviewed Tiãozinho at his home in Anápolis. He denied all the reports. He claimed that the accusations against him and João were opportunism. His lawyer, Jorge Barbosa Lobato, said the same. "Empty allegations, with no factual support, and unworthy of credibility."

The soap opera wasn't over. In November, João was found guilty in his fifth trial. This was for the rape of four women (with thirteen victims testifying) that occurred from 2009 to 2018. The sentence was for forty-four years in prison. The court ordered compensation for the victims from 20,000 to 75,000 reais per accuser, about 4,000 to 15,000 dollars each.

With this new conviction, his sentence reached one hundred and nine years in prison. Yet, he remained under house arrest.[262]

Ten additional cases had yet to be tried, and probably more would be filed. Many issues still need to be addressed, like his illegally gained assets and the continued functioning of the Casa, his nameless accomplices, and accountability regarding protectors in high places. What about the allegations of murder for hire, witness tampering, conspiracy with corrupt police, and bribery?

Are there unmarked graves on the grounds of the Casa? Or perhaps at his ranches or in the local cemetery? The police suspect so and have even done cursory searches for clandestine burials. How many falsified death certificates were issued on his behalf? How many autopsies should have been done but weren't? How many falsified police reports? How many poor souls were dumped at the entrance of hospitals in critical condition?[263]

How many people died while visiting the Casa or because of their visit? And, of course, what was his role in the years of torture and terror by his military cronies?

The office where he committed his many sexual assaults is also where he received important officials. Political figures and celebrities sat on the same sofa as his rape victims.

Many ghosts hide in the mystery of João's secret past. Secrets that many in power want to *disappear*. In this way, João Teixeira de Faria is Brazil's Jeffrey Epstein. A serial pedophile rapist and keeper of secrets of the powerful and corrupt. Who is implicated in his reign of crimes and abuse of power? To this day, only João can answer these questions.

Cognitive Dissonance and The Casa Cargo Cult

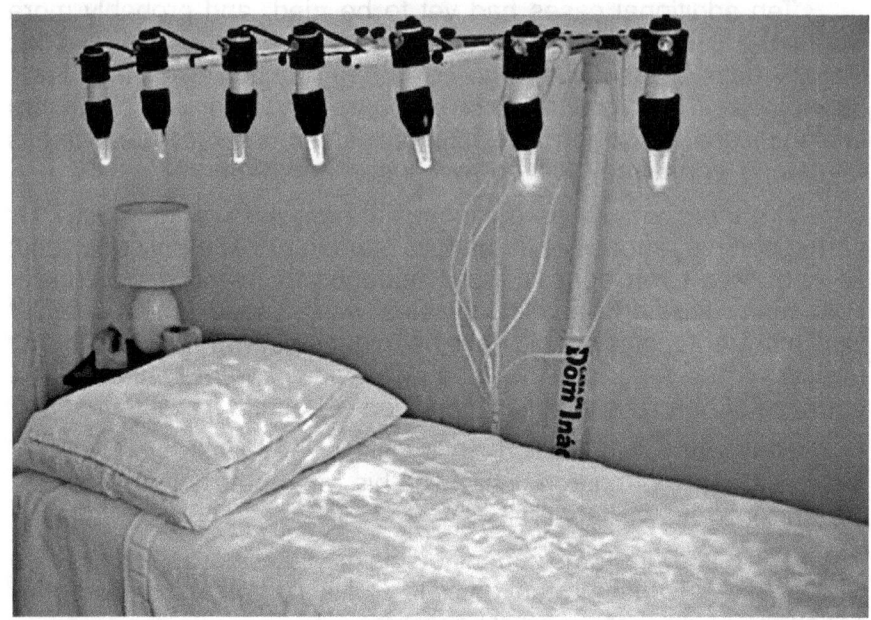

The Crystal Bed; now incorporating the Casa Entities? Photo: Casa archives.

From the beginning, the Casa staff and João's devotees have been in unequivocal denial. Not to mention his crew of lawyers, who shielded him over the decades. Children of the Casa pretend *there is nothing to see here* while trying to keep their business going. Several tour guides continued bringing guests, while many dropped out of the game. All of them have taken a tremendous financial loss. The staff-authored books and films are still for sale. I don't understand. Why must you persist?

There are many vested in perpetuating the Casa myth. The posada owners have faced their crises and are grasping for options. Renting or selling their posadas to drug rehabilitation clinics is one example.

Even his fans, who purchased homes and businesses in Abadiânia, have much at stake. The value of the real estate and rentals plunged by half in the first year after the Medium's arrest. By 2022, many properties lost eighty percent of their rental or sale value. Only a few of the more than 100 posadas were open. *For Sale* signs are plastered all over Barrio Lindo Horizonte. Some of their owners were left with enormous mortgages. The economy of the city of Abadiânia crashed along with the Casa. [264]

Those with reason to fear their implication in his crimes risk everything if exposed. They all are desperate to keep João out of trouble and out of the picture at any cost. They also have their reputation to defend. One has to stretch the limits of credibility to justify continued support for the convicted serial rapist of Abadiânia. It takes gumption to alter the facts to suit your business goals. Or to hide your complicity in heinous crimes.

Let's begin with the tour guides. As this scandal unfolded, most guides and Casa personalities defended the medium. When the mounting evidence soured their efforts, they turned to subterfuge to resolve the problem. When searching websites promoting Casa, there was no mention of his crimes. Or only a quick gloss over the truth or blunt denial of his guilt. They portrayed João as an innocent victim.

When João requested that the statue of Saint Rita be placed on his unoccupied throne, everything changed. The entire theme and sales pitch for the Casa shifted. The Medium was divorced from the Casa, at least publicly. He is no longer called João de Deus but Medium João. The statue of Santa Rita now incorporates the Entities.

Many people bailed out, took down their websites, and disappeared, as did most of the posadas and shop owners. Notorious players of the Casa game slipped out of town. Robert Pellegrino left a trail of defaulted loans and fraudulent real estate deals well before the scandal broke.

Also, a suspected suicide or arranged murder occurred at one of his rental properties. He was last heard of in Malaysia, then vanished for the past six years. What does he have to hide? Or Valdete Ferreira and her son, who packed up the Posada Dom Ingrid and fled as well? What did they know? Arturo Rios skipped town amidst accusations of embezzlement by his partner. Yes, many ran from the consequences of their decisions about the Casa.

Some major players in João's code of silence and web of protection continue to work and live in Abadiânia. Norberto Kist is João's staunch defender. Norberto is a smooth-talking posada owner with a double face. He is hand-in-glove with the Medium and in on all of his secrets. Kist still haunts the Casa.[265]

The Carlotto family, owners of the Posada Catarinense, saw it all. Oh, the stories they could tell. Each one of them got their hands dirty in the cesspool.

Martin and Fernanda Mosquera are the owners of the Pousada Irmão Sol e Irmã Lua. *"What a tangled web we weave when first we practice to deceive."*

Martin and Fernanda were two of the most powerful people in João's web of protection. They participated in most of João's international tours and were leaders in the Casa. Both have warm, outgoing personalities. They radiate kindness and sympathy. Martin is an educated, sophisticated man who is fluent in four languages. He has perfect teeth and manicured nails. He is notably handsome, even charismatic. Fernanda looks like an angel—a real sweetheart. Thousands of people love and respect them. Their Posada Irmão Sol e Irmã Lua was the most popular posada in town.

Of course, there is always a backstory. I am privy to this but reluctant to talk about it. But I can tell you this—their marriage was consistently tragic, often ugly, and the polar opposite of the happy, perfect family they projected for the public. This couple wears two faces. They also know *everything* that went on with João. They were among his closest disciples and, undoubtedly, his informants.

In 2019, Martin began promoting another healer. He hosts private events at his posada where people can stay (and pay) and receive treatment from the new miracle healer.

This man is called The Dreamer *(O Sonhador)*. His name is Jucelino Nóbrega da Luz. He is a psychic, author, and healer who has received a lot of publicity on Brazilian TV shows and in magazines. The Dreamer is middle-aged and well-dressed. He claims that he has predicted thousands of events. He writes down his prophecies and mails them to people he thinks might be able to prevent the predicted disasters.[266]

Some of the events he claims to have predicted with his letters include the World Trade Center attack in New York, the death of Michael Jackson, and the Asian tsunami on December 26, 2004.

He says he sued the US government during the Bush administration, asking to be paid their $25 million bounty on Hussein's head for having revealed the location of Saddam Hussein's hideout. He claims to have mailed the location to the U.S. consul in São Paulo and the director of the FBI well before Hussein's capture.

The Dreamer has been periodically treating participants in tour groups at Martin's posada for six years now (2019 to 2024). He is avoiding the Casa—or, more likely, is prohibited from using it. He performs "surgeries" without making cuts and treats the invisible wound with blessed water. The operation takes a few minutes, and the Dreamer claims that the work is done by the Holy Spirit.

The Dreamer denies that he is trying to replace João as the Casa healer. He says that he has an "energetic, personal connection with Abadiânia" and that we should forgive João. "Throwing stones is too easy. Forgiveness is something divine."

Martin and Fernanda are touring Europe with The Dreamer, Jucelino Nóbrega da Luz, attending venues in the same locations as João. The events are managed by a large German tour agency, Earth Oasis. A two-day "seminar" with the healer costs 200 Euros, not including food and lodging (it is held in large hotels). In August 2023, their entourage was visiting nine European cities. They have re-created the road show and the myth of Abadiânia as sacred ground. Martin and Fernanda are staff members at all Earth Oasis events.[267]

The same German tour agency, Earth Oasis, which had once heavily promoted João de Deus, now offers tours to Brazil that combine visits to several healers. These include sessions with The Dreamer, visits to the Casa de Dom Inácio, and surgery by Regis, a young medium channeling Dr. Fritz at the Spiritist Hospital of Palmelo. They also offer healing sessions with Pai Santo Lazaro, a priest of Candomblé from Bahia.[268]

Earth Oasis maintains a retreat center in Abadiânia named Oasis of Light. You can sign up for an additional week and attend a Santo Daime ayahuasca ritual in the Abadiânia church. The same agency offers extensive tours with psychedelic shamans in Peru.

The entire Casa crew is suffering from cognitive dissonance. The bottom fell out of their magical world. Since João's first arrest, dozens of friends of the Casa have been wrangling with reality. They are attempting to craft a New Casa. At first, they were hoping for some sort of successor to step in and take over the control of the Entities. That will never be.

João's staunchest defenders sent e-mails to their clients, uploaded YouTube interviews, and posted messages. They defiantly tried to explain away the sick reality.

An early e-mail from Josie Ravenwing to her worried fans echoed the Casa sentiment. Fake news and opportunistic phony victims framed João. Josie wrote, "What is ironic to me is that there are always women wanting to have sex with him [I guess association with power, charisma, whatever], and many hoping to be the next Mrs. John of God. Given all of that, John could pretty much have his pick, so why do what he is accused of doing?

"However, as he always says, he is just a man, and it is the loving spirits that work through him, all around the Casa and in distance work, that do the healing. None of the women making the accusations are denying the healing work of the Casa, but they are unhappy with the man. And the man, like all humans, is not perfect by any means."[269]

Gail Thackray posted a YouTube video from her perspective. She asserted she wouldn't support anyone who was a rapist or abuser. Thus, we should trust her on this one. João would never do such a thing. Besides, she questioned the Casa staff about all this. They assured her that nothing had happened. João was never alone with anyone in his private office—never. She reiterated this five more times in her production.[270]

She explained that he was never incorporated when he was in his office, so he couldn't give private healing sessions. Gail reminds us that João is illiterate. She said, "So how could he write a note requesting the girls to go to his office after the session?"

I guess she was unaware that this note always looked like the letter K, and his staff knew what this mark meant. They should escort the victim to his office. Even João can write the letter K.

Thackray continued, "If there really were private sessions, everyone would want one."

Sorry, Gail, you're out of your league and not his type. He would have been all over you if you were fourteen.

She implied that João had been attacked and persecuted forever. That the Bolsonaro government wants to destroy him. And the big pharmaceutical companies and the press have it out for him— the evil, fake news.

Thackray slandered Zahira Mous with questions about her integrity and testimony. She said, "If she was actually molested the first time, then why in the world did she return for a second assault in the same room?"

To add to the confusion, she said the Press set up the system for victims to file complaints against the Medium. Actually, it was the State Prosecutor's Office. Gail even claimed that the hundreds of victims archived by the Victim's United group were all fake. The fake news comes from the Casa staff, not the press.

She filmed this in her Los Angeles home, seated by a fireplace. If you scroll down the YouTube page for more videos of Gail, you will find several filmed by the same fireplace. She sits in the same chair, with the same hairstyle and a slight costume change.

The other films are promoting her recently released tell-all autobiography, *Running with Wolves* (wonder where she got the idea for that title). She tells tales of her life as a porn star and her multi-million-dollar pin-up picture empire. Gail regales us with stories about her life with Hugh Hefner, Bob Guccione (creator of Penthouse), and Hustler's Larry Flynt. She gets animated when mentioning the seventy-eight-year-old woman she directed in a porn film.

You can see that Gail loves this aspect of her double life. Certainly, *Running with Wolves* is far more interesting than *Gail Thackray's Spiritual Journeys: Visiting John of God.*

The videos defending João and her pornographic adventures were filmed at the same time. As I continued scrolling down her YouTube posts, I found an interview, *Gail Thackray—Taken Down by the Mob.*

This is a talk show conducted by Mancow Muller. He's an ex-radio personality with several streaming programs. One is *Mancow's Microaggressions,* which features this interview with Gail. Mancow is a fast talker, a very fast talker. He opens the segment with a promotional trailer created by Gail Thackray, highlighting her wild career as a porn queen. It certainly grabs one's attention.

In her interview, Gail explains she made the trailer hoping to land a series on Netflix. She appeared on his show to promote her new book.[271]

But Mancow has surprises for her. He shifts the interview from pornography, which she assumes will be the topic, to John of God. He tells her that, in his opinion, John of God is a black magician and a fraud. Mancow attended her Toronto event with João and became friends with her there. The twenty-minute interview is his rapid-fire questions coming from far-left field. She attempts to deflect a question as soon as she begins answering it. He interrupts her every time. Then, he launches into another uncomfortable query.

He says porn is the scourge of humanity. While appearing to be joking and having fun with his good friend, he is actually disarming her. He doesn't allow her to answer a single question—except one. He permits her to struggle to explain how the New York Mafia brought down her porno empire. She then stumbles all over herself. She is there to promote her book but is made the brunt of his jokes. She is befuddled by his aggressive approach.

We are treated to a takedown and smear of poor Gail. Mancow is a master at exposing double talk and pretense. He does not tolerate bullshit.

Another guide, Maytree Meliana, posted her opinion of the situation soon after João's fall. She authored *John of God: A Guide to Your Healing Journey with Spirit Doctors Beyond The Veil.*

She said, "I will continue to return to the Casa as my spiritual home one to two times a year and recommend others visit for their spiritual evolution if they feel so aligned. I would educate people differently on what to expect and how to develop their own personal relationship with the entities."

The twist in the plot begins here. Many of his defenders say, "João always said that it wasn't he who did the healings. It was God and the Entities." [272]

His devotees began claiming bragging rights to the Entities, pushing João out of the picture. Anyone can now access the Entities, so who needs João?

Another method his defenders used to silence their critics was Brazil's draconian libel laws. Some of his outspoken critics on social media were served defamation lawsuits. They accused several of João's associates of crimes. They lost their cases and had to pay hefty fines. They even sued Sabrina Bittencourt, *absentee,* alleging that she wasn't dead.

Josie Ravenwing and others then used these cases as proof that João was innocent. They altered the facts to suit their argument. The Facebook wars had begun.

Josie posted on Facebook: "Sabrina Bittencourt found guilty in court of fabricating the 600 victims and "baby farm" lies. She is ordered to post redactions on social media and pay a fine of R $30,000. Great news for John of God; it is now coming out that this was all a setup and how cruelly he was set up. He is not out yet, but with these many new court findings, we hope he will be found innocent soon." [273]

Does Josie know that in 2000, when she was there but unaware, João was charged with human trafficking and for selling babies—heard in the Federal Court in Brasilia?

Bittencourt was not found guilty of *fabricating* the 600 victims and "baby farm" lies. She was convicted of a civil libel lawsuit. I doubt she attended the hearing, and I'm sure they will never collect the fine. And she never published a redaction.

In Brazil, winning a defamation lawsuit does not prove the allegations false. It merely illustrates that the claims were not proven in a court of law. To accuse someone of a crime or an embarrassing behavior, *if unproven in court,* is slander in Brazil. Most judges would agree—in Brazil, you can sue a person for hurting your feelings.

This loophole in the law can further restrict free speech about the scandal. This archaic law from Napoleon's court protected the Royal Family (and Napoleon) from public criticism. It didn't give the ordinary citizen the same right. It was against the law to insult or criticize royalty.

The Lobo family (who filed this lawsuit and others) doesn't like to be publicly criticized. It's not cool to bring up their heavy involvement in the inner workings of the Casa. It isn't appropriate to imply that the dearly departed Chico Lobo was up to his nose hairs in João's cesspit.

Josie, who claims to be the first American Casa guide, led about 150 tour groups to Abadiânia from 1998 to 2020. She said, "Within a few years of beginning my work at the Casa, John of God and the entities asked me to accompany him on his rare healing events outside of Brazil and to oversee and direct the spiritual surgeries/interventions and blessings room during those events. I did this twice in New Zealand, several times in Europe, once in Canada, and I think it's been eleven times in the US." [274]

Then, the Casa's ex-press officer, Edna Gomes, weighed in on social media. She wrote, "[I have] witnessed nothing outside the natural course of things in the place.

"[I denounce] the human liquidation, lynching violence, and the immediate spectacle of the crucifixion before the judgment of justice." Later, she wept as she was charged with obstruction of justice and falsifying legal documents. Edna didn't know anything either. [275]

From 2019 to 2021, a couple of dozen guides still quietly offered tours to the Casa. American, French, German, Australian, and East European guides had put the same spin on their tours.

The new spiel, as outlined by American Casa guides Klaus and Gundi Heinemann, was:

"Dear Friends, who have formerly traveled with us to Abadiania... Something new has been arising from the ashes... something that does not condone any of the alleged transgressions while at the same time taking responsibility with an atmosphere of compassion and forgiveness, taking to heart what Master Jesus said to the angry mob about to kill the adulterer. Who among you is free of sin and will throw the first stone?

"The re-built Casa will then re-gain the trust of people all over the world as it does not condone any of the alleged transgressions of which Medium Joao is being accused. We pray that the 'New Casa' will be based on ABSOLUTE INTEGRITY." [276]

That will be the day, a Casa built on absolute integrity! We won't hold our breath. Others shared their vision for re-branding the village of Abadiânia as a sort of Sedona, like this post from Diane S. / a Casa guide:

"My dear Abadiânia family, I want to share some thoughts and ideas about the continual growth and promotion of *our village of Abadiânia*. We understand that Abadiânia exists because of the Casa... and the Casa needs the village of Abadiânia to support all who come. I want to put out there that we can help by offering and supporting creative retreats in Abadiânia. It is already known as a place of deep healing and spiritual growth at the Casa—so we can also promote the town as a place of incredible creative energy for personal growth."[277]

Diego Coppola, a leader of the ongoing cover-up, had a different perspective in the Casa Newsletter: The Casa's Financial Future—the Months and Years Ahead. "During this year, the Casa has reduced expenses and trimmed the staff to a skeleton crew. The Casa will definitely be open over the holidays and into next year.

"According to management, the Casa can stay open indefinitely if the current level of visitors continues. Historically, the months of December, January, and February have been very slow months for the Casa. If the number of visitors is reduced proportionately in these next months, it could create some serious difficulty for the Casa. One way to help the Casa navigate these weaker months is to purchase Casa products (e.g., a crystal bed—the Casa is offering a special ONE TIME R$3000 rebate on the regular [price of] R$12000 (about 2,200 dollars); Casa water; Casa herbs, crystals)."

Did I mention that Copolla owns the business selling the crystal beds or that he has maintained an official Casa website that has been a commercial venture from top to bottom for many years?[278]

Soon, all the guides and his fans living in Abadiânia were singing a new song. *The Wicked Witch of the West is dead, and now the Munchkins rule instead.* A sanitized Casa, forgetful of the smelly elephant in the room, was presented to the devotees. They elevated the Entities even higher than João had placed them. His Exus became *The Casa Angelic Spirits.*

Deb Court wrote in the *Friends of the Casa Newsletter.* "The Casa Current sessions are about two hours long, with people going through the lines to present their issues and receive the healing interventions and blessings directly from the Benevolent Entities of Light at the Casa.

"The Casa Angelic Spirits are working vigilantly with each one of us directly without the intersession of a single medium translating messages."[279]

And, of course, Gail Thackray had a good sales pitch: "While the Casa continues to be swarmed by paparazzi and John of God is still being held in custody, the Casa is open, and people report incredible energy and amazing healing. Of course, John has always said, 'I am just the medium. God is the one who heals.' It seems the healing work continues. One benevolent spirit is inside John of God, while thousands are actually working in the room.

"While The Medium [John of God] is away, people still line up and still write their requests, but they pass in front of his chair and leave their requests on the chair. Many say they can still feel the sense of love and thousands of spirits there. My friends at the Casa say the energy is extremely high, even higher than usual. So, it seems the spirits of the white light continue to give amazing healings."[280]

The collective fantasy of his remnant of a cult lives on, but the reality is quite different. They have patched together a Casa Cargo Cult from the warm remains of their beloved founder. All that spiritual kitsch is still for sale.

You can pay someone living in Abadiânia to put your name on the empty throne. They gather up your herbs and water and mail your healing back to wherever you live. A friend calls them "ticks, sucking blood from João's ass."

The Entities live on, but they no longer possess a medium. Now, they manifest in a statue and a sordid throne.

Now, they are in the crystal beds. Seriously, that is how they are promoted. They are in the triangles and blessed crystals; they're everywhere and all for sale. Now, you can have your own entity living in your home earning a passive income. Everyone looks up to the sky for more magical gifts that João and his phalange keep raining down.

We are missing important details. For example, they are selling herbs gung-ho, but remember, João's wife owns this business. Lots of folks still have their hand in the cash register. João's crystal store re-opened. The core staff still receive generous salaries. The guides still make a profit. And the Entities? They are the Casa Cargo Cult. One should be very careful what one prays for (or to).

There are persistent rumors that João is still running the show from his mansion, under a very lax house arrest. Are all these devotees incredibly naïve and foolish, or are they part of João's web of protection, his mafia? One has to wonder. The iron fist of João has not relaxed its grip on the Casa de Dom Inácio.

The Civil Police began an investigation in February 2019, which concluded in 2022, into misappropriated funds generated by the Casa. An Australian woman accused João of stealing property she owned in Abadiânia. He was indicted for embezzlement and charged with making financial transfers from the Casa account to his private accounts and of people and companies linked to him. One million reais were transferred from the herbal business account. Five hundred thousand reais from his bookstore and snack bar were transferred to his crystal business account. This was done while he was in prison. [281]

Another legal investigation demonstrated that Faria deposited almost 240 million reais (more than 80 million dollars at the time) in his bank accounts from 2009 to 2019. In parallel, he moved enormous amounts of cash and gems outside the banking system.

For four years, I kept constant watch on the Casa. Inertia and gravity tugged on their sleeve until I could barely feel the pulse.

A persistent and devastating pandemic cast a shroud over Brazil. The Casa closed off and on because of the quarantines. It didn't help when folks began catching Covid at the Casa. Brazilians stayed far away from the Casa.

After all, they could read Portuguese, while many of João's foreign devotees living in Abadiânia could not. The few who can read Portuguese have declined to digest what they call fake news. I suppose this is the most you can expect from people who believe that inbred lizard elites rule the world, Abadiânia is a sacred place, and spirits lurk in a hokey massage table light show.

These posers should encourage visitors to self-insert the hemostat up their noses. Then, the Entities can get their thrill and their blood sacrifice without needing Medium João.

So, is there truth in the rumor that João is still running the show? In the Newspaper O Popular, a reporter described how he arrived at the Casa unannounced in October 2021. While waiting for one of the staff to speak with him, he overheard this fellow receive a phone call, which his speakerphone amplified. He heard, *"Hi, Seu João."* He then received directions, responding using the words *boss and boss,* and hung up.

When questioned, the employee initially said that medium João was on the line and that he was doing very well. He said, "Seu João, he's different from us. He goes to bed sick and gets up in one piece."

When the reporter finally announced his credentials, the staff member changed his story. Now, he claimed it was João Augusto— João's son. "It was the son. I said boss because I asked how he was, and the son told me João was fine. He can't call, right? He doesn't even have a phone," he said.

João Faria and João Augusto are not allowed to have any contact with the Casa. Indeed, his entire family is under court order not to contact the Casa or the victims. João's lawyer, Anderson Van Gualberto, denied that his client manages the Casa de Dom Inácio. He claims that the Medium has only a symbolic position as president of honor.[282]

For two years, I have heard rumors that João is having Zoom conferences with the Casa crew. The guides, Klaus and Gundi Heinemann, also assert that he is still running the show behind the scenes. They reaffirm this with a post by a friend who claims the same thing. They, and others, allude to a secret internal battle to dethrone the Medium and disenfranchise him of his Casa and their businesses.

The Heinemanns posted remarks from Hervé Glon, who has lived in Abadiania since early 2018. He wrote,

"I have now been in Abadiania for three and a half solid years, and I have no intention or desire to be anywhere else at this time... Whatever happened with Medium Joao has no weight in my decision. I find the spirit at the Casa truly amazing, even though it doesn't seem to be able to shake itself out of the slump.

"The few of us who live here feel that we are most blessed to be able [and allowed] to live in a very privileged sanctuary. Many who have come for a few weeks ended up staying semi permanently. That's how good it feels here. We all love the Casa. The energy there is beautiful. There have been many miraculous healings since the departure of Medium Joao.

"Of course, the landscape has changed dramatically in the last 2 1/2 years since only a small fraction of visitors still dares to come. I feel that the vast majority of those who used to be here were coming, hoping to find a wizard who would magically pull a rabbit out of his hat and instantly fix all their problems. These people will never come back.

"Those who do have a deeper understanding of how the work at the Casa is done which makes it even more beautiful.

"*It appears that Medium Joao is still pulling all the strings from wherever he is, in prison or under house arrest, and making all the decisions regarding the operations at the Casa.*

"He was instrumental in creating the Casa, for which we must be grateful, but now his mission is over, the time has come to bow out.

"The Casa will never be again what it was before, contrary to what many still hope for, but it has a lot of potential; it is still a holy place. The land existed long before he arrived. That's why Chico Xavier told him to come and build the Casa in this area [Chico *never* said this]." [283]

Indeed, the landscape had changed dramatically. By late 2021, the weekly visitors to the Casa had plunged to fifty or less.

Only a few first-time visitors are present. Most of the attendees are local devotees. Only a few posadas remain open. News reached the Casa that they sentenced João to over 100 years in prison. The last glimmer of hope for resuscitating the Casa and its reputation was fading fast.

Heather Cumming, Gail Thackray, and Josie Ravenwing removed Casa tours from their websites. They erased any reference to João, although they all credit him when claiming their dubious healing powers. Their books are still for sale. Gail continues to promote her book, film, and Casa knick-knacks.

Josie Ravenwing moved to Naples, Florida, and changed her name to Josie Ann Tamarin. In this digital age, you can run but you can't hide. This should serve as a warning for the rest of the Casa crew who haven't jumped ship. You might be under investigation as accessories.

In 2021, Heather redesigned her website, removing any discussion of John of God. Although she does mention the phalange of entities and her training at the Casa, she no longer refers to it as the Casa and now calls it the Dom Inácio Spiritual Center with its Entities of Light.

Her curriculum vitae boasts of her attendance at elementary and high school, Michael Harner shamanic workshops, participation in the Hoffman Quadrinity Process (a five-day new-age therapy workshop), and Reiki certificates.

The first thing that caught my eye when I visited her renovated site was her logo. It is unusual, especially the inverted triangle. The inverted triangle is the ancient symbol of water and of the feminine. The symbol of the Casa is an erect triangle. What's going on here? At the top of her logo is an inverted triangle in very dark blue (it looks black). Below the triangle is the Greek symbol lambda, which is the same color. The lambda symbolizes a scale and its fulcrum. In Heather's logo, the lambda has been inverted and altered so that the downward point of the triangle replaces the fulcrum. Below this is a globe.

I used these common symbols to duplicate her logo:

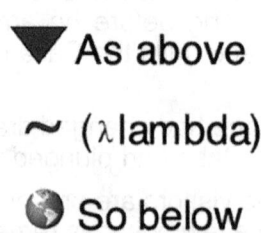

▼ As above

~ (λ lambda)

🌎 So below

Like the inverted pentagram, the inverted triangle is also a symbol of Satanism. In alchemy, the inverted triangle is associated with mercury, the God of financial gain, divination, luck, trickery, and thieves. Mercury also guides souls to the underworld.

An inverted black triangle was the patch the Nazi prison guards assigned to mark individuals considered "asocial." The category included lesbians, nonconformists, sex workers, gypsies and the insane. They were tattooed with this symbol as well. An inverted pink triangle was assigned to gay men. The gay community has adopted both symbols. The lambda was officially declared the international symbol for gay and lesbian rights by the International Gay Rights Congress. The lambda also has significance in chemistry, specifically because of its definition of *a complete exchange of energy.*

The phrase "As above, so below" also has ancient roots. It is rooted in hermeticism, something we have already visited regarding João and his Casa of black magic. When I Googled the phrase, the most common references were to an alchemical/hermetic tract called *The Emerald Tablet of Hermes Trismegistus.* A quote from Aleister Crowley, founder of The Golden Dawn and High Priest of black magic and its alchemical heritage, was equally common.

Now, we can decipher her logo. The inverted triangle with all its associated symbology is above, and the world is below—*as above, so below.* Heather's logo is a sigil, a magical symbol used to invoke alchemical transformation. It summons "what is above" to manifest as "what is below."

As I peeked into her website, I wasn't surprised to read her revised pitch: *The Entities were first introduced to Heather at the Centre of Dom Inácio. Over the years, she guided many, many people from all over the world to interact with these evolved Beings of Light. Her groups experienced the real, pure blessings that come from the Light. Today, as Heather incorporates spiritual mediumship into her practice, she closely associates with members of the phalange of St. Ignatius along with her Spiritual Guides and Mentors.*

Ordained in the Order of Melchizedek (you, too, can be ordained online for a mere $199), Heather assures us that she is the ideal teacher. She writes about *"The alchemical process of healing; an alchemist might be imagined as a very evolved being who lives as a hermit and devotes his or her life to literally transforming lead into gold. This is what empowers us. When we create peace, harmony, balance, equilibrium in our mind and heart, we find it in life. Let us live our lives with discipline, virtue, discernment, trust, integrity, faith and forgiveness of our self and others."*

In other words, Heather is offering her services as a medium incorporating the Casa Exus and practicing their hermetic brand of magic.[284]

As for the recreation of the Casa and a new set of ethics, we are still waiting. The cruel reality of commercialism is that Lindo Horizonte is being sold off to crack cocaine treatment internment centers. President Jair Bolsonaro created a law mandating involuntary hospitalization for drug addicts. This created an enormous surge in the private sector to profit from this. Many opened cheap centers for the overflow numbers of addicts for mandatory internment.[285]

The Agency overseeing this only licenses facilities that use a suitable existing building. Many abandoned posadas are ideal for these enterprises. Their sale or rental cost is up to 80% less than structures in neighboring cities. An eager (out-of-work) workforce is available in Abadiânia.

Six of the former posadas of Lindo Horizonte now function as treatment centers. The people now walking the streets are not dressed in white. Many are violent criminals, and others are at the rock bottom of their lives. Of course, they don't attend the Casa. I doubt the Casa folks would welcome them with open arms.

I suppose this is a just fate for the remaining Casa cultists. The presence of hundreds of crack addicts further reduces real estate values. After all, the posada owners were only in this for the money from the beginning. Money rules in Barrio Lindo Horizonte.

The former Posada Dom Ingrid is now a drug treatment center. Photo: Michael Bailot.

IX.
WHAT IN HELL HAPPENED HERE?

Well, I warned you. This story is like a fairy tale by Hans Christian Andersen. There was hell and terror to pay and a fight to the death between good and evil. In the end, the story has a moral and a truth that is hard to swallow. There is no happy ending. Yes, the story of João Faria is very difficult to swallow. Now we can relax and allow this heavy meal some time to digest. I tried my best to stay out of *his* story. But now it's my turn to express an opinion.

After researching his dirty laundry for four tedious years, I've had time to process it. It is not a pretty picture. I'll attempt to explain it through my eyes, soul, and truth.

Brazil is weird.

It is particularly weird when it comes to magic, cults, and trance possession. I can say the same for their religions, new age movements, and the thousands of men and women who founded their own tiny cults. They are everywhere. The city police chief, your barber, and the woman who owns the restaurant you frequent are participants in the cultish side of Brazil. The Casa de Dom Inácio was just one more cult center in a vast ocean of cults.

The term cult has a double meaning. It once signified a social group with common interests: a sect, a denomination, a church, or a spiritual movement. Nowadays, we tend to define a cult as a group that practices devotion to a particular person, deity, or object. A statue of Saint Rita or a crystal bed, for example.

A darker definition is a group sharing strange practices that frighten outsiders. These cults are considered crazy or evil by the public. Its leader is often demonized by the detractors and beatified by the devotees.

This applies to spirits as it does to people. A cult venerates the deity on the throne. What we have here is the cult of João de Deus and his phalange of entities. The Casa and its devotees are a cult in every regard.

Brazil is superstitious, yes, almost everyone.

They believe in all kinds of things North Americans and Europeans haven't considered possible or relevant. Brazil is a magical land, and Brazil loves magic. You practice Brazil's magic when you buy a candle at church and pray to a Saint to heal your cancer.

Or when you visit a local witch to put a curse on your husband's mistress. Brazilians are fond of the lottery for the same reason. Folks here believe in miracles and unexplainable supernatural events. This magic is embedded in their music, art, and souls. Magical thinking created the Casa—magical thinking of hundreds of thousands of regular Brazilians. João and his spirits created a cult of miracles and supernatural forces and a cult of João. The Casa teaches superstition. What he fashioned is Brazilian, through and through.

Brazil is corrupt.

Sorry, Brazil—I love you, heart and soul, but your bureaucracies are corrupt to the core. If it requires a document or a stamp, if it involves government funding or permission, you can find someone to bribe with a bit of effort.

João practiced bribery. The Casa's foundation is built on bribery and shared secrets. João practiced deceit and fraud his entire life. He isn't a good man who somehow got corrupted. No, he began his life journey on the wrong foot. His corruption reached the highest levels of government, courts, military, and police. João is a charismatic mafioso and the ultimate conman. He lured many people into his web of protection and deception and then sucked their souls dry.

By the way, in Brazil, it is easy to pay a hitman to take care of your dirty business. But these days, it costs a lot more than 300 reais.

But people were cured! The current was fantastic. It changed my life. I never saw him doing anything immoral or illegal. I had many beautiful experiences there.

I'm sure you did.

This must be uncomfortable for the people who benefited or were impressed by the work at the Casa. I'm pretty sure most of you won't ever read this book. But if you do, I'd like to assure you— yes, you did. You had a wonderful experience. But are you ready to face exactly what that experience was? Did you know that good spirits and harmful spirits are both capable of curing people? That demonic spirits can radiate love, create a fantastic current, and change your life? Are you certain the opening prayers at the Casa were prophylactic against evil?

Especially since João probably received a coerced blowjob-rape minutes before the prayer? Did the triangle or the framed painting of Jesus guarantee your safety?

Perhaps you saw nothing unethical or evil because you were shielded from it (lied to). Even as it penetrated your being while you sat in the Entities current. The conundrum of the Casa is this. If people were cured and had spiritual experiences, isn't this enough?

I suppose it is enough if you understand that black magic and dangerous spirits gave you this gift. And they will probably take it back one day. Do you understand that offerings of blood and semen secured the deal for you? Those young girls were raped for you to receive a cure from João's Exus. This is one of several enigmas that are difficult to face. For the non-believers, it's easy. Of course, this was some crazy and dangerous business. To the devotees, it is the end of their meme. How does one process this? A demon cured me. I adored a monster and a rapist. He conned me, and I paid dearly. Did I proselytize for a pedophile?

Who are the Entities?

Who owns their trademark? João owns their trademark. Only João incorporates these entities, and he forbids anyone else to do so.

Most rational people (albeit many visitors to Abadiânia are decidedly not rational) take one look at the cartoon-like portraits of the entities João claims to incorporate and are not impressed. These guys never existed. As I said, Brazil is weird.

To place these spirits on a pedestal, granting them omniscient powers, is a dangerous mistake. Let us clarify—no one but Seu João knows who and what these entities are, or even if they exist. Just as most of the attendees at the Casa do not understand who João and his cohorts really are. Didn't anyone notice how he winces in pain as he incorporates an entity (or mimics incorporation)? Does a spirit of light cause such agony? You'd think he would be ecstatic, with tears of joy on his face. And why are these superheroes all unsmiling and wearing mustaches?

José Valdivino   *José Penteado*   *Doctor Augusto*

So, these are the high angelical spirits of love and white light? Hmmm. The diminutive form of José is Zé: as in Zé Arigó and Zé Pilintra. Or perhaps, Exu Valdivino and Exu Penteado?

Gringos don't understand Portuguese.

Do you realize how much context and reality you lose if you can't speak the language? If you depend on your guide or the staff to explain everything—lead you about like a child? Can you understand this backwater Alabama of Brazil with so little information?

The gringos do not understand Brazilian culture and know nothing about João's or Brazil's secret history. Most of his foreign visitors wouldn't know Umbanda if it bit them on the nose.

They are unaware of the Casa Gestapo and intrigues. They are misled before they ever arrive in Brazil. Gringos are a brain-washed source of information about João. They have perpetuated the false claims and João's fake biography. They have no idea that they've joined a cult, are defending a serial rapist, or that there are no actual surgeries.

These enthusiasts would run away in fear and disgust if they knew who those entities were. All they know is what they've read and what their friends or guides have proclaimed. Those who "met" João for ten seconds at one of his traveling road shows know nothing about what they paid $800 for.

The Placebo Effect is a miracle maker.[286]

One of my favorite books about spiritual healing is *The Secret Teachings of the Espiritistas* by Harvey Martin. The Filipino Psychic Surgeons preceded João's Casa. They were at it long before Dr. Fritz showed up on the scene. The psychic surgeons became famous for seemingly opening a big hole in their patient's bodies. They put their hands into the bloody opening and performed surgeries. They appeared to close the wound with a pass of their hand, leaving no scar or evidence of surgery. This was filmed with shaky VHS cameras and blurred images. Tens of thousands of foreigners flocked to the Philippines in search of miracles. Shirley MacLaine was among them.

Harvey Martin researched these psychic surgeons. For many years, he filmed and documented their successes. He promoted them in America. Martin became vice president of their organization in Hawaii. The Filipino psychic surgeons have one significant difference from the work of Brazil's spirit doctors.

They are a Christian sect (a hybrid variety of Catholicism) and proclaim that they heal with the power of the Holy Spirit. They do not work with disembodied spirit doctors.

Their tradition reaches into the distant past before Catholic missionaries arrived. Its roots are in shamanism. The spiritists borrowed from the shamanic techniques of trance, hypnotism, psychodrama, and sleight of hand. These are almost universal in the world's shamanic traditions.

Harvey's mentors, among the Philippines' most famous psychic surgeons, such as Alex Orbito and Benjamin Pajarillo, let him in on a shocking secret. They revealed to him that the surgeries were sophisticated, sleight-of-hand tricks. Budding psychic healers were taught how to do this in special training groups, but only after they had mastered automatic writing and other spiritist techniques.

At the time of Harvey's travels, a scandal had surfaced about these psychic surgeons. Some of them amassed fortunes from their services. They were also exposed for their parlor tricks. In this atmosphere, the truth was revealed to Harvey. He was shocked and caught on the horns of a dilemma. How could he continue to promote these so-called miracles when he knew they were illusions? He began to doubt everything he believed.

Orbito and Pajarillo assured him that the Holy Spirit had indeed cured people. Their techniques were efficacious, even if they were magic tricks. What they, and shamans throughout the ages, understood was that the placebo effect is highly effective.

One of these shamanic techniques is extraction. The Filipino shamans of antiquity, the Mananamba, were among these practitioners. Shamans and folk healers worldwide have been documented sucking with their mouth, or through a tube, at the perceived site of the illness. This is done with much drama and vocalizations.

When they finish their work, they produce the object they extracted. Either an illness or an evil spirit. This might be something like a cockroach, a piece of meat, a pebble, or a nail. Producing the extracted cause of the disease sometimes affects a cure.

The world's first anthropologists noted these tricks early on. They misunderstood the theater of the trance state, mislabeling it as a type of psychosis. From that point on, shamanism was accused of charlatanism and superstition. The natives knew better. The patients demanded and expected the theater.

A significant amount of published scientific studies have proven that the power of the placebo has curative powers. For example, Harvey describes one of the first studies, by Dr. Henry Beecher, done in 1961. This study is one of many unethical research papers produced during the Cold War.[287]

These researchers did not advise the subjects that they were part of a study. Many of them risked the patient's life without their knowledge or permission. Eventually, this type of research was banned (we hope).

In Beecher's time, a controversy was being debated regarding the efficacy of a surgical technique claimed to reverse angina pectoris. This heart disorder causes attacks of heart pain because of insufficient blood flow to the heart muscle. Radical heart surgery was the prescribed technique. The problem was that many studies in the fifties revealed that this surgical technique often did not resolve the disorder.

Beecher's two double-blind studies illustrated this issue. Heart surgery usually involves breaking the sternum (sawing it open) to allow access to the heart. This is a bloody and dangerous procedure. In this case, he performed the actual surgery on 60% of the patients in his study.

The other 40% were given general anesthesia and told they would receive the operation. The surgeon made a shallow incision where a deep one would typically occur.

He did not break open the sternum or enter the heart cavity and didn't perform heart surgery. He stitched up the false incision and told the patients they had completed the operation. His two studies found that both groups had identical 50/50 results, whether it was a cure or not.

Dr. Leonard Cobb did a similar study around this time. He reported that 43% of those receiving the placebo surgery saw an improvement in their condition, while the people receiving the actual procedure reported only a 32% improvement rate.

In 1979, Norman Cousins published his book *Anatomy of an Illness as Perceived by the Patient.* The best-seller detailed his recovery from a life-threatening form of incurable degenerative arthritis. His self-prescribed regimen of positive thinking, laughter therapy, and massive doses of Vitamin C cured him.[288]

Professor Cousins detailed his theory: One's personal beliefs interact with the immune system, activating physiological processes. The power of one's beliefs and attitude can cure one.

He revived interest in the theory of the placebo effect. Hundreds of studies and dozens of books have since revealed its efficacy. The placebo is amplified exponentially when you factor in a group belief and support system. If many people are experiencing relief from a placebo, they pass this fervor on to others in their group. One sees this often with evangelical healing sessions. The Casa was a classic example of how the spiritual beliefs of like-minded people have curative effects.

But what about the surgeries?

What surgeries? During my internship at Casa, I was keen to witness a real surgical event. Opening the body, a deep probe to the internal organs, and the surgical removal of the problem area. Maybe a gallbladder or a baseball-sized tumor is expertly removed. There, in the surgical tray, for all to see. Of course, this never happened. João was a one-trick pony. Well, actually, a three-trick pony. He didn't go to the Philippines to master his tricks.

The Pincushion Man showed up at the Casa at least once a year. He came from Rio Grande do Sul. João always received him with open arms and would invite him to the stage for surgery on his tumors. I'm not sure why they called him the Pincushion Man.

João's Pincushion Man had a rare disorder that created several dozen lumps down his neck and back. They were the size of grapes and large marbles, with a ping-pong ball or two. João asked an assistant to fetch a pair of electrician's pliers.

The first time I saw the Pin Cushion Man was in one of those poorly shot VHS films the Casa once sold. This one was played every day as we waited for the stage show. I almost know it by heart. On VHS, it looks like João is really doing the bloody mess surgery I wanted to see. This led me to believe they might exist. It was as close as we would get. The older the videos, the bloodier it was. Those folks had to recuperate for weeks in the infirmary, injected with painkillers and antibiotics.

Mr. Pincushion, shirtless and in the flesh, was shocking enough. Benign tumors covered the entire length of his back. His disorder also damaged the nerves. He couldn't feel a thing if you messed with his tumors—there were no functioning nerves there.

João got right into it. With the man's back facing the audience, I had a bird's-eye view of the tragic landscape of his back. He sliced his scalpel around one of the bigger lumps, then secured the fat and gristle with the pliers. João tugged mercilessly until he tore out the entire lump. He displayed this with fanfare and self-satisfaction. He asked his victim if he felt any pain. Of course, he didn't. Then, he did the same to another tumor. João declared the man cured of his cancer and reminded him to come back again in one year for a checkup.

So, João's three tricks.

He probably learned The first one when he worked for a traveling carnival. We owe a magician, The Amazing Randi, for first pointing this out to the public, but his cry in the wilderness went unheeded.[289]

The carny trick has been practiced around the world for

centuries. It can be traced back to the Fakirs of India. It entered the worldwide circus circuit in the 1920s at many repertoires. It is now known as the Blockhead Trick.

The shill has his head leaned backward. Then the carney picks up a mallet and (gently) hammers a thick thirty-penny nail, about four inches long, up the guy's nose. A clear path that seems impossible. The trick is performed today by over a hundred performers in carnivals and sideshows around the world. The nail and the hemostat penetrate almost to the back of your throat, nowhere near your brain.

The Casa crew says the hemostat goes directly into your brain and stimulates your pineal gland, your third eye. He's also busy removing your breast tumor and bad liver; he just has to twist it a few extra times.

Let me show you where that 30d nail and João's torture instrument go. If you are one of the billions of people who got a nose swab test for COVID-19, that's the same avenue João takes. However, his probe is shorter than the Covid swab.

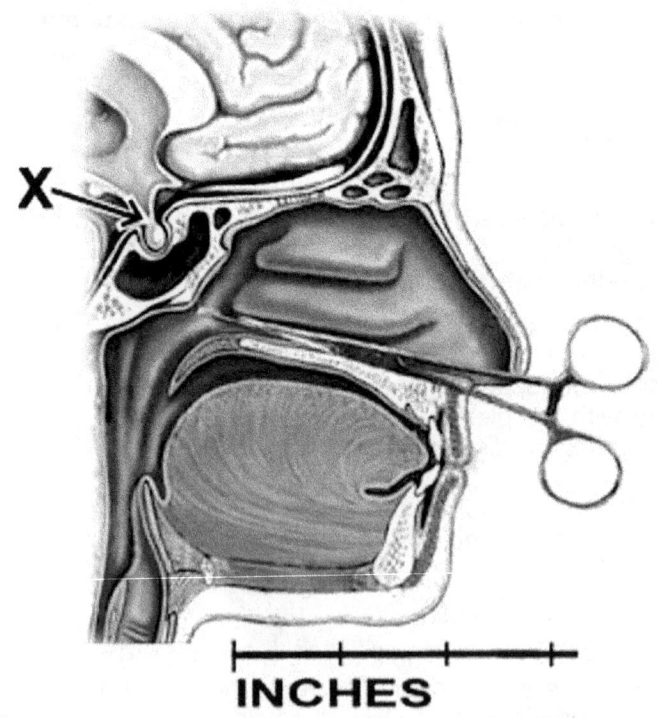

X = pineal gland. Hemostat enters only 2-3 inches; Illustration credit: James Randi Educational Foundation.

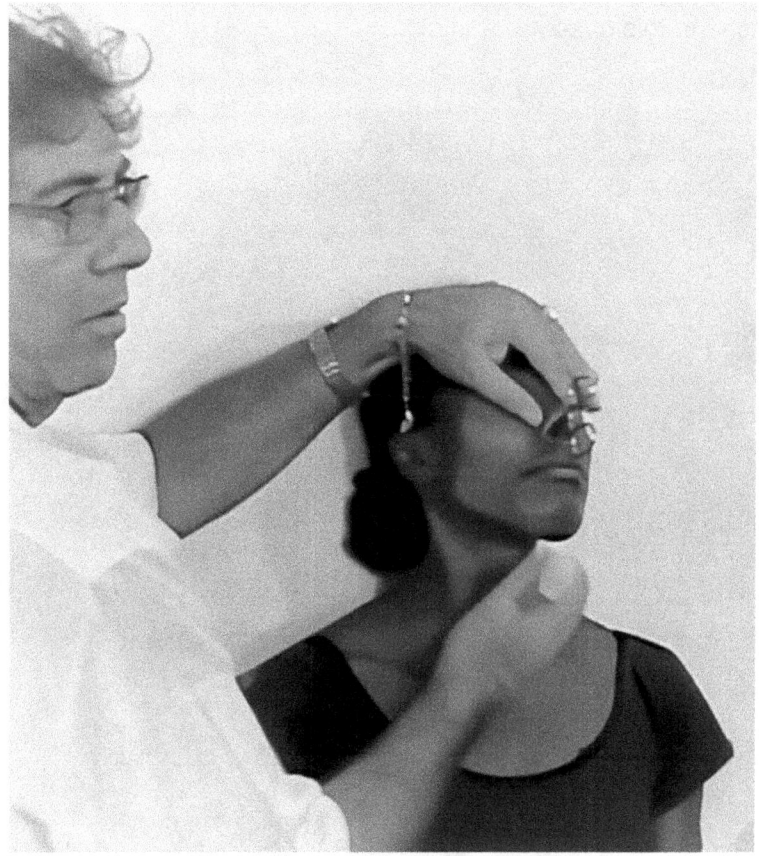

Nose job. Photo: Michael Bailot.

His second trick is the *cut*, which he calls surgery. There is no surgery. He makes a superficial cut, usually only one or two inches at most. Occasionally, he gets carried away and goes for three inches. But this would be a very shallow cut designed to show a thin line of blood more dramatically.

The cut is almost always into fatty tissue without veins or much blood. He likes to yank out a bit of fat to prove his great surgical skill. He needs blood, but only a little. Breasts, buttocks, and stomach flab are where he usually makes his cut—a place with few nerves and infection-resistant.

The cuts are made with a sterilized scalpel, freshly removed from its sealed wrapper. João was a tailor and shoemaker, so his stitching skill duplicates the curved needle technique used to pierce leather—in this case, fat and skin.

João's stage show with two hypnotized victims. Photo: Michael Bailot.

One day, Medium João performed surgery on Ultan O'Meara. He complained of pain and a bump on the top of his head. A berni caused this bump and pain. It begins when a botfly lays an egg on your exposed skin. The egg turns into a microscopic parasitic worm that penetrates your skin. It remains as thin as a hair for some weeks, and one barely notices it. Then, it turns into a bump the size of a maggot. It begins wiggling around under your skin and slowly eating your flesh with a mouth like a lamprey. When you realize you have a berni, it is past due time to remove it the best way you can. It is common in places like Abadiânia, where many cattle and livestock are its host.

When Ultan explained his discomfort to the Medium, the Entity told him he had a brain tumor. He would need to operate immediately. Ultan didn't know what a berni was (but João did) and had never had

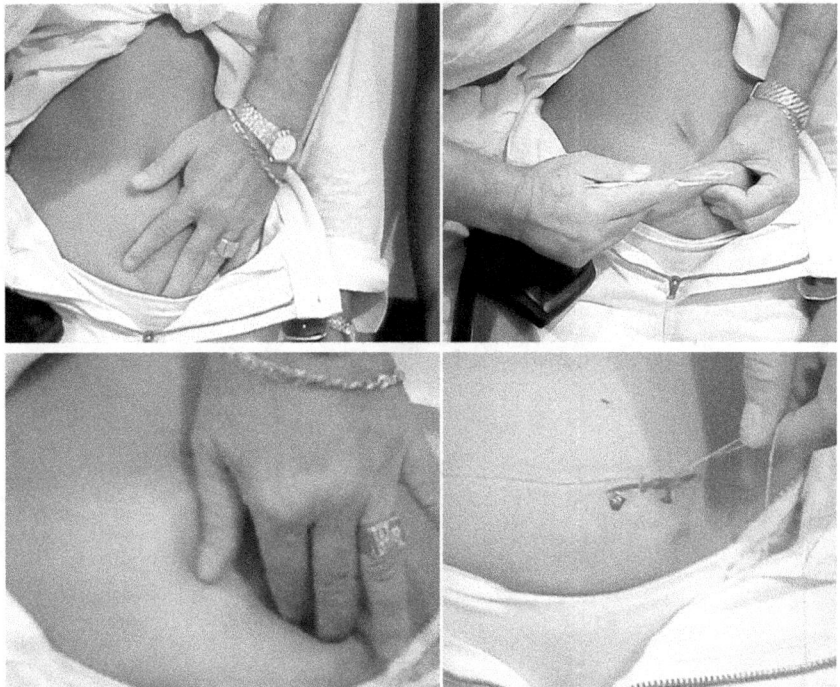

João makes a 1½" incision, sticks his finger in the hole, and wiggles it around. He stitches the wound in a minute. He is fond of the area above the pubic hairs—it looks like an ungloved finger probing a vagina. Photos: Michael Bailot

one. He submitted to brain surgery. When the Medium removed the berni, he waved it around for all to see, declaring it was the tumor he extracted. For many years, the rumor around Abadiânia was that Ultan had been cured of brain cancer.

As we discussed earlier, the tricks are João's stage show. They galvanize the crowd's attention. Then, hypnotic suggestions can be telegraphed across the current, enthralling the shocked audience. Almost every folk healer, evangelical faith healer, shaman, and born-again snake handler does this. Like the placebo effect, shock theater is a prerequisite to magical healing. A shaman needs to keep up the intensity of the theater and the shock throughout his performance. This can go on for hours, as does João's healing works.

The cut is the offering that guarantees cures for the people in the current, which is a current of blood. The blood must get on his hands and be cast to the ground. He does this every time he makes the cut. No blood, no axé, no cure.

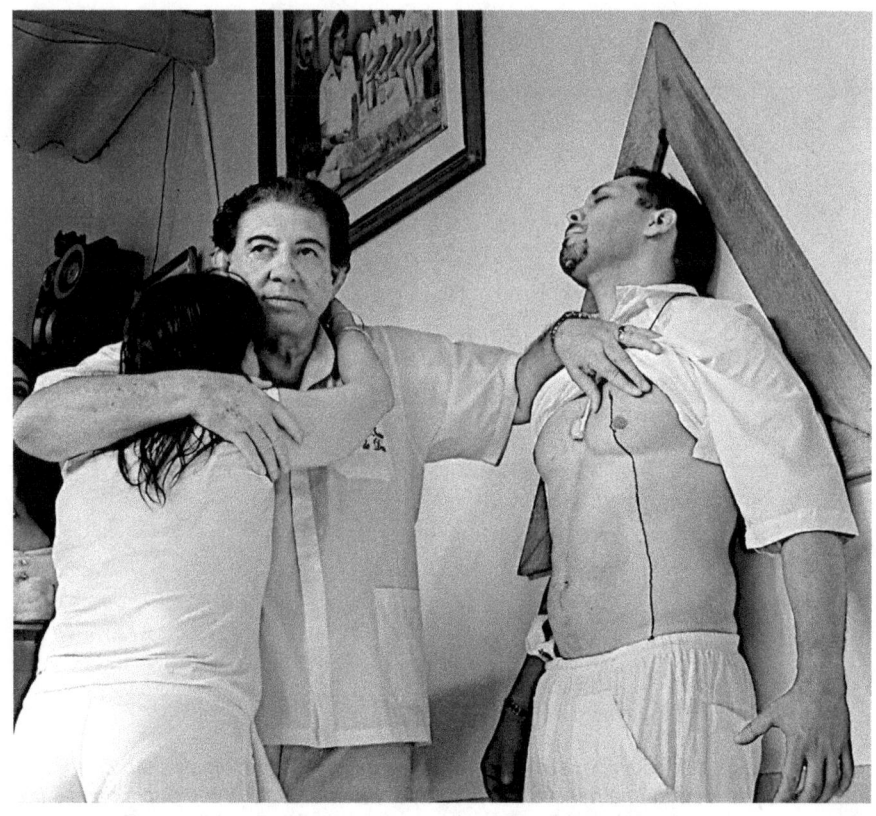

The Cut and the Triangle: Blood offerings occur before the Triangle. Photo: posted on Trip Advisor and attributed to Valdo F.

Eye scraping hurts. João pilfered the eye-scraping technique from Zé Arigó. This is the Casa's most shocking stage act. Why would anyone in their right mind allow this to happen? Violation of one's eye is the ultimate shock. It puts the recipient in an altered state, employing trauma to deliver a powerful message to both the victim and the audience. Here, we have crossed the line. Magician James Randi wrote this about João's surgeries:

"John of God will seat a subject for his visible surgery stunt and apparently scrape the eyeball of the patient with the edge of a knife. I believe that this is a variation of the usual trick—illustrated on page 177 of my book, *Flim-Flam!*—in which a knife blade is inserted under the eyelid of a subject with little or no resulting discomfort."

"With the Brazilian faker, the scraping motion gives it a much more fearsome aspect, but for several good reasons, I doubt that any contact takes place with the cornea. The sclera, the eye's white section, is relatively insensitive to touch. Try touching that area with a finger or any clean object; you'll see this is true. The cornea, however, is very sensitive—among the body's most sensitive areas.

"Most persons—and I'm one of them—have a difficult time watching the eye being touched. We tend to empathize with the situation, and I'm sure that some readers are at this moment involuntarily squinting in distaste as they read these words; we're that reactive to eyeball-touching. Few people will resist looking away when John of God seems to scrape an eyeball, and I note that he's furtively watching the camera position as he performs this stunt, blocking the view with his body when a close-up is sought." [290]

In the eye scraping and probes I have watched up close, João is scraping the white of the eye, not the cornea. Sometimes, he inserts a dull knife blade into the eye socket as well. Everyone I have questioned after the scraping experienced pain and inflammation. Marina Abramović's film, *The Space In-Between,* illustrates in detail how the scraping occurs only on the eye's sclera.

Every "surgery" João has performed is a variation of these three tricks. He does his other tricks in secret; rape of the vulnerable and surreptitious blood offerings to his exus.

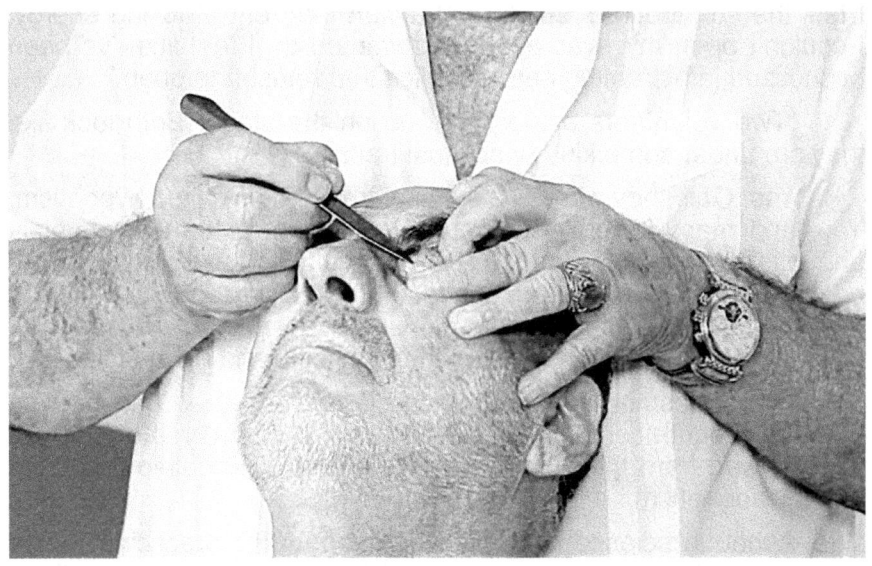

Eye scraping. Posted in an article by Vinicius Canova in Rondônia Jurídico. Photographer unknown.

There's no hypnotism here.

But why does no one feel any pain? Hypnotism is a subject and a phenomenon that has fallen in and out of fashion throughout history. We know the clichéd versions of hypnosis that we received through television and film. Someone swings a pocket watch or pendulum back and forth in front of the subject, suggesting they are getting very sleepy. Then they become stupidly suggestible and obey the hypnotist's every command. There is much more to hypnotism than this.

I was first hypnotized by a stage hypnotist when I was ten and fell into the deepest state possible. Afterward, he gave me a private session. He taught me how to self-hypnotize and hypnotize others. I took to it like a duck to water. I have a pretty good idea of what hypnotism is and how to spot it when it occurs.

Hypnotism is trance. Anyone from João's camp insisting that no hypnotism occurs in his treatments is not paying attention. Many interviewees have commented on the trance people enter before he performs their surgeries.

Even Gail Thackray noticed this as she was being prepared for her "surgery." She said, "The beautiful Brazilian guide is speaking softly and calmly, praising God and the spirits and talking us through a little meditation in a mixture of Portuguese and English. Gently, I feel the soft touch of spirits and a warm current of loving energy. I couldn't open my eyes even if I'd wanted to. I feel like I've been hypnotized into creating heavy eyelids that refused to open."

"Two volunteers are brought up on the stage. Both look like they are under some kind of spiritual trance." [291]

Yes, Gail, they were in a spiritual trance. It is called hypnotism. You, and many others, were put into a hypnotic trance, privately and without your knowledge. This was done in the Entities' Room before being brought out on the stage for your surgery. Hypnotism is the time-honored technique of shamans and yogis. They used it for millennia to influence and control their subjects and even animals.

Franz Mesmer, a German physician, "discovered" mesmerism in the eighteenth century. He was certain that some type of mystical force flowed from the hypnotist to his subject. He called this force animal magnetism.

Although science debunked his theory, any practicing trance medium would likely agree with his ideas. Axé (animal magnetism) can be passed from one person to another.

Trained mediums can put a susceptible person into a trance merely by reaching out and touching them. João did this many times, often captured on film. Trance and hypnotism are kissing cousins.

I would suggest that João's stage show is group hypnotism-- as is sitting in the current and passing through the current line. He knows exactly what he is doing.

One of the most important applications of hypnotic trance is its ability to deaden pain. Hypnotism gained credence in the medical profession precisely because of this effect. Hypnotism is a proven pain reduction technique.

Dentists and surgeons have used it as a substitute for anesthesia with varying success. Hypnotic suggestions can sometimes result in psychological effects as well. These include weight loss, remission of conditions, and release from addictions and neurotic behavior (at least temporarily).

Milton Erickson (1901-1980) was one of the most influential modern hypnotists. His Ericksonian therapy employed indirect suggestion and confusion techniques instead of formal hypnotic induction. He could produce hypnotic phenomena in a clinical setting. These included hallucinations, anesthesia, catalepsy, and regression as far back as infancy. He insisted that all these effects could be produced by light trance only. The subject didn't even realize they were in a hypnotic state.[292]

I encourage my readers to Google street hypnosis (essentially Ericksonian hypnosis). See how easily and covertly an unsuspecting public can be hypnotized and made subject to the whim of the hypnotist. You'll be surprised.

Another form of hypnotism is the practice of hypnosis for sexual purposes. But not in a therapeutic context. It has become popular in the fetishism of sadism, masochism, and bondage. It can even be performed over video conferencing or text chat. Hypnotic suggestions can freeze a victim in place or increase sexual arousal. One can seduce and entrap a person through hypnotism.[293]

Sadly, many of João's rape victims reported this. They felt like they couldn't move or speak. They remember coming out of a trance only to discover they were in a sex act. Several of them described the experience as being frozen. Many couldn't remember what had just happened. Others commented on his incantations or repetitious prayers or phrases. He even repeated The Lord's Prayer and Hail Mary to hypnotize his victims before the abuse.[294]

Irving Kirsch pointed out that hypnosis is a non-deceptive

placebo. With Medium João, we should disregard the non-deceptive part.[295]

The Encyclopedia Britannica (2004) defines the hypnotic state thus. "The hypnotized individual appears to heed only the communications of the hypnotist and typically responds in an uncritical, automatic fashion while ignoring all aspects of the environment other than those pointed out by the hypnotist. In a hypnotic state, an individual tends to see, feel, smell, and otherwise perceive in accordance with the hypnotist's suggestions, even though these suggestions may be in apparent contradiction to the actual stimuli present in the environment. The effects of hypnosis are not limited to sensory change; even the subject's memory and awareness of self may be altered by suggestion, and the effects of the suggestions may be extended (post-hypnotically) into the subject's subsequent waking activity."

Now, repeat after me, "I won't feel any pain when Medium João's entities perform surgery. No one has ever felt any pain during his operations. His procedure will cure me of whatever ails me. There will be no contraindications or infection."

Did you take the Passiflora Kool-Aid?

Passiflora (passionflower) and its fruit (maracuja) are well known for making one sleepy. It is listed as a hypnogogic (or oneirogenic) herb. This category of herbs contains drugs that can provoke hypnogogic dream states. These include waking dreams, lucid dreams, and nightmares.

They also produce hallucinations at the frontier between wakefulness and dream states and hypnic jerking as you approach sleep, as in the current room on a long, hot day. This creates a perfect state for hypnotic suggestions.

Yes, everyone attending the Casa was susceptible to hypnotism. Indeed, almost everyone was successfully hypnotized while in the current. I certainly was. I drank the Kool-Aid three times a day.

Don't believe everything you read.

Particularly if the author uses suspect sources or no sources at all. Nor if the author is using their book to pitch sales of their services. As a rule of thumb, don't blindly believe anything you read. Come to your own conclusions. We are beginning to see how books and media can misinform the public. Some give a spin and an opinion on a subject that is erroneous. Yet, please recognize good journalism for what it is—objective and factual with lots of provable notes and sources.

Pellegrino's first edition with a photo of Machu Pichu in the background.

Like a carnival barker, he touts the powers of the medium:

"He treats 3,000 people per day. Fifteen million people were treated.

He makes the blind see, and the quadriplegics walk again.

More operations in a day than in a large hospital in a month.

How does he remove tumors without touching the patient?"

And on the back cover, *"Could this be the second coming of Christ?"*

I'm a person with a lot of curiosity.

They warn you about this. When I worked at the Casa, I wanted proof of miracle cures. I'm sorry, but I'm skeptical when impossible claims are made.

If someone told me they had been cured of cancer by the Entities, I wanted details. Were you diagnosed with cancer by a doctor and with tests? Did you take conventional treatment or alternative therapies? What makes you think you are cured? Is it because the Entity told you so, or do you have definitive tests and x-rays to prove it? And, most importantly, was João the only healer and the only treatment you received?

No one passed my quiz. The Vatican has a long and drawn-out process to prove a miracle cure has occurred. It draws on reams of documentation and takes many years. They authenticate very few spiritual healings as miracles. If João's miracle cures went through the Vatican's process, I doubt he would have any cures at all.

We have to consider many variables. Spontaneous remission of cancer and almost all severe conditions and diseases exist statistically. Spontaneous cures occur often enough to credit or discredit miracles. Misdiagnosed diseases have an even worse track record. It is almost commonplace.

Then, some people have self-diagnosed and self-medicated themselves into a false sense of certainty. Many of the sufferers at the Casa have psychosomatic diseases.

I'm not denying the reality of chronic fatigue or the many orphan diseases floating around. But there sure was an inordinate amount of mystery maladies afflicting the visitors to Abadiânia, and I can't recall hearing about anyone cured of their ailment.

The Casa was crawling with incurable people who never got cured. Mentally and emotionally unstable folks visited there by the thousands. The Casa became renowned as a de-possession center, and rightfully so. Many became possessed during their visit. Others brought the spirits with them. Either way, possession looks a lot like many psychological disorders. These include anxiety attacks, bipolar disorder, borderline disorder, PTSD, and schizophrenia. João and his spirit guides could not tell the difference.

Do spirits even exist?

That's up to you to decide. As for me—yes, they do exist and even influence human life. Do João's spirits exist? That is also your decision. If spirits and João's spirits do not exist, then we have a classic case of fraud here. If they exist, we also have fraud. With the

Casa and its entities, everything is suspect. I believe João's spirits exist, and all of them are Exus.

Did you hear the rumor?

If you hear rumors that your guru is getting rich or having sex with his disciples—they are probably true.

If you hear tales that your guru is a rapist and a murderer, this might also be true, particularly if a friend or fellow devotee shares the rumor. We have quite a few recent examples proving this point. How many thousands of Casa visitors heard stories but disregarded them as sour grapes?

The buzzing meme.

Facebook, Instagram, Twitter, and YouTube promote memes and hysteria. You know what I'm talking about. Authorities, celebrities, and publicists wield the power of persuasion. We need to beware of them. They often manipulate our emotions and opinions to achieve their objectives.

The Casa tried to use these techniques to redeem their soiled reputation. The battle isn't over.

For example, as far as I know, there has been only one medical study of João's healing powers (not dozens or hundreds). It concluded: "The surgical procedures are real, but we couldn't evaluate the efficacy. It didn't appear to have any specific effect. Our findings are undoubtedly more of an exploratory kind than conclusive ones. Further studies are clearly necessary to cast light on this unorthodox treatment." [296]

This is hardly a published, peer-reviewed study. It is a master's thesis.

I'll have you killed.

How many hundreds of people received this threat from João or his bullies, and how many were ultimately on the receiving end? The Casa mafia exists. Quite a few are still lurking around the Casa and visiting João in his mansion. Police investigations did not destroy the veil of silence and secrecy, the web of protection, and the cult of fear. It is ongoing.

Rape is swept under the carpet here.

The subject and the desire for justice are almost taboo. In Brazil, *the minimum legal age for sexual consent is fourteen.* Sexual intercourse with an individual younger than fourteen years old is illegal. It's considered statutory rape.

Of course, rape without consent is illegal at any age. But, with many of João's rapes of vulnerability, he had technically secured their permission. It is a murky territory. Especially when the system turns a blind eye and questions the victims' statements. The defense attorneys tear them apart in court.

The police report that 30% of his victims, who were fourteen to seventeen years old, were raped through penetration. At least fifteen girls claim to have been victims before the age of thirteen.

Everyone knew.

Everyone living in Lindo Horizonte knew. Everyone across the highway in the real Abadiânia knew. The Judge knew. The Mayor knew, and the police knew. It was scary to know what João was doing. Everyone knew this, too.

Silence is a Prayer, the Casa motto, was the prayer on everyone's lips who walked in the Medium's shadow. Everyone knew, and they kept silent. Dead silent for forty long years.

Some of what they knew was rumor or hearsay. When several thousand people have heard the stories and gossip yet remain silent, this is either abject ignorance or fear. A cloud of fear (and ignorance) has always hovered over the Casa and the city.

Others knew the blunt end of João's rage, ego, sexual addiction, and ruthless power. Some of them are not with us anymore. The survivors have reasons to remain silent.

His goons, pistoleiros, managers, sidekicks, and crooked attorneys knew in another way. They abetted. As did the many authorities receiving João's bribes. His wives and family knew. The posada owners and the guides knew. The taxi drivers, chili pepper vendors, and hairdressers knew. The cowboys drinking at the bar knew. His banker knew. Everyone knew—except the tourists.

The locals never understood why the foreigners thronged to João. Imagine thousands of tourists dressed in white, avoiding contact with the locals—foreigners speaking English, insulated in their enclave. This was far removed from the day-to-day culture of Brazilian Abadiânia. No, the foreigners were a sight to see. But they spent a lot of money. Money silenced much of Abadiânia as efficiently as fear.

Wilson Francisco lived in Lindo Horizonte from 1997 to 2001. In an interview with Christina Fibe, Wilson said, "I saw him sitting in that position, on the throne of Dom Inácio's House, manipulating things of self-interest, as a man. At certain times, you knew it was the entity; at other times, it was John sitting there, fixing things for himself." He remembers waiting by the many buses parked at the Casa to watch the new batch of Brazilians disembark.

He and other men of Abadiânia placed bets on which young women João would sexually abuse. He said, "We'd see the women getting off and point out—that one there is going to be called to talk to João, that one too. We'd place bets to see who got it right the most. Everyone has ears, right? You could hear: *Medium João wants to talk to you after the work.*" Everyone knew.[297]

Rupert Drew, my friend from my Casa days, finally responded to my many requests for a conversation. He said, "It can't hurt to find out what you're after." He wasn't about to help one iota with my project, refusing any testimony—anonymous or otherwise. Nor would he agree to go to the police with information he likely could provide them. My persistence irritated him.

He finally agreed to at least watch the Netflix production. He said, "I watched the Netflix and saw that Joao is back in prison. For me, it is a dog and pony show. I am not interested in knowing what's going on, as I still live here... I found the show less dramatized and more sober [than the Globo interviews] if boring in the end.[298]

"Nothing new, though, just a lot more of the same repetitious talk from women. I can't blame them for being really angry and wanting to see him burn in Hell. Maybe they should get a bunch of gay criminal psychopaths to rape him and see how he feels about that."

We haven't been in touch since.

If he isn't a Catholic and isn't a spiritist, what is he?

Well, I hope we have already covered that in detail. He's a wizard. He's the Wizard of Oz.

Heather is the Wicked Witch of the West, with her phalange of demons. Martin is the tin man with his tin can heart. Pellegrino is the scarecrow (I wish I had a brain), and Diego Coppola is the cowardly lion. The Munchkin tour guides are waiting to escort Dorothy along the yellow brick road. We're off to see the *Emerald City* of the Grand Wizard. And Dorothy? She is the Wizard's next victim (my little pretty): Dorothy, the witch killer.

It is worse than you can imagine!

Corruption at every level kept João out of prison for decades. The Medium allegedly employed secret police vigilante groups and police mafias. He may have bribed public officials, including judges and district attorneys. Local police are said to have received cash payouts. No, it's even worse than all that. Sorry, but I'm too afraid to go there.[299]

João's fifty-year-long whine: "I've been unfairly persecuted my entire life."

To this day, João is crying about how he is a victim of the authorities. And running parallel to his whining is his rationalization for his deviant nature. One often heard the Medium say, "I must have had bad karma in my past lives. Now I am paying it off with my service to humanity." He said the same thing about his entities: "They are paying off their bad karma."

As Exu Lodo has said, "I was a doctor. I did harm to the slave, the maidservant, and the master. Today in Quimbanda, I have learned that charity transforms the darkness, the spell, and the evil."

One must investigate Faria's role in the torture culture to understand the sin he has unsuccessfully tried to pay off through so-called good deeds.

João and the military; there are no records! None.

My research for this book involved corresponding with military agencies. I wanted to confirm that João was enlisted or employed by one or more military branches. To my surprise, they could not (or more likely, would not) confirm that João was one of theirs.[300]

Both agencies overseeing these documents claim they have no record that he served in the military, nor was he employed as a tailor by them or was he under contract. There is no record of him being an intelligence agent and no documentation of his four years in Marabá. There is no document of enlistment, which is mandatory for all boys when they reach eighteen years of age. His nine-year association with the military at several bases hosting torture centers left no paper trail. This is food for thought.

My friend, who could verify that João had a tailor's shop in Marabá while the Casa Azul was functioning, got cold feet. He had been imprisoned and tortured. I hit a raw nerve.

Fear, fear, fear.

João, his mafia, his Casa, and his allies created a shroud of fear that forever permeates his history and Abadiânia. This fear hung over my shoulder for the four years I researched this book. I can't shake it loose, nor can his many victims.

Fear of reprisals, lawsuits, violence, or death. Fear of his demonic entities, his incantations, and macumba. Fear of his cronies, his thugs, his family. And we are still here, thousands of his victims. We live in fear of a powerful man with evil intentions and his deadly friends in high places.

João has remained under house arrest as of May 2022. His lawyer claims he will never return to prison. A judge in Abadiânia is responsible for this situation. The same judge that let him walk on other occasions.

Although João wears an electronic ankle bracelet and is imprisoned in his home, contact with people other than his victims and Casa staff is not restricted. Although cell phones are prohibited for inmates, they very frequently acquire them, and no one polices this. João could easily acquire non-traceable burner phones. He is not under surveillance. He could receive secret visitors and deliveries, and the police wouldn't know.

He cannot leave his home without permission from the court, which is not difficult to obtain. Recently, he requested the court to allow a former Supreme Court Judge and another politician to attend a barbeque at his home.

The last time he was in prison, he acquired a "legal" girlfriend. In May 2022, while under house arrest, he married her. This is his twelfth wife (or thirteenth—I've lost count).

His last wife, Ana Keyla, has divorced him. I couldn't find any records of divorce or separation. Like his previous wife, this one is also a lawyer thirty years younger than him. They live in his mansion, with every comfort imaginable.

His friends, lawyers, and folks of very questionable morals can visit—no one monitors this. João can enjoy his millionaire lifestyle. He can use what funds he has that were hidden away. He can do business. In theory, he could still hire thugs to intimidate people or even kill them. This man belongs in prison for life. He is a danger to the community and any woman crossing his path.

The journal O Popular reported, "The Public Ministry of the State of Goiás [MP-GO] believes that the recent marriage of medium João Teixeira de Faria, 80 years old, known as João de Deus, with lawyer Lara Cristina Capatto, 50, is another indication that he is in full physical and psychological condition to serve, in prison, the sentences related to the sexual crimes committed by him."

Prosecutor Luciano Miranda, responsible for the case, points out that, "Although the fact that he is getting married is not an illicit act, the MP-GO will analyze the issue to see if it is possible to file a request for João de Deus to return to jail. We have to analyze the procedural context, and after doing this analysis, we will verify the possibility of entering with any type of request.

"He is fully capable of serving the sentence of more than one hundred years that was imposed on him within the prison system. It is not only the MP-GO that understands this. The Court of Justice of the State of Goiás (TJ-GO) itself had already concluded in this same sense." [301]

Am I scared? You better believe it. I was waiting for Godot. He appeared but then vanished again. I will not wait any longer. It is time to confront the beast with seven heads. It is time for the truth to challenge the lie.

And the Casa?

It is still open and running on its usual schedule. My last visit to the Casa was in April 2022. It was my second visit since we fled for our lives twenty years earlier. The morning session was ending when I arrived. A few people in white exited. I had dressed in white for the occasion, slipping in like the invisible man. The herbs, water, and trinkets are still for sale. I purchased a couple of biographies in Portuguese to complete my João de Deus book collection. I took some more photos in the trophy room, nervous as ever.

The triangle was still there, as it had been in December 2018, yet the Casa was very different. It's a ghost town—a haunted one. The Casa is among the living dead. Lindo Horizonte was devoid of all but a few visitors.

The shops, including João's fancy crystal shop and Frutti's, were closed. A few posadas were open but empty. Not even a taxi driver was hanging around.

Several drug treatment centers have replaced some of the major hotels and posadas, including Posada Dom Ingrid, Hotel Amazonas, and Hotel Brasil.

I remembered the ambiance and miasma of my time in Abadiânia. But now, I saw it without rose-colored glasses.

The Casa is a perverse and frightening place. The village continues to sulk in silent fear of what happened. The medium had bullied everyone who came to his attention. Hundreds of people employed because of the Casa lived in fear, including his closest staff.

And many unnamed young women took that fear home with them, and it never left their side again. I don't feel safe in Abadiânia, and I never will. I won't be returning.

Nor will the tourists and seekers of a miracle. It's over. The Casa websites have stopped posting for over a year. Most of the guides are no longer bringing groups or touting their association with João; any mention of him has been erased from their Facebook pages and websites. His grandiose sideshow has vanished into thin air.

The New Age is a perverse commercialization of the sacred.

It is long overdue that those involved with the so-called New Age question its ethics—especially their underlying monetization of anything sacred. New Age publicity and philosophy enabled João to continue raping women for decades with impunity.

The loss of innocence is a necessary evil.

Even João will be judged for his sins. His proponents must come clean, admit they were wrong, and shut down the Casa. Much like Charlie Manson's girls, the hangers-on at the Casa need to be rounded up and charged as his accomplices. What a farce to insist that the Casa is clean and pure after all the filth perpetrated there *and encouraged by the entities.* Women were abused within this Casa for forty years. The Casa is so saturated with this stain that it can never be removed. The Casa needs to be leveled, and a monument to his victims erected in its place. Goodbye, Casa Azul.

In time, João will be brought to justice for the remaining pending charges against him. More crimes will come to light. The court will then liquidate his multi-million-dollar empire to pay reparations, unpaid taxes, and court costs. His lawyers will try to grab all they can, as will his ex-wife and offspring. The Casa will be closed one day, and the rats will be chased out. And then the civil lawsuits will commence.

Ghost Casa on a busy day in 2022. Photo: Michael Bailot.

*"Do not go gentle into that good night.
Rage, rage against the dying of the light."* Dylan Thomas.

*"Horror always lurks at the bottom of the magical world
And everything 'holy' is always mixed with horror."*
From a page underscored by Adolf Hitler in his copy of
Ernst Schertel's occult work, Magic: History, Theory, and Practice (1923).

"Pride goes before destruction, and haughtiness before a fall."
From King Solomon's *Proverbs 16:18.*

Santa Rita, stand-in for the Entities, on João's throne. Photo: Casa archives.

"Ad Majorem dei Gloriam"—For the greater glory of God.
The Latin motto of the Jesuits—Implying that anything goes if done for God—even bloodshed.

POSTSCRIPT

In early 2023, I completed the final draft of this book. João was back in the news. In December 2022, he was tried in three separate cases with thirteen victims. One of the victims had put public pressure on the Judge for the long delay in hearing these cases. Faria was found guilty of all charges, and nearly 110 years was added to his tally. The victims were awarded compensation totaling 100,000 reais. Despite this decision, João will remain under house arrest.[302]

In February 2023, another case was tried. This involved five women. He was convicted and sentenced to an additional 48 years. The victims were awarded 60,000 reais in damages. This brings the total years he is sentenced to 270+ years. I don't imagine he will live that long, but the *maximum time* for serving any prison sentence in Brazil is just forty years (even first-degree murder).[303]

In March, Faria was accused of consumer fraud for selling expired bottles of passiflora and bottled water without documentation of the source.

A new case was tried on July 10, 2023, and Faria was sentenced to an additional 99+ years, and must pay 100,000 reais in damages to the eight victims who were abused between 2010 and 2018. This brings his total sentence to 370 years.[304]

Then, on September 15, 2023, a decision was made on his final pending cases involving eighteen people. João was found guilty in three cases related to sex crimes and sentenced to an additional 118 years in prison. This brought his total sentence to more than 489 years, and the victims were awarded 100,000 reais in damages. He was found guilty and sentenced in all seventeen cases brought against him.[305]

In an interview with Cristina Fibe, author of *João de Deus–O Abuso da Fé,* she speaks of the frustration of his victims. Numerous cases in the past involving murder for hire and other serious crimes have not been reopened for investigation. Of his many victims, only sixty-six had their cases heard and a judgment made.[306]

His case is under wraps of secrecy. Accusations of money laundering, murder for hire, human trafficking, intimidation of witnesses, fraud, bribery, and military coverups have vanished into the thin air of the Brazilian judicial system. And there he is, a newlywed in the luxurious comfort of his home—earning a living from the Casa, still in the saddle. It makes you wonder.

The Netflix series *John of God, Crimes of a Spiritual Healer,* trended for three years after its release. It was still among the most popular on their trending list in 2023.

Brave women are continuing the fight, but the press ignores them. João is old news now. My hope is that a Brazilian investigator will go the extra mile and complete my work—someone with more courage and resources than I have. The missing years in the military and many unanswered questions about his web of protection and abettors beg to be examined in more detail.

God bless all who suffered in this maniac's hands. The wicked witch is dead, but his phalange lives on.

END NOTES

I.
A Long Time Ago in a Very Strange Land

1. I researched this book for four years. If I learned anything about João Teixeira de Faria, it was that the account of his youth and early adulthood was a myth that wandered far from the truth. In sequence, one biographer after another quoted a simplistic narrative. João repeated the same stories to the press in numerous interviews. As for his biographies, it all began with *João de Deus: The Phenomena of Abadiânia,* published in 1994. The author, Liberate Póvoa, was João's sidekick and lawyer for many years, accompanying the Medium on several of his roadshows in the early days. Póvoa is also a professor of law and a judge.

His book is like the New Testament's Gospel of Matthew. As the first written gospel, those that followed made a great effort to stay with the original storyline. And like the gospels, there is much more myth than historical substance. Póvoa laid down the myth.

Liberate Póvoa. *Joao de Deus: O Fenômeno de Abadiânia. Belo Horizonte:* Self-Published, 1994.

Like the gospels, the following biographers embellished here and there with additional tidbits provided by João or children of the Casa. They all stick to the fable. Throughout my study, I refer to this group of books as the "official story." And yes, I read every one of them. I have used their timeline. These are more of the *gospels* in order of publication:

Robert Pellegrino-Estrich. *The Miracle Man: The Story of João de Deus.* Australia, Self-Published, 1997 thru 2016.

Josie Ravenwing. *The Book of Miracles: The Healing Work of João de Deus.* Self-Published, US 2000, 2002, 2014.

Emma Bragdon. *Spiritual Alliances: Discovering the Roots of Health at the Casa Dom Inácio.* NY, Lightning Up, 2002.

Heather Cumming and Karen Leffler. *John of God: The Brazilian Healer Who's Touched the Lives of Millions.* NY, Simon & Schuster, Inc, 2007.

Ismar Estulano Garcia. *Curas Espirituais.* Goiânia: Abeditora, 2009. Garcia is another attorney who worked for João. He also represented João's wife in the case about illegal guns. His book is, by far, the most boring of them all. However, he lets slip some details about the

Medium that he probably wishes he hadn't.

Gail Thackray. *Gail Thackray's Spiritual Journeys: Visiting João de Deus.* US, Indian Springs Publishing, 2012.

Alfedina Arlete Savaris. *The Mentalist: John of God and Spiritual Healing.* Horizonte Grafica e Editora, 2014.

Maria Helena P. T. Machado. *João de Deus: Um médium no coração do Brasil.* São Paulo, Fontanar, 2016.

Cristina Rocha. *John of God: The Globalization of Brazilian faith healing.* New York, Oxford University Press, 2017.

2. Of note is Maria Helena P.T. Machado's in-depth history of Brazil in the era of João's childhood and the harsh realities of Goiás. Although she cited various authors listed above, her additional material as a historian is an important adjunct to his story.

Other sources I read to understand the history of these times were:

Levine, Robert M. The History of Brazil. US, Greenwood Press, 1999.

Roque, Paulo (Org.) A Colonização do Cerrado: Savana e Celeiro do Mundo. São Paulo, Prêmio, 2006.

Fausto, Boris and Segio. A Concise History of Brazil. NY, Cambridge University Press, 1999/2004.

Reid, Michael. Brazil: The Troubled Rise of a Global Power / Yale University Press, 2014.

Schwarcz, Lilia and Starling, Heloisa. Brazil: A Biography / NY Farrar, Straus and Giroux.

3. Citing Pellegrino-Estrich, Josie Ravenwing, Cristina Rocha, Chico Felitti, and Sebastião Lima.

4. One of Dona Yucca's prayers..... Also, "My son is not like a dog to be given away." And... Enraged at the lack of respect, the priest excommunicated the ten-year-old boy. Machado, Maria Helena P. T. João de Deus: Um médium no coração do Brasil.

5. Childhood friends reminisced about wild times drinking cachaça (sugar cane alcohol) with João as young boys and their frequent visits to the local prostitutes. From O Silêncio é Uma Prece, directed by Candé Salles. Paris Films / 2018, and from John of God; Crimes of a Spiritual Healer. NETFLIX, 2021. Interviews with Lindolfo Bento de Macedo.

Vagabond John: Taking a Spin

6. *The family trained young João in the tailor's trade.* Machado, Povoa, Pelligrino, Ravenwing, Felitti, etc., all mention the João the tailor tale.

7. *His trajectory begins in Campo Grande, in the State of Mato Grosso do Sul.* All of João's biographers and many interviews mention the events at Campo Grande. They all stick to the story.

8. *Kubitschek believed he was the reincarnated Egyptian Pharaoh Akhenaten. See: From Akhenaton to JK—from the Pyramids to Brasília* by Iara Kern, professor of Egyptology at the University of Brasília. Her thesis explores the uncanny similarities between ex-president Juscelino Kubitschek and Pharaoh Akhenaton (fourteenth century BC) and similarities between the master plan of Brasilia and Akhenaton's ancient capital, Achetaton.

9. *"I sold oranges on the streets of Cidade Livre."* From an interview with Severino Francisco, and Ana Dubeux of Correio Braziliense, April 23, 2017.
https://www.correiobraziliense.com.br/app/noticia/cidades/2017/04/23/interna_cidadesdf,590391/perdoe-sempre-recomenda-joao-de-deus-em-entrevista-ao-correio.shtml

10. *Twice a month, trucks loaded with prostitutes would visit the construction sites.* Alex Shoumatoff. *The Capital of Hope: Brasilia and Its People.* NY Random House, 1980, 1990.

11. *Filthy dormitories infested with vermin.* Professor Nair Bicalho writes, "They were housed in sheds that had ten to fifteen rooms with bunk beds from two to three floors. The toilets were a hole dug in the ground and secured with a canvas door. The camp also had a water shortage problem.

"Their beds were grass mattresses, and there was a huge lack of hygiene: fleas, bedbugs, and lice spread throughout the environment, making it necessary to burn the mattresses several times. Canteens had long lines because of the large number of workers in the barracks, which left hungry workers waiting a long time for breakfast, lunch, or dinner.

"This situation of discomfort and deprivation resulted in countless times in canteens breaking down because of raw, spoiled food or small dead animals in the food." Professor Nair Bicalho, from the University of Brasília (UnB), author of the book *Constructores de Brasília*.

Also hilariously helpful was an article titled *Tropical Millennium/ The Cult (and Cults) of Brasilia* by Julian Dibbell in 1992. julian@mostly.com

Dibbell writes: "Brasília, in other words, has come into its own as a masterwork of retro kitsch, still gamely proclaiming itself the shape of things to come while the past into which it was born cloaks it like a fake leopard- skin wrap.

"The smell of that past hangs everywhere, but for a really good whiff, nothing beats the pharaonic tomb of Juscelino Kubitschek, a marble-plated, trapezoidal traffic island rising amid eight lanes of superhighway slicing through the city center. Just outside the entrance sits Kubitschek's trusty Galaxy 500, enshrined in a glass case, and inside the tomb, a steady Muzak flow bathes the president's mortal remains in the hits of his city's heyday: "Love Me Tender," "Strangers in the Night," "Michelle," "The Theme From A Man and a Woman."

"But the centerpiece of this time capsule is the photographs that run along one wall, like hieroglyphs inside a pyramid, telling the story of the ruler's heroic acts: Kubitschek turning on a newly constructed hydroelectric plant; Kubitschek in a tractor clearing vegetation for his new capital; Kubitschek among maps and graphs, presenting to the public Brazil's first Global Development Plan, the scheme that lay behind all this activity."

12. *Mysteriously, there are no records that confirm his registration.*

Copies of my correspondences with two agencies overseeing military records, and their reply that no records exist for João Teixeira de Faria in their systems, can be found in the notes of the final chapter.

Quimbanda João

13. *I referenced dozens of books and academic papers on Candomblé. Some of them include the following:*

Parés, Luis Nicolau. *The Formation of Candomblé; Vodun History and Ritual in Brazil.* The University of North Carolina Press, 2013.

Voeks, Robert A. *Sacred Leaves of Candomblé.* The University of Texas Press, 1997.

Alonso, M.; Smith, Norman K. *The Development of Yoruba Candomble Communities in Salvador, Bahia, 1835-1986* (Afro-Latin@ Diasporas). Palgrave Macmillan / US, 2014.

Araújo, Alex. *Candomblé: Across the Margin of Religious Syncretism—A History of Black Resistance in Brazil.* Exu Edições Virtuais, Brasil, 2022.

Karade, Baba Ifa. *The Handbook of Yoruba Religious Concepts*. Red Wheel / Weiser, US, 1994, 2020.

Encyclopedia of the Yoruba. Indiana University Press, 2016. Carneiro, Edson.

Candomblés da Bahia. Rio de Janeiro, Civilização Braisileira, 1978.

14. Brazil was built on a deep foundation of slavery.

Hall, Gwendolyn Midlo. *Slavery and African Ethnicities in the Americas*. The University of North Carolina Press, 2005.

Editors; Pares, Luis Nicolau / Sansi, Roger. *Sorcery In The Black Atlantic*. The University Of Chicago Press, 2011.

Wikipedia, *Slavery in Brazil*.

15. Exus can open or close the roads of fate, to help or to harm.

Wafer, Jim. *The Taste of Blood, Spirit Possession in Brazilian Candomblé*. Page 14. Philadelphia: the University of Pennsylvania Press. 1991.

16. Blood contains Axé in its most concentrated form; thus, blood offerings have the most efficacy.

Johnson, Paul Christopher. *Secrets, Gossip, and Gods: The Transformation of Brazilian Candomblé*. Page 136. Oxford and New York: Oxford University Press. 2002.

Also, Voeks, Robert A. *Sacred Leaves of Candomblé: African Magic, Medicine, and Religion in Brazil*. Page 73. Austin, TX: the University of Texas Press. 1997.

17. Another influence in the styling of João Curador was Espiritismo. I drew on several sources regarding Spiritism:

Greenfield, Sidney M. *Spirits with Scalpels; The Cultural Biology Of Religious Healing In Brazil*. Taylor & Francis, Routledge, Vt, 2008 and 2016.

Francisco Cândido Xavier; Waldo Vieira; André Luiz (Espírito). *The Mechanics Of Mediumship (Life In The Spirit World Collection Book 11)*. Brazilian Spiritist Federation, 2018.

Foster, Brian. 51 *Disclosures From Spiritism – The 3rd Revelation*.

Kardec, Alan (Author), Dutra, E.G. (Translator). *The Spirits' Book (New English Edition)* Luchnos Media Llc, 2021.

Kardec, Alan. Book On Mediums: *The Guide for Mediums and Invocators*. White Crow Books, 2011.

18. Umbanda set out to resolve the issue, taking syncretism to

another level.

My first-hand experience as a practitioner of Umbanda for the past twenty years helped me understand the many nuances of this path.

I would like to acknowledge and thank my Madrinhas, who instructed me in the practice of Umbanda and mediumship: Baixina, Lucia, Clara, the three Corrente sisters, Maria Alice, and Madrinha Conçeicão.

My favorite overview of Umbanda is Hale, Lindsay. *Hearing the Mermaid's Song: The Umbanda Religion in Rio de Janeiro.* University of New Mexico Press, 2009.

Other research sources for Umbanda:

Lima, Valdir. *Cultos Afro-Paraibanos: Jurema, Umbanda e Candomblé — Fundamentos de Axé.* Editora Aruanda, Rio de Janeiro, 2020.

Guevara, Florencio. *Mesa Blanca / White Altar.* UR Link Print & Media, U.S., 2019.

Silva, Luiz Carlos de Oliveira. *Feitiços – Do Candomblé e na Umbanda.* Leqashy, Rio de Janeiro, Brasil.

De Souza, Leal. *Encruza Livros O Espiritismo, A Magia E As Sete Linhas De Umbanda.* Encruza Livros. Sao Paulo, Brasil 2019.

An excellent introduction to Quimbanda is: Laffitte, Stefania Capone. *Searching for Africa in Brazil; Power and Tradition in Candomblé.* Duke University Press / London 2010.

19. *The Exus have a supreme leader.*

Initiates understand him to be Lucifer; one of his syncretic aliases is the biblical figure of King Solomon. *"Exu Rei is an office that can be assumed by a handful of the Exus in the upper reaches of the hierarchy. Usually, this equates to Exu Mor, Exu Rei das Sete Encruzilhadas, or Exu Lucifer."* Exu Mor is syncretic with King Solomon. Exu Mor is also associated with Beelzebub and Baphomet. *"Exu Mor, who is basically the erratic and lustful element in Quimbanda, is the fire of embers drenched in blood and sperm."*

De Mattos Frisvold, Nicholaj. *Exu & the Quimbanda of Night and Fire.* Scarlet Imprint / Bibliothèque Rouge. Mentioned in other books as well.

20. *As João began his saga of the sixties, one of his points of reference was Master Yokaanam.*

I used several sources to research Yokaanam including:

Yokaanam, o Solitário. Evangelho de umbanda eclética. 5. ed. Cidade Eclética: Academia Eclética Esotérica do la Santuário Essênio do

Brasil, s/d.

Also, Dibbell, Julian. *Tropical Millennium / The Cult (and Cults) of Brasilia,* 1992. julian@mostly.com

Dibbell writes, "Where we are standing is an hour's drive southeast of Brasília, on the steps of a Neo-classical temple camped incongruously amid the red dirt and deep greens of the capital's surrounding countryside."

"Inside the temple, the poor, the pious, and the put-upon from near and far consult with a battalion of full-fledged, white-robed mediums possessed by the shades of long-dead Indians and black slaves, who bring healing power from the spirit world and words of wisdom from their lord Jesus Christ. Outside, scattered around the temple, lie the buildings of a self-sustaining, cashless community of some 600 spiritual seekers—the City of the Universal Spiritualist Eclectic Brotherhood, First Essene Sanctuary of Brazil and the Americas."

"The Eclectic City is older than Brasília, but not by much. It was founded in 1956, when the disciples of self-made messiah Master Yokaanam (formerly Lieutenant Oceano de Sa of the Brazilian Air Force) followed him into the wilderness of the Central Plateau, just months before the new capital's construction got underway. Members of the brotherhood like to suggest a causal link between the two events, but if it was part of Yokaanam's plan to bring the national capital along with him when he left Rio de Janeiro, that was merely a small first stage on the way to a much more ambitious goal: to establish here the nucleus of a great, global civilization, ruled by cosmic justice and love."

Rodrigues De Mello, Gláucia Buratto. Os Peregrinos Eclécticos Cristãos, a paper about Yokaanam and his pilgrimages, was helpful as well.

Yokaanam is also mentioned in detail by Maria Helena P. T. Machado.

21. Another influence in João's style was the Spiritist community of Palmelo, Goiás. They are mentioned by Povoa, Ismar Garcia, and Machado.

Palmelo is known as the Capital of Spiritism in Brazil. You can find a good overview at: https://diariodegoias.com.br/centro-espirita-que-deu-origem-a-cidade-de-palmelo-completa-93-anos/212276/

And here also: https://www.palmelo.com.

Most of these people needed their eyeglasses and canes the next day. They expelled him from the center. Machado and Felitti.

22. *João Goulart. He ruled until 1964, when he was overthrown by a U.S. ARMY/CIA--sponsored military coup.*

I read several books, dozens of papers, and websites to research the military dictatorship. These were particularly helpful:

Skidmore, Thomas. *The Politics of Military Rule in Brazil 1964-1985* / Oxford University Press, 1988.

Charles River Editors. *Operation Condor: The History of the Notorious Intelligence Operations Supported by the United States to Combat Communists across South America* / Charles River Editors.

Klein, Naomi. *The Shock Doctrine: The Rise of Disaster Capitalism* / Henry Holt and Co., 2007.

Anderson, Perry. *Brazil Apart 1964-2019*, NY. Verso, 2019.

Ghedine, André Luiz, and three others. *40 Anos de Golpe/ Cronologia.* (a chronology of the military regime and dictatorship). Empresa Folha da Manhã Ltda. 2004.

http://almanaque.folha.uol.com.br/ditadura_cronologia.htm

O Projeto Memória e Resistência (The Memory of Resistance Project).
https://paineira.usp.br/memresist/?page_id=285

Presidência da República. *Direito à Memória e à Verdade: histórias de meninas e meninos marcados pela ditadura* / Secretaria Especial dos Direitos Humanos. Brasília, 2009.

Wikipedia / *Golpe de Estado no Brasil em 1964*

https://www.google.com/
search?client=safari&rls=en&q=.+https%3A%
2F%2F+pt.m.wikipedia.org%2Fwiki%2FGolpe_de_Estado_no_
Brasil_em_1964&ie=UTF-8&oe=UTF-8

Comissão Nacional da Verdade (CNV) volumes 1 thru 3, 2014. Dados Internacionais de Catalogação na Publicação (CIP)

Biblioteca da Comissão Nacional da Verdade.

http://cnv.memoriasreveladas.gov.br/torturas-em-instalacoes-militares.html#topo (The National Truth Commission has published many volumes regarding Brazil's troubled history with military rule and torture.)

23. *His biographers explain that during the sixties João was persecuted and accused of charlatanism, and of practicing curanderismo (folk healing) and black magic.* Most of João's biographers note his history in Bahia with Umbanda and Quimbanda:

"João acted as a seer and began organizing open-air works where, under the label of umbanda and quimbanda, trance-related rituals, he held his own healing sessions." Machado.

"Accusations against him of practicing medicine without a license or practicing witchcraft arose frequently. Joao gravitated north to the state of Bahia, still known today for its high percentage of people of African heritage. Among their Umbanda and Macumba temples, he was able to do his mediumistic work with less interference."

"The practitioners of those paths already did trance medium healing and Joao's activities did not attract so much attention there." Josie Ravenwing.

"For some years he lived in the northern state of Bahia, where the population is predominately of black African origin whose ancestors were bought there as slaves to work the sugarcane fields. The slaves were subjected to horrendous cruelty by their masters, so they retaliated with **their black spirit rituals, Quimbanda and Macumba,** which their ancestors brought from Africa. **Here he was only able to carry on his work by disguising his healing in these rituals;** meeting groups of people at clearings on the edge of town to provide them with cures and spiritual guidance." Robert Pellegrino.

24. *Apparently, the money was pretty good, and João, who was also a pool shark during this time, leveraged his earnings gambling at the pool tables and, according to him, always winning. Although João was a participant in African trance cults, he didn't take his mediumship seriously and ignored the advice of other mediums who wished to train him properly.* Maria Helena P. T. Machado.

25. *Another place where João lived during these times was Cana Brava... and Barreiras, Bahia.* Povoa, Garcia, Pellegrino-Estrich, Ravenwing.

26. I visited the home of Santa Dica twice and had the good fortune of meeting one of her close friends who assisted Dica as a medium in her healing center. Divina Soares told me much of Dica's story. Most folks in this region can tell you tales about Santa Dica. Also, good documentaries have been made.

An article by Mauro Cruz can be accessed at this site: https://pirenopolis.tur.br/cultura/historia/santa-dica

Also: Robson Rodrigues Gomes Filho *O Movimento Messiânico De "Santa Dica" E A Ordem Redentorista Em Goiás (1923-1925)* Mariana, MG 2012
http://www.repositorio.ufop.br/jspui/handle/123456789/2432

27. Zé Arigó. John G. Fuller. *Arigo: Surgeon of the Rusty Knife.* Thomas Y. Crowell Co. NY.

A good biography in Portuguese is *Arigó: Vida, Mediunidade e Martírio,* Herculano Pires / Editora Paidéia Ltda. Brazil.

28. *It was the incubator that hatched João Curador and his Caboclo Gentil. Shall we take a peek down that rabbit hole?*

My peek down the rabbit hole was quite unpleasant. To understand the Casa de Dom Inacio, one must investigate Quimbanda and the left-hand paths. Some of my sources:

Souza, Laura de Mello e. *The Devil and the Land of the Holy Cross: Witchcraft, Slavery, and Popular Religion in Colonial Brazil.* The University of Texas Press, 1986/2003.

Pares, Luis Nicolau, and Sansi, Roger, editors. *Sorcery in the Black Atlantic.* University of Chicago Press, 2011.

De Mattos Frisvold, Nicholaj. *Pomba Gira and the Quimbanda of Mbùmba Nzila.* Scarlet Imprint / Bibliothèque Rouge, Brasil, 2011.

Simas, Luiz Antonio; Rufino, Luiz. *Fogo no Mato; A Ciência Encantada das Macumbas.* Mórula Editorial. Rio de Janeiro, 2019.

De Oxóssi, Diego. *Traditional Brazilian Black Magic: The Secrets of the Kimbanda Magicians.* Inner Traditions / Bear & Company, US, 2018, 2021. A good overview and explanation.

Brum, Helio. *Quimbanda Vermillion.* Corrente 72, Brazil.

Taussig, Michael. *The Magic of the State.* Routledge. NY, 1997.

De Oxóssi, Diego. *Desvendando Exu: O Guardião dos Caminhos.* Arole Cultural. Brasil.

De Bourbon-Montenegro, Carlos Antonio. *The Devil's Garden, King Of The Witches.* Morning Star, Los Angeles, 2012.

De Mattos Frisvold, Nicholaj. *Exu & the Quimbanda of Night and Fire.* Scarlet Imprint / Bibliothèque Rouge. This proved a rich source on the history of Quimbanda and its pantheon of Exus.

29. *This was João's world, the domain of the Trickster.*

In Quimbanda, the Major Exus are named by their qualities:

Peterson, Joseph H. (ed.), *The Lesser Key of Solomon: Lemegeton Clavicula Salomonis.* Weiser Books, 2001.

Also, Wilby, Kevin (ed.) *The Lemegetton. A Medieval Manual of Solomonic Magic.* Silian, Lampeter: Hermetic Research Series, 1985.

30. *...one of João's older brothers, Valdivino, had become a communist. He joined a popular peasant movement led by José Porfirio...* Machado and Wikipedia.

31. *He also told how he was jailed and severely beaten in Bahia.*

He also told how he was jailed and severely beaten in Bahia. All of João's bigraphers mention this. It is part of his myth.

32. *Blood calls Caboclo Gentil and the Exu he obeys.* Academic papers and books I researched regarding Caboclo Gentil:

Batista, Milena Xibile. *Angola, Jeje e Ketu: Memórias e identidades em Casas e nações de candomblé na Região Metropolitana da Grande Vitória (ES).* Master's thesis, 2014.

Silva, Jerônimo da Silva e *Cartografia de afetos na encantaria: narrativas de Mestres da Amazônia Bragantina.* Doctor's dissertation, Universidade Federal do Pará, 2014.

Rabelo, Miriam C.M. *Entre a Casa e a Roça: trajetórias desocialização no candomblé de habitantes de bairros populares de Salvador.* Artigos • Relig. soc. 28 (1) • Jul 2008 •
https://doi.org/10.1590/S0100-85872008000100009

Silva, Lucineide Almeida da. *Quem Não Vai Pelo Amor, Vai Pela Dor": as identidades étnicas dos adeptos do terreiro ogum de ronda na umbanda e gira de caboclos, na cidade de Jitaúna- Bahia.* Dissertação de mestrado apresentada ao Programa de Pós-Graduação em Relações Étnicas e Contemporaneidade da Universidade Estadual do Sudoeste da Bahia - UESB. Jequié, 2020.

Candomblé de Caboclo is a type of candomblé that, in addition to the worship of orixás, voduns or inquices, also worships Amerindian spirits, called entities, catiços (or boiadeiro caboclos) and gentileiros.
https://pt.wikipedia.org/wiki/Candomblé_de_caboclo

Ferretti, Mundicarmo Maria Rocha. *Terra de Caboclo.* São Luís: Plano Editorial SECMA. 1994.

Mendes, Andréa Luciane Rodrigues. *Sua Bandeira na Aruanda Está de Pé. Caboclos e espíritos territoriais centro-africanos nos terreiros e comemorações da Independência (Bahia, 1824-1937)* Doctor's thesis. – Universidade Estadual de Campinas, Instituto de Filosofia e Ciências Humanas. 2018.

Wikipedia—Catimbó.
https://pt.wikipedia.org/wiki/Catimbó-Jurema#Exu

Brandão, Maria do Carmo Tinóco and Rios do Nascimento, Luís Felipe. *O Catimbó-Jurema.* Universidade Federal de Pernambuco - UFPE 2020.

Prandi, Reginaldo; Vallado, Armando; Souza, André Ricardo de. *Caboclo Candomblé in São Paulo.*

Prandi, Reginaldo. *Brazilian Enchantment: the book of the masters, caboclos and enchanted.* Rio de Janeiro: Pallas, 2004.

The Ewe/Fon peoples. The influence of the Jeje peoples for Afrodescendants. You can find an interesting overview of the vodun cult of Jeje at this site: http://www.irdeb.ba.gov.br

Meneses Da Paz, Adilson. *Pedrinha Miudinha Em Aruanda Ê, Lajedo: O Modo De Vida Da Umbanda.* Doctor's Thesis, Universidade Federal Da Bahia, 2019.

Silva, Lucineide Almeida Da. Quem Não Vai Pelo Amor, Vai Pela Dor": *As Identidades Étnicas Dos Adeptos Do Terreiro Ogum De Ronda Na Umbanda E Gira De Caboclos, Na Cidade De Jitaúna-Bahia / Jequié,* 2020. Master's Dissertation, Universidade Estadual Do Sudoeste Da Bahia - Uesb, 2020.

33. *They all had code names.*

de Magalhães, Marionilde Dias Brepohl *Revista Brasileira de História - A Lógica da Suspeição: Sobre os Aparelhos Repressivos à época da Ditadura Militar no Brasil* Universidade Federal do Paraná.* On-line version ISSN 1806-9347 Rev. bras. Hist. vol. 17 n. 34 São Paulo http://dx.doi.org/10.1590/S0102-01881997000200011

34. *Two hundred and forty-two secret detention and torture centers.* Universidade Estadual de Campinas, Jornalda Unicamp, Março de 2001.

https://www.unicamp.br

35. *...he found refuge with the military.* I was citing Pellegrino, all other biographers, and João himself.

II.
GI João: Tailor for the Military

36. Sources for this chapter:

Archdiocese of São Paulo, Brazil. *Torture in Brazil: A Shocking Report on the Pervasive Use of Torture by Brazilian Military Governments, 1964-1979, Secretly Prepared by the Archiodese of São Paulo.* University of Texas Press, 1998. Originally published as Brasil: Nunca Mais by Editora Vozes Ltda., Petrópolis, 1985.

Godoy, Marcelo. *A Casa da Vovó (Grandma's House); Uma biografia do DOI-Codi (1969-1991), o centro de sequestro, tortura e morte da ditadura militar,* São Paulo, Alameda Casa Editorial, 2014.

Alves, Maria Helena Moreira. *State and Opposition in Military Brazil (Latin American Monographs).* The University of Texas Press, 1985.

Kucinski, Bernardo. *'K'*. Editora Expressão Popular, São Paulo, Brazil, 2011. English translation by Practical Action Publishing with Latin American Bureau.

Octavio de Lima, Luiz. *Os Anos de Chumbo*. Planeta, 2020.

Green, James N. *We Cannot Remain Silent; Opposition to the Brazilian Military Dictatorship in the United States* / Duke University Press, London, 2010.

Meirelles, Renata. *State Violence, Torture, and Political Prisoners On the Role Played by Amnesty International in Brazil During the Dictatorship (1964–1985)*. Routledge, NY, 2020.

Keilt, Karen. *The Parrot's Perch*. She Writes Press, CA, 2019.

Jornal da Unicamp Universidade Estadual de Campinas Março de 2001. https://www.unicamp.br

Quadrat, Samantha Viz, *The Training of Information Agents and the Civil-Military Dictatorship in Brazil (1964-1985)*. Article by Professora Adjunta de História da América Contemporânea Pesquisadora do Núcleo de Estudos Contemporâneos (NEC) Universidade Federal Fluminense / *VARIA HISTORIA, Belo Horizonte, vol. 28, no 47, p.19-41: Jan/Jun 2012*.

Figueiredo, Lucas. *Ministério do Silêncio; a História do Serviço Secreto Brasileiro de Washington Luís a Lula (1927-2005)*. Rio de Janeiro: Record, 2005.

Fico, Carlos. *Como Eles Agiam; os subterrâneos da ditadura militar; espionagem e polícia política*. Rio de Janeiro: Record, 2001.

Joffily, Mariana. *No Centro da Engrenagem; os Interrogatórios na Operação Bandeirante e no DOI de São Paulo (1969-1975)*. São Paulo: EDUSP, 2013.

Costa, Edmilson, *Remembering the Years of Lead under Brazil's military rule: AI-5 never again!* Translated for Liberation School by Silvio Rodrigues, December 23, 2019.

Inventário da Coleção Informante do Regime Militar, Rio de Janeiro, 2008 Arquivo Nacional.

Direito à Verdade e à Memória: Comissão Especial Sobre Mortos e Desaparecidos Políticos / Brasília: Secretaria Especial dos Direitos Humanos, 2007.

37. *Many wealthy and middle-class people supported the coup.*

Wikipedia: *Military Dictatorship in Brazil*. "The coup was planned and executed by the most forefront commanders of the Brazilian Army and received the support of almost all high-ranking members of the military, along with conservative elements in society, like the Catholic Church... influential politicians, media moguls, landowners, businessmen, and the middle class... Internationally, it was supported by the State Department of the United States through its embassy in Brasilia." https://en.wikipedia.org/wiki/ Military_dictatorship_in_Brazil

38. *The military set him up with at least one tailor shop.*

I mentioned my research to a Brazilian friend, a professor from Tocantins. He told me he knows a Senator in Pará, along with friends in his hometown of Marabá, who remember João's tailor shop there in the 1970s. My friend promised to put me in touch with the Senator who could give me the contacts in Marabá. However, he kept putting me off. When I asked him about the military government and torture in Pará, he told me he had been a communist but not with the group in Pará. My friend had been imprisoned for a couple of years, tortured, and exiled to Russia. He grew nervous and said he couldn't help me.

39. *The CIA guided the CIE, strategizing their every act of repression.*

"Brazilian president, Ernesto Geisel, to continue with summary executions of dangerous subversives, under certain conditions," says an April 11, 1974 memo sent by the director of the CIA, the US intelligence agency, to then- Secretary of State Henry Kissinger. The document, revealed by the US State Department's Bureau of Public Affairs, exposes that the top brass of the Brazilian military government (1964-1985) knew about the exceptional actions taken against opponents of the regime."

"This is the most disturbing secret document I have ever read in twenty years of research," described researcher Matias Spektor, coordinator of the Center for International Relations at Fundação Getúlio Vargas. Spektor drew attention on Thursday to reports made available by the US government ... "In this regard, General Milton reported that some 104 persons in this category had been summarily executed by CIE during the past year, or a little over a year."

"Figueiredo supported this policy and defended its continuation." Rudolfo Borges—Documento da CIA relata que cúpula do Governo militar brasileiro autorizou execuções. / El Pais, São Paulo, May 10, 2018.

"On June 17, 2014, Joe Biden, then vice-president during Barack Obama's administration, landed in Brasilia with a special object in his luggage: a hard drive containing 43 documents produced by US authorities between 1967 and 1977. Based on information provided not only by victims, but also by informants within the Armed Forces and the repression services, the American reports detailed information about censorship, torture, and murders committed by the military regime in Brazil."

"Until that moment, most of the documents were considered secret by the United States government, which supported and collaborated with the dictatorship during most of the period in which the military was in power."

The 'secret documents' brought by Joe Biden to Brazil that challenge Bolsonaro's version of dictatorship. Mariana Sanches / From BBC News Brazil in Washington October 9, 2020.

Also see: Ribeiro do Valle, Maria. 1964–2014: *Golpe Militar, História, Memória E Direitos Humanos.* Laboratório Editorial Da Fcl, Sao Paulo, 2014.

Muckrock published an article by Lucas Smolcic Larson, Brazil's military dictatorship leaves a paper trail in the CIA archives, October 24, 2018.

https://www.muckrock.com/news/archives/2018/oct/24/cia-brazil-piece/

40. *João mentioned being stationed in Bahia. My jaw dropped when I heard this.* Narrated by João in the documentary *O Silêncio é Uma Prece*, directed by Candé Salles, also confirmed by other biographers, including Povoa, Garcia, Machado, and Salvaris.

I matched the places where João said he was stationed and other locales mentioned by his biographers and calculated a timeline that took into account details gleaned from diverse sources. The puzzle of João has many pieces, but when they are all assembled, he has a very different face than the one presented to the public.

Throughout the chapters on the military government, I used this publication for the week-by-week timeline of the regime: *Inventário da Coleção Informante do Regime Militar,* Rio de Janeiro, 2008 Arquivo Nacional.

I used another timeline at:

http://almanaque.folha.uol.com.br/ditadura_cronologia.htm

Additional sources:

Brasilia:

Os Espiões Da Ditadura Militar. Gilberto De Oliveira Mello, Agente Plantado Na Ufrj. 2018

https://documentosrevelados.com.br/Tag/Espioes/

Bahia:

Ditadura Militar na Bahia Novos Olhares, Novos Objetos, Novos Horizontes Volume I Salvador EDUFBA 2009 Brito, Antonio Mauricio Freitas. *Militância estudantil e memórias dos anos 1960.* Revista

Pernambuco:

Da Silva Filho, Nivaldo Gerôncio *O Embate Entre Os Movimentos Sociais E O Estado: A História De Pernambuco Durante O Regime Militar (1964 – 1966)* Sociólogo e Mestrando (MDU- UFPE).

Recife, Pernambuco. *Secretaria da Casa Civil Comissão Estadual da Memória e Verdade Dom Helder Câmara: relatório final: volume I / Secretaria da Casa Civil.* Recife : CEPE. 405p. 2017.

Silva, José Rodrigo de Araujo. *Colonia de ferias de Olinda: presos politicos e aparelhos de repressão em Pernambuco (1964).* Dissertcao Mestrado UFPB/CCHLA. 2013.

Koury, Mauro Guilherme Pinheiro. *Rural protests in Pernambuco, Brazil: 1964 to 1968.* Sociology, Problems and Practices [Online], 64 I 2010, posted online on 12 May 2013, consulted 26 July 2021.

http://journals.openedition.org/spp/

Piauí:

Lima, Jéssika Maria (UFPI). *A Resistência Do Movimento De Educação De Base No Piauí Durante O Regime Militar.* Pós Graduanda No Programa De Pós-Graduação Em História Do Brasil Na Universidade Federal Do Piauí. 2019.

Steinke, Sabrina. *A repressão política, durante a ditadura civil- militar de 1964, no Piauí relatada no acervo da Comissão de Anistia.* UFPI, pós-doutoranda em História, bolsista PNPD/ CAPES.

De Oliveira, Marylu Alves. *You Are Under Arrest, Commie! Brief Observations On Anti-Communist Practices In Piauí, Right After The 1964 Civil-Military Coup.* Revista Crítica Histórica Ano V, No 10, Dezembro/2014 Issn 2177-9961.

Belem, Pará:

Comissão Nacional da Verdade. Agência Senado, reportagem de Marília Coêlho December 17, 2013. This site contains hundreds of papers and documents regarding the crimes of the military government.
http://cnv.memoriasreveladas.gov.br/

Marabá, Pará:

Rodrigues, Alan. *A tropa do extermínio. Documentos e depoimento de oficial revelam como o Exército cercou, torturou camponeses e aniquilou os guerrilheiros do PCdoB no Araguaia. Jornal Istoé / Edição No 2734 16/06,* 11/12/08.

Corrêa, Carlos Hugo Studart. *Em Algum Lugar Das Selvas Amazônicas: As Memórias dos Guerrilheiros do Araguaia (1966-1974).* Doctor's Thesis Departamento de História da Universidade de Brasília, 2013.

Cunha, Bruno Domingues. *História da Esquerda em Goiás: 1960-1979.* Master's Dissertation – Universidade Federal de Goiás, 2001.

Carneiro, Ana and Cioccari, Marta. *Retrato da Repressão Política no Campo – Brasil 1962-1985 – Camponeses torturados, mortos e desaparecidos –* Direito à Memória e à Verdade Brasília, 2011.

Tocantinopólis, Tocantins:

Dos Santos, Fernanda Gonçalves. *Memories Of A "Rapazola" On The Margins Of Araguaia: The Marks Of The Araguaia Guerrilla In The Life Of A Survivor.* Monograph / Uft - University Federal Do Tocantins, University Campus Of Tocantinópolis, 2020.

Imperatriz, Maranhão:

Filgueiras, Otto. *My Leg is My Class.* Repórter Brasil, 2005.

Alencar, Fábio Aquiles Martins de. *O leviatã e a coruja sob os olhos de Minemósine: a ditadura civil militar nas trincheiras da memória.* Masters dissertation. Universidade Estadual do Maranhão, 2016.

Anápolis / Goiânia, Goiás:

Abreu, Vandre. *Terror Das Torturas Na Capital,* a report in the journal, Politica, April 3, 2013.

Machado, Vinícius Felipe Leal. *Ditadura Militar Em Goiás: Um Perfil Dos Trabalhadores Rurais Sindicalistas A Partir Dos Documentos Do Dops-Go.* Universidade Estadual de Goiás Anápolis/GO 2009.

João also claims he was stationed at **Niterói, State of Rio de Janeiro, and Rio Grande de Sul,** also DOI-CODI torture centers. A few references regarding activities there:

Bettamio, Rafaella Lúcia de Azevedo Ferreira. *O DOI-CODI carioca: memória e cotidiano no "Castelo do Terror."* Master's dissertation, Centro De Pesquisa E Documentação De História Contemporânea Do Brasil – CPDOC, 2012.

Hofmeister, Naira. *Reencontro Com 1970, O Ano Do Terror Em Porto Alegre.* El País, December 22, 2019.

Adamczyk, Guilherme Luís. *Memórias Sobre Ditadura Militar No Norte Do Rio Grande Do Sul: O Destacamento Volante Da Brigada Militar (1964).* Master's Dissertation, Universidade Federal Da Fronteira Sul – Uffs, 2018.

About Secret Agencies and DOI-CODI torture centers:

A very helpful source is by Square, Felipe de Faria. *Surveillance without uniform: internal espionage in the civil dictatorship*. Military through DEOPS / Felipe de Faria Quadrado. Frank: [sn], 2014 118 f. / Universidade Estadual Paulista, 2014.

Wikipedia. O Centro de Inteligência do Exército (CIE).

A website from Universidade Federal de Minas Gerais, *Brasil Doc. / Arquivo Digital*, is a treasure chest of documents and articles regarding the military wrongdoings of this era.

https://www.ufmg.br/brasildoc/

Another informative source is *Os Espiões Da Ditadura Militar*. Gilberto De Oliveira Mello, Agente Plantado Na Ufrj - Documentos Rev:

https://documentosrevelados.com.br/os-espioes-da-ditadura-militar-gilberto-de-oliveira-mello-agente-plantado-na-ufrj/

"Codi-DOIs were created in São Paulo, Rio de Janeiro, Recife, and Brasília and in 1971 in Belo Horizonte, Curitiba, Salvador, Belém, and Fortaleza, with all the leading positions occupied by officers of the Armed Forces, with the exception of administrative positions... in direct articulation with the Army Information Center—CIE.

"The DOI-Codi ended up sharing the coordination of repression actions with the secret services of the Navy and of the Air Force, and even with the state Political and Social Order Police Departments."

De Magalhães, Marionilde Dias Brepohl. *A lógica da suspeição: sobre os aparelhos repressivos à época da ditadura militar no Brasil*. Universidade Federal do Paraná, Rev. bras. Hist. vol. 17 n. 34 São Paulo 1997.

O Memorial da Democracia website: *DOI-CODI, A Máquina De Torturar E Matar*.

http://memorialdademocracia.com.br/card/doi-codi-a-maquina-de-torturar-e-matar

Shootings and interrogations: the dictatorship in the view of a DOI-Codi military retired colonel Pedro Ivo Moézia de Lima in testimony to the National Truth Commission. By Fabrício Faria-09.sep.2014/ CNV Diego Toledo Collaboration for UOL, in São Paulo 13/12/2018.

https://noticias.uol.com.br/politica/ultimas-noticias/2018/12/16/doi-codi-regime-militar-ditadu

Figueiredo, Lucas. *Ministério do silêncio; a história do serviço secreto brasileiro de Washington Luís a Lula (1927-2005)*. Rio de Janeiro: Record, 2005.

Fico, Carlos. *Como eles agiam; os subterrâneos da ditadura militar; espionagem e polícia política*. Rio de Janeiro: Record, 2001.

Quadrat, Samantha Viz. *Poder e informação: o sistema de inteligência e o regime militar no Brasil.* Rio de Janeiro: UFRJ/ PPGHIS, 2000.

Lemos, Caroline Murta. *Arquitetando o terror: um estudo sensorial dos centros de detenção oficiais e clandestinos da ditadura civil-militar do Brasil (1964-1985)* / Caroline Murta Lemos; orientador Andrés Zarankin. – Laranjeiras, 2019. 384 f.; il. Tese (Doutorado em Arqueologia) – Universidade Federal de Sergipe, 2019.

41. During João's nine-year career as a "tailor," he explored many types of cults found in these regions.

The key to understanding João's roots in Quimbanda is the entity Caboclo Gentil and his biographers' vague references to the Oriental Line and the Gypsy Line (of Quimbanda). The places where he was stationed had their preferred style of regional Quimbanda. By tracing the names of João's entities to specific regions and times, I could discern their respective cults. I researched numerous books and academic papers. Some of the sources for this chapter include:

In Bahia:

Parés, Luis Nicolau. *A formação do candomblé: história e ritual da nação jeje na Bahia.* Campinas, SP: Ed. UNICAMP, 2006.

In Pernambuco, João and his Caboclo Gentil would be welcome to incorporate in the local terreiros:

Motta, Roberto. *Xangô, Jurema and Umbanda: Notes on Three Forms of Popular Religion in the Recife Region.* Universidade Federal de Pernambuco, Brasil. 2020.

https://www.redalyc.org/journal/2433/243364810018/html/

In Recife, one could find many terreiros working with Xango (the Orixá of iron, war, and justice).

Campos, Zuleica Dantas Pereira. *Religiões Afrodescendentes No Recife: Uma Trajetória De Modernização E Reinvenção De Tradições Na História.* Anais do XXVI Simpósio Nacional de História – ANPUH • São Paulo. 2011.

Nascimento, Morôni Laurindo do. *O nosso axé é africano... Mas o caboclo é mais bonito : um estudo antropológico sobre o culto do caboclo no terreiro Santa Cecília (AL).* Recife: Dissertação (mestrado) - Universidade Federal de Pernambuco. 2012.

Rodrigues, Michelle Gonçalves and Campos, Roberta Bivar Carneiro. Paths Of Visibility: *The Rise Of Worship To Jurema In The Religious Field Of Reef.* Doctoral Dissertation in Anthropology at the Federal University of Pernambuco, 2013.

There are over 400 umbanda/quimbanda terreiros in Teresina, Piauí.

Lima, Sabrina Verônica Gonçalves. *As Faces Da Umbanda No Piauí: Política, Festa e Criminalidade (1960-1978)*. Dissertação, Teresina-PI, 2017.

Sena, Luana. *Na Força Do Rito: Teresina, The Most Catholic Capital Of The Country, Is Home To More Than 400 Umbanda And Candomblé Temple Groups*. Vista Revestrés #24-–abril/maio de 2016.
https://revistarevestres.com.br/reportagem/na-forca-do-rito/

The states of Pará and Maranhão are notorious for their left-hand cults.

Campelo, Marilu Márcia and Tavernard de Luca, Taissa. *As Duas Africanidades Estabelecidas no Pará*. Revista Auelas. 2007.

Wikipedia: *Tambor de Mina*.
https://pt.m.wikipedia.org/wiki/Tambor_de_mina

Wikipedia: *Babaçuê*. https://pt.m.wikipedia.org/wiki/Babaçuê

Jorge de Melo, Diogo. *Festas De Encantarias: As Religiões Afro- Diaspóricas E Afro-Amazônicas, Um Olhar Fratrimonial Em Museologia*. Doctor's thesis Universidade Federal do Estado do Rio de Janeiro, 2020.

42. *A cleansing of Umbanda and all the Afro-Brazilian sects ensued.* Military agencies now regulated these cults.

Souza, Fabíola Amaral Tomé de. *Umbanda e Ditadura Civil-Militar relações, legitimação e reconhecimento*. Doutoranda em História pela UFRRJ.

Silva, Márcia Andréa Teixeira da. *Liberdade de culto: uma abordagem do processo de diminuição às perseguições policiais em terreiros de Culto Afro-Brasileiro em São Luís na década de 1960*. Monograph, Universidade Estadual do Maranhão, 2008.

43. *The first year he is accused of rape and attempted murder.* From an interview with "Maria" on Fantástico / TV Globo, 2019. Maria also appears in the Globo/Play series.
https://globoplay.globo.com/v/7482465/

The Parrot's Perch & The Parrot's Beak: Casa Azul—The Blue House of Terror

44. *"For four years, João resided at a military base in Marabá,"* Maria Helena P. T. Machado. This was also mentioned by João and several authors.

Professor Heloísa Starling of the Federal University of Minas Gerais wrote, "The case of Casa Azul was very impressive because, probably, it was the largest clandestine center [that existed]. Studies show that the house located in southeastern Pará was not a simple interrogation center... There is something very interesting: all the time, you have a military observer from Planalto [The Federal Capitol] inside Casa Azul. This shows the direct link to the High Command [of the Armed Forces]."

45. *"All soldiers who participated in military operations in the region witnessed and were aware of the torture,"* National Commission of Truth, 2014: page 796. The report is by Manuel Messias Guido Ribeiro, a former Army soldier who served in the Blue House (Casa Azul) between 1974 and 1980.

46. *João was stationed at several places in the Bico do Papagaio that were known torture centers. Let's begin with Marabá, Pará.*

Rodrigues, Alan. *A Tropa do Extermínio. Documentos e depoimento de oficial revelam como o Exército cercou, torturou camponeses e aniquilou os guerrilheiros do PCdoB no Araguaia.* Istoé, 11/12/2008.

Another sobering report was published by Folho de São Paulo, Sunday, May 1, 2005, by De Souza, Josias, and Michael, Andréa. *Testimonies from 36 witnesses show that terror tactics were decisive in Araguaia/Former soldiers report torture by the army against the guerrillas.*

https://www1.folha.uol.com.br/fsp/brasil/fc0105200502.htm

Wikipedia, *Araguaia Guerrilla War.*

https://en.wikipedia.org/wiki/Araguaia_Guerrilla_War

Square, Felipe De Faria. *Surveillance Without Uniform: Internal Espionage In The Civil Dictatorship Military Through Deops.* Quadrado. 2014.

https://Documentosrevelados.Com.Br/Tag/Espioes/

Macêdo Luiz, Janailson - Fernandes Inácio Reis, Naurinette Naurinette-Santiago-Santiago Da Silva, Idelma. *The Dictatorship And The Trails Of Repression In The Southeast Paraense: Unveiling Memories About The Blue House.*

Segredos Da Mata, Report About Major Curio, Secret Agent. Veja November 12, 1980.

Morais, Tais and Silva, Eumano. *Operação Araguaia: Os Arquivos Secretos Da Guerrilha.* São Paulo: Geração Editorial, 2005.

47. *A cleansing of Umbanda and all the Afro-Brazilian sects ensued.*

Military agencies now regulated these cults.

Souza, Fabíola Amaral Tomé de. *Umbanda e Ditadura Civil-Militar relações, legitimação e reconhecimento.* Doutoranda em História pela UFRRJ.

Silva, Márcia Andréa Teixeira da. *Liberdade de culto: uma abordagem do processo de diminuição às perseguições policiais em terreiros de Culto Afro-Brasileiro em São Luís na década de 1960.* Monograph, Universidade Estadual do Maranhão, 2008.

48. *"I was barbarously tortured."* From *National Commission Of Truth.*

João and the Indian Genocide of the 1970s

49. João became a participant in the Grande Carajás Program.

Dave Treece wrote, "Occupying an area of eastern Amazonia the size of Britain and France combined, the Carajás Program turned the region into a massive agro-industrial park of mines, smelters, dams, railroads, charcoal- burners, ranches and plantations, and transformed its people into a destitute, landless labor pool. The $62 billion scheme is not the monopoly of a single colonial power.

"Many governments, financial institutions and companies are sharing in the spoils, from the European Economic Community (EEC) and the World Bank to Japanese and North American banks and state and private companies within Brazil itself. They regard the region's 13,000 Indians as expendable."

Treece, David. Bound in Misery and Iron: The Impact of the Greater Carajas Program on the Indians of Brazil. Survival International, 1987. Informative and heartbreaking.

50. The actual figures are higher and unreported.

National Commission of Truth / Violations of the human rights of indigenous peoples.

Also: DAVIS, Shelton H. Vítimas do Milagre; o desenvolvimento e os índios do Brasil. São Paulo: Zahar, 1978.

Amazonia Real, a journal published in Manaus, has valuable reports of Indian abuses of this time. www.amazoniareal.com.br

Valente, Rubens. *Os Fuzis e as Flechas*. Companhia das Letras, São Paulo, 2017. An excellent source.

MARTINS, Edilson. *Nossos índios, nossos mortos*. Rio de Janeiro: CODECRI, 1978.

HEMMING, John. Die If You Must: Brazilian Indians in the Twentieth Century. London: Macmillan, 2003.

Benitez Trinidad, Carlos. The indigenous quest under the military dictatorship: from imagining to dominating. P. 257-284. 2018.

https://doi.org/10.4000/aa.2986

51. The Figueiredo Report.

Watts, Jonathan; Rocha, Jan. Brazil's 'Lost Report' into Genocide Surfaces after 40 Years.

https://www.theguardian.com/world/2013/may/29/brazil-figueiredo-genocide-report

Lost report exposes Brazilian Indian genocide. Survival International. www.survivalinternational.org.

Norman Lewis's article led to the founding of Survival International. Scribd archive.

Zema de Resende, Ana Catarina. O Relatório Figueiredo, as violações dos direitos dos povos indígenas no Brasil dos anos 1960 e a justa memória. Encontro Nacional do CONPEDI/UFS 2015 : Aracaju, SE.

52. "...an integrated Indian is one who becomes labor."

Violations of the human rights of indigenous peoples of the Truth Commission report.

Brasílio, Liza, Sousa, and Karina, *Human rights and diversity* / L. Karina Sousa, Demarchi, André and Morais, Odilon (orgs). Palmas/TO: Universidade Federal do Tocantins EDUFT, 2018.

53. Soon the Indians were writhing in burning pain, paralyzed and dying.

Truth Commission Report, the chapter "Violations of the Human Rights of Indigenous Peoples."

54. Joao lived in Vila Rondon, Tucuruí, Tocantinópolis, and Imperatriz from 1976 to 1980....

According to Liberato Póvoa, "He lived in the current state of Tocantins, more precisely in the cities of Colinas do Tocantins, Guaraí, and Tocantinópolis; in the city of Imperatriz, in Maranhão, and in the State of Pará: in Vila Rondon, Belém, Marabá and Tucuruí." (Póvoa, 2016, p.30). Also collaborated by Ismar Garcia.

Liberato Póvoa, who lives in Palmas, Tocantins, is a Judge of the Court of Justice of the State of Tocantins. He was President of the Permanent Commissions for Selection and Training, Jurisprudence and Documentation and Systematization of that Court. He was a Professor of International Law at the University of Tocantins Foundation.

55. In Pará, the first and largest hydroelectric dam project in the Amazon was shaping up, and João was there as well.

See Unexamined Synergies: dam building and mining go together in the Amazon by Zoe Sullivan/ June 2017. Mongabay.

https://news.mongabay.com/2017/06/unexamined-synergies-dam-building-and-mining-go-together-in-the-amazon/

56. Tocantinópolis was a military base with a landing strip used on bombing missions.

De Almeida Teles, Janaína. Memórias dos cárceres da ditadura: os testemunhos e as lutas dos presos políticos no Brasil. Doctor's thesis, Universidade de São Paulo, 2011.

Fernanda Gonçalves Dos Santos. Memories Of A "Rapazola" On The Margins Of Araguaia: The Marks Of The Araguaia Guerrilla In Life Of A Survivor. Monograph Presented To Uft - University Federal Do Tocantins, 2020.

57. In Tocantinópolis, João had access to a variety of terreiros offering exotic left-hand paths.

Caetano Venâncio, Sariza Oliveira and Ferretti, Mundicarmo. *Os Antigos Que Trabalhavam Perfeitamente Morre - Ram: A Memória Da Umbanda Em Araguaína.*

Barros Dos Santos, Bruno and De Carvalho Veras, Rogério. Maria Bonita De Tocantinópolis: História De Vida De Uma Mãe- De-Santo Do Norte Tocantinense. Revista Escritas Do Tempo – V. 2, N. 4, Mar-Jun/2020 – P. 222-245.

III.
João the Garimpeiro: The Gold Digger

58. Pelligrino says that 1976 was the year João left the military. Robert Pellegrino-Estrich. *The Miracle Man: The Story of João de Deus.* Most of his biographers use this date.

59. Rocha, Cristina. *John of God (pg 62-63).* Oxford University Press.

60. *Nineteen-seventy-six finds João in Tocantinópolis, where he sexually assaults a minor.* As reported by the Public Ministry of the State of Maranhão CCOM-MPMA, December 2018.

61. Machado and several other biographers.

62. *The line of the gypsies (ciganos) is at least three separate cults.*

Macedo, Lívia Alves dos Santos. *Estradas sem fim: a linha do Oriente e o povo cigano na umbanda.* Universidade De São Paulo, 2014.

Sudare, Lívia. *Romani People in Brazil. From Exile to the Search for Social Rights.* GRIN / Verlag.

Torres, Ramona. *Secret of Gypsy Magic.* Published by Pallas, Brazil. Goes into detail about the gypsy line.

Several of João's biographers mention his alignment with the Gypsy Line of Umbanda. A study of their cult resonates and echoes with the work at the Casa.

"The secrets of the Eastern Line are many as these entities are adherents of the occult. Because it has little public knowledge, there are few terreiros dedicated to this line of action. This is mainly because Roma culture is markedly oral and mysterious.

"Gypsy people passed on their knowledge from parent to child, by word of mouth, and share very little of their mystical secrets with other ethnic groups... The Cigana do Oriente line is formed by spirits that work mainly in physical and emotional healing processes.

"They are deeply connoisseurs of alchemy, astrology, tarot, oriental medicine, and many other aspects of ancient knowledge. Although

common sense speaks of Gypsies of the East as a synonym for the Oriental line, this auxiliary line of Umbanda embraces many more people. In addition to the Gypsies, Arab, Japanese, Chinese, Mongolian, Egyptian, Gallic, and Roman entities participate in the Orient line."
https://www.wemystic.com.br/cigana-do-oriente/

Another related link: https://www.facebook.com/105577044130500/posts/156723512349186/

Marsicano, Alberto and Vieira, Lourdes de Campos. *Os Ciganos na Umbanda.*, Ed. Madras, Brasil.

63. *The Oriental Line:*
"One woman who had been with the healer for over 20 years finally confirmed that he belonged to the Oriental Line of Umbanda, a line of healing, and had become a follower while living in the northern state of Pará." Rocha, Cristina. *John of God* (p. 64).

The Oriental Line is also discussed in Machado's biography of João. Wedge, Welthon Rodrigues. *The Eastern Line in Umbanda: the buildup of a religious symbolic field.* Goiânia: Catholic University of Goiás, 2004.

Marsicano, Alberto and Vieira, Lourdes de Campos. A Linha do Oriente in Umbanda. Ed. Madras, Brasil.

You can find many details regarding the Oriental line at: https://www.casavovojoaquina.com.br.

"The Phalange of Astral Physicians is an Egregore composed of hundreds of spiritual workers. Most of the time, they were in their last lives, doctors, healers, and prayers. This charitable army is classified into seven groupings or Legions (some call them Peoples)."

I - Legion of Medical Doctors: Composed by doctors of conventional Western medicine or homeopaths: Dr. André Luiz, Dr. Rodolfo de Almeida, Dr. João Correia, Dr. José Gregório Hernandéz, among others.

II - Legion of Oriental Physicians: Oriental therapists, specialists in herbal medicine, acupuncture, massage, and in the main traditional medical disciplines of Asia: Ramatis, Master Agastyar, Babaji.

III - Legion of Healers: Native healers and shamans from the Americas, Africa, and Oceania: caboclos and old blacks, traditional sorcerers, some exus - such as Exu Curador, Seu Maramael.

IV - Legion of Prayer: Praying people, healers, and practitioners of religious or spiritual medicine. Here we find all those who healed by the laying on of hands, faith, and prayer: Father João Maria de Agostinho, Father João de Camargo, Grandma Nhá Chica, Master Philippe de Lyon, Abbot Julio.

V - Legion of Roots: Practitioners of folk medicine and regional magic. They are the Brazilian master juremeiros, the herbalists or callers of the Americas, and all the specialists in curative flora, fauna, and minerals: Dom Nicanor Ochoa, Mestre Inácio, Mestre Carlos de Oliveira, Mestre Rei Heron.

VI - Legion of Kabbalists and Alchemists: Spirits of the old Kabbalists and alchemists who knew the secrets of plants and crystals: Pai Isaac da Fonseca (first Brazilian Kabbalist), Nicolau Flamel, Paracelsus, Pai Jaco. VII - Legion of the Holy Trustees: Catholic saints celebrated as doctors, healers, or specialists in the cure of any disease: Saint Lucia - eyes, Saint Agata - breasts, Saint Lazarus - skin diseases, Saint Benedict - poisonings.

"The preparation: Long before the gates of the spiritual house open or the mediums arrive, the environment destined for treatments is already being cleaned and prepared. The procedures begin with the isolation of the house, which is surrounded by teams of spiritual vigilantes **(the exus)**, who prevent the entry of disturbing spirits and make the fluid cleaning of the incarnates that arrive." **If this is necessary, they can even cause a malaise or another situation in order to drive away people** who come to the spiritual house with bad intentions or are involved in fluids that can disturb the work."

64. Dr. Augusto brags, *"My phalange is not constituted of ten, or a hundred, but of millions. I am the one who goes to the depths of the abyss to save a soul."* Most of João's biographers quote this phrase. Quimbanda also has seven phalanges.
http://maedenise.comunidades.net/linhas-da-quimbanda

65. *The terreiros of Maranhão (and of Pará and Tocantins) are renowned for practicing black magic.*

Prandi, Reginaldo (Org). *Encantaria Brasileira: the book of the masters, caboclos and enchanted.* Rio de Janeiro, Pallas, 2001.

Maggie, Ivonne. *In Fear of the Spell: Relationships between Magic and Power in Brazil.* Thesis, National Archive 1992.

Barretto, Maria Amália Pereira. *The Voduns of Maranhão.* São Luís: Cultural Foundation of the Maranhão, 1977.

Leacock, Seth and Ruth. *O Tambor de Flores; uma análise da Federação Espírita Umbandista e dos Cultos Afro- Brasileiros do Pará (1965-1975),* Master's dissertation. Campinas, UNICAMP, 1976.

66. *This association was part of the apparatus that led to legalizing Umbanda under the military regime.* This was the same federation being used by the hundreds of macumba cults of Maranhão in their attempt to become invisible to persecution. Some of my research: Sabrina, Verônica Gonçalves Lima. *Faces Of Umbanda In Piauí: Politics, Party and Criminality (1960-1978).*

Master's dissertation. Universidade Federal do Piauí - UFPI, Teresina-PI, 2017.

Ortiz, Renato. *A morte branca do feiticeiro negro: Umbanda e sociedade brasileira.* São Paulo: Brasiliense. 1999.

Silva, Márcia Andréa Teixeira da. *Liberdade de culto: uma abordagem do processo de diminuição às perseguições policiais em terreiros de Culto Afro-Brasileiro em São Luís na década de 1960.* Universidade Estadual Do Maranhão / São Luis, 2008.

Souza, Fabíola Amaral Tomé de. *Umbanda e Ditadura Civil-Militar relações, legitimação e reconhecimento.* Doutoranda em História pela UFRRJ / Revista Angelus Novus, 2016.

Cordovil, Daniela. *A Atuação Política De Afro-Religiosos Em Belém, Pará: Da Guerra Mágica Ao Fórum Social Mundial.* Revista Observatório Da Religião, Jan/June 2014.

Figueiredo, Aldrin Moura de. *A Cidade dos Encantados: pajelanças, feitiçarias e religiões afro-Brasileiras na Amazônia.* Belém: EDUFPA, 2008.

Silva, Anaíza Vergolino. *O tambor das flores: uma analise da*

Federação Espírita Umbandista e dos cultos afro-brasileiros do Pará. Master's dissertation in Anthropology, Unicamp, 1976.

Ferretti, Mundicarmo Maria Rocha. *Pajelança do Maranhão no século XIX.* São Luís: CMF; FAPEMA, 2004.

Bemerguy, Telma de Sousa. *Afro-brasileiros do Estado do Pará em Santarém.* Santarém, 2014.

67. Chico Felitti *A Casa: A História da Seita de João de Deus.* São Paulo, Todavia, 2020.

68. In February 1979, João #1 was thrown out of Abadiania. Also, The police named João as a murder for hire suspect. Chico Felitti / *A Casa: A Historia da Seita de João de Deus.*

69. GloboPlay Interview.

Serra Pelada: Naked Mountain Bonanza

70. João was embarking on a forty-year career in illegal gold and gemstone mining. According to João, he struck it rich at Serra Pelada. As recounted by João, several biographers, and many journals and TV reports.

Tavares de Moura, Salvador. *Serra Pelada: experiência, memórias e disputas.* Master's thesis, Pontificia Universidade Católica De São Paulo PUC-SP, 2008.

Wikipedia, *Serra Pelada.*

TIME magazine; Sep. 08, 1980. *The Treasure of Serra Pelada.*

Sayuri, Juliana. *Como foi o garimpo em Serra Pelada?* Super Interessante Magazine, December 9, 2016.

Kotscho, Ricardo. *Serra Pelada: Uma Ferida Aberta na Selva.* Biblioteca de Fotografia do IMS Paulista. São Paulo, Brasiliense, 1984.

Lavarda, Marcus Túlio Borowiski. *Desmontando o "formigueiro humano": uma leitura barthesiana das fotografias de Serra Pelada por Sebastião Salgado.* Doctor's thesis, Pontifícia Universidade Católica de São Paulo, 2017.

71. *Powaqqatsi,* Godfrey Reggio's 1988 documentary.

Link: https://youtu.be/EoOdhKYj8Bc?si=-Ll3gHTwqKR6SWS

72. In its heyday, thousands of underage girls, as young as twelve,

arrived for work, with the hope of a better future, as prostitutes. Jornal Hiper Cultura. Serra Pelada: história e fotos do maior garimpo a céu aberto do mundo.

Memória Globo. *Corrida do ouro em Serra Pelada.* https://memoriaglobo.globo.com/jornalismo/coberturas/corrida-do-ouro-em-serra-pelada/noticia/corrida-do-ouro-em-serra-pelada.ghtml

73. *Curió arrived with fanfare by helicopter.* Tavares de Moura, Salvador. *Serra Pelada: experiência, memórias e disputas.* Master's dissertation, Pontifícia Universidade Católica de São Paulo, 2008.

74. *João would lead dozens of miners in morning rituals where they linked hands and created a corrente (current) to invoke good luck.* As reported by Chico Felitti in *A Casa:* "I met João in Serra Pelada, says George Grunupp, who at the time also gambled on the gold reserve in Pará."

"Before starting the day's work, he would make a prayer chain, with dozens of miners joining hands," says Elke Maravilha's younger brother, who made a fortune in the gold mine that he spent in the following years. Among the 80,000 miners who lived in Curionópolis, it was rumored that Faria had only spent three weeks there. "They said he found the biggest gold nugget and left without saying goodbye to anyone," says Grunupp. "He just disappeared."

75. *João Américo França Vieira is an airplane pilot, garimpeiro, and smuggler who flew miners into Serra Pelada and various other illegal mines.*

Fuhrmann, Leonardo. *João Américo França Vieira was a partner of Rambo do Pará, killed by the Military Police of Pará in 1992. Both worked in Castelo dos Sonhos, a district of Altamira immersed in conflict over land and minerals.* De Olho nos Ruralistas 04/08/2019.

https://deolhonosruralistas-com-br.translate.goog/2018/12/20/braco-direito-de-joao-de-deus-fez-parte-de-grupo-que-aterrorizou-garimpos/?_x_tr_sl=pt&_x_tr_tl=em&_x_tr_hl=em&_x_tr_pto=sc

76. *Known as Rambo do Pará, he was killed by the Pará Military Police in 1992.*

Veja Magazine, Folha de S. Paulo. Also, Revista Ihu On-Line Instituto Humanitas Unisinos *Marcados para morrer no Castelo de Sonhos.*

Torres, Mauricio. *Dono é quem desmata : conexões entre grilagem e desmatamento no sudoeste Paraense São Paulo : Urutu-branco;* Altamira : Instituto Agronômico da Amazônia, 2017.

Campbell, Jeremy M. *Brazil's deferred highway: mobility,*

development, and anticipating the state in Amazonia. Boletín de Antropología Universidad de Antioquia, vol. 27, núm. 44, 2012, pp. 102-126 Universidad de Antioquia. Medellín, Colombia.

Campbell writes eloquently about the region of Castelo de Sonhos, its history, and what it is like today (scary). This is a good look at serious criminal activities impacting the Brazilian Amazon in Pará.

77. Savaris, Alfredina Arlete *The Mentalist/John of God and Spiritual Healing.*

78. *In 1979, the Casa had just been founded when he began abusing a girl whose family attended the Casa.* O Popular 12/18/2018.

IV.
Doctor John the Night Tripper; Babalaô João

79. *So, what in the world is a Babalaô?*

Eyiogbe, Frank Baba. *Babalawo, Santería's high priests: fathers of the secrets in Afro-Cuban ifá.* Llewellyn Worldwide, LTD. 2015.

Capone, Stefania. *The Holy Father And Babalaô: Religious Interaction And Ritual Rearrangements In The Religion Of Orishes.* Director of Anthropology, University of Paris.

Ifá versus Ocha. June 3, 2012, Santeria Church.

http://santeriachurch.org

Verger, P. *Notas sobre o culto aos orixás e Voduns na Bahia de todos os santos, no Brasil, e na Antiga Costa dos escravos, na África.* Editora da Universidade de São Paulo.

Handerson, Joseph. *Vudú são Haití – latino-am são Brasil: sistemas religiosos como concepciones del mundo afro- atino-americano.* VII Congreso Chileno de Antropología. Colegio de Antropólogos de Chile A. G, San Pedro de Atacama, 2010.

Bemerguy, Telma de Sousa. *História, regras e sentidos: a Federação Espírito Umbandista e dos cultos.*

80. *According to Chico Felitti, João befriended an herbalist in Anápolis, an older woman, who identified all the endemic cerrado healing plants for João, and taught him how to prepare the tinctures.* Chico Felitti, *A Casa.* Covered extensively in the chapter: *The Absent Father of the Sons of the House.*

81. *He had her pretend she was paralyzed, and stand up and proclaim a cure to the audience.* Chico Felitti, *A Casa*, in the chapter: *The Absent Father of the Sons of the House.*

82. *Some people did not recover, returned home and died.* From an interview with Julia Pascali (a child of the Casa at that time) by Chico Felitti, *The Casa,* page 49. Liberato Povoa also confirms that patients were given injections of antibiotics and painkillers and that some did not get cured.

83. *Abuses of Faith, A year of the João de Deus Case.* Lu Sudré. Brazil de Facto. São Paulo, 12/7/2019.

84. *"An entity has arrived, and he insists on possessing you sexually."* Jornal O Popular, December 13, 2018 / p 14.

85. *This was the year he began penetration rape of his daughter Dalva, who was now 11 years old and still under his care in Anápolis.* GloboPlay series, Veja and other interviews.

86. *Left on their own when João was absent, the Casa was their bedroom in the evening.* Chico Felitti, *A Casa,* in the chapter: *The Absent Father of the Sons of the House.*

87. *He and João Américo opened another illegal mine in 1980 in Santa Terezinha, Goiás, this one for emeralds.*

Alexandria, Katherine. *Negócios escusos em garimpos chamam atenção no caso João de Deus.* Jornal O Popular, 12/22/ 2018.

Morais, Rodrigo. *Me, garimpeiro.* Jornal Papo de Homen, September 25, 2011.

Bergamelli De Brito, Ivanildes. *Políticas públicas de apoio as famílias impactadas pela crise mineradora em Santa Terezinha de Goiás.* Master's thesis Biblioteca Faculdades ALFA.

88. *Other places in Goiás where João was involved in illegal mining:*

João's biographer, Ismar Garcia, lists two mining camps where João lived in the 1970s and 1980s: Colinas (TO), and Presidente Kennedy (TO). Povoa mentions Guarari, and Campos Belos, Goias.

An article in Galileu Magazine on 12/25/2008 by Pablo Nogueira quotes João as saying he also lived in Cotegipe (BA), and Wanderley (BA)—perhaps ranches. Wanderley didn't exist before 1985.

"A large quantity of emeralds was found in one of his 'bunkers' by the civil police, who are investigating the cases of rape and other criminal offenses. Weapons and dollars were also found.

"The emeralds found by the civil police were already cut and may have come from the Capoeirana mine, assured an experienced miner from Itabira, who asked not to be named for fear of reprisals.

"He said it has long been known among the region's miners that João de Deus is a partner in a mine in the district of Capoeirana, in the neighboring municipality of Nova Era, on the side of the MGC-120 highway that connects Itabira to the old São José da Lagoa.

Povoado de Capoeirana, district of Nova Era, where João de Deus' mining operation would be located. 'They say that he is a partner of the prospector Geraldinho, who owns a mine there,' he said, and then added. 'There is no point in looking for Geraldinho. He has been missing since João de Deus was arrested. The Capoeirana mine was closed last year for being illegal and for not complying with environmental legislation. "But the 'curiango' runs wild,' says the same miner. Curiango is the name given to the miner who, secretly, in the dead of night, steals the green precious stones, coveted since the time of the bandeiras of Fernão Dias Paes Leme, who allegedly confused tourmalines with emeralds when he was mining in Minas Gerais.

"According to another source, who for the same reason asks not to be identified, João de Deus also explores emeralds in the mines of Santa Terezinha, in Goiás.

"He worked 'miracles' with high-ranking people from the former DNPM and the Ministry of Mines and Energy in exchange for a concession to exploit the precious stones, says the same miner.

"For him [João de Deus], mining was good because those who seek find the miracle. He is the true 'hollow wood saint', who also worked miracles around Itabira and Nova Era." Source: Vila de Utopia, 12/26/2018.

https://viladeutopia.com.br/joao-de-deus-e-socio-de-garimpo-em-capoeirana-nova-era-assegura-garimpeiro/

Oswald, Vivian. *New Gold Cycle.* Jornal O Globo, Economia. 11/20/2011, p. 29-31.

Cerrados Magazine (Unimontes). *Overview And Consolidation Of The Mineral Sector In Goiás.* Vol. 14, no. 1, pp. 96-124, 2016, Montes Claros State University.

Also, *Recursos Minerais Do Estado De Goiás E Distrito Federal.* A comprehensive list of all mineral deposits in Goiás. Using this reference, I was able to determine what minerals were being mined in the epoch that João lived there and when the illegal mines were active.

Ribeiro De Padua, Wilian. *As Dinâmicas Socioespaciais No Garimpo De Esmeraldas Em Campos Verdes, GO (1981-2017).* Master's Thesis, Universidade Federal de Goiás, Goiânia 2020.

89. *Edson Cavalcante Queiroz was the most famous of the new Doctor Fritzs.*

Wilson Garcia. *Edson Queiroz, the conflicts of healing mediumship.*

Dubugras, Elsie. *A tragic end for Edson Queiroz.* São Paulo: Revista Planeta, no. 230, November 1991, p. 47-49.

Tourinho, Nazareno. *Edson Queiroz, the new Arigó of the spirits (2nd ed.).* São Bernardo do Campo (SP): Correio Fraterno, 1991.

Nuñez, Sandra. *The Homeland of Curadors: A History of Medicine and Spiritual Healing in Brazil.* São Paulo: Thought, 2013.

90. *Another medium at Palmelo was the shocking Antonio de Palmelo.* An interesting interview with Anna Sharp in the NETFLIX series, episode one, shows footage of her husband and the scar from the saw surgery. She said it was a Makita circular saw with a rusty blade.

A brief history of Antonio de Palmelo. *Psychic operates with blood and has death predicted by Chico Xavier.* Alexandre Pollara / The Folha Database.

https://f5.folha.uol.com.br/saiunonp/2014/11/1548495-medium-opera-com-sangue-e-tem-morte-prevista-por-chico-xavier.shtml?_x_tr_sl=pt&_x_tr_tl=são&_x_tr_hl=são&_x_tr_pto=sc

This paper has a graphic description of Antonio de Palmelo: Greenfield, Sydney M, Ph.D. *A Model Explaining Brazilian Spiritist Surgeries And Other Unusual, Religious-Based Healings.*

https://journals.sfu.ca/seemj/index.php/seemj/article/viewFile/181/146

91. *Rubens de Farias Junior began to work as Fritz in Rio de Janeiro soon after the death of Edson Queiroz.* Folho de São Paulo/Sergio Torres/ São Paulo, 2/10/1999.

Maki, Masao. *In Search of Brazil's Quantum Surgeon: The Dr. Fritz Phenomenon.* VIZ Media LLC; 1998.

Moreira, William. *Dr. Fritz The Phenomenon of the Millenium: The author's true story between the spiritual and material worlds.* Self-published, 2002.

92. *He wrote to the famous channeler Chico Xavier, and asked his advice.* Several of his biographers mention this. The original "letter" is on display at the Casa.

93. *Another problematic wife to deal with.* Bianca Corona of Grifa Films provided me with a long list of alleged crimes of João, which was passed to her by the Prosecutor's office. Ligia Bueno was listed as a suspected murder by the civil police on 2/1/1983 (unsolved case). Dalva also mentions this in her interviews, including VEJA of December 19, 2018, edition no. 2613.

94. *I think she drank some poison first and shot herself in the head afterward.* From an interview with Sandro Teixeira, December 16, 2018, in the Jornal O Popular/ Cidades, by Galtiery Rodrigues. The link has been removed.

95. *Meanwhile, Dalva decides to escape. She discovers she is pregnant with João's baby. She is 14.* Interview with Dalva on Globo and Netflix, a radio interview, and various Journals. In some interviews, she says the

child was her boyfriend's, but in later interviews confesses it was her father's child.

96. *João got involved with smuggling. He became part of an organized crime group.* Globo/Play 3/24/2019

https://globoplay.globo.com/v/7482465/

Also, Veja Magazine, *It Got Scarier.*

https://veja.abril.com.br/brasil/ficou-mais-assustador/?+_x_tr_sl=pt&_x_tr_tl=en&_x_tr_hl=en&_x_tr_pto=sc

João's JuJu

97. The Medium was on a mission and liked to say that he made a deal with his spirit guides—take care of him financially, and he'd promise to do their work for the rest of his life. João mentioned this frequently. His biographers repeated it.

Like most left-hand terreiros João had attended, the house was commanded by a king, in this case, King Solomon.

"In the Sacred Jurema, the great king Solomon does not incorporate in his consecrated disciples, but his science and wisdom is present in all the works.

"This great monarch, son of King David, was one of the great connoisseurs of the occult sciences of his time, such as; Kaballah, astrology, alchemy, and the art of Goeticism. He was initiated into the mysteries of Goeticism by the great Queen of Sheba, whom he later married.

"In the Sacred Jurema, he and the Queen of Sheba are rulers of the enchanted Kingdom of the Seven Pits, or kingdom of Urukunda, which is the kingdom where the cabalistic magicians, alchemists, and the Gypsy people from Turkey dwell." From the Facebook page of Amantes da Jurema.

https://www.facebook.com/AmantesDaJurema/posts/812662885754044/

Wikipedia link to all you might want to know about Goeticism:

https://en.wikipedia.org/wiki/The_Lesser_Key_of_Solomon

Reginaldo, Prandi, André Ricardo de Souza. *Encantaria Brasileira: O Livro dos Mestres, Caboclos E Encantados.*, Pallas Editora, 2001.

Reginaldo, Prandi. *In the footsteps of Voduns: a mine drum terreiro in São Paulo.* Articles, theses, and publications; Spirituality and Society.

www.espiritualidades.com.br.

Wikipedia; Encanteria. *Well-researched article explaining several left-hand cults.*

98. *In the cults he frequented in Maranhão and Pará, there are a large variety of entities that go by the name of Dom.*

Mundicarmo Ferretti, Doctor of Anthropology at UFMA, was a fantastic source of information about the cults of the enchanted, the doms, and the gentiles:

Ferretti, M. *Tambor de Mina, Cura e Baião na Casa Fanti-Ashanti (MA).* São Luís, SECMA, 1991.

Maranhão Encantado: *Encantaria maranhense e outras histórias.* São Luís, EDUFMA, 2000.

Encantaria de "Barba Soeira": *Codó, capital da magia negra?.* São Paulo: Siciliano, 2001.

Pajelança do Maranhão no século XIX: o processo de Amélia Rosa. São Luís: CMF/FAPEMA, 2004.

A Representação de reis portugueses encantados no Tambor de Mina. São Luís. Mundicarmo Maria Rocha Ferretti is a retired professor from the Federal and State Universities of Maranhão (UFMA and UEMA).

Sacred Jurema, Master and Mistress of Catimbo.

https://santajuremasagrada.blogspot.com/2016/03/salomao.html

"Exu Mor is tied to King Solomon... When the infernal hosts are called, and spirits such as Amazael, Aziel, Anathana, Azael, Tyer, Lucifer, Ashtaroth, Belial, Troglis, it is always done by the virtue of St. Michael, St. Cyprian or King Solomon...

"Those who undergo immediate transfiguration are known as encantados, charmed ones who vanish in nature and remain in proximity to the earth as Masters and Teachers of certain people or small communities. The cult of Catimbó is particularly rich with these spiritual phenomena, but some Exus are also encantados and are therefore known as catiços." Frisvold, Nicholaj de Mattos. *Exu And The Quimbanda Of Night And Fire.* Scarlet Imprint, 2012.

https://vdoc.pub/documents/exu-and-the-quimbanda-of-night-and-fire-70r4essp4n40

99. *The last style of Quimbanda that caught João's eye was the Esoteric Line.*

Carneiro, João Luiz and Carneiro, Érica Jorge. *Umbanda Esotérica não é Esoterismo na Umbanda.* Revista Brasileira de História das

Religiões. May/September 2017.

Olavo Ortiz Solera, Osvaldo. *A Magia Do Ponto Riscado Na Umbanda Esotérica* Master's Dissertation, Pontifícia Universidade Católica São Paulo 2014.

Serra, Ordep. *No Caminho De Aruanda: A Umbanda Candanga Revisitada.* Journal Afro-Ásia, #25-26 (2001), pages 215-256.

Cordovil, Daniela And Dos S. De Castro, Luis Paulo. *Indigenous Spirits In Esoteric Umbanda: A Complex Web Of Meanings.* Plura, Revista De Estudos De Religião, Vol. 9, No 1, 2018, Temática Livre.

Zacarias França, Bianca. *Umbanda Esotérica: Uma Etnografia Sobre O Encontro Da Religiosidade Afro Com A Nova Era Em Um Terreiro De Belo Horizonte.* Revista Calundu – Vol.3, N.2, July/ December, 2019.

100. "Santa Rita inside Umbanda: Santa Rita is regarded as one of the most powerful figures within the line of Oxalá, **being extremely feared for her low spirituality,** as she managed to abdicate herself and ask Christ-Jesus himself to take, that is, to kill her children. Thus, she heads as chief the third phalanx of the first Line of Faith, the line of Oxalá, being directly subordinated to Jesus.

"This phalanx is composed of a majority of entities [spirits and enchanted ones] of a feminine nature. They work within religious spaces [terreiros, gardens, churches, and others] promoting harmony. They also always balance disputes at home and in the family, **working for the conversion of sins into benefits and gifts."**

https://perdido-co.translate.goog/2016/05/santa-rita-de-cassia/?_x_tr_sl=pt&_x_tr_tl=en&_x_tr_hl=en&_x_tr_pto=sc

Wikipedia. *Rita of Cascia.*

Santa Rita de Cássia and Obá - Syncretism. Vida Urbana May 22, 2014. Post from Rozzi Brazil.

Blood, Semen, and Tears

101. *All the left-hand paths that João traversed are sometimes referred to as Crossed Line Umbanda. This term signifies that the cult continues to make a blood sacrifice the centerpiece of their rituals.*

Barros Gama, Ligia. *KOSI EJÉ KOSI ORIXÁ: Simbolismo e representações do sangue no Candomblé.* Master's dissertation, Universidade Federal De Pernambuco, 2009.

Lemos Soares, Rodrigo and Marcos Bussoletti, Denise. *Rituais de sangue na quimbanda: diálogos entre memórias, pedagogias culturais e produção de corporeidades.* Centro Universitário Ritter dos Reis, 2017.

Rogério, Janecléia Pereira. *Se não há sacrifício não há religião. Se não há sangue, não há.* Master's dissertation, Universidade Federal de Pernambuco, 2008.

Barros, Sulivan Charles. *A simbólica da violência e da transgressão no universo da quimbanda.* Caminhos, Goiânia, v. 5, n. 1, pp. 107-127, jan./jun. 2007.

Azevedo Corral, Janaina. *O Livro Da Esquerda De Umbanda.* Universo Dos Livros, Brasil, 2010.

102. *The most shocking offering that Medium João introduced to the Casa is one that only a man can make.*

A YouTube presentation by a self-proclaimed practitioner of the Umbanda of Ciganos: https://www.youtube.com/watch?v=e_RJBu92QjM

What Umbanda line uses semen as an offering? Quimbanda.

Oliveira Trajano Gomes, Adriano. *Narrativas Sobre Dinâmicas Sexuais De Exu No Território Sagrado Da Umbanda Nos Terreiros De Viçosa, Alagoas.* Doctor's Thesis, Universidade Federal Da Paraíba, 2019.

Urban, Hugh B. *Magia Sexualis: Sex, Secrecy, and Liberation in Modern Western Esotericism.* Journal of the American Academy of Religion Vol. 72, No. 3 (Sep. 2004), pp. 695-731: Oxford University Press.

Sorceress Cagliastro. *Menstrual Blood And Semen, A Sorcery Manual.* Iron Ring Publishers, 2015.

Another Interesting Link:

https://misticos-blogs-sapo-pt.translate.goog/magia-sexual-2910?_x_tr_sl=pt&_x_tr_tl=en&_x_tr_hl=en&_x_tr_pto=s

103. *In 1987, João was featured on a popular national television show hosted by Luiz Gasparetto, a medium famous for his channeled paintings in the styles of artists like Picasso, Monet, and Renoir.* Luiz Antonio Gasparetto Entrevista João de Deus.

https://www.youtube.com/watch?v=6vpC0PhkOnY

104. *When the sympathy level was at its peak, he pulled off a grand publicity stunt. He operated on himself!*

Explained by most of his biographers as a miracle cure. Felitti is the exception. *A Casa* pages 49-50.

105. One of them, reported by Fantástico, says she was raped about ten times when she was just 11 years old, always at the Casa. TV program Fantástico, GloboPlay. 12/9/2018. https://globoplay.globo.com/v/ 7220890/

106. Link: https://globoplay.globo.com/v/7482465/

107. *Urubatan was caught having a sexual affair with two underage sisters at the same time.* Sarah Teófila. *Crime de 1988 não foi esquecido em Abadiânia* – O Popular, 12/11/2018, Goiânia.

https://www.opopular.com.br/noticias/cidades/crime-de-1988-não-foi-esquecido-em-abadiânia-1.1721799

108. *João said he wanted to marry her, that in past lives they had also been married. He called her his wife.* Interview with Dalva Teixeira. Published in VEJA on December 19, 2018, edition no. 2013.

109. *In 1991, the American actress, Shirley MacLaine, made an unannounced and incognito visit to the Casa.* The Contigo! Magazine, 4/11/1991. Many of João's biographers mention this visit.

110. *As soon as he caught sight of her in the line, his eyes were glued on her.* Cristina Fibe / *João de Deus – O Abuso da Fé*, p.104-106. Globo Livros.

111. Liberato Póvoa, Chico Felitti, and other biographers cover this.

112. *Edson was dead, stabbed to death by his groundskeeper. João was on his way to becoming the most famous healer in the world.*

Dubugras, Elsie. *A tragic end for Edson Queiroz.* São Paulo: Revista Planeta, no. 230, November 1991, p. 47-49.

Tourinho, Nazareno. *Edson Queiroz, the new Arigó of the spirits.* São Bernardo do Campo (SP): Correio Fraterno, 1991.

113. *This is the story of Simone Soares Silva.*

Soares, Simone. *A Outra Face Do João (The Other Side of João).* Self-published, Brazil, 2019. An interview with Chico Felitti and news reports confirm her account.

114. *Exu do Lôdo is a phalange of exus with dark, dense energy. Most of his phalange were priests, witches, and sorcerers in past lives.*

De Mattos Frisvold, Nicholaj. *Exu & the Quimbanda of Night and Fire.* Scarlet Imprint / Bibliothèque Rouge.

De Oxóssi, Diego. *Desvendando Exu: O Guardião dos Caminhos.* Arole Cultural. Brasil.

Exu do Lôdo: "His aspect resembles an elderly witch. His line includes sorcerers, witches, wizards and also bishops, and priests, who, when dealing with the sacred, end up dealing with the magical aspect of nature as well. Because he is an Exu from souls and the scope of his wisdom in the medical field, he is a guardian capable of curing very severe diseases. You know those diseases that don't seem to have a solution, that doesn't have any adequate remedy? Those in which the patient is already disillusioned? That's where he seeks to work, and people come to him for that kind of help."

https://blog.vidatarot.com.br/exu-do-lodo/?+_x_tr_sl=pt&_x_tr_tl=en&_x_tr_hl=en&_x_tr_pto=sc

115. *João was treated like a head of state, and after the works in Puna, he was secretly flown to doctor Peru's new dictator, Alberto Fujimori.* Liberato Póvoa, João de Deus O Fenômeno de Abadiânia.

116. *Most people think of a charlatan as a conman or a quack. In Brazil, it is the legal term for a practitioner of black magic, something that João was charged with multiple times.*

Pellegrino and most biographers use the word charlatan.

The original penal code is Charlatanismo Article 283 – *Inculcar ou anunciar cura por meio secreto ou infalível*—inculcating or advertising healing by secret or infallible means.

The "secret" part refers to black magic. Brazilian law still protects freedom of religion diligently. Charlatanism is a *commercial* crime against the health of Brazil's citizens.

If you make money by promising magical or impossible cures, this is charlatanism. If you pretend you are a doctor or a pharmacist or illegally ply their trade, you are a curandero. This is also against the law, Article 284.

The law has evolved since the days authorities were chasing João. More recently, it has been enforced for bogus remedies, therapies, and even products making false claims.

The President of Brazil, Jair Bolsonaro, was charged by the higher court with charlatanism when he thwarted attempts to get Covid vaccines for Brazil promptly and recommended Ivermectin and Hydroxychloroquine as viable remedies.

117. *"João was the one who had the plane sabotaged because he had found out that Urubatan was stealing from him."* Simone Soares, *A Outra Face Do João*.

118. *He handed her a glass of water suffused with rose petals and told her to drink it. She lost consciousness and claimed he drugged her.* Related by Prosecutor Alline Matos Pires Ferreira of the 8th

Prosecutor's Office of Imperatriz (2018).
https://henriqueaires-wordpress-com.translate.goog/2018/12/20/imperatriz-duas-mulheres-denunciam-medium-joao-de-deus-ao-mpma/?_x_tr_sl=pt&_x_tr_tl=en&_x_tr_hl=en&_x_tr_pto=sc

119. *Then he took her to her mother's house and asked her if it would be ok if Dalva went to Abadiânia for two weeks while he helped her sort her life out.* My Father Is A Monster. Interview with Dalva published in VEJA on December 19, 2018, issue no. 2613.

120. *He had her sons beaten by thugs because they knew of his abuses and protested.*
https://g1.globo.com/go/goias/noticia/2019/05/06/neto-de-joao-de-deus-denuncia-que-foi-vitima-de-perseguicao-em-anapolis.ghtml

121. *As if all this wasn't enough for one year, he and his gang faced charges on trafficking cocaine.* Veja Magazine, It Got Scarier.
https://veja.abril.com.br/brasil/ficou-mais-assustador/?+_x_tr_sl=pt&_x_tr_tl=en&_x_tr_hl=en&_x_tr_pto=sc

122. *The episode of violence allegedly took place inside the Civil Police Station of Abadiânia in the presence of police officers."* Jornal O Popular 12/10/2010.

See more about Éder Martins at:
https://globoplay.globo.com/v/7482465/
Also in *Veja, It Got Scarier.*
https://veja-abril-com-br.translate.goog/brasil/ficou-mais-assustador/?_x_tr_sl=pt&_x_tr_tl=en&_x_tr_hl=en&_x_tr_pto=sc
"In her opinion, the prosecutor Cristiane Marques de Souza considered that the investigation was not sufficient." O Popular, 12/10/2010.

123. *Simone, now seventeen years old, is irresistibly drawn back to the Casa after a five-year absence.*
Simone Soares/*The Other Side of João.* She also mentions details in YouTube postings, in an interview with Chico Felitti, and in media interviews.

124. *Pellegrino-Estrich, a mustachioed flim-flam man, was single-handedly responsible for the spectacular fraud that João was about to perpetuate.* Robert Pellegrino-Estrich. *The Miracle Man: The Story of João de Deus.*

125. *One of my anonymous contacts in Abadiânia told me a story that the locals know well.*

My source is a good friend who has lived near the Casa for 25 years. My friend shared many stories with me, which I confirmed with others in the community who also wished to remain anonymous. It's a small town. When something happens to your neighbor, the word gets out. Unfortunately, the police and prosecutors are not interested in stories. Because of this, they ignored dozens of criminal acts right under their noses. Widely shared rumors are often correct, especially in Abadiânia.

126. He said, *"He charged a minimum (monthly) wage from each inn. And the taxi drivers paid half a salary per month during that period."* GloboPlay series, Netflix, episode two, *A Casa,* Chico Felitti, and other interviews.

V.
ME AND THE MEDIUM

127. He wielded an enormous veterinary syringe, dipping it repeatedly in a bucket at his feet. The bucket was a mixture of kerosene, alcohol, and bleach. Maki, Masao. *In Search of Brazil's Quantum Surgeon: The Dr. Fritz Phenomenon.* VIZ Media LLC; 1998.

128. *"I was very sick and sad, desperate with the doctors, disillusioned, with a terrible disability, when someone advised me to look for João."* Casa De Dom Inácio. Local country music duo, from their album *Casaco de Frio, Alberto & Albano,* copyright 1983, Loirinho/ Alberto/ Albano. https://youtu.be/PTqnJYuii2k

City of Sycophants

A Sycophant is a person who acts obsequiously toward someone important in order to gain an advantage. Denoting an informer.

129. *The triangle within a triangle is a well-known magical device used to trap low spirits for their eventual enslavement and control.* It is called a demon trap. A variation of this is a triangle within a circle. Solomon's seal is another demon trap. King Solomon was notorious for trapping demons and enslaving them within various "seals" (geometric symbols). His technique was very similar to Pontos Riscado.

Waite, Arthur Edward. *The Book of Ceremonial Magic.* London, 1913.

Ferre, Lux. *Magic Triangle.* Journal Occult World, 4/9/2019.

https://occult-world.com/magic-triangle/

"A magic triangle is in ceremonial Magic, an inscribed triangle into which a spirit or Demon is evoked into physical appearance and is contained. The magic triangle, also called the Triangle of Art, is a symbol of the manifestation of the invisible into the visible, or the powers of darkness and night into daylight. The points of the magic triangle are bounded by three great names of God.

"As long as a spirit is inside a magical triangle, it is subject to the commands of the magician, who remains protected inside a magic circle. The spirit must be discharged or dismissed from within the triangle. It is considered dangerous to allow a spirit to escape the triangle."

130. *The Casa holds many esoteric secrets.*

"He writes his prescriptions with speed in a spirit shorthand which looks like a squiggly line and a few ticks." Pellegrino-Estrich, Robert. *The Miracle Man,* location 85.

Olavo Ortiz Solera, Osvaldo. *A Magia Do Ponto Riscado Na Umbanda Esotérica.* Master's Dissertation, Pontifícia Universidade Católica, São Paulo, 2014.

Laffitte, Stefania Capone. *Searching for Africa in Brazil: Power and Tradition in Candomblé.* Duke University Press, 2010.

Itaoman, Mestre. *Pemba: A Grafia Sagrada dos Orixas.* Thesaurus Publications, Brasilia, 1990.

Wikipedia. *Pontos Riscado.*

131. *"In this terreiro, the caboclo is seated after knowing his Pontos Riscado..."* https://cabanadocaboclogentil.wordpress.com/

132. Crimes that he said, "Had the connivance of the judicial police of that locality." From an article by Sarah Teófilo in O Popular, 3/25/2019.

133. *The other cases denounced João Teixeira de Faria for sexually enslaving women until they were pregnant and then marketing their babies......* Prosecutor Valeria Scaranzzi from the Public Prosecutor's Office in São Paulo, said that the reports had a wealth of evidence. Source: investigative research gathered for NETFLIX series on João. The case was prosecuted by the Federal Police in Brasilia but thrown out by the civil police with encouragement from the military police of Goiania.

The current situation in Brazil with human trafficking at the illegal gold mines is covered in this BBC report:

https://youtu.be/md9Ieeq4LvE?si=ljmsJPH4Uh5Pk6TJ

Child of the Casa

134. *Then he said, "Our group is coming with Heather Cumming."* The group was the board of directors of The Foundation for Shamanic Studies. In this group was Sandra Ingerman, one of the principals, who teaches workshops on shamanism and has authored several books. She shared her reflections on her trip to Brazil in 2001 in her newsletter archives of June and July 2001.

www.shamanicvisions.com/ingerman_folder/ingerman01.html

Once again, we have a person who should have known better, endorsing the Casa with practically no understanding of what was going on. She quotes Heather Cumming extensively.

135. *"I have to remark that when it comes to the sexual behavior, other than the seemingly petty molestations, about which I'm currently not getting upset, all the serious cases have questions hanging over them. All the women involved have had histories of sexual abuse."* Email sent to me by Ultan O'Meara 4/26/2001.

The account of my experience working at the Casa is reinforced by a daily journal that I kept during this time, several additional emails that I mentioned in this chapter, and many conversations that occurred during this time.

136. *Joao then told the group of people that he consistently—through exerting his own spiritual power and with God's help—was able to keep closed a particular spiritual portal that existed above the Casa and surrounding area. If left open, this portal would allow all kinds of negative entities to attack and create problems for those coming to the Casa seeking healing.* Josie Ravenwing, *The Book of Miracles*. See the triangle within a triangle mentioned previously.

VI
Waiting for Godot

137. We will never know how many people took his advice and died or made matters worse by doing so. GloboPlay series, In the Name of God.

https://globoplay.globo.com/v/8633380/?s=0s

138. Another woman died while in the Casa's care in 2003, Leigh Hopkins. GloboPlay series, In the Name of God.

https://globoplay.globo.com/v/8633380/?s=0s"

Santo de Pau Oco: The Hollow Log Saint

139. In 2005, the famous new age guru Ram Das (Richard Alpert) arrived from the States to visit João, one of a growing number of celebrities endorsing his work. https://youtu.be/jt_wx_JECDA

140. *"I was totally shocked on my visit there to learn that John of God is sexually molesting girls as young as 12 years old."* This letter, sent to many guides, posada owners, and children of the Casa used a pseudonym. There is no Amy Bryant, and she isn't a tour guide — but the allegations are true. The person who wrote this is a friend of mine, associated with the Casa for many years, and this episode happened to the twelve-year-old sister of a friend as they both stood outside the Medium's office waiting for the girl as she had her private session. "Amy" also mentions a website and Australian friends with similar stories. This was altered as well. The friends are real, and the allegations happened, but these are Austrians, not Australians. Amy was very afraid when she penned this email and felt a need to conceal her identity.

141. *One of these victims was an American in her early thirties.*

https://www-brasildefato-com-br.translate.goog/especiais/abusos-da-fe-or-um-ano-do-caso-joao-de-deus?_x_tr_sl=pt&_x_tr_tl=en&_x_tr_hl=en&_x_tr_pto=sc

142. *His daughter was a petite young woman, five feet tall and 23 years old. She had just received her law degree.*

As reported by Lu Sudré in *Brasil de Fato São Paulo (SP)*, December 7, 2019. Widely covered in the press.

143. *Caritas prayer.* The Caritas Prayer, often said at the opening of *Umbanda* sessions and always at the beginning of the Casa ritual (and frequently, soon after João had raped young women in his office):

God our Father, you who are all power and goodness

Give strength to him who is in trial

Give light to him who seeks the truth

Put compassion and charity in the heart of man.

God, Give the traveler the guiding star

To the afflicted, consolation

To the sick, rest.

Father, give repentance to the guilty
To the spirit, the truth
To the child, the guide
To the orphan, the father.
Lord, may your goodness extend over all you have created
Mercy, Lord, for those who do not know you
Hope for those who suffer
May your goodness allow the consoling spirits
Spread peace, hope, and faith everywhere.
God, one ray, one spark of your love can scorch the earth
Let us drink at the fountains of this fruitful and infinite goodness
And all tears will dry, all pains be soothed.
One heart, one thought will rise to you
Like a cry of recognition and love
Like Moses on the mountain
We await you with open arms
Oh goodness! Oh, beauty! Oh, perfection!
And we want somehow to reach your mercy
God, give us the strength to help progress in order to ascend to you.

144. *A German tourist had been murdered just behind the Posada Catarinense.* Sarah Teófilo reporting for O Popular, *3/25/2019.* https://opopular.com.br/cidades/morte-de-alemã-em-abadiânia-vem-à-tona-após-denúncia-1.1760619?_x_tr_sl&_x_tr_tl=en&_x_tr_hl=en&_x_tr_pto=sc

145. *"Barbaric homicide by subduing the old victim and firing a shot at close range in the face."* Fantastico/Rede Globo, O Popular.

146. The case was reopened in 2019. Journal O Popular, *Death of German in Abadiânia comes to light after complaint,* by Sarah Teófilo, 3/25/2019. https://opopular.com.br/noticias/cidades/morte-de-alemã-em-abadiânia-vem-à-tona-após-denúncia-1.1760619

147. *Heather Cumming promoted the US event at a church in Atlanta, Georgia.* Matthew Remski, *The Conspirituality Report. John of Fraud: How did slack journalism and New Age earnestness help a monster*

globalize?

https://matthewremski.medium.com/john-of-fraud-c5e92acb786d

148. Afterward, he was interviewed for the ABC Primetime program, appearing on American television for the first time. He was introduced as John of God.

https://abcnews.go.com/Health/Primetime/story?id=482292&page=1

See James Randi's scathing comments on this show, where his skeptical interview was cut entirely from the program:

https://web.randi.org/home/from-the-archives-randis-inside-scoop-into-abc-news-john-of-god-investigation-2005

149. *The couple was threatened with death and fled Abadiânia abruptly, abandoning their group!* Ultan O'Meara and other residents told me this.

150. *In 2007, The Discovery channel covered João. The Extraordinary is the name of the special that Discovery Channel broadcasted from August 19 to 24, 2007.*

151. *The result was that the Omega Institute hosted João for nine visits between 2007 and 2017.* An interview with the CEO of Omega Institute and valuable research about the Omega events can be found here:

https://matthewremski.medium.com/john-of-fraud-c5e92acb786d

152. *Heather Cumming, who is at his side for most of his foreign tours, is rewarded for her loyalty.* Chico Felitti, *A Casa*.

Link to PDF of Healing Quests Llc Spiritual Tours To John Of God. Promotional Material From Heather Cumming:

https://silo.tips/download/healing-quests-llc-spiritual-tours-to-john-of-god

Hotel Rei Davi:

https://www.tripadvisor.com/Hotel_Review-g2440582-d2664581-Reviews-Hotel_Rei_Davi-Abadiania_State_of_Goias.html

153. *Around the same time, João was being accused of hiring someone to kill Ilion Fleury Junior; a high profile Doctor, from an influential family in Goiás.*

https://portalcontexto-com.translate.goog/morte-do-medico-ainda-e-um-misterio/?_x_tr_sl=pt&_x_tr_tl=en&_x_tr_hl=en&_x_tr_pto=sc

154. *A sixteen-year-old girl suffering from anxiety attacks was brought to the Casa by her father.* This was first covered by Veja Brasília magazine on September 4, 2013, and also interviewed on TV Globo's Fantástico program and the GloboPlay series on João.

Also: https://www.metropoles.com/brasil/brasilenses-relatam-terror-de- abusos-sexuais-feitos-por-joao-de-deus

155. *Criminologist Aisla Carvalho writes about João, "The danger of perversity resides in the subtle form applied by the agent, who savors the agony it arouses in the victim."* Published by Canal Ciência Criminal by Aisla Carvalho.

156. *She reported she was abused by João de Deus about twenty times from 2009 to 2010. All of them occurred during services at the Casa. She had recorded all of this in her daily diary, which she displayed for the camera, and which is now evidence in the case.* FANTASTICO/GLOBO TV series.
https://g1.globo.com/fantastico/noticia/2018/12/23/diario-escrito-por-jovem-revela-que-joao-de-deus-dava-presentes-para-seduzir-suas-vitimas.ghtml

John the Con: The Wizard of Oz

"You can fool people for one or two years, but you cannot fool people for fifty years." **João de Deus**

157. *Gail Thackray, now that's a character.* Wikipedia has a great biography of Gail Harris (Thackray's porno queen stage name).
https://en.wikipedia.org/wiki/Gail_Harris

158. *"I now find myself about to be face to face with the great spirit that is incorporated in John of God."* Gail Thackray's Spiritual Journeys: Visiting John of God, chapter five, first page.

159. *Elisabetta Dami is the creator of the internationally best-selling series for children, the Geronimo Stilton adventure stories, which have been translated into 49 languages and have sold over 161 million copies around the world.* Wikipedia comes through once again.
https://en.wikipedia.org/wiki/Elisabetta_Dami

160. *A young woman appeared at the Sedona police department in December.* Netflix, GloboPlay, Chico Felitti, Dangerous Diane Blog: https://dangerousdiane.blogspot.com/2008/01/john-of-god-from-i-dont-believe-it-file.html.

161. *João was accused of twenty sexual assaults, including two girls from his center in Rio Grande de Sul.*
https://opopular.com.br/cidades/morte-de-alemã-em-abadiânia-

vem-à-tona-após-denúncia-1.1760619? x_tr_sl& x_tr_tl=en& x_tr_hl=en& x_tr_pto=sc

162. *Gail Thackray films a vanity travelogue about her adventures in the jungles of Brazil, João de Deus: Just a Man (2013).* Full video: https://www.youtube.com/watch?v=gkc7ZPIEm6Q

163. *Brazil's megastar Xuxa landed in Abadiania by helicopter.* Chico Felitti and many news reports:

https://espiritualidade.hi7.co/casa-de-dom-inacio-recebe-a-apresentadora-xuxa-5642db1925493.html

164. *João told the author, "You are well." Dyer died four years later.*

https://matthewremski.medium.com/john-of-fraud-c5e92acb786d

165. *"More often than not, they would be taken by tour guides (and the event organizers were also guides) in package tours."* Rocha, Cristina. *John of God (pp. 165-166).*

166. *"We saw that the only thing going on was to make money."* Post on Dangerous Diane blog for João's victims.

https://dangerousdiane.blogspot.com/2008/01/john-of-god-from-i-dont-believe-it-file.html

167. *"Bewildered and not remembering how she had entered this shocking moment, she looked up to see Heather—who was grinning at her."* Ultan O'Meara told me about this shortly after it happened. His source was the guide this had happened to. After the scandal about João surfaced, I wrote to Ultan suggesting he make a statement to the police as he knew about many events at the Casa. He refused. I asked for help with this book, particularly for help getting a contact for this guide/victim. He refused. Over the next two years, he refused to help me with details about any events he had related to me.

168. *"The Civil Police of Abadiânia opened an investigation into the death of an 80-year-old Austrian woman at the request of the Public Ministry."* G1 Portal - February 10, 2012, with information from TV Anhanguera. The civil police first investigated this as a murder. Occurrence: 112/2006-IP72-2006

169. *With her stamp of approval, João and his Casa entered international celebrity status.* This was covered in depth by Cristina Rocha and Maria Machado.

Also: *Oprah's Visit with John of God: You Are Exactly Where You Need to Be,* by Oprah Winfrey. http://www.oprah.com/

O, Oprah's Magazine article: *Leap of Faith: Meet John of God by Susan Casey.* December 2010 issue.

Read more: http://www.oprah.com/spirit/oprahs-experience-with-john-of-god-oprah-on-lifes-journey-ixzz5ZBsodGDD

Insightful:

https://medium.com/@ryanjones_81455/oprah-john-of-god-an-explosive-hypothetical-theory-for-why-oprah-is-trying-to-convince-the-9c655ece902f

Link to the TV program with Oprah.

https://www.imdb.com/title/tt2773058/

170. *The young woman sexually assaulted while her father sat with his eyes closed three meters away in 2006 finally had her day in court six years later._*

https://www.brasildefato.com.br/especiais/abusos-da-fe-or-um-ano-do-caso-joao-de-deus?+_x_tr_sl=pt&_x_tr_tl=en&_x_tr_hl=en&_x_tr_pto=sc

171. *When João arrived to testify, the court staff exited in fear of retribution.* Chico Felitti, *O Casa,* page 104.

172. *On his next visit to Rio Grande do Sul, the fathers, husbands, and leaders of the Casa in Três Coroas warned him never to return or that he would be killed.* Reported in Globo, by Luís Guilherme Julião. 12/10/2018.

173. *Martin Mosquera's wife, Fernanda, and another daughter of the Casa, Tãnia Appel, were sent to Três Coroas to attempt damage control (they come from there).* Maria do Carmo, Vitimas Unidas writes in a personal email:

"Fernanda was also the person who went to Rio Grande do Sul along with Tãnia Appel to try to put some heat on the story of the two girls who were abused there in Abadiânia and who were daughters of the Director of Casa Dom Inácio de Loyola Sul. But they didn't succeed. At the meeting, one of the owners, until today, of the land where the Casa in the South was, is police officer Delmes Feiten, who, together with his son, also a policeman, did not give João the order to be arrested. They only expelled him from the Casa no sul and Delmes started to frequent the house there in Abadiânia. I have photos and the document that he still owns the land."

174. João told her it was because she couldn't get pregnant and told her she needed to "get this thing out of you." Interviewed by Chico Felitti, page 122.

Also, https://diariogaucho.clicrbs.com.br/?_x_tr_sl&_x_tr_tl&_x_tr_hl

VII.
The Enchanted Realm of Abadiânia

175. *"In Switzerland, João was prohibited from entering the country, as there was a report of a sexual crime against him."* Maria do Carmo, Vitimas Unidas, in personal communication.

YouTube advertisement for the event in Switzerland.

https://www.youtube.com/watch?v=7CyKRBFFzzU

Josie Ravenwing, Martin and Fernanda Mosquera, Norbert Kist, Diego Coppola, Bob Dinga, Diana Rose, and Heather Cumming were usually assisting João at these events. Link to the booklet, *John of God in Switzerland:*

https://dokumen.tips/download/link/booklet-john-of-god-switzerland

176. *"John of God is world renowned for his healing powers. People swear by him. Oprah has visited him. Acclaimed author Wayne Dyer credits him with healing his leukemia."* Quoting Gail Thackray, sponsor of the event. A video Gail produced to promote the event:

https://www.youtube.com/watch?v=HQsOT4GzySY

177. *"Readers report actually feeling the energy coming through the book, and some even say they have received a healing just from having the book by their bedside."* John of God Interview with Gail Thackray / Lori Bosworth—TORONTOCITY, February 18, 2013.

178. *"I have reason to believe that Elisabetta Dami wants to open a Casa of John of God or something like this near my town in Northern Italy."* https://dangerousdiane.blogspot.com/2008/01/john-of-god-from-i-dont-believe-it-file.html

179. A volunteer at the Casa for 20 years, filed a police complaint accusing the Medium of sexual assault. Testimony from Victims Unidas.

180. *"At night, I had a horrible dream. João de Deus appeared in black beside my bed and sucked all my energy with his hands under my face."* Businesswoman Aline Saleh, 29, who reports sexual abuse of the medium *João de Deus in Goiás* - Edition no 2613 Alberto Rocha/ Folhapress.

https://www1-folha-uol-com-br.translate.goog/cotidiano/2018/12/quem-tem-de-sentir-vergonha-e-ele-nao-eu-diz-ex-paciente-de-joao-de-deus.shtml?_x_tr_sl=pt&_x_tr_tl=en&_x_tr_hl=en&_x_tr_pto=sc

181. *"There are three distinct lines of work: trips to the Worlds of Enchantments, the manifestation of Masters, caboclos, trunqueiros, kings, and enchanted of Jurema and other entities such as pretos-*

velhos, exus, and pomba-giras." Catimbó And The Enchanted Masters / Gutta Monteiro, www-wemystic-com-br.

182. *When I watched the video interviews with Zahira Mous, I wept.* GLOBO interview with Bial / December 2018.
https://globoplay.globo.com/v/7218772/

183. *"As I walked toward people, some people would begin to weep and some would fall down and ..."* Paul Simon interview in SOJOURNERS by Cathleen Falsani June 6, 2016. Paul Simon's Spiritual Fascination.
https://sojo.net/articles/paul-simons-spiritual-surgery

184. *"Nine such events between 2007 and 2017 may have grossed as much as $4.5 million USD."*
https://matthewremski.medium.com/john-of-fraud-c5e92acb786d
Contract and information for 2014 event:
https://www.eomega.org/sites/default/files/resources/2014_jog_event_details_letter.pdf

185. *In October, the TV show 60 Minutes Australia visited Abadiânia.* Full program on YouTube:
https://www.youtube.com/watch?v=NtsNfy1eVMA
Soon afterward, João brought his theater to Sydney. A debunker comments:
https://www.ratbags.com/rsoles/comment/faithhealer.htm

186. *In front of dozens of guests, the priest said he wouldn't hold the wedding if João attended.* Chico Felitti, *A Casa*.

187. *Much later, I would learn that Erika Beira, who inherited the homestead after the death of Israel, also had confrontations with João.* Maria do Carmo in personal communication.

188. *The chemotherapy wasn't enough to cure João's cancer.* VEJA: *Como o médium João de Deus venceu o câncer. Ele já ofereceu ajuda a mais de 5 milhões de pessoas, mas manteve sob reserva sua batalha pessoal para superar um tumor agressivo no estômago.* Adriana Dias Lopes e Egberto Nogueira 7/2/2016.
https://veja.abril.com.br/saude/como-o-medium-joao-de-deus-venceu-o-cancer/
Also, several biographers and Chico Felitti, *A Casa*.

189. *In February 2015, one of the Casa attendees was found dead in her apartment in Abadiânia. The local police considered this a suicide.* (Ocorrencia #85-2015-03.03.2015).

Her husband wrote, "The money will be used for the funeral home expenses in Brazil, the flight to get her home, and having to hire a lawyer in Brazil to facilitate Amy's trip home to her family. Any money left over will be donated to the Wounded Warrior Project and the USO, which serves service men and women worldwide."

"To all of Amy's friends and family, I want to thank all of you for helping give Amy the best memorial possible this past Saturday morning... God bless all of you, Bob Nole."

190. *In February 2016, João was featured in a special edition of Newsweek. TECH & SCIENCE John of God, the Miracle Healer.* Newsweek Special Edition 2/27/16.

https://www.newsweek.com/miracle-worker-430163

191. *The Space in Between, a film by the world-famous performance artist Marina Abramović, debuted in May 2016. Marina Abramović in Brazil: The Space in Between.* You can stream this on Prime Video, Apple TV, and Vimeo.

https://vimeo.com/ondemand/thespaceinbetween

192. *Her thesis (published in 2018) was to be an analysis of the judicial proceedings brought against the medium, "which has not been examined in detail and analytically in any research so far."*

Professor Mesquita */ Me Too e as Decisões: Diário e diálogos sobre a sexualidade em João de Deus (Me Too and the Decisions: Diary and Dialogues on Sexuality of John of God).* You can download her pdf file here: http://anpocs.org.br

https://www.contemporanea.ufscar.br/index.php/contemporanea/article/view/871/pdf

193. *Professor Maria Machado, who had done field research at the Casa for four years. João de Deus: Um Médium no Coração do Brasil.*

194. *In 2016, she had a series of dreams where she was at the Casa and speaking directly to João about Jesus. Simone Soares, A Otra Face de João.*

195. *One of them entangled João, his son Sandro, a police officer, a lawyer, and Edna the Casa publicist in a criminal case that was brought to trial in 2020.*

https://opopular.com.br/cidades/morte-de-alemã-em-abadiânia-vem-à-tona-após-denúncia-1.1760619?

ENDNOTES

Silence is a Prayer

196. *Dalva's two sons, Paulo and João Paulo, now adults, sued their grandfather João Teixeira de Faria, in 2017. For the first time, he was publicly accused of abusing their mother.*

"After complaints, grandchildren of João de Deus are subjected to DNA testing. Exams were carried out this Friday (12/14/2018) after the psychic's daughter denounced that she suffered sexual abuse from her father." Juliana Moraes, from R7, with information from RecordTV, 12/15/2018.

His grandsons were threatened and even beaten by thugs in response to their denunciations. *Neto de João de Deus denuncia que foi vítima de perseguição em Anápolis*, report by Alessandro Vieira and Vanessa Martins, TV Anhanguera e G1 GO, 5/6/2019.

https://g1.globo.com/go/goias/noticia/2019/05/06/neto-de-joao-de-deus-denuncia-que-foi-vitima-de-perseguicao-em-anapolis.ghtml

197. *Later, the Casa posted this video on their Facebook page, denouncing Dalva as an insane drug addict.*

Video link: https://www.youtube.com/watch?v=fX7yfXaVGIY.

Also covered in the NETFLIX series, episodes 3 and 4.

198. *"I was there to heal," she said, "there to forgive the man that had nearly destroyed my life."* Chico Felitti, *A Casa*. Page 96.

199. *Rocha said, "Following the approaches of experiential anthropology, anthropology of humanism and of consciousness, if people tell me that they have been healed by religious practices—be they prayer, rituals, or spiritual surgeries—I accept it."* Rocha, Cristina. *John of God* (p. 16). Oxford University Press.

Also, *"The sharp disconnect between the image of the healer as an enlightened, generous, loving being, painted by his followers in books and chats, and the reality of his absolute power caught me by surprise."* Rocha, Cristina. *John of God* (p 28). Oxford University Press.

200. *A few days after the Omega event, João and crew attended the premiere screening of O Silêncio é Uma Prece, directed by Candé Salles (Silence is a Prayer). Paris Films, 2017. Although this film has been removed from distribution and streaming media, I have a copy and have viewed it several times.*

201. *Unsurprisingly, the documentary does not include a single person in doubt about John's practices or an eventual unsuccessful surgery.* Review of O Silêncio é uma Prece, awarded two stars for Adoro Cinema, *The Proof Through Image,* by Bruno Carmelo.

202. *In one memorable scene (I think it was filmed at the Swiss event), João picks up a glass next to his throne and begins eating it!* You can see this trick on episode three of the NETFLIX series John of God: The Crimes of a Spiritual Healer.

Also, at this link: https://www.youtube.com/watch?v=Bm7pYt0upKY

Also, *In the Name of God* GLOBOPLAY series. "A great-nephew of João de Deus reveals that the glass he chewed (when he had his mediumship under suspicion) was made of crystalized sugar."

https://noticiasdatv.uol.com.br/noticia/daniel-castro/farsa-de-joao-de-deus-inaugura-nucleo-de-documentarios-de-pedro-bial-na-globo-38208

203. *"John of God, known in Brazil as Joao de Deus, received the Order of Malta (Maltese Cross) in a special ceremony held on May 4, 2018, in Brazil."* The Casa Newsletter of 2018.

204. *The group is actually a secretive international Military Order with a long and bloody history and unique status under international law.* Wikipedia. *Knights of Malta.*

205. *In 2006, a newspaper article in the United Arab Emirates claimed that the Knights were "directly influencing U.S. policy in Iraq and Afghanistan, reprising the Crusades." Who Are the Knights of Malta and What Do They Want?* By Joshua E. Keating / Foreign Policy 1/19/2011.

206. *In July, their lawyer, Segio Beze Prates, was shot point blank while sitting in his car conversing with a client, killing the attorney and wounding his passenger.*

https://g1.globo.com/go/goias/noticia/2018/07/18/advogado-e-morto-a-tiros-e-cliente-dele-e-baleado-dentro-de-carro-em-goiania.ghtml

207. *In late August, one of João's staunchest allies, a high profile Brazilian billionaire by the name of Marcos Eduardo Elias, was arrested in Switzerland and extradited to the US, where he was arrested by the FBI and faced charges for embezzling $750,000 from a New York bank.*

Maria do Carmo, in an email dated 7/11/2021: "Martin and Fernanda were with João in Miami when Marcus Elias [Daslu and Parmalat's owner] was arrested in Brazil, and the four of them fled together. But I can't prove it (no written documentation)."

See: https://www.moneytimes.com.br/gestor-brasileiro-e-preso-pelo-fbi-por-fraude-bancaria/

"Brazilian Man Sentenced To 3 1⁄2 Years In Prison For Defrauding

Manhattan Financial Institutions And Aggravated Identity Theft." Department of Justice US Attorney's Office Southern District of New York, July 25, 2019.

https://www.justice.gov/usao-sdny/pr/brazilian-man-extradited-switzerland-defrauding-financial-institutions-and-identity

"Laep Investments, a company that made a BRL 5 billion coup: Headquartered in a PO box in the Bermuda Islands and ghostly partners, it was the biggest loss to the Brazilian capital market in history." Thiago Bronzatto for Globo/ÉPOCA Magazine, 3/7/2015.

https://epoca.globo.com/tempo/noticia/2015/07/laep-investiments-uma-empresa-que-deu-um-golpe-de-r-5-bilhoes.html

You can gather an earful about this at Wikipedia: *LAEP Investments.* https://pt.wikipedia.org/wiki/Laep_Investments

208. *"I was not ready to see what I saw on that day in September 2018."* This is the only footnote that I cannot place with a source or a link. It was lost in the clutter of thousands of notes. It came from one of these two sources and was part of a much longer group of postings: https://www.facebook.com/Vitimasunidas/ or, https://www.facebook.com/coamebr

209. *We probably will never know which type of situation trapped Gigi in João's spider web.* Gigi died in Abadiania 10/30/2018. The police determined it was murder—case # 8173323.

VIII.
The Shit Hits the Fan

Throughout this book, I have used a timeline provided by the Prosecutor's Office in Goiania. It graphs the number of denunciations they are investigating from 1973 to 2018, listing the rape victims that had come forward by early 2019. Much more needs to be added, and the years before 1973 are now being investigated. They are cloaked in secrecy as these are the years of the dictatorship. Apparently, they have military documents.

Source: Public Ministry of the State of Goiás.

210. A television special about João, on Brazil's most popular channel, had aired the night before, exposing João as a rapist to almost everyone's surprise. Conversa com Bial /TV Globo 7/12/2018.
https://globoplay.globo.com/v/7218663/?s=0s

211. Amy Biank has a lot of explaining to do. In her published remarks, it becomes apparent that she knew of these sexual assaults for some years yet continued to bring tour groups.

http://intuitionunlimitedbyamybiank.blogspot.com/2011/07/john-of-god-in-brazil.html

Posted in 2011: Amy Biank said...

I have been a guide at the Casa for many years, here is my take on what is happening. Is Joao (John) highly charged sexually? Yes. Has he taken advantage of his position as a healer to seduce women and girls into allowing him to take sexual liberties? Yes.

Healing and sexual energy go hand in hand. They are the same. It takes great personal strength for a healer to use one and put the other aside. Even good, kind people can be corrupted by the strength of this energy. It is up to you as a spiritual explorer to develop the life skills to not lose yourself in the energy of a healer and to protect and teach those who do not have those skills!

Is the Casa an instrument of financial gain for Joao? No.

I know for a fact that Joao does not care about the money the Casa brings in outside of the enormous cost of running such a large enterprise. Once as a tour guide, I handed him $10,000 cash (donations from a large tour) and 5 minutes later I saw a ragged nun leave his office, tears streaming down her face, with the whole wad *of cash!*

Are there any "safe" "holy" places in the world? No. You are only as safe as your own poise and discretion can allow.

Is the healing at the Casa a fraud? No.

The Casa is a hospital that turns no one away! Thieves, con artists, perverts, the mentally ill, delusional people, stubborn people, egotistical people and people with all physical illness are treated. Everything is real, nothing is real. God is so loving he allows us the freedom to explore ourselves and our world in any fashion we choose, and always there is the opportunity to heal!

What would I wish for...

I wish for every person in the world to have an adventure, a pilgrimage, a sacred journey. I wish that people would be strong, know themselves, stay in their bodies and make wise choices about their journeys. I wish that people would have the courage to tell the truth to each other and their children without embroidering it with emotional detail. I wish for all people to draw wisdom from experience rather then expression. I wish for people to not abdicate their human rights for the illusion of safety. I wish for people to be so wise that they can experience life without the need for laws or government.

In a YouTube interview, https://youtu.be/e5nb2u0vpZo

212. *João de Deus—A Medium in the Heart of Brazil.* Jornal Opção, Euler de França Belém. 11/12/2018.

https://www.jornalopcao.com.br/imprensa/companhia-das-letras-suspende-distribuicao-de-biografia-de-joao-de-deus-152768/

213. *João de Deus–Silence is a Prayer.* Jornal De Brasília:

https://noticias.r7.com/brasil/comercializacao-de-documentario-sobre-joao-de-deus-e-suspensa-29062022

214. *The authorities also froze his primary bank account.* Link reporting on his enormous assets and the freezing of them by authorities:

https://www1-folha-uol-com-br.translate.goog/cotidiano/2018/12/joao-de-deus-acumula-27-imoveis-em-berco-espiritual-no-valor-de-r-20-milhoes.shtml?_x_tr_sl=pt&_x_tr_tl=en&_x_tr_hl=en&_x_tr_pto=sc

215. *His group finally gained access to the stage, and he addressed the crowd and a wall of cell phones, cameras, and microphones. The medium claimed he was innocent.* Dramatic film coverage of this event can be found in the second episode of the NETFLIX production, John of God: The Crimes of a Spiritual Healer. Most Brazilian media covered this event live, and some were slugged by

João's bodyguards.

216. In a matter of a few days, our poor, illiterate farmer had acquired one of the most sought-after criminal lawyers (and most expensive) in Brazil. The defense attorney for João de Deus, Alberto Zacharias Toron, and his stellar crew began the battle with opening salvos of writs of habeas corpus.

https://opopular.com.br/noticias/cidades/quem-é-o-advogado-de-joão-de-deus-1.1680908

They argued he should be allowed to continue to work at the Casa while awaiting his trials.

https://jovempan.com.br/noticias/brasil/ele-esta-sendo-vitima-de-uma-grande-injustica-alega-defesa-de-joao-de-deus.html?+_x_tr_sl=pt&_x_tr_tl=en&_x_tr_hl=en&_x_tr_pto=sc

Also see:

https://oglobo.globo.com/epoca/brasil/quem-alberto-toron-rei-dos-habeas-corpus-23995097

217. Marcos Elias, Brazil's brash hedge fund billionaire, along with publicist Nizan Guanaes, paid the bills.

https://glamurama.uol.com.br/negocios/nizan-guanaes-e-marcus-elias-estao-entre-os-empresarios-que-estao-ajudando-joao-de-deus-entenda/

218. Marcos Elias's Laep Investments is known as the largest stock market fraud in Brazilian history.

https://epoca-oglobo-globo-com.translate.goog/tempo/noticia/2015/07/laep-investiments-uma-empresa-que-deu-um-golpe-de-r-5-bilhoes.html?_x_tr_sl=pt&_x_tr_tl=en&_x_tr_hl=pt-BR&_x_tr_pto=sc

He was also convicted of defrauding a New York bank and sentenced to 3 1/2 years in prison.

https://www.justice.gov/usao-sdny/pr/brazilian-man-sentenced-3-years-prison-defrauding-manhattan-financial-institutions-and

219. The prosecutors said, "Women heard by the Public Ministry stated that some employees of the medium João de Deus were colluding with the sexual abuse committed during the spiritual sessions in Abadiânia." Brazilian media covered this extensively. Two interviews with survivors of João's assaults mention Chico Lobo and Heather Cumming, as employees colluding with the abuser. Several others on the staff were named in interviews as someone who told them that this was not a molestation but a healing or that they should stay quiet and leave town immediately. NETFLIX episode 3 is a good example.

220. On December 16th, his attorneys met the police on a secluded rural road near the Casa, where João surrendered.
https://g1.globo.com/go/goias/noticia/2018/12/16/medium-joao-de-deus-e-preso-suspeito-de-abusos-sexuais.ghtml

221. The cops were spooked. Fábio Fabrini. Interrogation of João de Deus has broken keyboard, screams, burned wire and injured agent, Folha de S.Paulo,12/17/2018.
https://www1-folha-uol-com-br.translate.goog/cotidiano/2018/12/depoimento-de-joao-de-deus-tem-teclado-quebrado-gritos-fio-queimado-e-agente-ferido.shtml?_x_tr_sl=pt&_x_tr_tl=en&_x_tr_hl=en&_x_tr_pto=sc

222. The same day, armed police dressed in black swarmed the Casa. They entered several of João's homes and ranches with search warrants.
https://g1.globo.com/go/goias/noticia/2019/01/16/prisao-do-medium-joao-de-deus-completa-1-mes-veja-linha-do-tempo.ghtml

223. Around the middle of December, an exclusive interview was published in VEJA, Brazil's equivalent of Newsweek or Time. It was Dalva on their front cover, out of rehabilitation and with her terrible tale.
https://veja.abril.com.br/brasil/meu-pai-e-um-monstro/

224. By the 19th of December, the police had received over 500 accusations of sexual assault.
https://pt-globalvoices-org.translate.goog/2018/12/20/mais-de-500-mulheres-acusam-famoso-medium-brasileiro-de-abuso-sexual/?_x_tr_sl=pt&_x_tr_tl=en&_x_tr_hl=en&_x_tr_pto=sc

225. By New Year, it was a ghost town. https://www-metropoles-com.translate.goog/brasil/apos-denuncias-de-estupro-centro-de-joao-de-deus-tenta-manter-se-vivo?_x_tr_sl=pt&_x_tr_tl=en&_x_tr_hl=en&_x_tr_pto=sc

226. They used the terms invisible web of protection, law of silence, and conspiracy to conceal crimes.
https://globoplay.globo.com/v/7482465/
https://opopular-com-br.translate.goog/noticias/cidades/morte-de-alemã-em-abadiânia-vem-à-tona-após-denúncia-1.1760619?_x_tr_sl=pt&_x_tr_tl=en&_x_tr_hl=en&_x_tr_pto=sc
https://g1.globo.com/go/goias/noticia/2019/03/25/policia-investiga-suposta-rede-de-protecao-a-joao-de-deus.ghtml

227. The State Attorney revealed the first bad news.

https://www1.folha.uol.com.br/cotidiano/2018/12/maioria-das-denuncias-contra-joao-de-deus-expirou-prazo-legal-diz-delegada.shtml?+_x_tr_sl=pt&_x_tr_tl=en&_x_tr_hl=en&_x_tr_pto=sc

228. Chico Lobo told the police that about 10,000 people attend the Casa per week.

https://www-jornalopcao-com-br.translate.goog/reportagens/um-mes-apos-denuncias-contra-joao-de-deus-comerciantes-de-abadiania-fecham-as-portas-156973/?_x_tr_sl=pt&_x_tr_tl=en&_x_tr_hl=en&_x_tr_pto=sc

229. Brasilia; "Judge Liciomar Fernandes da Silva, who ordered the arrest of João de Deus for illegal possession of firearms [a serious charge in Brazil] on Friday, stated that investigations show that the medium heads a criminal organization that operates mainly in the city of Abadiânia."

Judge says medium João de Deus led a gang. The magistrate who ordered João de Deus's arrest claims that he 'heads a criminal organization' that operated in the city of Abadiânia, in Goiás, Jornal Estado de Minas,12/24/2018.

https://www.em.com.br/app/noticia/politica/2018/12/24/interna_politica,1015828/juiz-diz-que-medium-chefiava-quadrilha.shtml?+_x_tr_sl=pt&_x_tr_tl=en&_x_tr_hl=en&_x_tr_pto=sc

230. The lawyer Antônio Carlos de Almeida Castro, famous for defending those accused of Operation Lava Jato, joined the defense team of the medium João de Deus.

https://noticias.uol.com.br/cotidiano/ultimas-noticias/2018/12/24/kakay-joao-de-deus-habeas-corpus-stf-dias-toffoli.htm?_x_tr_sl=pt&_x_tr_tl=en&_x_tr_hl=en&_x_tr_pto=sc

231. *In early January, João, and his wife, Ana Keyla, were charged with illegal possession of firearms, the second case to be brought against him.* Vanessa Martins, Raquel Morais e Paula Resende, Juiz dá nova ordem de prisão contra João de Deus, por posse ilegal de armas. G1 GO 12/21/2018.

https://g1.globo.com/go/goias/noticia/2018/12/21/juiz-acata-novo-pedido-de-prisao-contra-joao-de-deus-por-porte-ilegal-de-armas.ghtml

232. *João's son, Sandro Teixeira, is the same son I read about on the front page of the newspapers in 2002. He was arrested, along with his girlfriend, for sexually molesting and torturing her three-year-old child. She lost custody of the child, and he was imprisoned.* Source: Maria do Carmo interviews with Sandro's girlfriend and my recollection.

233. Chico Felitti. *A Casa A história da seita de João de Deus.*

Todavia, 2020.

234. Fifteen of them were three years old or younger at the time of the assaults. https://www.brasildefato.com.br/especiais/abusos-da-fe-or-um-ano-do-caso-joao-de-deus

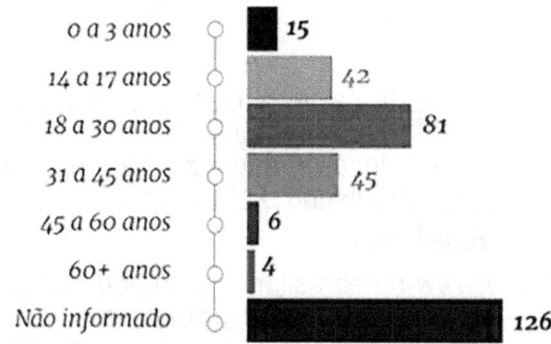

The chart is courtesy of the Public Ministry of Goiás. Statistics on about 300 of his victims.

235. One investigator is Maria do Carmo dos Santos, a co-founder of Vítimas Unidas (Victims United) with Vana Lopes.
https://www.facebook.com/Vitimasunidas/
Maria do Carmo is also a founder of COAME, a group assisting victims of sexual abuse in religions and spiritual cults. Maria do Carmo Santos, victims' psychologist, Master in History, and Ph.D. in Education. President of Grupo Vitimas Unidas.
https://www.facebook.com/coamebr

236. "Respondents repeat several times that, in Abadiânia, there are many rumors that the medium has already murdered or ordered the murder of women whom he raped so as not to be denounced." By Lu Sudré, for Brazil de Facto. São Paulo, December 7, 2019.

237. "We have received reports from the adoptive mothers of these children who were sold for $20,000 to $50,000 in Europe, the US, and Australia." said Bittencourt in a video posted on Facebook. Manoela Albuquerque. Activist accuses João de Deus of trafficking babies and enslaving women. Metropoles, 7/1/2019.

https://www-metropoles-com.translate.goog/violencia-contra-a-mulher/ativista-acusa-joao-de-deus-de-traficar-bebes-e-escravizar-mulheres?_x_tr_sl=pt&_x_tr_tl=en&_x_tr_hl=en&_x_tr_pto=sc

Sabrina Bittencourt made the international press with her allegations and suspicious 'suicide.' These are links about her and her controversial life:

Wikipedia:

https://pt-m-wikipedia-org.translate.goog/wiki/Sabrina_Bittencourt?_x_tr_sl=pt&_x_tr_tl=en&_x_tr_hl=en&_x_tr_pto=sc

Globo report:

https://revistamarieclaire-globo-com.translate.goog/Noticias/noticia/2019/02/sabrina-bittencourt-mulher-que-ajudou-desmascarar-joao-de-deus-comete-suicidio.html?_x_tr_sl=pt&_x_tr_tl=en&_x_tr_hl=en&_x_tr_pto=sc

Rede Brasil Atual:

https://www-redebrasilatual-com-br.translate.goog/politica/2019/02/ativista-que-denunciou-abusos-em-todo-o-mundo-disse-em-mensagem-final-que-2018luta-continuara2019/?_x_tr_sl=pt&_x_tr_tl=en&_x_tr_hl=en&_x_tr_pto=sc

Bittencourt's famous video alleging baby trafficking and sex slaves: https://youtu.be/vTJ20ZFSjU0

Sabrina was having a battle of video accusations with another YouTube figure. He was well known in Brazil as a radical right-wing proponent.

Cited in a letter from Sabrina Bittencourt, Paulo Pavesi says he will ask the PF to investigate "alleged suicide." Revista Forum, 3/2/2019:

https://revistaforum-com-br.translate.goog/brasil/2019/2/3/citado-em-carta-de-sabrina-bittencourt-paulo-pavesi-diz-que-pedira-pf-para-investigar-suposto-suicidio-52461.html?_x_tr_sl=pt&_x_tr_tl=en&_x_tr_hl=en&_x_tr_pto=sc

YouTube link to a Pavesi video: https://youtu.be/1ld2Tr0Arnk

Many videos pertaining to Bittencourt have been removed from both of their accounts.

Bittencourt also posted this WhatsApp text shortly before her disappearance:

https://www-diariodocentrodomundo-com-br.translate.goog/quem-e-paulo-pavesi-citado-na-ultima-mensagem-de-sabrina-bittencourt-por-sacramento/?_x_tr_sl=pt&_x_tr_tl=en&_x_tr_hl=en&_x_tr_pto=sc

Her last post before her death forgave Pavesi for his behavior. Article here: https://www-diariodocentrodomundo-com-br.translate.goog/quem-e-paulo-pavesi-citado-na-ultima-mensagem-de-sabrina-bittencourt-por-sacramento/?_x_tr_sl=pt&_x_tr_tl=en&_x_tr_hl=en&_x_tr_pto=sc"

Full text of her final letter: *Sabrina Bittencourt quotes Marielle Franco before she died.*

https://catracalivre.com.br/cidadania/sabrina-bittencourt-cita-marielle-franco-antes-de-morrer/

238. *Sabrina committed suicide, according to her teenage son. This looked suspicious from the very beginning.*

Bruna de Lara. *Sabrina Bittencourt's Body Hunt.* The Intercept Brasil, 2/5/2019.

https://theintercept-com.translate.goog/2019/02/05/imprensa-suicidio-de-sabrina-bittencourt/?_x_tr_sl=pt&_x_tr_tl=en&_x_tr_hl=en&_x_tr_pto=sc

Also,

https://ohoje-com.translate.goog/noticia/cidades/n/163043/t/familia-e-amigos-acreditam-que-sabrina-bittencourt-esta-viva/?_x_tr_sl=pt&_x_tr_tl=en&_x_tr_hl=en&_x_tr_pto=sc

https://www.pragmatismopolitico.com.br/2019/02/amiga-de-sabrina-bittencourt-suicidio-falso.html?+_x_tr_sl=pt&_x_tr_tl=en&_x_tr_hl=en&_x_tr_pto=sc

https://www.cjr.org/analysis/brazilian-activists-alleged-suicide-sparks-coverage-controversy.php

239. *"They are powerful people, who are now in control, and who silenced our heroine."* The YouTuber published a long text about Sabrina Bittencourt, in which he says goodbye to his friend and says he spoke to her before the suicide. Raphael Campos reporting in Metrópoles, 2/3/2019.

Wikipedia:

https://pt-m-wikipedia-org.translate.goog/wiki/Felipe_Neto?_x_tr_sl=pt&_x_tr_tl=en&_x_tr_hl=en&_x_tr_pto=sc

240. VEJA, the same magazine that had covered his daughter's story, was granted a prison interview. The Newsroom 3/8/2019 Marcelo Camargo/Brazil Agency.

https://veja-abril-com-br.translate.goog/brasil/todos-me-tratam-bem/?_x_tr_sl=pt&_x_tr_tl=en&_x_tr_hl=en&_x_tr_pto=sc

241. Fantástico quoted the Public Ministry as saying, "The complaints against João indicate he had a protection network made up of authorities from Abadiânia, including the police."

"Investigations by the Public Ministry and the Civil Police lead to the suspicion that the medium João Teixeira de Faria was shielded by the authorities so that he could continue committing crimes. The investigation led to a complaint in court for the misrepresentation of the captain of the PM Reginaldo Gomes do Nascimento, the lawyer João José Elias, and the journalist Edna Ferreira Gomes. The former delegate of Abadiânia and current councilor

Éder Martins (PTB) is under investigation, in addition to a delegate whose identity was not revealed."

242. The group of hundreds of homeless squatters had occupied his farm since soon after his arrest in December. Integrantes do MST ocupam fazenda de João de Deus em Goiás. Sílvio Túlio, Paula Resende e Lis Lopes reporting in G1/GO, 3/13/2019.
https://g1.globo.com/go/goias/noticia/2019/03/13/integrantes-do-mst-ocupam-fazenda-de-joao-de-deus-em-goias.ghtml

243. One report posted a photograph of him in an ambulance, looking longingly at a very young medical attendee sitting beside him. His hand is planted firmly on her inner thigh. Photo widely distributed through the Brazilian Press, credited to Global 1 TV.

244. Also in May, COAF (Council for Control of Financial Activities), gained access to the emails of people the prosecutors call 'the healer's gang.'. GLOBO reportage and https://opopular.com.br/cidades/jo-o-de-deus-movimentou-r-240-milh-es-em-dez-anos-1.2439838

245. Regarding the death of Chico Lobo:

"Chico Lobo, the right-hand man of João de Deus and former mayor of Abadiânia, dies. He had been hospitalized for weeks due to pneumonia. For more than two decades, he was the one who managed Casa Dom Inácio de Loyola." Bruna Lima reporting for Correio Braziliense, 7/4/2019.

https://www-correiobraziliense-com-br.translate.goog/app/noticia/cidades/2019/07/04/interna_cidadesdf,768227/morre-chico-lobo-braco-direito-de-joao-de-deus.shtml?_x_tr_sl=pt&_x_tr_tl=en&_x_tr_hl=en&_x_tr_pto=sc

Chico was João's *fixer*. The Casa rape victims who raised hell were directed to him. He was the Casa manager until his death. He also was an Abadiania City councilman for three terms and deputy mayor for two terms.

246. This was a blow to the Prosecutor's investigation, as Chico was their number one suspect after João in their efforts to reveal the Casa

crime organization. From an interview with several investigating detectives discussing the case in the NETFLIX series, episode 3.

In the Name of God

247. *At the end of June, Globoplay, Brazil's streaming equivalent of Netflix (and part of the Globo media empire), released a six-part series about João de Deus and the unfolding scandal. Em Nome de Deus (In the Name of God).* https://globoplay.globo.com/v/8633380/?s=0s

"In the Name of God, from Globoplay, reveals the strength of journalism in the case involving João de Deus." Adriana Izel reporting for Correio Braziliense, 6/28/2020.

https://blogs-correiobraziliense-com-br.translate.goog/proximocapitulo/em-nome-de-deus-do-globoplay-critica/?_x_tr_sl=pt&_x_tr_tl=en&_x_tr_hl=en&_x_tr_pto=sc

248. *On July 25th, João's entire crew of nine lawyers quit without explanation.* All Brazilian media covered this. Link to O Globo article by Guilherme Amado in their Época Magazine, 7/24/2019:

https://oglobo.globo.com/

249. *"...the need for preventive detention to ensure public order, in view of the amount of military material in the possession of João de Deus."* Consulto Juridico, Gabriela Coelho, 8/26/2019.

https://www-conjur-com-br.translate.goog/2019-ago-26/turma-stf-nega-liberdade-joao-deus?_x_tr_sl=pt&_x_tr_tl=en&_x_tr_hl=en&_x_tr_pto=sc

250. They discovered two mysterious documents. One was an identity card with his photograph, listing him as an agent of the Military Police Intelligence Unit of Goiás. Jornal O Popular. Jéssica Torres. *João de Deus tinha carteira policial, aponta investigação da Polícia Federal.* 8/7/2019.

http://www.ugopoci.com.br/joao-de-deus-tinha-carteira-policial-aponta-investigacao-da-policia-federal/

251. *My friend told me many rumors that were going around town. My friend, a Brazilian, has lived near the Casa for 25 years and has been challenged and harassed by João for most of this time.* This person wished to remain anonymous, as do several friends who confirmed these rumors.

252. *In late September, Faria complained of chest pains. He was admitted to the public hospital in Goiânia for observation.* Globo,

9/27/2019.

253. *The press covered an event that had occurred in prison. VEJA / John of God says to continue to work miracles in jail. According to lawyers, the medium claims to have exorcised demons.* Hugo Marques, 11/20/2019, edition no 2661.

https://veja.abril.com.br/brasil/joao-de-deus-diz-continuar-a-operar-milagres-na-cadeia/

254. *The news is a continuing soap opera of revelations.* Antônio de Olivos Guatambu. Jornal Argumento, 11/19/2019.

https://jornalargumento.com.br/denuncias/familia-de-joao-de-deus-quer-dinheiro-de-volta/

255. *UOL, another Brazilian media company,*

https://www.uol.com.br/play/videos/2020/11/25/poder-e-silencio-como-as-denuncias-contra-joao-de-deus-destruiram-abadiania.htm

256. *A Casa visitor living there for the past two years, Hitomi Akamatsu, was found murdered at the Casa's sacred waterfall.* "The body of Hitomi Akamatsu, 43, was found amidst stones and earth, on land owned by João de Deus, in Abadiânia, where she was undergoing spiritual treatment. The suspect, who confessed to the crime, is in prison. Judge holds suspect of robbing and killing Japanese woman in Casa Dom Inácio waterfall." Novaonda, 11/19/2020.

https://www.novaonda.fm.br/site/noticias/corpo-de-japonesa-morta-em-cachoeira-da-Casa-dom-inacio-de-loyola-segue-no-iml-tres-dias-apos-ser-localizado

257. *He gave interviews, including one for the upcoming Netflix series.* The brief interview is filmed at his home, the woman who is now his wife was already living with him. He continues to insist that he is innocent of all allegations and convictions—Netflix episode 4.

258. *They exposed his vast real estate holdings and wealth.*

https://opopular.com.br/noticias/cidades/joão-de-deus-movimentou-r-240-milhões-em-dez-anos-1.2439838

259. *In August, a new book about João appeared (in Portuguese).*

https://www.amazon.com.br/João-Deus-abuso-Cristina-Fibe-ebook/dp/B09FRW8XSY

260. *Netflix debuted its four-part series.* My interview is in the second part.

https://www.netflix.com/br-en/title/81103570

261. João's sidekick of forty years, Secretary of the Casa and second in command, Sebastião de Lima, was now in the headlines. *Men accuse Tião de Lima, assistant of João de Deus, of sexual abuse at Casa Dom Inácio.* Chico Felitti, Mirelle Pinheiro, Metrópoles, 01/10/2021.

https://www-metropoles-com.translate.goog/brasil/homens-acusam-tiao-de-lima-assistente-de-joao-de-deus-de-abuso-sexual-na-casa-dom-inacio-de-loyola?_x_tr_sl=pt&_x_tr_tl=en&_x_tr_hl=en&_x_tr_pto=sc

262. *With this new conviction, his sentence reached one hundred and*

nine years in prison. Yet, he remained under house arrest.

https://noticias.uol.com.br/cotidiano/ultimas-noticias/2022/12/08/joao-de-deus-condenacao-109-anos-de-prisao-crimes-sexuais.htm

263. *Are there unmarked graves on the grounds of the Casa?* "Without taking their eyes off the ground, two men scour the surroundings of the waterfall that the House considers sacred. Sometimes they crouch down to get a better look at something...

"The men are plainclothes Civil Police agents, and they are searching the ground for evidence. Evidence of a clandestine cemetery at the back of the Casa, the final resting place for those who might have died during spiritual treatment. This information comes from anonymous complaints...

"But even in the city's official cemetery, there are also issues linked to the House. On the entrance wall, a plaque warns *ATTENTION: By order of the Public Ministry and the City Hall, we cannot do burial without a burial certificate and burial guide Law 6.015-73 Article 77.* And that's because Abadiânia had the habit of saying goodbye to its dead without notifying the public authorities." Chico Felitti, A Casa. Page 53-54.

Cognitive Dissonance and the Casa Cargo Cult

264. *The economy of the city of Abadiânia crashed along with the Casa. Properties close to Casa de Dom Inácio that were worth R$5 million are offered for R$1.5 million. Demand has ceased to exist, say brokers.* Galtiery Rodrigues for Metrópoles, 04/27/2021.

https://www-metropoles-com.translate.goog/brasil/casas-milionarias-perdem-valor-em-abadiania-apos-caso-joao-de-deus?_x_tr_sl=pt&_x_tr_tl=en&_x_tr_hl=en&_x_tr_pto=sc

Also, *"Since the medium's arrest, the economy of Abadiânia has experienced an unprecedented ruin in its 66 years.*

"At City Hall, the communications director reports that, in 2019, between 1,500 and 2,000 people lost their jobs; 55 of the 63 commercial establishments in Joao's side of town [inns, restaurants, and shops] closed their doors."

https://paulosampaio-blogosfera-uol-com-br.translate.goog/2019/12/07/um-ano-apos-escandalo-entidade-joao-de-deus-ainda-assombra-abadiania/?_x_tr_sl=pt&_x_tr_tl=en&_x_tr_hl=en&_x_tr_pto=sc

265. Norberto Kist:

https://www.facebook.com/nkistpousada/?locale=pt_BR

266. *The Dreamer, Jucelino Nobrega da Luz:*

https://www.jucelinodaluz.com.br/livros/789-the-dreamer-jucelino-s-premonitory-dreams-os-sonhos-premonitorios-de-jucelino

http://bilogangbuwanniluna.blogspot.com/2008/07/sleeping-false-prophet.html

267. *Our friends Martin and Fernanda from Abadiania, who came with the team from Brazil to all our healing events, warmly recommended him to us four years ago. And vouches for his truthfulness and integrity: Jucelino Nobrega da Luz, who foresees future events in nightly dreams.* Earth Oasis:

https://www.jucelinodaluz.com.br/2-paginas-principais/1308-jucelino-luz-orientador-espiritual-palestrante-clarividente-e-curador-espiritual-energetico-segunda-jornada-europa-2023

https://earth--oasis-de.translate.goog/seminare/?_x_tr_sl=de&_x_tr_tl=en&_x_tr_hl=en&_x_tr_pto=sc

268. The same German tour agency, Earth Oasis, that had once heavily promoted João de Deus, now includes tours to Brazil that combine visits to several healers.

https://earth--oasis-de.translate.goog/heilungsimpulse/?_x_tr_sl=de&_x_tr_tl=en&_x_tr_hl=en&_x_tr_pto=sc

269. *An early e-mail from Josie Ravenwing to her worried fans echoed the Casa sentiment.* I was quoting my personal copy.

270. *Gail Thackray quickly posted a YouTube video from her perspective.*

https://www.youtube.com/watch?v=_EQjQ15tsg8

The other films are promoting her recently released tell-all autobiography, Running With Wolves (wonder where she got the idea for that title). https://youtu.be/j173a8O6YO0

271. He opens the segment with a promotional trailer created by Gail Thackray, highlighting her wild career as a porn queen. It certainly grabs one's attention. https://www.youtube.com/watch?v=6I4r7viRII8

272. *John of God: A Guide To Your Healing Journey With Spirit Doctors Beyond The Veil.* Her current website declares: "I help women become goddesses. I teach and mentor women and women leaders like you to: heal from trauma, liberate yourself from patriarchy, find your voice, speak your truth, embody your power and passion, and live your Soul Purpose. Connect with the Divine Feminine." She no longer mentions João and has removed archives regarding him from her blog.

Her book, however, is still for sale: *Meliana, Mytrae John of God: A Guide to Your Healing Journey with Spirit Doctors Beyond the Veil.* Blue Leopard Press.

Her website: https://mytraemeliana.com

273. *Josie posted on Facebook*

https://m.facebook.com/JohnOfGodLive/posts/2536095656512091?d=m&s=100001663009946

274. *Josie, who claims to be the first American Casa guide, led about 150 tour groups to Abadiânia from 1998 to 2020.*

Facebook:

https://files.constantcontact.com/8c4aea7c001/5a4c3132-3acf-4fb4-8537-cf0e3a96248c.pdf

Another post:

https://peoplelifepoliticsandbullshit.com/2018/03/22/1165/

275. *Then, the Casa's ex-press officer, Edna Gomes, weighed in on social media.* https://www.odemocrata.com.br/

276. "The re-built Casa will then establish good press in its own right and attract people from all over the world to come to Abadiania to experience the undiminished healing activities by the Good Entities, without the expectation that Medium Joao is the facilitator, or even the healer who he himself — according to his own assurances — never was." Klaus and Gundi Heinemann / *Tenets for a New Casa*

posted 1/5/2019.

https://www.healingguidance.net

277. We understand that Abadiãnia exists because of the Casa... Diane S. / a Casa Guide.

https://www.healingguidance.net

278. *"The Casa's Financial Future — the Months and Years Ahead."* Diego Coppola is a native of Peru, works as a volunteer and translator for John of God in Brazil, and was part of the entourage at many of the John of God Events worldwide. Posted on his commercial website, *Friends of the Casa*. Also, https://www.healingguidance.net

279. *The Casa Angelic Spirits are working vigilantly with each one of us directly without the intersession of a single medium...* Casa Newsletter by Deb Court.

https://myemail.constantcontact.com/Friends-of-the-Casa-Newsletter---November-2019.html?soid=1102861739208&aid=ATb3tbKZQUY

Also, https:/www.healingguidance.net

280. *"While the Casa continues to be swarmed by paparazzi and John of God is still being held in custody, the Casa is open and people report incredible energy and amazing healing."* Letter from Gail Thackray posted on Casa website.

https://myemail.constantcontact.com/Friends-of-the-Casa-Newsletter---November-2019.html?soid=1102861739208&aid=ATb3tbKZQUY

281. The Civil Police began an investigation in February 2019, which concluded in 2022, into misappropriated funds generated by the Casa. By Vitor Santana, g1 Goiás 18/04/2022.

"It is demonstrated that João Teixeira de Faria unduly appropriated the money of the private association Centro Espírita Dom Inácio de Loyola, a non-profit entity, remitting money from this association to his personal account, to his wife's account, to the account of his company Cristais Dom Inácio LTDA and to third parties," said police officer Thiago Martimiano.

https://g1.globo.com/go/goias/noticia/2022/04/18/joao-de-deus-pegava-indevidamente-de-dinheiro-da-casa-dom-inacio-de-loyola-e-transferia-para-sua-conta-diz-policia.ghtml

Márcio Leijoto, from O Popular, writes: "Documents raised by the Civil Police show that the medium João Teixeira de Faria, the 79-year-old João de Deus, received in his bank accounts almost R$240 million between 2009 and 2019, but that in parallel he moved a large volume of resources outside financial institutions, whether in cash, jewelry or other means. Part of these amounts he obtained through the donations of people who were convinced to seek spiritual help in his care center in Abadiânia, the Casa Dom Inácio Loyola, a nonprofit entity."

https://opopular.com.br/noticias/cidades/joão-de-deus-movimentou-r-240-milhões-em-dez-anos-1.2439838

282. So, is there truth in the rumor that The Medium is still running the show? From an article in O Popular by Márcio Leijoto, *João de Deus still has a strong "presence" in the Dom Inácio house, in Abadiânia* 10/22/2021.

https://opopular.com.br/cidades/joão-de-deus-ainda-tem-presença-forte-na-casa-dom-inácio-em-abadiânia-1.2341623?_x_tr_sl&_x_tr_tl=en&_x_tr_hl=en&_x_tr_pto=sc

Also: *John of God's Business Desk, by Vicente Vilardaga Jornal Istoé, 10/04/2019.*

https://istoe-com-br.translate.goog/o-balcao-de-negocios-de-joao-de-deus/?_x_tr_sl=pt&_x_tr_tl=en&_x_tr_hl=en&_x_tr_pto=sc

283. *"It appears that Medium Joao is still pulling all the strings from wherever he is, in prison or under house arrest, and making all the decisions regarding the operations at the Casa."* Hervé Glon posted October 2021 on the website of German guides Klaus and Gundi Heinemann. https://www.healingguidance.net/log

284. Heather's website: https://healingquests.com/

285. The cruel reality of commercialism is that Lindo Horizonte is being sold off to crack cocaine treatment internment centers. *"Six outpatient units for this patient profile were installed on the avenue, which is also named after João Teixeira's mother, Francisca Teixeira Damas."*

https://opopular-com-br.translate.goog/noticias/cidades/joão-de-deus-ainda-tem-presença-forte-na-casa-dom-inácio-em-abadiânia-1.2341623?_x_tr_sl=pt&_x_tr_tl=en&_x_tr_hl=en&_x_tr_pto=sc

IX.
What In Hell Happened Here?

286. *The Placebo Effect is a miracle maker.* Martin, Harvey. The Secret Teachings of the Espiritistas. Metamind Publications, US 1998.

287. *...one of the first studies, one by Dr. Henry Beecher, done in 1961. This experiment was one of many unethical research papers produced during the Cold War.* This was reported in a paper by O'Regan, Brandan, and Hurley, Thomas. *Psychoneuroimmunology: The birth of a new field.* The Institute of Noetic Sciences, 1984.

Also: *Placebo, The Hidden Asset in Healing,* 1985.

288. Professor Cousins detailed his theory; one's personal beliefs interact with the immune system, activating physiological processes. Cousins, Norman. *Anatomy of an Illness as Perceived by the Patient: Reflections on Healing and Regeneration.* W.W. Norton & Company, Inc., 1979.

These books were helpful:

Dispenza, Joe. *You Are the Placebo.* Hay House, 2014.

O'Sullivan, Suzanne. *Is It All in Your Head?* The Random House Group Ltd, 2015.

Vance, Erik. *Suggestible You.* National Geographic Society, 2016.

289. We owe The Amazing Randi for first pointing this out to the public, but his cry in the wilderness went unheeded. "John of God will seat a subject for his visible surgery stunt and apparently scrape the eyeball of the patient with the edge of a knife." *Flim- flam! Psychics, ESP, unicorns, and other delusions.* James Randi.

An excellent interview with James Randi regarding an ABC coverage of João: https://web.randi.org/home/from-the-archives-randis-inside-scoop-into-abc-news-john-of-god-investigation-2005

Another related book by James Randi: Randi, James. The Faith Healers. James Randi Educational Foundation, 2011.

290. *Flim-flam! Psychics, ESP, unicorns, and other delusions.* James Randi.

291. *"Two volunteers are brought up on the stage. Both look like they are under some kind of spiritual trance."* Thackray, Gail. *Gail Thackray's Spiritual Journeys: Visiting John of God.* Chapter four, Indian Springs Publishing, 2014.

292. His Ericksonian therapy employed indirect suggestion and confusion techniques instead of formal hypnotic induction. *My Voice Will Go with You: The Teaching Tales of Milton H. Erickson.* W. W. Norton & Company, 1982.
Wikipedia is a rich resource regarding *Milton H. Erickson.*
https://en.wikipedia.org/wiki/Milton_H._Erickson
I encourage my readers to Google street hypnosis.
https://www.google.com/search?q=street+hypnosis+videos+on+youtube

293. Another form of hypnotism is the practice of hypnosis for sexual purposes. Wikipedia, *Erotic Hypnotism:*
https://en.wikipedia.org/wiki/Erotic_hypnosis

294. He even repeated The Lord's Prayer and Hail Mary to hypnotize his victims during the abuse.
https://br.noticias.yahoo.com/rezava-o-pai-nosso-e-obrigava-masturba-lo-diz-vitima-de-joao-de-deus-144309550.html

295. Irving Kirsch pointed out that hypnosis is a non-deceptive placebo. With Medium João, we should disregard the non-deceptive part. Kirsch I (October 1994). Clinical hypnosis as a non-deceptive placebo: empirically derived techniques. The American Journal of Clinical Hypnosis. 37 (2): 95–106.

I recommend a paper regarding hypnosis and Brazil's spiritist surgeons by Doctor Greenfield (he has published many books and articles on these subjects): Greenfield, Sydney M, Ph.D. *A Model Explaining Brazilian Spiritist Surgeries And Other Unusual, Religious-Based Healings.*

296. For example, as far as I know, there has been only one medical study of João's healing powers (not dozens or hundreds). A.M. de Almeida, T.M. de Almeida. *Cirurgia espiritual: uma investigação* Gollner Instituto de Psiquiatria do Hospital das Clínicas da FMUSP. Departamento de Patologia da Faculdade de Medicina da Universidade Federal de Juiz de Fora, MG.
https://doi.org/10.1590/S0104-42302000000300002

297. He and other men of Abadiânia placed bets on which young women João would sexually abuse. Fibe, Cristina. *João de Deus - O Abuso da Fé* (pp. 199). Globo Livros.

298. *"For me, it is a dog and pony show."* Email response from Rupert Drew, 7/2021.

299. *No, it's even worse than all that. Sorry, but I'm too afraid to go there.*

But someone *who has gone there* is Maria do Carmo Santos. She explained in an email: "Hi Michael, I have been trying to get away from Operations Sixth Commandment and Malavita, but many things led me from João to these two operations. Even these two operations had two great characters that denounced those involved, among them a Priest and a Teacher. This Teacher was tortured, raped, and trafficked. Today we have been trying to keep her secret outside the country since her children are still in Goiás, and if this gets out, they could be killed. The priest the Vatican took out of Brazil. But I got a connection much earlier than these Operations, which was the death of a famous Radicalist in Brasilia also involving people who were later caught in Operation Sixth Commandment.

So more and more, I think you are right in researching where João was during the military period. I have a Post Cad, in audio, that the person who is going to interview Writer Chico Felitti from *A Casa* talks about João's connection with the military period and torture. I will try to reach this person. I was very impressed because she said it with immense assurance.

"In the case of Operation Sixth Commandment, politicians were involved. And look at the case of the murder of the radio broadcaster Valério Luiz and look at the connection between the corrupt police officer who was his best friend and the former Senator Demostenes Torres."

In Cristina Fibe's book *João de Deus - The Abuse of Faith,* she interviews the ex-Governor of Goiás, Marconi Perillo, who was in office during these scandals. Perillo was a friend of João, as were many other politicians, including three Brazilian Presidents (pp 203-206).

Operation Sixth Commandment (Thou shalt not kill) was an internal investigation of the Military Police of Goiás. It led to a scandalous and shocking trial. Twenty Military Police officers were convicted of murder, torture, kidnapping, and "assisting in suicides"—some of them high-ranking. What they uncovered was a secret organization within the Military Police—*an extermination group* that had been operating in Goiás for almost a decade and that included many other military police officers who were not accused. They were tried and found guilty of more than forty homicides. This organization's members were all hitmen— uniformed hitmen. They operated in several cities in Goiás (including Anápolis) and were available for hire. The trial and investigation did not go anywhere near far enough.

https://www-jornalopcao-com-br.translate.goog/reportagens/onde-esta-o-resultado-da-operacao-sexto-mandamento-9648/?_x_tr_sl=pt&_x_tr_tl=en&_x_tr_hl=en&_x_tr_pto=sc

Operation Malavita was another internal investigation of the Military and Civil Police of Anápolis in 2014. Nineteen officers were tried and convicted of organized crime, extortion, murder, and torture. They were a large secret group within the police who ran a drug empire and hit squad in the city. This is, of course, João's hometown—convenient.

https://www-dmanapolis-com-br.translate.goog/noticia/52749/promotores-de-anapolis-pedem-informacoes-sobre-morte-de-pm-durante-cumprimento-de-mandado-de-prisao-pela-policia-civil?_x_tr_sl=pt&_x_tr_tl=en&_x_tr_hl=en&_x_tr_pto=sc

https://www-mpgo-mp-br.translate.goog/portal/noticia/302047?_x_tr_sch=http&_x_tr_sl=pt&_x_tr_tl=en&_x_tr_hl=en&_x_tr_pto=sc

300. *João and the military; there are no records! None.* After several false starts, I was directed to the military agency that provides records of enlistees and military contractors. I sent them this inquiry (written in Portuguese):

"I am a writer researching the biography of João Teixeira de Faria. Can you help me verify the veracity of some details of his life?

"In several interviews with Mr. Faria, it was mentioned that he served the army or provided tailoring services for the armed forces. He states that he served the military for nine years (or more) and that he was assigned to the following bases:

- Marabá, Pará (1970-1974)

- Imperatriz, Maranhão (1970-1974)

He also claims to have served in the following locations: Pernambuco, Bahia, Piauí, Tocantinopolis, Rio Grande de Sul, Brasília, Anápolis, Nitaroi, and Belém.

"Could you confirm or correct these statements? Could you also kindly share other details of Mr. Faria's military background?

"The information I have so far:

João Teixeira de Faria

Born 16/06/1941

Cachoeira de Goiás, GO

Father: José Nunes de Faria

Mother: Francisca Teixeira Damas

CPF 100.854.591-00 — ID: 387.895-SSP-DF

Required Military Enlistment: 1959/1960 (18 years old).

"I need the following information: What year he enlisted in the army? In which city was he enlisted? Was he drafted immediately, or did he wait for some time? What year was he discharged?

Thank you in advance for your attention, Michael Bailot"

They replied, *"Your request for access to information was successfully processed and received the protocol number 60143.004007/2020-50. To obtain details of the information request, click on the protocol number informed; a username and password may be required to access the system.*

Your request for information must be processed within 20 (twenty) days, as established in art. 11, § 1, of Law 12.527/2011, and this period may be extended for another 10 (ten) days, with express justification, as provided for in art. 11, § 2, of the aforementioned Law. The status of your request can be checked whenever you wish through the option "My Manifestations" in the system menu.

If there is no response to your request, you can file a complaint. Attention: the deadline for filing a complaint is 10 (ten) days and begins 30 (thirty) days after the registration of your request.

https://www.gov.br/acessoainformacao/pt-br

This agency dragged out its reply to the last day allowed by law. The claimed to have no information about João Teixeira de Faria. They referred me to another agency.

This was Fala BR - Plataforma Integrada de Ouvidoria e Acesso à Informação.

https://sistema.ouvidorias.gov.br/publico/Manifestacao/RegistrarManifestacao.aspx?idFormulario=3&tipo=8&origem=idp&modo=

This agency also waited until the last day permitted to respond. Their reply: *"No records found."*

Responsible Type Publication

12/01/2020 2:21 PM Conclusive Answer SIC

Stock history Date/Time Action

11/14/2020 17:02 Registration 12/01/2020 2:21 pm Registration Answer: Referrals: No records found.

Extensions: No records found.

Answers to satisfaction surveys: No records found.

I filed an appeal but received no response.

301. *"He is fully capable of serving the sentence of more than 100 years that was imposed on him within the prison system."* O Popular, by Mariana Carneiro.

https://opopular.com.br/cidades/defesa-de-jo-o-de-deus-diz-que-argumentac-o-do-mp-n-o-procede-1.2450026

Postscript

302. *Faria was found guilty of all charges, and a total of nearly 110 years was added to his tally.*

https://noticias.uol.com.br/cotidiano/ultimas-noticias/2022/12/08/joao-de-deus-condenacao-109-anos-de-prisao-crimes-sexuais.htm

303. *He was convicted and sentenced to an additional 48 years.*
https://noticias.r7.com/cidades/joao-de-deus-e-condenado-a-mais-de-48-anos-de-prisao-por-crimes-sexuais-04022023

304. *A new case was tried on July 10, 2023, and Faria was sentenced to an additional 99+ years.*

https://www-em-com-br.translate.goog/app/noticia/nacional/2023/07/10/interna_nacional,1518373/joao-de-deus-e-condenado-a-100-anos-de-prisao.shtml?_x_tr_sl=pt&_x_tr_tl=en&_x_tr_hl=en&_x_tr_pto=sc

305. *This brought his total sentence to more than 489 years and the victims were awarded 100,000 reais in damages.*

https://www-uol-com-br.translate.goog/universa/noticias/redacao/2023/09/15/joao-de-deus-condenado-118-anos-prisao-crimes-sexuais-quase-500-anos.htm?_x_tr_sl=pt&_x_tr_tl=en&_x_tr_hl=en&_x_tr_pto=sc

306. *In an interview with Cristina Fibe:*

https://www.uol.com.br/universa/noticias/redacao/2023/03/31/joao-de-deus-mp-go-faz-nova-denuncia-contra-medium-por-venda-de-passiflora.htm

ABOUT THE AUTHOR

I *lived* this horrifying story. No one else has dared to step forward and reveal the secrets of John of God. I am in a unique position because I studied and participated in the arcane subjects I cover. When I discuss Afro-Brazilian religions, it comes from experience. My portrayal of the life of João de Deus and the culture of Brazil is the fruit of twenty-five years of study in the Brazilian school of hard knocks. I know the people I discuss in this book. I am a closet anthropologist with bookshelves to prove it.

The *Cult of John* entailed four years of research, reading hundreds of dissertations, documents, and victim interviews. Personal journals from my time at the Casa were referenced, as were over a dozen books written about João. I have reliable sources who gave first-hand accounts. I live in the region of this story and read every newspaper and journal account about João I could find. I gave a four-hour-long deposition to the Chief of Military Police investigating the case, and an insider provided me with details of the case as they were revealed via the District Attorney's office. I speak and read Portuguese. I have a lifetime's experience with obscure cults, shamanism, hypnotism, mediumship, meditation, and alternative folk healing. I know a con when I see one and a Saint when I meet one. All this helped in compiling *Cult of John*.

Thank you for reading Cult of John. Please leave a review – I'd appreciate it. You can also post reviews on Goodreads and any other applications you use.

www.ingramcontent.com/pod-product-compliance
Lightning Source LLC
Chambersburg PA
CBHW060449030426
42337CB00015B/1528